GRAMMATIK KOMPLETT
ENGLISCH

Das große Übungs- und Nachschlagebuch

PONS GmbH
Stuttgart

PONS

GRAMMATIK KOMPLETT
ENGLISCH

Das große Übungs- und Nachschlagebuch

von
Darcy Bruce Berry und Dr. Alexander T.Bergs (Grammatik)
Samantha Scott (Verbtabellen)
Claudia Heidieker unter Mitarbeit von Esther Lorenz-Bottke (Übungsgrammatik)

Auflage A1 $^{5\ 4\ 3\ 2\ 1}$ / 2012 2011 2010 2009

© PONS GmbH Stuttgart, Rotebühlstraße 77, 70178 Stuttgart, 2009
Internet: www.pons.de
E-Mail: info@pons.de
Alle Rechte vorbehalten.

Logoentwurf: Erwin Poell
Logoüberarbeitung: Sabine Redlin, Ludwigsburg
Einbandgestaltung: Schmidt und Dupont
Titelfoto: fotolia (Danimotxo)
Layout: andrea grundmann kommunikationsgestaltung, Karlsruhe; belugadesign, Stuttgart (Übungsgrammatik)
Satz: Satz und mehr, Besigheim
Illustrationen: Palmer-Lorenz Illustrationen, Steinbach
Anpassung der Illustrationen: Norberto Lombardi, Campana
Tonstudio: Ton in Ton Medienhaus, Stuttgart
Digital Mastering: ARTist Tonstudio, Pfullingen
Druck und Bindung: L.E.G.O. S.p.A., in Lavis (TN)
Printed in Italy
ISBN: 978-3-12-561249-5

Gesamtinhaltsverzeichnis

1. Grammatik 5

2. Verbtabellen 147

3. Übungsgrammatik 253

Willkommen in der Welt der englischen Sprache

PONS Grammatik Komplett Englisch ist ein umfassendes Nachschlage- und Übungswerk, das Sie in ihrer gesamten Sprachlernlaufbahn begleiten wird.
Es bietet Ihnen als Sprachanfänger oder fortgeschrittenem Lerner die Möglichkeit, die wichtigsten Bereiche und Aspekte der englischen Grammatik nachzuschlagen und zu üben:

- **Grammatik**

In diesem Kapitel finden Sie die wichtigsten Grammatikregeln an zahlreichen Beispielen sinnvoll veranschaulicht. Leicht verständliche Erklärungen und nützliche Tipps helfen Ihnen, typische Fehler zu vermeiden.

- **Verbtabellen**

Dieses Kapitel bietet Ihnen übersichtliche Konjugationstabellen der wichtigsten Verben. Zusätzlich finden Sie eine ausführliche Verbliste mit Verweisen auf das jeweilige Konjugationsmuster. Für einen besseren Überblick sind die Besonderheiten in den Konjugationen farbig hervorgehoben.

- **Übungsgrammatik**

In diesem Teil trainieren Sie mit einer modernen, kommunikativen Lernmethode intensiv die englische Grammatik und lernen, diese in lebensnahen Situationen anzuwenden. Die Lösungen und Tipps tragen dazu bei, dass Sie als Selbstlerner die englische Grammatik schnell beherrschen.

Viel Spaß und Erfolg beim Englischlernen!

1 | Grammatik

Grammatik

Inhalt

Einleitung	9
Erklärung der Grammatikbegriffe	10
1 Verbs – Verben	**11**
Vollverben	11
Tenses – Zeitformen	12
Auxiliaries – Hilfsverben	24
Modalverben	29
Spezielle Verben	35
2 Prepositions – Verhältniswörter	**42**
Zeitangaben	42
Ortsangaben	45
Richtung	47
3 Phrasal Verbs – Partikelverben	**51**
Allgemeines	51
4 Nouns – Hauptwörter	**55**
Groß- und Kleinschreibung	55
The Plural – Mehrzahl	55
Possessive – besitzanzeigende Form	57
Zählbare und nicht zählbare Nouns	60
Pair Nouns	61
Proper Names: Titles	62
5 Pronouns – Fürwörter	**64**
Personal Pronouns – persönliche Fürwörter	64
Possessive Forms – besitzanzeigende Formen	67
Reflexive Pronouns – rückbezügliche Fürwörter	70
Demonstrative Pronouns – hinweisende Fürwörter	73
6 Articles and Related Words – Artikel und verwandte Wörter	**79**
Der unbestimmte Artikel	79
Der bestimmte Artikel	81
Demonstrativpronomen	83
Andere artikelähnliche Wörter	84
7 Quantities and Measurements – Mengen- und Maßangaben	**87**
8 Adjectives – Eigenschaftswörter	**90**
Allgemeine Bemerkungen	90
Steigerungsformen	91
Adjectives in the Noun Phrase	94

Grammatik

Adjectives nach Verben	95
Good – well	96
Own	96
Than	97
Vergleiche mit as ... as	98
Am meisten	98
Allgemeine Fragen	99

9 Adverbs – Umstandswörter **101**

Der Unterschied zwischen Adjective und Adverb	101
Die Bildung von Adverbs	101
Die Steigerung	105
Verb- und satzbeschreibende Adverbs	106

10 Coordinating Conjunctions – Bindewörter **108**

Einzelwörter	108
Mehrwortbildungen	109

11 Sentence Construction – Satzbau **110**

Der Aussagesatz	110
Nebensatz-Fragen	111
Indirect Speech – Indirekte Rede	112
Pronouns – Fürwörter	113
Adverbiale Nebensätze	114
Wenn-Sätze	115
Verbformen mit if-Sätzen	116
Andere adverbiale Nebensätze	118
Infinitivsätze	119
Adverbiale Anwendung	121
ing-Sätze	121
Lassen	125
Let – erlauben, zulassen	126
Have – veranlassen, in Auftrag geben	126
Make – veranlassen, zwingen	127

12 Question Words – Fragewort-Fragen **128**

Liste der englischen Fragewörter	128
Anwendung	128

13 Relative Clauses – Relativsätze **131**

Relative Pronouns – Relativpronomen	132
That	135
Free Relatives – freie Relativsätze	136

Grammatik

14 Negation – Verneinung **138**
    Negative Ausdrücke 138
    Any-Wörter 138

15 Glossary – Glossar **140**

Stichwortregister 144

Einleitung

Sie wollen die Regeln der englischen Sprache auf einfache und verständliche Weise erlernen oder wiederholen, Sie möchten zu speziellen Fragen aber auch schnell und gezielt nachschlagen können.

Das Kapitel **Grammatik** bietet Ihnen eine **übersichtliche Darstellung** der aktuellen englischen Sprache in Nordamerika und Großbritannien. Die Regeln werden anhand **zahlreicher englischer Beispielsätze** mit deutschen Übersetzungen veranschaulicht.

Das Kapitel **Grammatik** warnt vor typischen Fehlern, die gerade deutschsprachigen Englischlernenden häufig passieren.

Bei der Arbeit mit diesem Kapitel helfen Ihnen die folgenden Hervorhebungen:

> Hier wird auf eine **Regel** oder eine **Besonderheit** hingewiesen, die man nicht übersehen sollte.

> Kleine **Tipps** verraten Ihnen an dieser Stelle, wie Sie sich die Regeln besser merken können.

> Hier werden Unterschiede zwischen dem Deutschen und dem Englischen aufgezeigt, die Sie besonders beachten sollten.

> Hier finden Sie **Varianten**, die im amerikanischen Englisch vorkommen.

▶ Hier wird auf ein anderes Grammatikkapitel verwiesen, z.B. ▶ **Kapitel Verbs – Verben.**

Wenn Sie etwas gezielt nachschlagen wollen, führt Sie das **ausführliche Stichwortregister** im Anhang schnell zur richtigen Stelle.

Viel Spaß und Erfolg!

Erklärung der Grammatikbegriffe

Englisch	Latein	Bedeutung
active	Aktiv	Tätigkeitsform
adjective	Adjektiv	Eigenschaftswort
adverb	Adverb	Umstandswort
article	Artikel	Begleiter
auxiliary	Hilfsverb	Hilfs-Tätigkeitswort
conjunction	Konjunktion	Bindewort
consonant	Konsonant	Mitlaut
continuous tense	Kontinuativ; Progressive Form	Verlaufsform
demonstrative pronoun	Demonstrativpronomen	hinweisendes Fürwort
future	Futur	Zukunft
gerund	Gerundium	ing-Form
imperative (form)	Imperativ	Befehlsform
imperfect (tense)	Imperfekt	einfache Vergangenheit
infinitive	Infinitiv	Grundform des Verbs
intransitive verb	intransitives Verb	Tätigkeitswort ohne direkte Ergänzung
noun	Nomen, Substantiv	Hauptwort
object	Objekt	Ergänzung
participle	Partizip	Mittelwort
passive	Passiv	Leideform
perfect (tense)	Perfekt	vollendete Gegenwart
personal pronoun	Personalpronomen	persönliches Fürwort
plural	Plural	Mehrzahl
possessive (pronoun)	Possessivpronomen	besitzanzeigendes Fürwort
preposition	Präposition	Verhältniswort
present (tense)	Präsens	Gegenwart
progressive (tense)	Progressive Form	Verlaufsform
pronoun	Pronomen	Fürwort
reflexive pronoun	Reflexivpronomen	rückbezügliches Fürwort
relative pronoun	Relativpronomen	bezügliches Fürwort
singular	Singular	Einzahl
subject	Subjekt	Satzgegenstand
transitive verb	transitives Verb	Tätigkeitswort mit direkter Ergänzung
verb	Verb	Tätigkeitswort
vowel	Vokal	Selbstlaut

1 Verbs | *Verben*

Vollverben

Verbarten

Es gibt zwei Arten von Verben: transitive und intransitive Verben.

- transitive Verben brauchen mindestens ein, manchmal zwei Objekte. Verben, die ein Objekt benötigen, heißen monotransitive Verben, solche mit zwei Objekten ditransitive Verben:

Monotransitive Verben
Anne likes dogs.   *Anne mag Hunde.*
Peter kissed Mary.   *Peter küsste Mary.*

Ditransitive Verben
Jeremy wrote me a letter.   *Jeremy schrieb mir einen Brief.*
Paul gave me a book.   *Paul gab mir ein Buch.*

- intransitive Verben brauchen dagegen kein Objekt:
Anne slept.   *Anne schlief.*
Usually Jeremy drives.   *Normalerweise fährt Jeremy.*

Manche Verben können sowohl transitiv als auch intransitiv sein:
John is reading a book.   *John liest gerade ein Buch.*
John is reading.   *John liest gerade.*

Regelmäßige und unregelmäßige Verben

Bei regelmäßigen Verben braucht man nur den Infinitiv (die erste Form, oder Grundform) um alle anderen Formen abzuleiten:

1. Form Infinitiv/Grundform	2. Form Simple Past	3. Form Past Participle
(to) call	called	called
(to) kiss	kissed	kissed

Grammatik

Bei unregelmäßigen Verben reicht der Infinitiv nicht, da sich das Simple Past bzw. Past Participle nicht ableiten lassen:

1. Form Infinitiv/Grundform	2. Form Simple Past	3. Form Past Participle
(to) sing	sang	sung
(to) see	saw	seen

Tenses | *Zeitformen*

Einfache Formen

Von den Zeiten werden nur die einfache Gegenwart und die einfache Vergangenheit ohne Hilfsverb gebildet:

Simple Present | *Einfache Gegenwartsform*

Das Simple Present ist bei fast allen Verben in allen Personen außer der dritten (**he/she/it**) gleich dem Infinitiv (der Grundform). Vollverben in Sätzen mit Subjekten in der dritten Person haben in der Regel ein **-s** am Ende.

I **like** hairy spiders.	*Ich mag haarige Spinnen.*
You **need** a haircut.	*Du musst zum Friseur.*
He/she **watches** TV every night.	*Er sieht jeden Abend fern.*
Theresa **prefers** white wine.	*Theresa trinkt lieber Weißwein.*
Tom and Martha **want** a new car.	*Tom und Martha wollen ein neues Auto.*

Lediglich bei den Hilfsverben **be** und **have** und den Modalverben **may**, **can**, **will**, **should** usw. gibt es Abweichungen: (▶ Hilfsverben)

Grammatik

BE (sein)	
I **am** tired.	*Ich bin müde.*
You **are** tired.	*Du bist müde.*
He/she/it **is** boring.	*Er/Sie/Es ist langweilig.*
Ballet **is** boring.	*Ballett ist langweilig.*
Peter, Paul, and Mary **are** here.	*Peter, Paul und Mary sind hier.*

HAVE (haben)	
I **have** a car.	*Ich habe ein Auto.*
You **have** a nice jacket.	*Du hast eine hübsche Jacke.*
Mary-Jane **has** a flat tire.	*Mary-Jane hat einen Platten.*
They **have** a swimming-pool.	*Sie haben einen Swimming-Pool.*

Die Modalverben (▶ Modalverben) haben immer die gleiche Form:

I/you/he/she/it/they **may** be here now.	*Ich/Du/Er/Sie/Es könnte jetzt hier sein.*

Simple Past | *Einfache Vergangenheitsform*

Die regelmäßige Form des Simple Past fügt **-ed** ans Ende des Infinitivs. Dies gilt für jedes Subjekt, d.h. alle Personen.

I **wanted** a new car.	*Ich wollte ein neues Auto.*
My colleagues **worked** yesterday.	*Meine Kollegen arbeiteten gestern.*

Grammatik

Einige der wichtigsten unregelmäßigen Verben:

Infinitive	Simple Past	Past Participle	Übersetzung
be	was	been	*sein*
begin	began	begun	*beginnen*
bring	brought	brought	*bringen*
buy	bought	bought	*kaufen*
catch	caught	caught	*fangen, erwischen*
choose	chose	chosen	*auswählen*
come	came	come	*kommen*
cost	cost	cost	*kosten*
cut	cut	cut	*schneiden*
do	did	done	*tun, machen*
drink	drank	drunk	*trinken*
drive	drove	driven	*fahren*
eat	ate	eaten	*essen*
fall	fell	fallen	*(hin)fallen*
feel	felt	felt	*(sich) fühlen*
fly	flew	flown	*fliegen*
forget	forgot	forgotten (UK) forgot (US)	*vergessen*
get	got	got (UK), gotten (US)	*kriegen, werden*
give	gave	given	*geben, schenken*
go	went	gone	*(hin)gehen*
have	had	had	*haben*
hear	heard	heard	*hören*
keep	kept	kept	*behalten*
know	knew	known	*wissen, kennen*
leave	left	left	*weggehen, verlassen*
lend	lent	lent	*ausleihen*
lose	lost	lost	*verlieren*
make	made	made	*machen*
pay	paid	paid	*(be)zahlen*
put	put	put	*stellen, (hin)legen*
read	read	read	*lesen*

Grammatik

ride	rode	ridden	*reiten, (mit)fahren*
ring	rang	rung	*läuten, ringen*
run	ran	run	*laufen*
say	said	said	*sagen*
see	saw	seen	*sehen*
sell	sold	sold	*verkaufen*
sing	sang	sung	*singen*
sit	sat	sat	*sitzen*
sleep	slept	slept	*schlafen*
take	took	taken	*(mit)nehmen*
teach	taught	taught	*lehren, unterrichten*
tell	told	told	*erzählen, sagen*
think	thought	thought	*denken, glauben*
wake	woke	woken	*erwachen, aufwecken*
write	wrote	written	*schreiben*

Dazu gibt es Verben, die im Amerikanischen regelmäßig sind (also mit **–ed** gebildet werden), im britischen Englisch aber wie folgt:

Infinitive	Simple Past	Past Participle	Übersetzung
dream	dreamt (UK)	dreamt (UK)	*träumen*
	dreamed (US)	dreamed (US)	
lean	leant	leant	*(sich) anlehnen*
learn	learnt	learnt	*lernen*
spell	spelt	spelt	*buchstabieren*
spill	spilt	spilt	*verschütten*
spoil	spoilt	spoilt	*verderben, verwöhnen*

Das einzige Verb, wo dies umgekehrt passiert, ist **to dive** (*tauchen, hechten*):

Infinitive	Simple Past	Past Participle	Übersetzung
dive	dove (US)	dived (US)	*tauchen, hechten*
	dived (UK)	dived (UK)	

Grammatik

Zusammengesetzte Formen

Zusammengesetzte Formen bestehen aus mindestens einem Hilfsverb und der entsprechenden Form des Vollverbs.

Progressive | *Die Verlaufsform*
Um eine Progressive Form zu bilden, braucht man die richtige Form von **be** als Hilfsverb und die *ing*-Form des Vollverbs. Zur Bildung der *ing*-Form hängt man einfach **-ing** an den Infinitiv (die Grundform) des Vollverbs.

Present Progressive:	
The cat **is sleeping**.	*Die Katze schläft gerade.*
They **are learning** English.	*Sie lernen gerade Englisch.*

Past Progressive:	
George **was wearing** a bow tie.	*George trug eine Fliege.*
You **were** all **driving** me crazy.	*Ihr habt mich alle verrückt gemacht.*

Perfect Tenses | *Perfektformen*
Perfect Tenses bildet man immer mit dem Hilfsverb **have** und der dritten Form (dem Past Participle) des Vollverbs. Man unterscheidet zwischen dem gegenwarts-bezogenen Present Perfect und der Vorvergangenheit, dem Past Perfect.

Present Perfect:	
I **have seen** her before.	*Ich habe sie schon einmal gesehen.*
Carla **has hidden** my shoes again.	*Carla hat wieder meine Schuhe versteckt.*

Past Perfect – Vorvergangenheit:	
Deanna **had chosen** a large SUV.	*Deanna hatte sich einen großen Geländewagen ausgesucht.*
Wally **had slipped** on a banana peel.	*Wally war auf einer Bananenschale ausgerutscht.*

In der gesprochenen Sprache ist es üblich, die Gegenwarts- und Vergangenheitsformen von **have** zusammenzuziehen und an das Subjekt anzuhängen:

You have gone.	▶	You've gone.	*Du bist (fort)gegangen.*
She has gone.	▶	She's gone.	*Sie ist (fort)gegangen.*
We had gone.	▶	We'd gone.	*Wir waren (fort)gegangen.*

Future | *Zukunft:*

Englisch hat viele verschiedene Zukunftsformen, die sehr schwer zu unterscheiden sind (▶ Wie man über die Zukunft spricht). Sehr häufig aber bildet man die Zukunftsform einfach mit dem Hilfsverb **will** (das nie verändert wird) und dem Infinitiv (der Grundform) des Vollverbs:

| They **will move** next year. | *Sie werden nächstes Jahr umziehen.* |
| She **will** never **meet** him again. | *Sie wird ihn nie wieder sehen.* |

Passive Forms | *Passiv*

Das normale englische Passiv wird mit dem Hilfsverb **be** und dem Past Participle (der dritten Form) gebildet:

| That song **is sung** at services. | *Dieses Lied wird beim Gottesdienst gesungen.* |
| The dishwasher **was repaired** today. | *Die Spülmaschine wurde heute repariert.* |

Oft benutzt man auch eine Phrase, die zeigt, wer oder was etwas getan hat. Diese Phrase wird von **by** eingeleitet:

| The dessert is brought **by the butler**. | *Der Nachtisch wird vom Butler gebracht.* |
| He was greeted **by many people**. | *Er wurde von vielen Leuten gegrüßt.* |

Kombinationen von Hilfsverben

Es ist möglich, verschiedene Hilfsverben nach Bedarf aneinander zu reihen. Dabei bleibt die Reihenfolge gleich, man muss aber auf die richtigen Formen achten:

Modalverb – **have** *(perfect)* – **be** *(continuous)* – **be** *(passive)* – Vollverb

She **had been** promoted.	*Sie war befördert worden.*
They **will have been being** taught French for a year now.	*Sie werden jetzt wohl seit einem Jahr in Französisch unterrichtet.*
He **can't be** eating again!	*Er kann doch nicht schon wieder beim Essen sein!*

Used to | *früher*

Um vergangene Zustände und Gewohnheiten zu beschreiben, verwendet man häufig **used to**. Dies drückt dann ungefähr das gleiche aus wie das deutsche *früher*. Sehr oft beinhalten Formen mit **used to** den Hinweis, dass der Zustand bzw. die Gewohnheit nicht mehr gilt:

But you **used to** like spinach.	*Aber früher hast du Spinat doch gemocht.*
Mr. Jones **used to** go for a walk every day.	*Früher ist Herr Jones jeden Tag spazieren gegangen.*

Man setzt **used to** wie ein Hilfsverb zwischen das Subjekt und das Vollverb. **Used** ist dann das erste Verb des Satzes.

Zu beachten ist außerdem, dass **used to** im Kontext **be used to** + *ing*-Form *etwas gewöhnt sein* bedeutet (▶ **be used to, get used to**):

Carlos is **used to washing** up the dishes.	*Carlos ist es gewöhnt, das Geschirr abzuwaschen.*

Grammatik

Anwendung der verschiedenen Formen

1. Simple Present and Present Progressive
Simple Present wird hauptsächlich für Tatsachen und Gewohnheiten in der Gegenwart verwendet:

I like chocolate ice cream.	Ich mag Schokoladeneis.
The church bells ring every hour.	Die Kirchenglocken läuten jede Stunde.
The children watch TV every night.	Die Kinder sehen jeden Abend fern.

Present Progressive dagegen wird für momentan andauernde Zustände gebraucht. Solche Zustände können auch sich wiederholende Ereignisse sein:

I'm eating chocolate ice cream.	Ich esse gerade Schokoladeneis.
It's raining.	Es regnet.
What are you thinking about?	Woran denkst Du gerade?

2. Present Perfect
Present Perfect verwendet man für Zustände und Ereignisse, die in der Vergangenheit angefangen haben, in der Gegenwart als noch nicht abgeschlossen gelten, oder für diese immer noch größere Bedeutung haben:

The plumber has been here since 9 a.m.	Der Klempner ist (schon) seit 9 Uhr morgens da.
We've lived in London for five years.	Wir leben seit fünf Jahren in London.
Pete has called me twelve times last month.	Pete hat mich zwölf Mal letzten Monat angerufen.
I've worked all day, and now I want to relax.	Ich habe den ganzen Tag gearbeitet, und jetzt will ich mich entspannen.

Man verwendet das Present Perfect auch für Neuigkeiten:

Beatrice has written another novel.	*Beatrice hat noch einen Roman geschrieben.*
Playboy Clark has married for the seventh time.	*Der Playboy Clark hat (gerade) zum siebten Mal geheiratet.*

3. Present Perfect and Simple Past

Wie oben beschrieben kann man das Present Perfect nur dann verwenden, wenn ein Ereignis oder ein Zustand irgendwie aktuell ist. Wenn aber das Ereignis oder der Zustand abgeschlossen ist und eine Zeitangabe hierfür getroffen werden kann, muss man das Simple Past verwenden:

I have lived in London for five years.	*Ich lebe seit fünf Jahren in London. (Und tue dies immer noch!)*
I lived in London for five years.	*Ich habe fünf Jahre lang in London gelebt. (z.B. als ich ein Kind war!)*
We've met before.	*Wir sind uns schon mal begegnet. (irgend wann, ohne feste Zeitangabe)*
We met at a party last week.	*Wir haben uns letzte Woche auf einem Fest kennengelernt. (abgeschlossen, Zeitangabe)*

Im amerikanischen Englisch können einige Ausdrücke, die auf aktuelle Zustände hindeuten (z.B. **just, already**) auch mit dem Simple Past stehen:

He has just left the hotel. (UK)	*Er hat gerade das Hotel verlassen.*
He just left the hotel. (US)	*Er hat gerade das Hotel verlassen.*

Grammatik

Wenn man einen Zeitausdruck benutzen will, der einen Zeitraum oder einen Zeitpunkt in der Vergangenheit bezeichnet, kann man das Present Perfect nicht verwenden:

I saw that play last year.	*Ich habe dieses Theaterstück letztes Jahr gesehen.*
I paid that bill on the first of the month.	*Ich habe diese Rechnung am Monatsersten bezahlt.*

4. Simple Past and Past Progressive

Einerseits verwendet man das Simple Past für Allgemeinheiten und Gewohnheiten in der Vergangenheit, ähnlich wie **used to**:

Leonard's cat liked spaghetti. **Leonard's cat used to like spaghetti.**	*Leonards Katze mochte Spaghetti.*
Professor Roberts always wrote on the blackboard. **Professor Roberts used to write on the blackboard.**	*Professor Roberts schrieb immer an die Tafel.*

Andererseits verwendet man das Simple Past auch für einzelne Ereignisse in der Vergangenheit:

Their daughter ran off with a hobo.	*Ihre Tochter ist mit einem Landstreicher durchgebrannt.*
Several plates fell off the shelves.	*Mehrere Teller fielen aus dem Regal.*

Dagegen verwendet man das Past Progressive für Ereignisse, die zu einem Zeitpunkt in der Vergangenheit gerade abliefen:

At that moment she was thinking about her problems at work.	*In dem Moment dachte sie gerade über ihre Probleme bei der Arbeit nach.*
When I saw him, he was dipping doughnuts in his coffee.	*Als ich ihn sah, war er dabei Doughnuts in seinen Kaffee zu tunken.*

Grammatik

Solche Zustände können auch sich wiederholende Ereignisse sein. Durch das Past Progressive deutet man an, dass der Zeitraum dieser Ereignisse nicht allzu lang dauerte:

At that time we were talking on the phone every day.	Zu der Zeit telefonierten wir jeden Tag.
In those days they were buying real estate like crazy.	Damals haben sie Immobilien wie verrückt gekauft.

5. Wie man über die Zukunft spricht

Wie unter den Verbformen schon erwähnt, bildet man in der Regel das Future Tense mit dem Hilfsverb **will**. Allerdings wird diese Zeitform nicht so häufig angewandt, wie man sich denken könnte. Die Zukunft mit **will** verwendet man hauptsächlich für Ereignisse, die nicht geplant werden, sondern einfach so passieren oder passieren könnten:

It **will rain** soon.	Es wird bald regnen.
If you aren't careful, you**'ll fall**.	Wenn du nicht aufpasst, fällst du hin.
Business **will improve** during the Christmas season.	Das Geschäft wird in der Vorweihnachtszeit besser laufen.

Außerdem verwendet man diese Zukunftsform für Vorschläge und Ideen bei der Planung:

I'll buy the drinks for the party.	Ich kann die Getränke für das Fest kaufen.
Marty will drive Al home after the meeting.	Marty fährt Al nach der Besprechung heim.
Jon will take the car tomorrow, and we'll take the bus.	Jon nimmt morgen das Auto mit, und wir fahren mit dem Bus.

Wenn etwas aber schon geplant ist, so ist das Future Tense nicht üblich. Das gilt besonders für die gesprochene Sprache. Dann muss man auf andere Ausdrucksweisen ausweichen:

Be going to ist die allgemeine Zukunftsform der gesprochenen Sprache: man kann sie für geplante wie ungeplante Ereignisse (aber nicht für Vorschläge) verwenden:

I'm going to marry in April.	*Ich werde im April heiraten.*
It's going to rain.	*Es wird bald regnen.*

Present Progressive
Für fest geplante Ereignisse kann man auch das Present Progressive nehmen:

Mabel is flying to Hawaii tomorrow.	*Mabel fliegt morgen nach Hawaii.*
My parents are moving next year.	*Meine Eltern ziehen nächstes Jahr um.*

Future Progressive
Das Future Progressive ist eine Kombination aus **will** und Progressive (**be** + *ing*-Form). Diese Bildung verwendet man, wenn das Ereignis sowieso passieren wird, also nicht extra geplant werden muss:

I can ask Randy. I'll be seeing him tonight.	*Ich kann Randy fragen. Ich sehe ihn heute abend sowieso.*

Simple Present
Man kann das Simple Present für Ereignisse in der Zukunft verwenden, wenn es um einen fest geplanten Zeitpunkt geht:

My cousin arrives on Monday.	*Meine Kusine kommt am Montag an.*
Dr. Curtis and her husband travel to Moscow on the 27th.	*Dr. Curtis und ihr Mann reisen am 27. nach Moskau.*

6. Zukunft in der Vergangenheit
Manchmal ist es notwendig, aus der Perspektive der Vergangenheit von etwas zu berichten, das damals noch in der Zukunft lag.

Yesterday morning Sue was going to be late.	*Gestern früh war Sue drauf und dran zu spät zu kommen.*

Grammatik

Hierzu kann man natürlich die oben erwähnten Zukunfsformen in entsprechende Vergangenheitsformen umwandeln. Allerdings geht dies nicht immer. Man kann z.B. **would** als die Vergangenheit von **will** normalerweise nur in der indirekten Rede benutzen:

Harold said that Sue would be late.	*Harold sagte, dass Sue später kommen würde.*

Ansonsten hat **will** überhaupt keine Vergangenheitsform. Deshalb muss man auf einen Ersatz, eine Umschreibung zurückgreifen, nämlich **going to**:

Last week they were going to drive me crazy.	*Letzte Woche waren sie auf dem Weg mich in den Wahnsinn zu treiben.*

Wenn man das Simple Present in das Simple Past verwandelt, hat der Satz nur eine normale Vergangenheitsbedeutung:

My cousin arrived on Monday.	*Meine Kusine kam am Montag an.*

Hier ist es also besser entweder **going to** oder das Past Progressive zu verwenden:

My cousin was going to arrive on Monday.	*Meine Kusine wollte/sollte am Montag ankommen.*
My cousin was arriving on Monday.	*Meine Kusine wollte/sollte am Montag ankommen.*

Auxiliaries | *Hilfsverben*

Hilfsverben im Englischen stehen zwischen dem Subjekt und dem Vollverb:

The dog has eaten my homework.	*Der Hund hat meine Hausaufgaben gefressen.*
They are looking for Easter eggs.	*Sie suchen gerade Ostereier.*

Unentbehrliche Hilfsverben

Bestimmte grammatische Strukturen können ohne Hilfsverb nicht gebildet werden. Wenn kein Hilfsverb vorhanden ist (nämlich bei einfacher Gegenwart oder Vergangenheit), muss man das Spezialhilfsverb **do** nehmen. Dieses merkwürdige Hilfsverb hat keine Bedeutung! Es erfüllt nur diese Erfordernis der Grammatik.

Yes-No Questions | *Ja-Nein-Fragen*

Fragen, auf die man mit ja oder nein antwortet, werden mit einem Hilfsverb eingeleitet. Wenn das Hilfsverb im entsprechenden Aussagesatz schon vorhanden ist, setzt man es einfach an den Satzanfang. Wenn aber der Aussagesatz nur ein Vollverb enthält, muss das Spezialhilfsverb **do** einspringen:

Have you seen the new film?	*Hast du den neuen Film gesehen?*
Do you want to marry me?	*Willst Du mich heiraten?*
Does he like chocolate?	*Mag er Schokolade?*

Die entsprechenden Aussagesätze sind:

You have seen the new film.	*Du hast den neuen Film gesehen.*
You want to marry me.	*Du willst mich heiraten.*
He likes chocolate.	*Er mag Schokolade.*

Der erste Aussagesatz enthält das Hilfsverb **have**, das dann an erster Stelle in der Frage steht. Der zweite und der dritte Aussagesatz enthalten kein Hilfsverb. Da man die Frage ohne Hilfsverb gar nicht anfangen kann, setzt man die passende Form von **do** an den Satzbeginn. Bei zwei oder mehr Hilfsverben in der Aussage wird nur die erste vorangezogen.

Grammatik

Aussage:	
The letters have been sent.	*Die Briefe sind abgeschickt worden.*
Frage:	
Have the letters been sent?	*Sind die Briefe abgeschickt worden?*

Eine kleine Besonderheit findet sich bei Ja-Nein Fragen mit **have** bzw. **have got** (*haben, besitzen*). Im britischen English werden entsprechende Aussagesätze häufig mit **have got** gebildet. Dann ist das erste Hilfsverb für die Frage **have**. Im amerikanischen Englisch werden die entsprechenden Aussagesätze eher mit dem einfachen **have** gebildet. Dies gilt dann natürlich als Vollverb und braucht zur Fragebildung noch das Hilfsverb **do**:

Aussage:	
She has got a red car. (UK)	*Sie hat ein rotes Auto.*
She has a red car. (US)	*Sie hat ein rotes Auto.*
Frage:	
Has she got a red car? (UK)	*Hat sie ein rotes Auto?*
Does she have a red car? (US)	*Hat sie ein rotes Auto?*

Negation | *Verneinung*

Die normale Satzverneinung mit **not** verlangt ein Hilfsverb. Dabei steht **not** zwischen dem Hilfsverb und dem Vollverb:

The guests had not arrived yet.	*Die Gäste waren noch nicht angekommen.*
We did not like the beer.	*Wir mochten das Bier nicht.*

Ohne **do** (in diesem Fall die Vergangenheitsform **did**) hätte der zweite Satz kein Hilfsverb. Der entsprechende nicht verneinte Satz lautet nämlich:

We liked the beer.	*Wir mochten Bier.*

Grammatik

Diesen Satz kann man nicht verneinen, indem man nur **not** in den Satz einschiebt!

In der gesprochenen Sprache verwendet man das volle Wort **not** nur zur ausdrücklichen, betonten Verneinung und sonst eher selten. Stattdessen verwendet man die reduzierte Form **-n't**, die an das Hilfsverb angehängt wird:

The guests **hadn't** arrived yet.	*Die Gäste waren noch nicht angekommen.*
We **didn't** like the beer.	*Wir mochten das Bier nicht.*

Wenn man nun eine **Yes-No Question** mit einem verneinten Satz bilden will, muss man das Hilfsverb voranziehen. Dabei geht **-n't** mit.

Didn't you like the beer? | *Habt ihr das Bier denn nicht gemocht?*

Kurzantworten

Wenn man eine Frage gestellt bekommt, ist es meist nicht notwendig mit einem vollständigen Satz zu antworten. Bei einer **Yes-No Question** kann man natürlich einfach nur **yes** oder **no** sagen. Dies wird aber oft als abgehackt und unhöflich empfunden. Daher hat man die Möglichkeit, einen abgekürzten Satz hinzuzufügen.

Bei der Antwort **yes** besteht der abgekürzte Satz nur aus Subjekt und Hilfsverb:

Did you see the film on Monday?	*Hast du am Montag den Film gesehen?*
Yes, I **did**.	*Ja, habe ich.*
Can you pass me the salt?	*Kannst Du mir das Salz geben?*
Yes, I **can**.	*Ja, kann ich.*

Grammatik

Bei der Antwort **no** besteht der abgekürzte Satz aus Subjekt und Hilfsverb mit angehängter Verneinung (**-n't**):

Did you see the film on Monday?	*Hast du am Montag den Film gesehen?*
No, I **didn't**.	*Nein, habe ich nicht.*
Can you pass me the salt?	*Kannst Du mir das Salz geben?*
No, I **can't**.	*Nein, kann ich nicht.*

Sehr wichtig bei Kurzantworten ist, dass das Hilfsverb immer dasselbe ist wie in der vorangegangenen Frage.

Es gibt auch noch spezielle Kurzantworten auf Subjektsfragen, d. h. Fragen, bei denen das Fragewort das Subjekt ist. Hier besteht die Kurzantwort aus dem Subjekt und dem entsprechenden Hilfsverb.

Who's [= has] been to Paris?	*Wer war schon mal in Paris?*
Terry and Larry **have**.	*Terry und Larry waren schon mal dort.*
Who bought the present for Susan?	*Wer hat das Geschenk für Susan gekauft?*
Harry **did**.	*Harry hat das gemacht.*

Tag Questions | *Frageanhängsel*

Eine sehr übliche Bildung im Englischen ist der Aussagesatz mit **Tag Question**. Das **Tag** (Anhängsel) hat die Form von einer Kurzfrage: Hilfsverb + Subjekt.

Laura hasn't taken my sweater, **has she**?	*Laura hat meinen Pullover nicht mitgenommen, oder?*

Das Subjekt der **Tag Question** ist immer das Pronomen, das dem Subjekt der vorangegangenen Aussage entspricht:

The children have returned, haven't they?	*Die Kinder sind zurück, oder?*

Wenn das einzige oder erste Verb in der Aussage kein Hilfsverb, sondern ein Vollverb ist, verwendet man **do** im **Tag** (Anhängsel).

You know my friend Sebastian, don't you?	*Du kennst meinen Freund Sebastian schon, nicht wahr?*

Wichtig ist, dass hinter einer bejahenden Aussage das verneinende **Tag** (Anhängsel) steht, und hinter einer verneinenden Aussage das bejahende **Tag** (Anhängsel).

Billie had left, hadn't she?	*Billie war schon gegangen, nicht wahr?*
Billie hadn't left, had she?	*Billie war noch nicht gegangen, nicht wahr?*

Formal betrachtet ist das Frageanhängsel eine Bitte um Bestätigung.

Modalverben

Formen

Modalverben sind eine Untergruppe der Hilfsverben und verhalten sich meist auch wie diese. Die wichtigsten Modalverben des Englischen sind **can, could, will, would, shall, should, may, might** und **must**. Es wird oft gesagt, dass die meisten dieser Hilfsverben sich in Gegenwarts-Vergangenheits-Paare einordnen lassen:

Grammatik

Gegenwartsform	Vergangenheitsform	Übersetzung
can	could	können
will	would	werden, wollen
shall	should	werden, sollen
may	might	dürfen, können

Diese Behauptung stimmt bezüglich der indirekten Rede. Ansonsten stimmt die Aussage in der Regel nicht. Nur **could** wird tatsächlich manchmal als Vergangenheitsform von **can** verwendet:

Gegenwart:	
You can open the door.	*Du kannst die Tür aufmachen.*
Vergangenheit:	
You could open the door, after all.	*Du konntest die Tür doch aufmachen.*

Es ist viel einfacher, die Bedeutungen der einzelnen Formen auswendig zu lernen.

can	*kann*	could	*konnte, könnte*
will	*wird*	would	*würde*
shall	*wird, soll*	should	*sollte, soll, dürfte*
may	*darf, kann*	might	*könnte*
must	*muss*		

Das englische **will** ist im modernen Sprachgebrauch nicht gleich dem deutschen *will* (*wollen*). Das deutsche Verb *wollen* wird mit dem Vollverb **want** übersetzt.

They will have dinner soon.   *Sie werden bald zu Abend essen.*
They want to have dinner soon.   *Sie wollen bald zu Abend essen.*

Parallel dazu heißt **would** *würde* (und nicht *wollte*).

Ms. Fielding would do it.	Frau Fielding würde es tun.
Ms. Fielding wanted to do it.	Frau Fielding wollte es tun.

Wenn man über eine Zeit in der Vergangenheit spricht, so kann man would auch einsetzen, um Gewohnheiten auszudrücken:

He would go in and order five hamburgers.	Er ging einfach rein und bestellte fünf Hamburger.

Gerade in der gesprochenen Sprache wird **will** oft zu **'ll** bzw. **would** zu **'d** verkürzt und an das Ende des Subjekts angehängt:

I'll bring my special tuna and ketchup salad.	Ich bringe meinen Tunfisch-und-Ketchup-Spezialsalat mit.
They'd buy a yacht if they had the money.	Sie würden sich eine Jacht kaufen, wenn sie das Geld hätten.

Fehlende Formen und Alternativen

Bei den Modalverben gibt es ein besonderes Problem: sie besitzen nicht alle nötigen Formen. Ein Modalverb kann immer nur das erste Verb im Satz (Haupt- oder Nebensatz) sein und es kann nicht hinter **to** stehen:

We can bake the cookies.	Wir können die Kekse backen.

Aus diesem Grund ist der Gebrauch von Modalverben natürlich ziemlich eingeschränkt. Trotzdem kommt es vor, dass man die Bedeutung eines Modalverbs an einer problematischen Stelle ausdrücken möchte. Dafür gibt es verschiedene Alternativen, mit denen man Modalverben ersetzen kann:

Modalverb	Alternative	Übersetzung
can, could	be able to	können
will, shall	be going to	werden
may	be allowed to	dürfen
must	have to	müssen
should	be supposed to	sollen

We have been able to to bake the cookies.	Wir konnten die Kekse backen.
They hoped to be able to bake the cookies.	Sie hofften, die Kekse backen zu können.

Verneinte Formen

Formen mit der verkürzten Version von **not** gibt es auch bei den Modalverben. Im Allgemeinen hängt man **n't** wie bei **have** und **do** an das Ende des Modalverbs an. Aber in ein paar Fällen muss man eine besondere Form verwenden:

can	+	n't	=	can't
will	+	n't	=	won't
shall	+	n't	=	shan't

Man beachte, dass **won't** manchmal die Bedeutung *will nicht* (im Sinne einer Verweigerung) haben kann:

The gardener won't rake the leaves.	Der Gärtner will das Laub nicht zusammenrechen.
The car won't start.	Das Auto will nicht anspringen.

Parallel dazu bedeutet **wouldn't** manchmal *wollte nicht*:

The gardener wouldn't rake the leaves.	Der Gärtner wollte das Laub nicht zusammenrechen.
The car wouldn't start.	Das Auto wollte nicht anspringen.

Gebrauch im Satz

Die Modalverben unterscheiden sich von den anderen Verben darin, dass ihre Form sich bei einem **he/she/it**-Subjekt nicht verändert:

I can go.	Ich kann hingehen.
She can go.	Sie kann hingehen.

Modalverben kommen an denselben Stellen im Satz vor wie andere Hilfsverben. Das Modalverb verlangt, dass das nächste Verb in der einfachen Grundform steht:

James can meet you at the airport.	*James kann dich vom Flughafen abholen.*
James can't meet you at the airport.	*James kann dich nicht vom Flughafen abholen.*
Should Cathy take her car?	*Soll Cathy mit ihrem Auto kommen?*
No, she shouldn't.	*Nein, das soll sie nicht.*
They'll just do it again, won't they?	*Sie werden es einfach wieder tun, oder?*

Das modalverbähnliche **ought (to)** bedeutet ungefähr das gleiche wie **should**. Im Gegensatz zu den Modalverben folgt aber immer ein Infinitiv mit **to**:

You ought to bathe sometimes.	*Du solltest dich ab und zu baden.*

Sonderfunktionen der Modalverben

Oft setzt man Modalverben ein, um klarzustellen, dass es sich bei einer Äußerung um eine Vermutung handelt. Die Wahl des Modalverbs zeigt die Wahrscheinlichkeit der Aussage an.

May und **might** können beide eine Möglichkeit ausdrücken. Dabei ist **may** ein bisschen sicherer oder wahrscheinlicher als **might**.

Ms. Young may know.	*Frau Young weiß es vielleicht.*
Ms. Young might know.	*Frau Young weiß es vielleicht.*

In **should** steckt die Annahme, dass ein Zustand existieren müsste oder sollte:

Ms. Young should know.	*Frau Young sollte es wissen.*
Walter should be feeding the cat now.	*Walter müsste jetzt die Katze füttern.*

Grammatik

Must ist stärker als **should** und bedeutet entweder eine starke Verpflichtung, oder dass der Sprecher annimmt, dass etwas der Fall sein muss (z.B. aufgrund von sichtbaren Beweisen):

Ms. Young must know.	*Frau Young muss es erfahren!*
The thief must have forgotten the money. There's still some of it lying on the floor.	*Der Dieb muss das Geld vergessen haben. Da liegt immer noch etwas auf dem Fussboden.*

Bei Verbketten, die aus einem Modalverb gefolgt von einer Perfektform bestehen, gibt es zwei Bedeutungsklassen. Die Bedeutung hängt immer vom Modalverb ab.

Vermutung:	
They **will have** paid the conman.	*Sie werden den Schwindler bezahlt haben.*
They **may have** paid the conman.	*Sie könnten den Schwindler bezahlt haben.*
They **might have** paid the conman.	*Sie können den Schwindler vielleicht bezahlt haben.*
They **must have** paid the conman.	*Sie müssen den Schwindler bezahlt haben.*
They **can't have** paid the conman.	*Sie können den Schwindler nicht bezahlt haben.*

Unwirkliches in der Vergangenheit:	
They **would have** paid the conman.	*Sie hätten den Schwindler bezahlt.*
They **could have** paid the conman.	*Sie hätten den Schwindler bezahlen können.*
They **should have** paid the conman.	*Sie hätten den Schwindler bezahlen sollen.*
They **might have** paid the conman.	*Sie hätten den Schwindler doch bezahlen können.*

Dabei sieht man, dass nur **might** in beide Klassen fällt.

Höflichkeitsformen

Would und **could** gelten in bittenden Fragen als besonders höflich:

Would you please close the door?	*Würden Sie bitte die Türe schließen?*
Could you bring me one too?	*Könntest du mir auch eins bringen?*

Spezielle Verben

Be | *Formen*

Simple Present		Simple Past	
I am	*ich bin*	I was	*ich war*
you are	*du bist*	you were	*du warst*
he/she/it is	*er/sie/es ist*	he/she/it was	*er/sie/es war*
we are	*wir sind*	we were	*wir waren*
you are	*ihr seid*	you were	*ihr wart*
they are	*sie sind*	they were	*sie waren*

In der gesprochenen Sprache verwendet man gern Kurzformen in der Gegenwart:

I am	▶	I'm
she is	▶	she's
you are	▶	you're
They are	▶	they're

I'm here – under the table!	*Ich bin hier – unter dem Tisch!*
She's nice.	*Sie ist nett.*
You're not alone.	*Du bist nicht allein.*

Grammatik

Anwendung

Be kann auch als Vollverb eingesetzt werden. Dann verbindet es das Subjekt mit einer anderen Phrase:

John **is** in the kitchen.	*John ist in der Küche.*
Such problems **are** normal.	*Solche Probleme sind normal.*
Susan **is** an excellent ice hockey player.	*Susan ist eine ausgezeichnete Eishockeyspielerin.*

Im Normalfall muss ein Vollverb in gewissen Situationen wie z.B. Verneinung oder **Yes-No-Questions** von einem Hilfsverb begleitet werden (▶ Hilfsverben). Bei **be** ist es anders – auch als Vollverb verhält sich **be** wie ein Hilfsverb: **be** steht vor **not**, leitet Fragen ein und taucht in Kurzantworten und Frageanhängseln auf:

Verneinung:	
John **isn't** in the kitchen.	*John ist nicht in der Küche.*
Ja-Nein-Frage:	
Is John in the kitchen?	*Ist John in der Küche?*

Kurzantworten:	
Yes, he **is**.	*Ja, ist er.*
No, he **isn't**.	*Nein, ist er nicht.*
Frageanhängsel:	
John **is** in the kitchen, **isn't** he?	*John ist in der Küche, oder?*

Be wird als Hilfsverb im Passiv und in den Progressive Formen benutzt, aber nicht im Present Perfect:

Food **is prepared** here.	*Hier wird Essen zubereitet.*
Frank **was reading**.	*Frank las gerade.*

There is/There are

There is (Singular) und **there are** (Plural) drücken meist Existenz, Anwesenheit oder Erscheinen aus:

There is a squirrel in the garden.	*Ein Eichhörnchen ist im Garten.*
There are squirrels in the garden.	*Ein paar Eichhörnchen sind im Garten.*
There are twelve months in a year.	*Das Jahr hat zwölf Monate.*

Bei dieser Verwendung handelt es sich um unbestimmte Dinge. Das bedeutet, dass man in der Regel keine bestimmten Artikel, Demonstrative oder Eigennamen nach **there is/there are** benutzen darf:

There was a stranger at the party.	*Da war ein Fremder auf dem Fest.*

There is/there are kann auch bei Aufzählungen verwendet werden:

Frage:	
What chores do you still have to do?	*Was musst du noch an Hausarbeit machen?*
Antwort:	
Well, there's the washing and the ironing. Then there are the dishes.	*Also, da wäre das Waschen und Bügeln. Dann muss ich auch noch abspülen.*

Have und have got | *Gegenwartsformen von have*

I have	*Ich habe*
you have	*Du hast*
he, she, it has	*Er, sie, es hat*
we have	*Wir haben*
you have	*Du hast*
they have	*Sie haben*

Grammatik

Anwendung

Have kann ebenfalls als Vollverb gebraucht werden. Am häufigsten bedeutet **have** *haben* im Sinne von *besitzen, bei sich haben*, usw.:

The Smiths have a yellow car.	*Die Smiths haben ein gelbes Auto.*

Eine Alternative zu diesem **have** ist **have got**:

The Smiths have got a yellow car.	*Die Smiths haben ein gelbes Auto.*

> Im Amerikanischen gilt **have got** als umgangssprachlich und wird in formellen Situationen nicht verwendet.

Have mit und ohne Hilfsverb

Das tückische bei **have** sind die Situationen, in denen man ein Hilfsverb braucht und keines vorhanden ist. (Die englischen Muttersprachler sind sich nämlich nicht einig, wie man die Sätze bilden soll!)

Strategie 1: **have** wird wie ein Hilfsverb gebraucht:

They haven't a bicycle.	*Sie haben kein Fahrrad.*
Have you a car?	*Hast du ein Auto?*

Obwohl diese Strategie wohl am einfachsten ist, bringt sie gewisse Probleme mit sich: Erstens wird sie im Amerikanischen nur noch in ein paar alten Ausdrücken überhaupt verwendet und kommt den Leuten fremd vor. Zweitens kommt sie in Großbritannien auch aus der Mode; dort wird sie hauptsächlich von älteren Leuten benutzt.

Strategie 2: **have** wird wie ein Vollverb gebraucht:

Dies ist die gängige Strategie des Amerikanischen. Sie hat zur Folge, dass man **do** einsetzt, wenn ein Hilfsverb gebraucht wird:

They don't have a bicycle.	*Sie haben kein Fahrrad.*
Do you have a car?	*Hast du ein Auto?*

Grammatik

Strategie 3: **have** wird durch **have got** ersetzt:

They haven't got a bicycle.	*Sie haben kein Fahrrad.*
Have you got a car?	*Hast du ein Auto?*

Diese Strategie stellt die moderne Lösung in Großbritannien dar. Sie hat den Vorteil, dass man sie in der Umgangssprache überall anwenden kann. Im Amerikanischen gehört sie zum lockeren Sprachgebrauch; in der Standardsprache muss man Strategie 2 nehmen.

Weitere Bedeutungen von have

Have wird auch in anderen Zusammenhängen und festen Verbindungen verwendet, die man am besten auswendig lernt:

We have breakfast at 8:00.	*Wir frühstücken um 8.00.*
I had a cup of coffee.	*Ich habe eine Tasse Kaffee getrunken.*
Lisa is having a baby.	*Lisa bekommt ein Kind.*
Keith had a smoke.	*Keith rauchte eine.*

Bei den obigen Beispielen muss man Strategie 2 anwenden:

Did they have breakfast with you?	*Haben sie mit euch gefrühstückt?*
I didn't have a cup of coffee.	*Ich habe keine Tasse Kaffee getrunken.*
Keith didn't have a smoke.	*Keith hat nicht geraucht.*

Do | *Gegenwartsformen*

I do	*Ich mache*
you do	*Du machst*
he/she/it does	*Er/sie/es macht*
we do	*wir machen*
you do	*Ihr macht*
they do	*Sie machen*

Grammatik

Anwendung

Do ist nicht nur das Spezialhilfsverb, das bei den Vollverben aushilft, sondern wird auch selbst als Vollverb eingesetzt:

The children did their homework.	*Die Kinder machten ihre Hausaufgaben.*
What are you doing?	*Was machst du?*

Wenn nun ein Hilfsverb unentbehrlich ist und nur das Vollverb **do** zur Verfügung steht, muss man auch das Hilfsverb **do** einsetzen. Dann enthält der Satz zweimal **do:**

The children didn't do their homework.	*Die Kinder haben ihre Hausaufgaben nicht gemacht.*
What did you do?	*Was hast du gemacht?*

Get

Get ist ein meist umgangssprachliches Verb mit der Grundbedeutung *kriegen* bzw. *bekommen*:

I got a watch for my birthday.	*Ich habe eine Uhr zum Geburtstag bekommen.*
We finally got the door open.	*Endlich haben wir die Tür aufgekriegt.*
I couldn't get the cat down from the tree.	*Ich habe die Katze nicht vom Baum runterkriegen können.*

Get kann aber auch *werden* bedeuten:

We were getting tired.	*Wir wurden allmählich müde.*
It gets hot here in summer.	*Es wird hier im Sommer heiß.*
Tony got hit by car.	*Tony wurde von einem Auto angefahren.*

Be used to und get used to

Die Phrase **be used to** bedeutet *etwas gewöhnt sein*. Sie wird mit **be** verwendet um einen Zustand des Gewöhntseins auszudrücken:

She's used to the noise. Ms. Thompson is used to teaching large classes.	*Sie ist den Lärm gewöhnt.* *Frau Thompson ist es gewöhnt große Klassen zu unterrichten.*

Get used to hingegen bedeutet *sich an (etwas) gewöhnen*.

She got used to the noise quickly. I can't get used to English pronunciation. Ms. Thompson is getting used to teaching large classes.	*She gewöhnte sich schnell an den Lärm.* *Ich kann mich an die englische Aussprache nicht gewöhnen.* *Frau Thompson gewöhnt sich daran große Klassen zu unterrichten.*

2 Prepositions | *Verhältniswörter*

Zeitangaben

- Die Uhrzeiten werden mit **at** angegeben:

I'll be home at seven.	*Ich bin um sieben Uhr wieder zu Hause.*
We had lunch at noon.	*Wir aßen um zwölf zu Mittag.*

- **Morning, afternoon** und **evening** verlangen die Präposition **in** und den bestimmten Artikel **the**:

Stretch before you get up in the morning.	*Strecken Sie sich, bevor Sie morgens aufstehen.*
The children always play in the afternoon.	*Nachmittags spielen die Kinder immer.*
In the evening we went out.	*Am Abend gingen wir aus.*

- **Night** verlangt meist die Präposition **at** und tritt dann ohne Artikel auf:

Owls hunt at night.	*Eulen gehen nachts auf die Jagd.*
My friend Steve, a catburglar, works at night.	*Mein Freund Steve, ein Fassadenkletterer, arbeitet nachts.*

Vorsicht, denn der Abend wird auch sehr häufig als **night** bezeichnet:

What did you do last night?	*Was habt ihr gestern Abend gemacht?*
When I get home at night, I make dinner.	*Wenn ich abends nach Hause komme, mache ich das Abendessen.*

Grammatik

- Wochentage werden häufig mit **on** angegeben:

I have an appointment on Wednesday.	*Ich habe am Mittwoch einen Termin.*
Most museums are closed on Mondays.	*Die meisten Museen sind montags geschlossen.*

Jedoch kann man **on** in der gesprochenen Sprache auch weglassen:

I have an appointment Wednesday.	*Ich habe am Mittwoch einen Termin.*
Most museums are closed Mondays.	*Die meisten Museen haben montags zu.*

In Großbritannien sagt man **at the weekend**, in Nordamerika stattdessen **on the weekend**.

- Einzelne Feiertage brauchen normalerweise **on**:

We get half the day off on Christmas Eve.	*Heiligen Abend bekommen wir den halben Tag frei.*
Many people go to church at sunrise on Easter.	*An Ostern gehen viele Leute bei Sonnenaufgang in die Kirche.*

At oder **over** weisen nicht nur auf den Feiertag hin, sondern auch auf die Zeit um den Feiertag herum:

I saw my aunt and uncle at Christmas.	*Ich habe meine Tante und meinen Onkel zu Weihnachten gesehen.*
I'm flying home over Easter.	*Ich fliege zu Ostern nach Hause.*

Grammatik

- Monate und Jahreszeiten werden mit **in** angegeben:

It happened in July.	*Es ist im Juli passiert.*
The neighbors barbecued every day in August.	*Im August grillten die Nachbarn jeden Tag.*
In winter we need to heat the house.	*Im Winter müssen wir das Haus heizen.*

- Man braucht **in** auch immer bei Jahreszahlen:

In 1492 Columbus discovered America.	*1492 entdeckte Columbus Amerika.*
Sales figures fell in 1996.	*Die Verkaufszahlen sind 1996 gefallen.*

Während

In der Regel wird *während* mit **during** ausgedrückt:

I fell asleep during the opera.	*Ich bin während der Oper eingeschlafen.*
She arrived during the winter.	*Sie kam im Laufe des Winters an.*

Als Übersetzung für *während des/der ganzen ...* nimmt man meist **throughout**:

The postal service is very busy throughout the Christmas season.	*Die Post hat während der ganzen Weihnachtszeit sehr viel zu tun.*
Evergreens stay green throughout the year.	*Immergrüne Pflanzen bleiben das ganze Jahr über grün.*

Bei **day, night, month, year** geht es ohne Präposition – man setzt einfach all davor:

The cats sang outside my window all night.	*Die Katzen haben die ganze Nacht vor meinem Fenster miaut.*
Evergreens stay green all year.	*Immergrüne Pflanzen bleiben das ganze Jahr über grün.*

For gibt an, wie lange ein Ereignis dauert:

Nigel and Joo didn't talk to each other for a year.	*Nigel und Joo sprachen ein Jahr lang nicht miteinander.*
They worked for five more hours.	*Sie arbeiteten fünf weitere Stunden.*

Das deutsche Wort *vor* hat zwei verschiedene Übersetzungen. Wenn sich *vor* auf einen Zeitpunkt bezieht, übersetzt man es mit **before**:

Before the flood we lived in the valley.	*Vor der Überflutung lebten wir im Tal.*
We had to get up before daybreak.	*Wir mussten vor Tagesanbruch aufstehen.*

Wenn man stattdessen eine Zeitspanne nennt, verwendet man im Englischen keine Präposition, sondern setzt **ago** nach dem Zeitraum:

We met six years ago.	*Wir haben uns vor sechs Jahren kennen gelernt.*
Three days ago my car broke down.	*Vor drei Tagen ist mein Auto kaputtgegangen.*

Ortsangaben

Die wichtigsten Präpositionen für die Ortsangabe sind **in** und **on**:

We stayed in New York.	*Wir wohnten in New York.*
There's a frog on my desk.	*Auf meinem Schreibtisch ist ein Frosch.*

Man muss **on** (*auf*) und **at** (*an*) unterscheiden:

We all sat down on the table.	*Wir setzten uns alle auf den Tisch.*
We all sat down at the table.	*Wir setzten uns alle an den Tisch.*

Grammatik

An den obigen Beispielsätzen sieht man, dass Phrasen wie **sit down, lie down, set down, lay down** nicht immer zu den jeweiligen Präpositionen passen. Man lernt daher diese Phrasen in ihren einzelnen Zusammensetzungen am besten auswendig.

At verwendet man auch für Anwesenheit in Läden und auf Veranstaltungen:

I ran into Ralph at the pharmacy.	*Ich traf Ralph in der Apotheke.*
The adults are at the circus,	*Die Erwachsenen sind im Zirkus,*
but the children are at the museum.	*aber die Kinder sind im Museum.*
Who was at the party?	*Wer war alles auf der Party?*

Problemfälle

Der Ausdruck **at home** heißt immer *zu Hause*:

I often stay at home.	*Ich bleibe oft zu Hause.*

Bei einer Ortsangabe bedeutet **by** *ganz in der Nähe von*, nicht *bei*:

Vera lives by Jonathan.	*Vera wohnt ganz in der Nähe von Jonathan.*
Vera lives at Jonathan's.	*Vera wohnt bei John.*

In der Nähe von heißt auf Englisch oft einfach **near**:

Newark is near New York City.	*Newark liegt in der Nähe von New York.*
There's a telephone booth near the church.	*In der Nähe der Kirche ist eine Telefonzelle.*

Richtung

Into (*in/hinein*) und **onto** (*auf*) zeigen die räumliche oder zeitliche Richtung oder Orientierung eines Geschehens. Im Gegensatz zu **on** oder **in** steht hier das jeweilige Verb bzw. Geschehen im Mittelpunkt.

The rabbit jumped into a hole.	*Das Kaninchen ist in ein Loch gesprungen.*
Jeff got into trouble.	*Jeff geriet in Schwierigkeiten.*
Bonzo fell onto my foot.	*Bonzo fiel mir auf den Fuss.*

Manchmal kann man aber auch **into** und **onto** mit **in** und **on** ersetzen:

We got into/in the car.	*Wir sind ins Auto gestiegen.*
She put chocolate in/into the cake.	*Sie hat Schokolade in den Kuchen getan.*
The ball rolled onto/on the street.	*Der Ball rollte auf die Strasse.*

To deutet an, dass sich etwas nicht nur in eine Richtung bewegt, sondern auch ankommt:

We went to the supermarket.	*Wir sind zum Supermarkt gegangen.*
Let's go to Switzerland!	*Fahren wir in die Schweiz!*

To wird auch häufig anstatt des Wemfalles (Dativ) verwendet:

The librarian showed the visitor the books.	*Die Bibliothekarin zeigte dem Besucher die Bücher.*
▸ The librarian showed the books to the visitor.	*Die Bibliothekarin zeigte dem Besucher die Bücher.*
She explained the problem to me.	*Sie erklärte mir das Problem.*
They recommended a cheap restaurant to me.	*Sie haben mir ein billiges Restaurant empfohlen.*

Grammatik

Die Phrase **go to (someone)** bedeutet, dass man zu der Person als solche gegangen ist, nicht zu deren Wohnung o.ä.:

I went to Mary and told her the story.	*Ich ging zu Mary und erzählte ihr die Geschichte.*

From sagt uns, woher jemand oder etwas kommt:

Kyle is from Athens, Georgia.	*Kyle stammt aus Athens in Georgia.*
We drove from the bank to the restaurant next door.	*Wir sind mit dem Auto von der Bank zum Restaurant nebenan gefahren.*

From verwendet man auch bei Entfernungen:

Oakville is five miles from here.	*Oakville liegt fünf Meilen von hier entfernt.*
It's four inches from the doorframe to the wall.	*Vom Türrahmen zur Wand sind es etwa zehn Zentimeter.*

Of ist ein vielseitiges Wort. Besonders schriftsprachlich muss man meist **of** anstelle des Besitzfalles (Possessive) bei Besitzern und Verursachern verwenden, wenn etwas nach dem Kernwort der Noun Phrase steht:

Possessive:	
The funny young man's favorite aunt	*Die Lieblingstante des komischen jungen Mannes*
Tom's advice	*Toms Rat*
Of-Phrase:	
The favorite aunt of the man wearing a silk suit	*Die Lieblingstante des Mannes im Seidenanzug*
The advice of a stranger	*Der Rat eines Fremden*

Eine sehr wichtige Anwendung von **of** drückt Zugehörigkeit oder Zuordnung aus:

An association of scientists was having a meeting.	*Eine Gruppe Wissenschaftler tagte gerade.*
The man was standing naked on the roof of the house.	*Der Mann stand nackt auf dem Dach des Hauses.*

Man verwendet **of** zusammen mit Mengen- und Inhaltsangaben:

a pinch of salt	*eine Prise Salz*
a box of matches	*eine Schachtel Streichhölzer*
a glass of water	*ein Glas Wasser*
I ate a bowl of soup, a slice of bread, and a can of beans, and drank two big glasses of grape juice.	*Ich aß einen Teller Suppe, eine Scheibe Brot und eine Dose Bohnen und trank zwei große Gläser Traubensaft.*

Das Wort **pair** (**of**) bezieht sich immer auf zwei Gegenstände oder Leute:

Rene bought a pair of socks.	*Rene kaufte ein Paar Socken.*
They made a pretty pair.	*Sie waren ein hübsches Pärchen.*

Häufig markiert **of** die entsprechende Phrase nach dem verwandten Nomen (*Noun*):

The delay of the flight worried the passengers.	*Die Verspätung des Fluges beunruhigte die Passagiere.*
The classification of bats is a difficult business.	*Die Klassifizierung von Fledermäusen ist ein schwieriges Unterfangen.*
The baking of cookies leads to overeating.	*Das Plätzchenbacken führt dazu, dass man zu viel isst.*

Of gibt auch die Todesursache an:

My grandmother died of old age.	*Meine Großmutter ist an Altersschwäche gestorben.*
Timothy Toast almost died of overeating.	*Timothy Toast starb fast an zuviel Essen.*

By drückt aus von wem oder was etwas gemacht worden ist:

I'm reading an exciting book by Sara Paretsky.	*Ich lese gerade ein spannendes Buch von Sara Paretsky.*
Who's the article by?	*Von wem ist der Artikel?*

Komplexe Präpositionen

Einige wenige Präpositionen bestehen aus zwei oder mehr Wörtern:

because of	*aufgrund, wegen*
in spite of	*trotz*
instead of	*(an)statt*
out of	*aus*
from under	*von unter*

The game was cancelled because of the snowstorm.	*Das Spiel wurde wegen des Schneesturms abgesagt.*
In spite of their promise, they behaved badly.	*Trotz ihres Versprechens haben sie sich schlecht benommen.*
Clint came out of the bathroom half dressed.	*Clint kam halb angezogen aus dem Bad.*
Betsy crawled out from under the bed.	*Betsy kam unter dem Bett hervorgekrochen.*

3 Phrasal Verbs | *Partikelverben*

Allgemeines

Phrasal Verb wird oft als ein Überbegriff für mehrere Bildungstypen aus einem Verb und mindestens einem zusätzlichen Element verwendet. Dabei muss man zwischen zwei Arten von ähnlichen zusätzlichen Elementen unterscheiden: Präpositionen und Partikel. Präpositionen verlangen immer eine *Noun Phrase*, mit anderen Worten ihr eigenes Objekt. Dieses Objekt muss – außer in Fragewort-Fragen, Relativsätzen u.ä. – nach der Präposition stehen. Partikel treten zwar häufig zusammen mit Noun Phrases auf, aber die Noun Phrase ist nicht das Objekt der Partikel und muss daher nicht dahinter stehen. Das Schwierige bei der Sache ist natürlich, dass Präpositionen und Partikel oft gleich aussehen! Ein relativ einfacher Test ist die Verschiebbarkeit des Elements. Kann es hinter der Noun Phrase oder dem Fürwort (Pronoun) stehen, so ist es ein Partikel. Muss es immer vor der Noun Phrase oder dem Pronoun stehen, ist es eine Präposition.

Präposition:	
The woman pushed the stroller up the street.	*Die Frau schob den Sportwagen die Straße hoch.*
Partikel:	
The woman looked up the telephone number. **The woman looked the telephone number up.**	*Die Frau schlug die Telefonnummer nach.*

Es gibt auch verschiedene Kombinationsmöglichkeiten:

Verb	+	Partikel				
Verb	+	Partikel	+	Noun Phrase		
Verb	+	Präposition	+	Noun Phrase		
Verb	+	Partikel	+	Präposition	+	Noun Phrase

Grammatik

Beispiele für Verb + Partikel

come along	mitkommen	grow up	aufwachsen, erwachsen werden
get in	einsteigen (ins Auto)		
get on	einsteigen (in den Bus, Zug, Flugzeug)	make up	sich versöhnen
		run away	weglaufen
get up	aufstehen	sit down	sich hinsetzen
go along	mitgehen	take off	abheben, abfliegen, sich davonmachen
go away	weggehen		
go back	zurückgehen	wake up	aufwachen

Die Partikel steht unmittelbar nach dem Verb:

I have to **get up** so early every morning!	*Ich muss jeden Morgen so früh aufstehen!*
The others wanted to go to the party without me, but I **went along** anyway.	*Die anderen wollten ohne mich auf die Party, aber ich bin trotzdem mitgegangen.*
The unhappy teenager **ran away** from home.	*Der unglückliche Teenager ist von zu Hause weggelaufen.*

Beispiele für Verb + Partikel + *Noun Phrase*

bring along	mitbringen	put on	anziehen
bring back	zurückbringen	ring up	anrufen (UK)
call off	absagen	run over	überfahren
call up	anrufen (US)	stand up	versetzen, sitzen lassen
let in	hereinlassen	take along	mitnehmen
look up	nachschlagen	take off	ausziehen
make up	schminken; (Geschichte) erfinden	turn down	kleiner oder leiser stellen
		turn off	ausschalten
pick up	abholen	turn on	einschalten

In der Wortfolge stehen Partikel und Noun Phrase nach dem Verb und vor anderen Elementen wie z. B. Adverbien. Bei voller Noun Phrase ist es grammatisch gesehen egal, ob die Partikel vor der Noun Phrase steht oder umgekehrt – obwohl manchmal die eine oder andere Wortfolge üblicher wird. Wenn aber die Noun Phrase ein Pronomen (Fürwort) ist, muss sie vor der Partikel stehen.

Judith **stood up** Mel.	*Judith hat Mel sitzen lassen.*
Judith **stood** Mel **up**.	*Judith hat Mel sitzen lassen.*
Judith **stood** him **up**.	*Judith hat ihn sitzen lassen.*

Casey **called** us **up** last night.	*Casey hat uns gestern Abend angerufen.*
Lenny **made** that story **up**.	*Lenny hat diese Geschichte erfunden.*
When they **called off** the wedding, the make-up artist was already **making up** the bride.	*Als sie die Hochzeit absagten, war die Visagistin schon dabei, die Braut zu schminken.*

Beispiele für Verb + Präposition + *Noun Phrase*

call for	*rufen nach; fordern; abholen*	look at	*anschauen*
care for	*pflegen*	look for	*suchen*
do without	*auskommen ohne*	run after	*hinterherlaufen*
listen to	*zuhören; hören auf*	run across	*stoßen auf*
look after	*hüten; sich kümmern um*	run into	*zufällig treffen; rennen/ fahren gegen*

Man verwendet die Präposition genauso wie sonst, d.h. sie stehen immer vor ihrer Noun Phrase oder dem Pronoun:

You never **listen to** me!	*Du hörst mir nie zu!*
I can't possibly **do without** my waffle iron.	*Ich kann unmöglich ohne mein Waffeleisen auskommen.*
I was **looking for** a job and **ran across** an unusual advertisement.	*Ich habe nach einer Stelle gesucht und bin dabei auf eine ungewöhnliche Anzeige gestoßen.*

Grammatik

Die Präposition und ihr Objekt stehen meist vor anderen Phrasen, die hinten im Satz stehen können.

The babysitter looks after the children on weekdays.	*Die Babysitterin passt an Wochentagen auf die Kinder auf.*
A nurse cares for their sick child at their home.	*Eine Krankenschwester pflegt ihr krankes Kind bei ihnen zu Hause.*

Beispiele für Verb + Partikel + Präposition + *Noun Phrase*

catch up with	*einholen*	**look forward to**	*sich freuen auf*
do away with	*abschaffen; umbringen*	**look out for**	*achten auf; Ausschau halten nach*
fall back on	*zurückgreifen auf*		
	herumkommen um;	**put up with**	*sich gefallen lassen*
get out of	*herauskommen aus*	**rub off on**	*abfärben auf*
keep up with	*Schritt halten mit; mithalten mit*	**run out of**	*kein ... mehr haben*
		watch out for	*achten auf*
look down on	*herabsehen auf*		

Man muss die Wortfolge beachten: Nach dem Verb kommt zunächst die Partikel, dann die Präposition und erst dann die Noun Phrase.

Watch out for pickpockets at the fair!	*Achtet auf Taschendiebe auf dem Jahrmarkt!*
His bad mood rubbed off on the others.	*Seine schlechte Laune färbte sich auf die anderen ab.*
We ran out of milk yesterday.	*Uns ist gestern die Milch ausgegangen.*
My boyfriend is running out of excuses.	*Meinem Freund gehen langsam die Ausreden aus.*
I promised to go, and now I can't get out of it.	*Ich habe versprochen hinzugehen, und jetzt komme ich nicht mehr drum herum.*
Audrey is always on the run; no one can keep up with her.	*Audrey ist ständig auf Achse, keiner kann mit ihr mithalten.*

4 Nouns | *Hauptwörter*

Groß- und Kleinschreibung

Im Englischen werden die meisten Hauptwörter (Nouns) kleingeschrieben:

The boy bought a hamburger and a salad.	*Der Junge hat einen Hamburger und einen Salat gekauft.*

Eigennamen aber werden großgeschrieben:

In London, George and Marilyn went to see the Tate Gallery.	*In London haben George und Marilyn die Tate Gallery besucht.*

Die Namen der Wochentage, Monate sowie auch Nationalitäten, Sprachen und Religionen bzw. Religionszugehörigkeiten gelten als Eigennamen:

Mr. Firth normally comes on Mondays, but this Monday he wasn't there.	*Herr Firth kommt normalerweise montags, aber diesen Montag ist er nicht gekommen.*
It's nearly always cold in February.	*Im Februar ist es fast immer kalt.*
The Americans took pictures, while the New Zealanders talked.	*Die Amerikaner machten Fotos, während die Neuseeländer redeten.*
I speak English, German and Chinese.	*Ich spreche Englisch, Deutsch und Chinesisch*
In this part of town, Jews, Christians and Muslims live together peacefully.	*In diesem Stadtviertel leben Juden, Christen, und Muslime friedlich miteinander.*

The Plural | *die Mehrzahl*

Den regelmäßigen Plural bildet man mit **-s**:

The gardeners asked for pails, shovels, and rakes.	*Die Gärtner baten um Eimer, Schaufeln und Rechen.*

Grammatik

Wenn nun das Wort mit einem Zischlaut endet, kann man das **-s** (auch ein Zischlaut) nicht direkt an den ersten Zischlaut hängen, sondern man braucht einen kleinen Vokal dazwischen.

- Wenn der Singular mit einem ungesprochenen **e** endet, hängt man im Plural das **-s** einfach daran und spricht das **es** dann als eigene Silbe aus:

prince (einsilbig):	**princes** (zweisilbig)	*Prinze(n)*
garage (zweisilbig):	**garages** (dreisilbig)	*Garagen*

- Wenn der Singular nicht mit einem ungesprochenen Buchstaben endet, hängt man gleich **-es** daran und spricht dies genauso als eigene Silbe aus:

church (einsilbig):	**churches** (zweisilbig)	*Kirche(n)*
bush (einsilbig):	**bushes** (zweisilbig)	*Büsche*

- Wenn die Singularform einen Konsonanten und dann **-y** am Ende hat, wird das **-y** im Plural meist zu **ie** vor dem **-s**:

ferry	**ferries**	*Fähren*
copy	**copies**	*Kopien, Ausgaben (Bücher)*

Es gibt zwölf Nouns, die in -**f** oder -**fe** enden, und dieses gegen **-ves** tauschen, wenn sie in den Plural gesetzt werden:

wife	**wives**	*Ehefrauen*
wolf	**wolves**	*Wölfe*
thief	**thieves**	*Diebe*

(ebenso: **calf, half, knife, leaf, life, loaf, self, sheaf, shelf**). **Hoof, carf, wharf** können beide Formen **–s** oder **–ves** annehmen.

Das Englische hat darüber hinaus genau wie das Deutsche natürlich noch eine Reihe von unregelmässigen Pluralformen, die auswendig gelernt müssen:

man	men	*Männer*
woman	women	*Frauen*
foot	feet	*Füße*
mouse	mice	*Mäuse*
tooth	teeth	*Zähne*
child	children	*Kinder*
phenomenon	phenomena	*Phänomene*

Possessive | *besitzanzeigende Form*

Die besitzanzeigende Form wird normalerweise mit **'s** gebildet:

| **Cathy's mouse escaped.** | *Cathys Maus ist entkommen.* |
| **Bill's best friend's tennis racket broke.** | *Der Tennisschläger von Bills bestem Freund ist kaputtgegangen.* |

Wenn das Noun im Plural steht und deswegen ein **-s** am Ende hat, lässt man das **'s** der besitzanzeigenden Form weg. Dann hängt man nur **'** (einen Apostroph) ans Ende des Noun. Natürlich hört man danach keinen Unterschied zur normalen Pluralform, aber man sieht sie in schriftlichen Texten:

| **The boys' tennis rackets broke.** | *Die Tennisschläger der Jungen sind kaputtgegangen.* |
| **The boy's tennis racket broke.** | *Der Tennisschläger des Jungen ist kaputtgegangen.* |

Grammatik

Wenn der Plural nicht mit **-s** gebildet wird, benutzt man die besitzanzeigende Form des Plurals mit **'s**:

The children's toys are in the way.	*Das Spielzeug der Kinder steht im Weg.*
Those deer's antlers grow quickly.	*Das Geweih dieser Rehe wächst schnell.*

Bei manchen Eigennamen (vor allem bei berühmten Persönlichkeiten), die mit **-s** enden, lässt man das **s** der besitzanzeigenden Form wie bei dem **s**-Plural weg:

The Beatles' words always impressed their followers.	*Die Worte der Beatles beeindruckten ihre Anhänger immer.*

Dieselben Aussprachregeln wie beim Plural gelten auch beim Possessive **'s**.
Wenn das Kernwort der Noun Phrase einen Artikel hat, lässt man ihn weg:

The daughter of a queen is a princess.	*Die Tochter einer Königin ist eine Prinzessin.*
▶ **A queen's daughter is a princess.**	*Die Tochter einer Königin ist eine Prinzessin.*

Problemfälle

Folgende Bildung ist für die meisten Leute etwas unerwartet, kommt im Englischen aber häufig vor:

A friend of my mother's tapdanced at the wedding.	*Eine Freundin meiner Mutter steppte bei der Hochzeit.*
Two books of Helen's got lost.	*Zwei von Helens Bücher sind verloren gegangen.*

Grammatik

Man kann die Possessiv-Form alleine verwenden um die Wohnung der genannten Person zu bezeichnen.

There was a wild party at Leo's last night.	Bei Leo gab es gestern Abend eine wilde Party.
We're going to the Millers' for a meeting.	Wir gehen zu einer Besprechung zu den Millers.
I'll be at my mother's.	Ich werde bei meiner Mutter sein.

Viele Geschäfte werden nach demselben Prinzip benannt: sie bekommen den Namen des Inhabers in der besitzanzeigenden Form:

I bought all my dishes at Jenner's.	Ich habe mein ganzes Geschirr bei Jenner gekauft.
After breakfast at Tiffany's, we went to Sotheby's.	Nach dem Frühstück bei Tiffany sind wir zu Sotheby gegangen.

Man kann auch auf Geschäfte, Praxen usw. nach der Berufsbezeichnung des Inhabers hinweisen.

I spent the morning at the doctor's.	Ich habe den Vormittag beim Arzt verbracht.
I got this exotic orchid at the florist's.	Ich habe diese exotische Orchidee vom Floristen.

Man verwendet Possessive 's zusammen mit bestimmten Zeitangaben:

It was in Tuesday's paper.	Es war in der Zeitung vom Dienstag.
The older generation is agreed that today's youth is lazy – and their parents said the same thing 30 years ago.	Die ältere Generation ist sich darüber einig, dass die Jugend von heute faul sei – und ihre Eltern sagten vor 30 Jahren das gleiche.

Grammatik

Zählbare und nicht zählbare Nouns

Im Allgemeinen kann man Nouns in zwei Klassen einteilen: zählbare und nicht zählbare. Die zählbaren Nouns bezeichnen einzelne Dinge, die man zählen kann:

I want a pineapple.	*Ich möchte eine Ananas.*
I want three pineapples.	*Ich möchte drei Ananas.*

Die nicht zählbaren Nouns bezeichnen Sachen, die als Mengen oder Massen betrachtet werden. Man verwendet dabei immer den Singular:

The milk always goes off.	*Die Milch wird immer schlecht.*
The wheat is being harvested.	*Der Weizen wird gerade geerntet.*
I'd like some jam.	*Ich hätte gern Marmelade.*

Es ist möglich, manche von diesen Wörtern im Plural zu verwenden, wobei sie meistens als Portionen oder Sorten zu verstehen sind:

Two coffees and eight beers, please.	*Zwei Kaffee und acht Bier, bitte.*
They grow three different wheats here.	*Hier bauen sie drei verschiedene Weizensorten an.*
I've tried all the jams.	*Ich habe alle Marmeladensorten schon probiert.*

Trotzdem gibt es nicht zählbare Nouns, die so nicht verwendet werden können:

His information was always unreliable.	*Die Informationen von ihm waren immer unzuverlässig.*
She has had a lot of experience.	*Sie hat schon eine Menge Erfahrung gesammelt.*
The room was full of furniture.	*Der Raum war voller Möbel.*

Das Wort **news** (ebenso wie **mumps**) sieht aus wie Plural, ist aber Singular:

All the news in the paper was good that day.	An diesem Tag waren alle Nachrichten in der Zeitung gut.
The good news is that we have a spare tire; the bad news is that we don't have the necessary tools to mount it.	Die gute Nachricht ist, dass wir einen Ersatzreifen haben, die schlechte Nachricht ist, dass wir das notwendige Werkzeug nicht haben, um ihn zu montieren.

Es gibt unterschiedliche Verwendungsweisen für Bezeichnungen von Institutionen und Personengruppen (collective nouns) wie etwa **police, government, team, family**, je nachdem, ob man diese als Einheit oder eine Anzahl Individuen sieht:

Our family is the best.	Unsere Familie ist die beste.
Our family are wearing their motto shirts now.	Unsere Familienmitglieder tragen jetzt ihre Mottohemden.

Pair Nouns

Es gibt Nouns, die einen Gegenstand bezeichnen, aber trotzdem als Paare aufgefasst werden (**pair** = Paar). Normalerweise handelt es sich um Gegenstände, die aus zwei Teilen bestehen:

This pair of scissors is blunt.	Diese Schere ist stumpf.
Bring me a pair of pliers!	Bring mir eine Zange!
I need a new pair of glasses.	Ich brauche eine neue Brille.

Grammatik

Oft verwendet man sie ohne **pair of** im Plural:

These scissors are blunt.	*Diese Schere ist stumpf.*
Bring me the pliers!	*Bring mir die Zange!*
I need new glasses.	*Ich brauche eine neue Brille.*
I'm looking for a pair of paisley trousers.	*Ich suche eine Hose mit Paisleymuster.*
My pants have shrunk.	*Meine Hose (US)/Unterhose (UK) ist eingelaufen.*
These jeans don't fit.	*Diese Jeans passt nicht.*

Solche Wörter lassen sich nur paarweise zählen:

I'd like two pairs of green jeans.	*Ich hätte gern zwei grüne Jeans.*

Proper Names: Titles

> Abkürzungen von Titeln werden im britischen Englisch ohne Punkt und im Amerikanischen mit Punkt geschrieben.

Der allgemeine Titel für Männer ist **Mr.**:

Mr. Johnson	*Herr Johnson*

Bei den Frauen ist die Lage komplizierter: Es gibt zwei herkömmliche Titel – **Miss** für unverheiratete Frauen (z. B. **Miss Johnson** = *Fräulein Johnson*) und **Mrs.** für verheiratete (z. B. **Mrs. Johnson** = *Frau Johnson*, also die Ehefrau von einem **Mr. Johnson**). Inzwischen aber gibt es auch einen dritten, allgemeinen Titel für alle Frauen, ganz gleich, ob sie verheiratet sind oder nicht: **Ms.** (z. B. **Ms. Johnson** = *Frau Johnson*). **Ms.** ist auch der einzige korrekte Titel für Frauen, die in der Ehe ihren eigenen Nachnamen beibehalten haben.

Dr. und Prof.

In der englischsprachigen Welt werden Titel nicht vor dem Namen angesammelt: Man spricht eine Person mit nur einem Titel an. Mit anderen Worten gibt es keine Bildungen wie im Deutschen: *Herr Dr. Mayer* und *Frau Prof. Dr. Reis*.

Grammatik

Wer den Doktor- oder Professorengrad schon erreicht hat, verdient auch den dazugehörigen Titel. Also ist es höflicher, diesen Titel statt eines allgemeinen, geschlechtbezogenen Titels zu gebrauchen:

Dr. Beale and Prof. Sinclair arrived at the conference on Friday.	*Herr Dr. Beale und Frau Prof. Sinclair kamen am Freitag auf die Konferenz.*
Drs. Corcoran and Lowe, a husband-and-wife research team, have been invited to speak.	*Man hat Dr. Corcoran und Dr. Lowe, ein Forscherpaar, eingeladen einen Vortrag zu halten.*

5 Pronouns | *Fürwörter*

Pronouns ersetzen nicht, wie viele glauben, einzelne Nouns, sondern Phrases, die ein Noun als Kern haben. So eine Phrase nennt man eine Noun Phrase. Eine Noun Phrase kann schon aus einem einzigen Noun bestehen, aber dies ist nur Zufall: sie kann auch aus zehn oder mehr Wörtern bestehen:

William fell into a hole.	*William ist in ein Loch gefallen.*
▸ **He fell into a hole.**	*Er ist in ein Loch gefallen.*
The tall blond man wearing a yellow overcoat fell into a hole.	*Der große blonde Mann, der einen gelben Mantel trug, ist in ein Loch gefallen.*
▸ **He fell into a hole.**	*Er ist in ein Loch gefallen.*

Im ersten Satz ist **William** das Noun. Im zweiten ist **man** das Noun, während die volle Phrase aus **the tall blond man wearing a yellow overcoat** besteht. An diesem Beispiel kann man deutlich sehen, dass das Fürwort die ganze Phrase (und nicht nur das Noun) ersetzt.

Personal Pronouns | *persönliche Fürwörter*

Die Personal Pronouns sind die normalen Fürwörter, also diejenigen, mit denen man von *ich* oder *du* redet oder auch von bekannten Dritten.

Subject Pronouns

Singular		Plural	
I	*ich*	we	*wir*
you	*du, Sie*	you	*ihr, Sie*
he	*er*		
she	*sie*	they	*sie*
it	*es*		

Grammatik

Bei den persönlichen Fürwörtern sollte man sich gleich zwei Unterschiede zum Deutschen merken: Erstens gibt es nur eine Form für *du*, *ihr* und *Sie*: nämlich **you**. Das Fürwort **you** kann – der Situation entsprechend – Singular oder Plural ausdrücken. Im Englischen gibt es kein formelles Fürwort wie im Deutschen *Sie*:

You're mean!	*Du bist gemein!*
You two should do your homework.	*Ihr zwei solltet eure Hausaufgaben machen.*
Would you like coffee, tea, or juice?	*Möchten Sie Kaffee, Tee oder Saft?*

Zweitens sind **he**, **she** und **it** anders zu unterscheiden als im Deutschen. Während im Deutschen die Hauptwörter alle ihr eigenes Geschlecht haben, ist das im Englischen nicht so. Das Geschlecht, das zu einem Noun passt, entspricht einfach dem Geschlecht des bezeichneten Menschen oder Gegenstands in der Wirklichkeit.

The girl tried to laugh at his jokes.	*Das Mädchen versuchte, über seine Witze zu lachen.*
▶ **She tried to laugh at his jokes.**	*Sie versuchte, über seine Witze zu lachen.*

Nur Menschen und Tiere können in der Regel als **he** oder **she** bezeichnet werden (obwohl manche Leute andere Dinge wie z. B. ihr Auto als „Haustiere" betrachten und entsprechend bezeichnen). Alles andere bekommt das Fürwort *it*.

The table collapsed.	*Der Tisch brach zusammen.*
▶ **It collapsed.**	*Er brach zusammen.*

Im Gegensatz zu den Nouns haben die Personal Pronouns andere Formen für Objekte als für Subjekte.

Object Pronouns

Singular		Plural	
me	mich; mir	us	uns
you	dich; dir; Sie; Ihnen	you	euch; Sie; Ihnen
~~him~~ *him*	ihn; ihm	them	sie; ihnen
~~her~~ *her*	sie; ihr		
~~it~~ *it*	es; ihm		

Die Objektsformen verwendet man u. a. für Objekte (Noun Phrases direkt nach dem Verb) und nach Präpositionen:

Archibald took **them**.	Archibald hat sie genommen.
Thelma gave **her** a good scolding.	Thelma hat sie tüchtig ausgeschimpft.
I threw the stick, and Rover ran after **it**.	Ich habe den Stock geworfen, und Rover ist ihm nachgelaufen.
Paul fixed our car for **us**.	Paul hat uns unser Auto repariert.

Wenn man ein Fürwort allein verwenden will, gebraucht man die Objektform:

Who's there? – **Me**.	Wer ist da? – Ich.
It's **me**.	Ich bin's.
It's **them**.	Sie sind's.
Was it **you**?	Warst du es?

Grammatik

Possessive Forms | *besitzanzeigende Formen*

Jedes Personal Pronoun hat nicht nur eine, sondern zwei besitzanzeigende Formen!
- Eine Form benutzt man vor einem Noun in einer Noun Phrase.

Possessive Forms before Nouns

Singular		Plural	
My	*mein*	our	*unser*
your	*dein; Ihr*	your	*euer; Ihr*
his	*sein*		
her	*ihr*	their	*ihr*
its	*sein*		

My friend Barbara is getting divorced.	*Meine Freundin Barbara lässt sich scheiden.*
They wouldn't take **our** brilliant advice.	*Sie weigerten sich, unseren genialen Rat zu befolgen.*

Bei Körperteilen, Kleidung u. ä. von Individuen muss man besitzanzeigende Formen verwenden:

I broke **my** arm.	*Ich habe mir den Arm gebrochen.*
They took off **their** clothes but not **their** hats.	*Sie zogen sich die Kleidung aus, aber setzten ihre Hüte nicht ab.*
He touched **her** shoulder.	*Er berührte ihre Schulter.*
Our stomachs hurt.	*Wir hatten Bauchschmerzen.*

aber:

She kicked **him** in the stomach.	*Sie hat ihn in den Bauch getreten.*

- Die andere Form ist nicht vom *Noun* abhängig.

Grammatik

Independent Possessive Forms

Singular		Plural	
mine	meins, das meine	ours	unseres, das unsere
yours	deins, das deine, Ihres, das Ihre	yours	eures, das eure, Ihres, das Ihre
his	seines, das seine		
hers	ihres, das ihre	theirs	ihres, das ihre
(its)	seines, das seine		

Its wird sehr selten benutzt. Es darf nicht verwechselt werden mit **it's** (**it** + Apostroph) als Kurzform für **it has** oder **it is**.

Diese Form gilt als unabhängig, weil sie allein stehen kann:

My shirt's clean, but **hers** is dirty.	*Mein Hemd ist sauber, aber ihres ist schmutzig.*
Ellen has **her** own locker, but she likes to put **her** things in **his**.	*Ellen hat ihr eigenes Schließfach, aber sie stellt ihre Sachen gern in seines.*

Wie sagt man *ein Freund/eine Freundin von mir*? Eigentlich genau wie im Deutschen – aber mit der unabhängigen Form:

A friend **of mine** is coming to visit.	*Ein Freund/eine Freundin von mir kommt zu Besuch.*
A notebook **of mine** is missing.	*Ein Notizbuch von mir ist weg.*

Wenn es mal unpersönlich wird

Was macht man, wenn man *man* meint? Da gibt es zwei Lösungen.
In der gesprochenen Sprache sagt man meist **you**:

You have to be really stupid to do a thing like that.	*Man muss wirklich dumm sein, um so was Blödes zu machen.*
You can get good shoes and bags there.	*Man bekommt dort gute Schuhe und Taschen.*

Aber die „offizielle" Übersetzung von *man* ist **one**. Allerdings wirkt **one** ziemlich formell. Die besitzanzeigende Form von **one** ist einfach **one's**.

One should always wash **one's** hands before meals.	*Man sollte sich vor jeder Mahlzeit die Hände waschen.*
One needs to update **one's** wardrobe once in a while.	*Man muss seine Garderobe ab und zu der aktuellen Mode anpassen.*

Es ist ein Problem, wenn man von einer Person redet, die entweder männlich oder weiblich sein könnte. Früher wurde gelehrt, dass man in solchen Situationen das männliche Fürwort (personal pronoun) **he** verwenden soll, aber heutzutage wird dies als sexistisch und altmodisch betrachtet. Es ist viel besser, **he or she** zu sagen:

If the customer is not satisfied, **he or she** may return the item for a full refund.	*Wenn der Kunde/die Kundin nicht zufrieden ist, kann er oder sie die Ware gegen eine volle Rückerstattung des Kaufpreises zurückbringen.*
A typical fan wants to wear **his or her** favorite player's number.	*Der typische Fan will die Nummer seines Lieblingsspielers tragen.*

In der gesprochenen Sprache hat sich eine schlichtere Lösung entwickelt: man verwendet die Pluralform:

Apparently someone called up Harlan last night, and they started threatening him.	*Anscheinend hat gestern abend jemand Harlan angerufen, und der jenige hat angefangen, ihn zu bedrohen.*
If the person is hungry, they can get something at the fast-food place across the street.	*Wenn die Person Hunger hat, kann sie etwas beim Schnellimbiss gegenüber bekommen.*

Reflexive Pronouns | *rückbezügliche Fürwörter*

Das deutsche Wort *sich* ist etwas merkwürdig: eigentlich hat es eine ganze Reihe von Formen, aber außer *sich* sind alle gleich mit dem Wen- oder Wemfall (z. B. *mich, mir*). Deshalb: wenn man nicht sicher ist, ob man es in einem deutschen Satz mit einem *sich*-Wort zu tun hat, sollte man den Satz mit einem er/sie/es-Subjekt probieren. Wenn das Fürwort dann zu *sich* wird, ist es ein *sich*-Wort!
Sich hat mehrere Anwendungen. Wenn man mit dem Englischen zurechtkommen will, muss man diese auseinander halten.
Wenn ein *sich*-Wort ungefähr *dieselbe Person* bedeutet, wird es normalerweise mit speziellen Fürwörtern, den Reflexive Pronouns, übersetzt:

Reflexive Pronouns

Singular		Plural	
Myself	*mich; mir*	**ourselves**	*uns*
yourself	*dich; dir; sich*	**yourselves**	*euch; sich*
himself	*sich*		
herself	*sich*	**themselves**	*sich*
itself	*sich*		
oneself	*sich*		

Wie man an der Tabelle sehen kann, ist es sehr problematisch, wenn man immer versucht, alles direkt zu übersetzen. Am besten überlegt man, ob das Subjekt seine Handlung, sein Gefühl usw. auf sich selber richtet.

The man admired himself in the mirror.	*Der Mann bewunderte sich im Spiegel.*
I told myself I should be careful.	*Ich sagte mir, ich sollte aufpassen.*

Wenn man *sich selbst/selber* meint, kann man ein Reflexive Pronoun benutzen.

We're always laughing at ourselves.	*Wir lachen dauernd über uns selbst.*
Frieda was angry with herself.	*Frieda ärgerte sich über sich selbst.*

Manchmal sagt man *selbst* oder *selber* ohne *sich* um das Subjekt zu betonen. Im Englischen verwendet man auch hier die Reflexive Pronouns.

You know that yourself.	*Das weißt du doch selbst.*
Dean said so himself.	*Dean sagte es selbst.*

Wenn das *sich*-Wort *einander* oder *jeder den/dem anderen* bedeutet, verwendet man im Englischen meist **each other**. Dieser Ausdruck ist unveränderlich:

The two dogs chased each other.	*Die zwei Hunde jagten einander.*
Mark and Carla gave each other socks for Christmas.	*Mark und Carla schenkten sich Socken zu Weihnachten.*
We haven't seen each other for a long time.	*Wir haben uns schon lange nicht mehr gesehen.*

Grammatik

Es gibt auch etliche Verben im Deutschen, die ganz einfach ein *sich*-Wort verlangen. Manchmal übersetzt man das *sich*-Wort ins Englische, aber oft auch nicht. Folgende Ausdrücke haben kein Reflexive Pronoun im Englischen:

get dressed	*sich anziehen*	comb one's hair	*sich kämmen*
get/be angry	*sich ärgern*	open	*sich öffnen*
move; (Fitness) exercise	*sich bewegen*	close	*sich schließen*
		argue	*sich streiten*
concentrate	*sich konzentrieren*	meet	*sich treffen*
turn	*sich drehen*	change [one's clothes]	*sich umziehen*
remember	*sich erinnern an*		
be interested	*sich interessieren*		

Suddenly I remembered the cake in the oven.	*Plötzlich erinnerte ich mich an den Kuchen im Backofen.*
Aaron concentrated real hard.	*Aaron konzentrierte sich sehr.*
The wheel was turning.	*Das Rad drehte sich.*

Das Verb **meet** kann in Bezug auf Menschen folgende Bedeutungen haben:
- *zum ersten Mal kennen lernen*
- *sich zum ersten Mal kennen lernen*
- *treffen*
- *sich treffen*

I met my wife at a party.	*Ich habe meine Frau auf einer Party kennen gelernt.*
Don and Kelly originally met in Las Vegas.	*Don und Kelly haben sich in Las Vegas kennen gelernt.*
Guess who I met in town!	*Rate mal, wen ich in der Stadt getroffen habe!*
Let's meet at the pub.	*Treffen wir uns in der Kneipe.*

Verschiedene Wörter, die sonst als Adjektive, Adverbien usw., verwendet werden, finden auch Einsatz als Fürwörter.

Demonstrative Pronouns | *hinweisende Fürwörter*

Die Demonstrative Pronouns **this** (Plural **these**) und **that** (Plural **those**) können wie Artikel vor einem Noun stehen oder auch allein als Fürwörter:

These are the best plums I've ever eaten.	*Diese sind die besten Pflaumen, die ich je gegessen habe.*
I saw **that**.	*Das habe ich gesehen.*

All | *alles, alle*

Meist braucht **all** eine ergänzende Phrase hinter sich. Diese kann eine Noun Phrase sein:

The cats ate **all the fish**.	*Die Katzen fraßen den ganzen Fisch.*
All the visitors were cranky.	*Alle Besucher waren schlecht gelaunt.*

Bei persönlichen Fürwörtern stellt man **all** hinter das Pronoun!

I beat **them all**.	*Ich schlug sie alle.*
We all ordered cheesecake.	*Wir bestellten alle Käsekuchen.*

Man kann die Phrase auch mit **of** einleiten:

The cats ate **all of the fish**.	*Die Katzen fraßen den ganzen Fisch.*
All of the visitors were cranky.	*Alle Besucher waren schlecht gelaunt.*

Bei Subjekten besteht eine dritte Möglichkeit: Man setzt die Noun Phrase allein in die Subjektsposition und **all** danach – entweder gleich nach dem Subjekt oder nach dem (ersten) Hilfsverb:

The painters all went home early.	*Die Maler sind alle früh heimgegangen.*
The books have **all** fallen off the shelf.	*Die Bücher sind alle aus dem Regal gefallen.*
The parents all have written to the governor.	*Die Eltern haben alle dem Gouverneur geschrieben.*

Grammatik

Das Vollverb **be** verhält sich wie ein Hilfsverb, d. h. **all** darf dahinterstehen:

You were all there too.	Ihr wart auch alle da.
The employees were all happy.	Die Arbeitnehmer waren alle zufrieden.

Obwohl man **all** in ganz wenigen Fällen allein und ohne Bezug zu einer anderen Phrase verwenden kann, muss man im Normalfall jedoch auf die viel üblicheren Wörter **everything** (*alles*) und **everyone** bzw. **everybody** (*alle*) zurückgreifen:

Rex worries about everything.	Rex macht sich über alles Sorgen.
Everything was fine.	Alles war in Ordnung.
Everyone came.	Alle sind gekommen.
I gave one to everyone.	Ich habe jedem eins gegeben.
Everybody was talking about Roseanne's new nose.	Alle haben von Roseannes neuer Nase geredet.
Aunt Becky kissed everybody good-bye.	Tante Becky küsste alle zum Abschied.

Both | *alle beide*

Both betont, dass nicht nur eins von zwei, sondern alle beide gemeint sind.
Man kann **both** wie **all** vor einer Noun Phrase, vor einer **of**-Phrase oder wieder aufgreifend nach dem Subjekt einsetzen.

We met both her sons.	Wir lernten ihre beiden Söhne kennen.
Both our cars are old.	Unsere beiden Autos sind alt.
Both of the bottles exploded.	Alle beide Flaschen explodierten.
I gave both of the letters to Jess.	Ich gab Jess beide Briefe.
The eggs for the cake both broke.	Die Eier für den Kuchen zerbrachen beide.
Mac and Toni were both screaming.	Mac und Toni haben beide geschrien.
Now the teacher and the substitute were both sick.	Jetzt waren die Lehrerin und ihre Vertretung beide krank.

Im Gegensatz zu **all** kann **both** auch völlig allein stehen:

I was worried about the packages, but both arrived safely.	*Ich machte mir Sorgen um die Pakete, aber alle beide sind heil angekommen.*
Which flavor is better: chocolate or vanilla? – Both are good.	*Welcher Geschmack ist besser: Schokolade oder Vanille? – Alle beide sind gut.*

Each | *jedes, jeder, je*

Each kann vor einer **of**-Phrase oder auch nach dem Subjekt stehen. Es kann dagegen nicht vor einer Noun Phrase stehen:

Each of the pipes had to be repaired.	*Jede Leitung musste repariert werden.*
The boss spoke to each of the employees individually.	*Die Chefin sprach mit jedem der Mitarbeiter einzeln.*
Five robbers each decided to break into the same bank the same night.	*Fünf Räuber beschlossen in derselben Nacht jeweils in dieselbe Bank einzubrechen.*
Mandy, Phil, Candice, and Henry have each given us a toaster as a wedding gift.	*Mandy, Phil, Candice und Henry haben uns je einen Toaster zur Hochzeit geschenkt.*

Each betont, dass jeder als einzelnes Individuum bzw. jedes als einzelner Gegenstand gemeint ist.

Häufig bezieht sich **each** auf das erste von zwei Objekten. Dann steht **each** meist nach dem ersten Objekt:

The nurse gave the children each a toy.	*Die Krankenschwester gab jedem der Kinder ein Spielzeug.*

Aber wenn man die Zahl des zweiten Objekts hervorheben will, setzt man **each** (oder auch **apiece**) erst danach:

Uncle Willy gave the boys five dollars each.	*Onkel Willy gab jedem der Jungen fünf Dollar.*
We ate four muffins apiece.	*Jeder von uns hat vier Muffins gegessen.*

Grammatik

Bei Stückpreisen ist es üblich, **each** oder **apiece** (*pro Stück*) nach dem Preis zu sagen:

These pens are 95 cents each.	*Diese Kugelschreiber kosten 95 Cent pro Stück.*
The bouquets cost ten pounds apiece.	*Die Blumensträuße kosten zehn Pfund pro Stück.*

One | *eines*

One ist ein unbestimmtes Fürwort für zählbare Dinge im Singular. Es kann unabhängig oder mit einer **of**-Phrase auftreten:

Have one!	*Nimm eins!*
I had never seen an armadillo until we encountered one at the zoo.	*Ich hatte noch nie ein Gürteltier gesehen, bis wir eins im Zoo entdeckt haben.*
One of the books was about horse races.	*Eins der Bücher handelte von Pferderennen.*

Man kann **one** auch als eine Art Kleinfürwort für das Hauptwort nach einem Artikel verwenden. **One** ist hier oft völlig unentbehrlich:

Which one do you want?	*Welches willst du?*
I'll take the blue one.	*Ich nehme das blaue.*
Grace hoped for some chocolates when she got home, but Julie had eaten every one.	*Als Grace heim kam, hoffte sie noch ein paar Pralinen zu erwischen, aber Julie hatte alle aufgegessen.*

Either und neither

Either bedeutet soviel wie *entweder das eine oder das andere*:

Should we take the stew or the roast? – Either would be fine.	*Sollen wir den Eintopf oder den Braten nehmen? – Beides wäre gut.*
Either of the boys will be glad to help you – if you pay him.	*Jeder der beiden Jungen hilft dir gern – wenn du ihn bezahlst.*

Neither bedeutet *weder das eine noch das andere*:

Neither really appeals to me.	*Keiner der beiden sagt mir wirklich zu.*
Neither of them did a good job.	*Keiner der beiden hat seine Arbeit gut gemacht.*

Wenn **either** irgendwo hinter einem verneinenden Wort steht, ergibt sich die Bedeutung *keiner der beiden*:

The parrots **wouldn't** describe **either** of the robbers.	*Die Papageien wollten keinen der Räuber beschreiben.*
I **never** saw **either** of them again.	*Ich habe keinen der beiden jemals wieder gesehen.*

Some | *manche, einige, welche*

Das unbestimmte Fürwort **some** kann sich auf den Singular oder auf eine unzählbare Menge beziehen:

I'd like **some**, please.	*Ich hätte gern welche.*
Roger didn't really want licorice, but he bought **some** anyway.	*Roger wollte eigentlich keine Lakritze, aber er kaufte trotzdem welche.*
Some of the waiters were more elegant than the patrons.	*Einige Kellner waren eleganter als die Kunden.*

None | *keins, keiner*

Außer im formellen Sprachgebrauch sollte man **none** immer mit einer *of-Phrase* verwenden. Solche *none-Phrases* eignen sich hauptsächlich als Subjekte; sonst verwendet man lieber **not ... any**:

None of the mice likes cheese.	*Keine der Mäuse mag Käse.*
None of her furniture was comfortable.	*Keine ihrer Möbel waren bequem.*

Trotz seiner Verwandtschaft zu **one** kann man ein Verb im Plural nach einer *none-Phrase* bringen, vorausgesetzt, es handelt sich um ein zählbares Noun:

None of your greedy clients were there.	*Keiner deiner gierigen Klienten war da.*

Wenn man *keiner* im Sinne von *kein Mensch* sagen will, verwendet man **no one** oder **nobody**:

No one was home.	*Keiner war zu Hause.*
Nobody said you had to believe it.	*Niemand hat gesagt, dass du es glauben musst.*

Any

Nach dem Verb in negativen Sätzen muss man **any** anstelle von **some** verwenden. Im Deutschen sagt man in solchen Fällen *keine*:

I asked for secondhand computers, but they didn't have any.	*Ich verlangte gebrauchte Computer, aber sie hatten keine.*
I haven't heard from any of them.	*Ich habe bislang von keinem von ihnen gehört.*
My shoes weren't in any of the closets or under any of the beds in the house.	*Meine Schuhe waren in keinem der Schränke und auch unter keinem der Betten im Haus.*

6 Articles and Related Words
Artikel und verwandte Wörter

Artikel (articles) stehen am Anfang einer Noun Phrase. Die Wortfolge vor dem Noun innerhalb einer Noun Phrase ist

Article–Number–Adjective(s)–**Noun**

D. h. ein Artikel kann vor einer Zahl, einem Adjektiv oder dem Substantiv selber stehen, je nachdem, ob sich etwas zwischen dem Artikel und dem Substantiv befindet:

The marmot	*Das Murmeltier*
The sleepy marmot	*Das schläfrige Murmeltier*
The five marmots	*Die fünf Murmeltiere*
The five sleepy marmots	*Die fünf schläfrigen Murmeltiere*

Nicht nur der unbestimmte und der bestimmte Artikel, sondern auch noch verschiedene andere Wörter, z.B. Demonstrativpronomen wie **this, that, these** und **those** oder besitzanzeigende Formen wie **my, her, their** und **John's** können an dieser Stelle stehen.

This marmot	*Dieses Murmeltier*
My sleepy marmot	*Mein schläfriges Murmeltier*
Their five marmots	*Ihre fünf Murmeltiere*
John's five sleepy marmots	*Johns fünf schläfrige Murmeltiere*

Der unbestimmte Artikel

Der unbestimmte Artikel für zählbare Nouns im Singular ist **a**:

A passing car skidded to **a** stop.	*Ein vorbeifahrendes Auto rutschte und kam zum Halten.*
A monkey wrench is **a** useful thing to have.	*Es ist nützlich, einen Engländer* zu haben.* (**verstellbarer Schraubenschlüssel*)

Grammatik

Wenn man den unbestimmten Artikel vor einem Vokallaut gebraucht, hat er die Form **an**:

An anteater and an elephant went for a stroll.	*Ein Ameisenbär und ein Elefant gingen zusammen spazieren.*
Please buy me an orange and an apple.	*Kauf mir bitte eine Orange und einen Apfel.*
He was wearing an old shirt.	*Er trug ein altes Hemd.*

Das entscheidende Kriterium der Wahl zwischen **a** und **an** ist nicht der nächste Buchstabe, sondern der nächste Laut:

She intended to join a union.	*Sie hatte vor, in eine Gewerkschaft einzutreten.*
This graph shows an x-axis and a y-axis.	*Dieses Diagramm zeigt eine x-Achse und eine y-Achse.*

Anwendungstipps

Man verwendet den unbestimmten Artikel **a**, wenn man den Beruf einer einzelnen Person angibt:

Stephanie is a welder.	*Stephanie ist Schweißerin.*
Julian is a singer.	*Julian ist Sänger.*

Im Plural fällt dieser natürlich weg:

Liza and Victor are nurses.	*Liza und Victor sind Krankenpfleger.*

Man kann – besonders in informellen Situationen – **one** am Anfang von größeren Zahlen durch **a** ersetzen:

Simon just won a hundred thousand dollars.	*Simon hat gerade hunderttausend Dollar gewonnen.*
We expected a hundred people at the opening.	*Wir erwarteten hundert Leute bei der Eröffnung.*

In der Regel gebraucht man den unbestimmten Artikel nach **with** und **without**, wenn das Noun zählbar ist und im Singular steht:

The boss was wearing a blouse with a bow.	*Die Chefin trug eine Bluse mit Schleife.*
Al left the house without a jacket.	*Al ging ohne Jacke aus dem Haus.*
You can have the chicken with or without a salad.	*Sie können das Hähnchen mit oder ohne Salat haben.*

Nach **as** gebraucht man auch den unbestimmten Artikel bei einem zählbaren Noun, das im Singular steht:

As a politician, Lisle was successful; as a human being, he was not.	*Als Politiker war Lisle erfolgreich, als Mensch war er es nicht.*
Lillian came dressed as a witch, but no one realized that she was in costume.	*Lillian kam als Hexe verkleidet, aber keiner merkte, dass sie kostümiert war.*
We can use the bed as a couch.	*Wir können das Bett als Couch benutzen.*

Der bestimmte Artikel

Der bestimmte Artikel ist **the**. Im Gegensatz zum deutschen *der/die/das* wird er nie verändert:

This is the only bridge over the river.	*Das ist die einzige Brücke über den Fluss.*
The cats are sitting on top of the bookcase.	*Die Katzen sitzen oben auf dem Bücherregal.*

Grammatik

Anwendungstipps

- Gattungen oder Gruppen bezeichnet man eher ohne **the**:

Crows are intelligent, amusing animals.	*Krähen sind intelligente, witzige Tiere.*
Canadians speak a North American dialect of English.	*Die Kanadier sprechen eine nordamerikanische Variante des Englischen.*
Archaeologists like the outdoors.	*Archäologen sind gerne draußen.*

- Wochentage, Monate und die meisten Feiertage haben keinen bestimmten Artikel:

We could meet on Monday.	*Wir könnten uns am Montag treffen.*
January is a dreary month.	*Der Januar ist ein öder Monat.*
Easter would be a good day for a party.	*Der Ostersonntag wäre ein guter Tag für ein Fest.*

- Mahlzeiten bezeichnet man ohne bestimmten Artikel, außer wenn es sich um eine ganz bestimmte Mahlzeit als Ereignis oder um das servierte Essen handelt:

We had lunch at a restaurant.	*Wir haben in einem Restaurant zu Mittag gegessen.*
Joan invited me over for tea.	*Joan hat mich zu sich zum Tee eingeladen.*
The four of them met for dinner at Sophy's.	*Die vier trafen sich bei Sophy zum Abendessen.*
The charity dinner was a success.	*Das Abendessen für wohltätige Zwecke war ein Erfolg.*
I didn't like the lunch.	*Ich mochte das Mittagessen nicht.*

- Folgende Bezeichnungen für Einrichtungen verwendet man meist ohne **the: school** (*Schule,* auch *Hochschule, Berufsschule*), **college** (*Hochschule, Universität* bis zum ersten Abschluss), **jail/gaol** (*Gefängnis, Untersuchungsgefängnis*), **prison** (*Gefängnis*), **church** (*Kirche*). Im britischen Englisch erscheint auch kein Artikel vor **university** (*Universität*) und **hospital** (*Krankenhaus*):

My daughter has to go to school in the morning, unless she can think of a good excuse.	Meine Tochter muss morgens in die Schule gehen, es sei denn, sie lässt sich eine gute Ausrede einfallen.
The murderer escaped from prison.	Der Mörder ist aus dem Gefängnis ausgebrochen.
We go to church every Sunday.	Wir gehen jeden Sonntag in die Kirche.

Für alle Wörter gilt allerdings: wenn man ein bestimmtes Gebäude oder Gelände meint, gebraucht man den Artikel:

The school is fairly large.	Die Schule ist ziemlich groß.
The prison was always cold.	Das Gefängnis war immer kalt.
We went into the church.	Wir sind in die Kirche hineingegangen.

Demonstrativpronomen

Die Demonstrativpronomen **this** (Plural **these**) und **that** (Plural **those**) gebraucht man wie Artikel am Anfang der Noun Phrase:

With **this** drink you'll add ten years to your life.	Mit diesem Getränk verlängern Sie Ihr Leben um zehn Jahre.
These boots are killing me!	Diese Stiefel bringen mich um!
What does **that** man want?	Was will dieser Mann da?
Those two jokers had better watch out!	Die beiden Spaßvögel dort sollten sich in Acht nehmen!

Grammatik

Man wählt **this** bzw. **these,** um auszudrücken, dass das Bezeichnete in der direkten Nähe ist, z.B. dass man es bei sich hat. Umgekehrt wählt man **that** bzw. **those,** um auszudrücken, dass das Bezeichnete etwas weiter weg ist, z.B. weil es jemand anderes hat, oder es gerade nicht verfügbar ist. Distanz und Nähe kann man also auch im weiteren Sinn verstehen, z. B. zeitlich oder emotional.

This house is bigger than **that** house. **Those** applicants weren't as good as the current ones.	*Dieses Haus hier ist größer als das Haus da. Jene Berwerber waren nicht so gut wie die jetzigen.*

Beim Erzählen kann man **this** gebrauchen, um subtil anzudeuten, dass es sich um eine ungewöhnliche bzw. komische Sache handelt. Dies hilft oft, die Geschichte lebendiger zu machen:

Alison came in wearing **this** weird hat. And then she ate **this** huge chocolate cake right after lunch.	*Alison ist hereingekommen mit diesem merkwürdigen Hut auf dem Kopf. Und dann aß sie diesen riesigen Schokokuchen direkt nach dem Mittagessen.*

Andere artikelähnliche Wörter

Andere artikelähnliche Wörter stellt man auch an den Anfang einer Noun Phrase.

Some (*etwas, einiges, manches*) kann sich auf den Plural oder auf eine unzählbare Menge beziehen. Beim Singular eines zählbaren Hauptwortes gebraucht man **a** oder **one**:

Could I have **some** hot tea, please? **Some** drunks were singing outside my window.	*Könnte ich bitte etwas heißen Tee haben? Einige Betrunkene sangen vor meinem Fenster.*

In seiner Artikelfunktion deutet **all** auf die gesamte Menge von etwas hin. Daher sind Sätze mit **all** in der Regel allgemeine Aussagen:

Grammatik

All passengers must pay attention during the safety briefing.	*Alle Passagiere müssen während der Sicherheitsunterweisung aufpassen.*
The course covers **all** basic problems.	*Der Kurs behandelt alle elementaren Probleme.*

Every bedeutet jedes Mitglied einer Gruppe. Es steht immer im Singular.

In the US **every** town has at least one motel.	*In den USA hat jede Stadt mindestens ein Motel.*
Every person in the room stood up.	*Alle Leute im Raum standen auf.*
I think Ken knows **every** single rock on the shore.	*Ich glaube, Ken kennt jeden einzelnen Stein am Ufer.*

Each bezeichnet jedes Mitglied einer Gruppe und betont, dass die Mitglieder als Einzelne zu betrachten sind:

Each toy is inspected individually.	*Jedes Spielzeug wird einzeln untersucht.*
We admired **each** item in the window.	*Wir bewunderten jedes Stück im Schaufenster.*

Both bedeutet *alle beide*, d. h. es betont, dass jeder von zweien gemeint ist:

Both companies sell green sunscreen.	*Alle beide Firmen verkaufen grünes Sonnenschutzmittel.*
Each crook tried to blame the other, but in the end **both** men were convicted.	*Jeder der beiden Gauner versuchte, dem anderen die Schuld zu geben, aber schließlich wurden alle beide Männer verurteilt.*

Wenn man dies nicht betonen will, nimmt man stattdessen **the two**:

The two friends talked on the phone every day.	*Die beiden Freunde telefonierten jeden Tag miteinander.*
The two companies work together.	*Die beiden Firmen arbeiten zusammen.*

Grammatik

Either bezieht sich meistens auf *entweder der/das eine oder der/das andere*; d. h. es bezeichnet genau zwei Leute, Gegenstände usw., separat betrachtet:

Either dog would be good.	*Jeder der beiden Hunde wäre gut.*
You can have either one but not both.	*Du kannst das eine oder das andere haben, aber nicht beide.*
I don't care; you can give me either kind.	*Mir ist es egal, du kannst mir entweder das eine oder das andere geben.*

Manchmal aber bedeutet **either** *jeder von beiden*:

The actress came down the corridor with a bodyguard on either side.	*Die Schauspielerin kam mit einem Leibwächter auf beiden Seiten den Gang entlang.*

Neither bedeutet *keine/keiner/keins der beiden*:

Neither girl was interested in dolls.	*Keins der beiden Mädchen interessierte sich für Puppen.*
Neither textbook contains any useful information.	*Keins der beiden Lehrbücher enthält irgendwelche nützliche Informationen.*

No gebraucht man als negativen Artikel, aber im Gegensatz zu vielen artikelähnlichen Wörtern kann es nicht als Pronoun (Pronomen) allein stehen. Das entsprechende Pronoun ist **none**:

No news is good news.	*Keine Nachrichten sind gute Nachrichten.*
We waited for celebrities, but none showed up.	*Wir haben auf Berühmtheiten gewartet, aber Keiner tauchte auf.*

No findet hauptsächlich bei Noun Phrases Gebrauch, die Subjekte sind. Sonst gebraucht man normalerweise **not ... any**:

Having worked in a chocolate factory, I didn't like any cookies.	*Da ich in einer Schokoladenfabrik gearbeitet hatte, mochte ich keine Kekse.*

7 Quantities and Measurements
Mengen- und Maßangaben

Entscheidend für Mengen- und Maßangaben im Englischen ist der Unterschied zwischen zählbaren und nicht zählbaren Dingen. Wenn man z. B. fragt: *Wie viel Milch habt ihr gekauft?*, dann kann eine grammatisch korrekte Antwort nicht *zwei* lauten, weil man Milch nicht zählen kann. Dagegen ist *zwei* eine durchaus befriedigende Antwort auf die Frage: *Wie viele Hemden hast du gekauft?*

Fragen

Im Englischen fängt der Unterschied schon mit den Fragen nach Maß und Menge an. Man verwendet also **How many ...?**, wenn das Noun als einzelnes ohne weitere Mengenangabe wie Liter, Kilogramm, usw. zählbar ist. Wenn man eine maßangebende Antwort wie z.B. *drei Liter* hören möchte, benötigt man die Frage **How much ...? How much ...?** ist also für nicht zählbare *Nouns*:

How many **calves** are there?	*Wie viele Kälber sind es?*
How much **milk** have we got?	*Wie viel Milch haben wir noch?*

Oft kann man etwas Unzählbares sozusagen zählbar machen, indem man entsprechende Gefäße nennt, die einzeln zählbar sind.

How much **wine** should I buy?	*Wie viel Wein soll ich kaufen?*
How many **bottles of wine** should I buy?	*Wie viele Flaschen Wein soll ich kaufen?*

Wenn die Maßeinheit schon in der Frage genannt wird, und die Antwort somit auch zählbare Einheiten ergibt, ist auch **how many...?** zu verwenden:

How many **liters of wine** should I buy?	*Wieviel Liter Wein sollte ich kaufen?*

Money (*Geld*) ist im üblichen Sinn nicht zählbar:

How much **money** do you have on you?	*Wie viel Geld hast du dabei?*
How much **money** has that rich man got?	*Wie viel Geld hat der reiche Mann?*

Grammatik

Gleichzeitig aber werden Antworten auf Fragen nach Geldmengen oft in zählbaren Währungseinheiten angegeben:

How much money do you have on you?	
I have five dollars and twenty-five cents.	*Ich habe fünf Dollar und fünfundzwanzig Cent.*
He has three million pounds.	*Er hat drei Millionen Pfund.*

Bei zählbaren Nouns verwendet man **many** für *viele*, **few** für *nur wenige* und **a few** für *einige wenige, ein paar*:

That library has many good books.	*Diese Bibliothek hat viele gute Bücher.*
Many people disagree.	*Viele Leute sind anderer Meinung.*
Eleanor took few blouses along on her trip.	*Eleanor nahm nur wenige Blusen auf die Reise mit.*
Few people like to swim in cold water.	*Nur wenige Leute schwimmen gern in kaltem Wasser.*
A few coins fell on the floor.	*Einige Münzen fielen auf den Boden.*
There were a few candles in the drawer.	*Da waren ein paar Kerzen in der Schublade.*

Der Ausdruck **quite a few** bedeutet *relativ viele, nicht wenige*:

Ralph read quite a few books while he was recovering.	*Ralph hat nicht wenige Bücher gelesen, während er sich erholt hat.*
Quite a few people have read Shakespeare.	*Ziemlich viele Leute haben Shakespeare gelesen.*

Grammatik

Bei nicht zählbaren Nouns verwendet man **much** für *viel*, little für *nur wenig* und **a little** für *ein wenig, ein bisschen*:

There isn't much to eat in the house.	Es gibt im Haus nicht viel zu essen.
Don't make so much noise!	Mach nicht so viel Lärm!
The employees had little to do.	Die Mitarbeiter hatten nur wenig zu tun.
Olga ate little soup but much cake.	Olga hat wenig Suppe, aber viel Kuchen gegessen.
A little rest would do you good.	Ein bisschen Ausruhen würde dir gut tun.
Would you like a little milk with your coffee?	Möchten Sie ein bisschen Milch in Ihren Kafee?

A lot (of) ist ein umgangsprachlicher Ausdruck mit der Bedeutung *viel*, der sowohl für zählbare als auch für nicht zählbare Nouns geeignet ist. Besonders in positiven Sätzen hört er sich viel natürlicher an als **much**. Andererseits kann man **a lot** nicht mit **too** (*zu* im Sinne von *übermäßig*, z.B. *zu schnell*) verwenden:

We ate a lot of lasagna.	Wir haben viel Lasagne gegessen.
We talked to a lot of people that we knew.	Wir haben mit vielen Leuten gesprochen, die wir kannten.

aber:

We ate too much lasagna.	Wir haben zu viel Lasagne gegessen.
We talked to too many people.	Wir haben mit zu vielen Leuten gesprochen.

8 Adjectives | *Eigenschaftswörter*

Allgemeine Bemerkungen

Im Gegensatz zu deutschen Adjektiven haben englische *Adjectives* keine Endungen, die zwischen verschiedenen Fällen oder auch zwischen Singular und Plural unterscheiden. *Adjectives* im Englischen bleiben also in ihrer Grundform (▶ Kapitel Verben) immer gleich:

The hungry dog stole the sausage.	Der hungrige Hund hat die Wurst gestohlen.
I fed a hungry dog.	Ich habe einen hungrigen Hund gefüttert.
The two hungry dogs were fighting over some meat.	Die beiden hungrigen Hunde haben um ein Stück Fleisch gekämpft.

Adjectives werden oft aus Participles (Partizipien), wie etwa dem Past Participle gebildet. Das Past Participle, das man ja in der Passivbildung verwendet, hat als Adjective meist eine Passivbedeutung:

The lost keys turned up in the pocket of a thief.	Die verlorenen Schlüssel tauchten in der Tasche eines Diebes auf.
The needed funds were provided by a local millionaire.	Die benötigten Gelder wurden von einem hiesigen Millionär bereitgestellt.

Daher können solche Sätze mit Kombinationen aus Adjective (Past Participle) und Noun auch ganz einfach als Passivsätze ausgedrückt werden:

The keys that were lost turned up in the pocket of a thief.	Die Schlüssel, die verloren worden waren, tauchten in der Tasche eines Diebes auf.
The funds that were needed were provided by a local millionaire.	Die Gelder, die benötigten wurden, wurden von einem hiesigen Millionär bereitgestellt.

Die **ing**-Form eines Verbs ist auch ein Partizip. Wie in den Progressive Tenses (▶ Hilfsverben) deutet sie häufig aber nicht immer an, dass ein Ereignis im Gange ist. Sie hat immer eine Aktivbedeutung. Diese Form gleicht dem deutschen *-end*:

The **falling** tree hit Cassie's house.	*Der herunterfallende Baum traf Cassies Haus.*
Let **sleeping** dogs lie.	*Schlafende Hunde soll man nicht wecken.*

Manchmal ist aber die deutsche Übersetzung mit *–end* sehr eigenartig. In solchen Fällen übersetzt man besser z.B. mit einem Relativsatz:

The **losing** team must pay for the beer.	*Die Mannschaft, die verliert, muss das Bier bezahlen.*

Nationalitätsbezeichnende Adjectives werden wie die entsprechenden Nouns großgeschrieben (▶ Groß- und Kleinschreibung).

Let's order an **English** breakfast. Bobby finally woke up from the **American** dream.	*Bestellen wir uns ein englisches Frühstück. Bobby wachte schließlich aus dem amerikanischen Traum auf.*

Steigerungsformen

Viele Adjectives haben Steigerungsformen:

tall	*groß*	taller	*größer*	tallest	*am größten*
late	*spät*	later	*später*	latest	*am spätesten*

Grammatik

Neben der Grundform gibt es eine *mehr*-Form (comparative) und eine *meist*-Form (superlative). Das Comparative bildet man oft dadurch, dass man **-er** an das Ende der Grundform anhängt. Für das Superlative hängt man **-est** an die Grundform:

Vincent is tall, but Nick is taller.	*Vincent ist groß, aber Nick ist größer.*
That elephant is the biggest.	*Der Elefant da ist der größte.*
Harold's newest tie has red lobsters on a white background.	*Harolds neueste Krawatte hat rote Hummer auf einem weißen Hintergrund.*

Bei Adjectives, die mit Konsonant **+ y** enden, wird das **y** zu **ie**, wenn **-er** oder **-est** angehängt wird:

funny ▶ funnier ▶ funniest	*witzig, merkwürdig*
No one is funnier than Jerry Lewis.	*Keiner ist lustiger als Jerry Lewis.*

Es gibt aber auch einige unregelmäßig gebildete Steigerungsformen. Diese muss man auswendig lernen:

Grundform	*Comparative*	*Superlative*	Übersetzung
bad	worse	worst	*schlecht, schlimm*
good	better	best	*gut*
well	better	best	*gesund*
far	farther, further	farthest, furthest	*weit*
little	less	least	*wenig*
much	more	most	*viel*
many	more	most	*viele*

The patient looked better after a while.	*Nach einer Weile sah der Patient besser aus.*
That was the worst day of my life!	*Das war der schlimmste Tag in meinem Leben!*

Adjectives ohne Steigerungsformen

Die meisten Adjectives mit mehr als zwei Silben besitzen keine eigene Steigerungsformen. Trotzdem können solche Wörter gesteigert werden – durch die Umschreibung mit **more** und **most**:

It was the **most interesting** thing in the world!	*Es war das interessanteste Ding der Welt!*
The painting became **more beautiful** every day.	*Das Gemälde wurde jeden Tag schöner.*
This room is **most comfortable**.	*Dieser Raum ist am bequemsten.*

Bei zweisilbigen Adjektiven entscheidet oft eher das Sprachgefühl als die Regel:

I have never seen a plan that was **simpler**!	*Ich habe noch nie einen einfacheren Plan gesehen!*
I have never seen a plan that was **more simple**!	

Auch kürzere, aus dem Lateinischen oder Griechischen stammende *Adjectives* haben meist keine eigenen Steigerungsformen und benötigen **more** und **most**:

Her style has become **more modern**.	*Ihr Stil ist moderner geworden.*
Al isn't the **most patient** person.	*Al ist nicht der geduldigste Mensch.*

Adjectives, die von den Partizipformen der Verben abgeleitet sind, besitzen normalerweise ebenfalls keine Steigerungsformen:

The new clerk made the **most glaring** errors.	*Der neue Sachbearbeiter machte die schlimmsten Fehler.*
Ron thought geometry was **more boring** than biology, but Delia thought it was the **most fascinating** subject.	*Ron meinte, Geometrie sei langweiliger als Biologie, aber Delia meinte, es sei das faszinierendste Fach.*

Adjectives, die Zugehörigkeit zu Gruppen (Nationen, Religionen, Städte etc.) ausdrücken, brauchen auch **more** oder **most**:

The immigrants were more French than the French themselves.	*Die Einwanderer waren mehr französisch als die Franzosen selbst.*

Adjectives in the Noun Phrase

Meistens stehen Adjectives direkt vor dem Noun in der Noun Phrase:

The furious passenger wanted his money back.	*Der wütende Passagier wollte sein Geld zurück.*
The small TV is more expensive.	*Der kleine Fernseher ist teurer.*

Einige Adjektive verlangen eine von einer Präposition eingeleitete Phrase. Dies ist dann aber vor dem Noun zu viel, und das ganze Gebilde muss hinter das Noun gesetzt werden:

Parents proud of their children like to tell others about them.	*Eltern, die stolz auf ihre Kinder sind, erzählen gern anderen Leuten von ihnen.*
Anybody as furious about a delayed flight would want their money back, too.	*Jeder, der so wütend über einen verspäteten Flug ist, würde auch sein Geld zurückhaben wollen.*

Wenn das Noun überflüssig ist

Wenn es schon klar ist, um welches Noun es sich handelt, kann man im Deutschen das Substantiv einfach weglassen und nur das Adjektiv verwenden: z. B. *Ich nehme den Gelben*. Im Englischen kann man das meist nicht machen; man braucht eben immer ein Noun oder ein entsprechendes Fürwort. Es reicht zum Teil schon das Fürwort **one**:

I'll take the yellow one.	*Ich nehme den Gelben.*
Do you mean the fat one or the skinny one?	*Meinst du den Dicken oder den Dürren?*

Adjectives nach Verben

Man kann Adjectives auch nach gewissen Verben wie **be** (*sein*), **seem** und **appear** (*scheinen, vorkommen*), **get** und **become** (*werden*) oder **stay** und **remain** (*bleiben*) verwenden. Dabei passen **seem, get** und **stay** besser zur gesprochenen Sprache als **appear, become** und **remain:**

You're crazy!	Du bist verrückt!
The book on basket weaving seemed interesting.	Das Buch über Korbflechten schien interessant zu sein.
You won't get rich that way.	So wirst du nicht reich.
The class remained quiet.	Die Klasse blieb ruhig.

Besonders bei Farben verwendet man **turn** für *werden*:

Julia turned red with embarrassment.	Julia wurde rot vor Verlegenheit.
When I washed my new jeans, the water turned blue – and so did all the other clothes.	Als ich meine neue Jeans gewaschen habe, ist das Wasser blau geworden – und die andere Kleidung auch.

Andererseits kann man sie gut mit bestimmten Verben wie **look** (*aussehen*), **sound** (*klingen, sich anhören*), **taste** (*schmecken*), **smell** (*riechen*) und **feel** (*sich anfühlen*) verwenden:

Everyone looked great.	Alle haben toll ausgesehen.
This old Easter egg smells rotten.	Dieses alte Osterei stinkt.
It felt right.	Es fühlte sich richtig an.

Good/well

Als Eigenschaftswörter bedeuten **good** *gut, brav* und **well** *gesund*. **Good** ist ein sehr allgemeines Wort mit vielen Anwendungen, während das Adjective **well** sich nur auf die Gesundheit bezieht:

They enjoyed the good **meal.**	*Sie haben das gute Essen genossen.*
The children were being good.	*Die Kinder waren im Moment brav.*
I don't feel well.	*Ich fühle mich krank.*
His old mother isn't looking well.	*Seine alte Mutter sieht zur Zeit recht krank aus.*

Own

Das Adjective **own** kann nur nach einem besitzanzeigenden Fürwort (Pronoun) stehen:

She makes all her own **hats herself.**	*Sie macht ihre Hüte alle selbst.*
I feel like a stranger in my own **house.**	*Ich fühle mich wie ein Fremder im eigenen Haus.*

Vergleichende Anwendungen

Man verwendet das Comparative (**-er, more**), wenn man zwei Dinge vergleicht, während man das Superlative (**-est, most**) verwendet, wenn man mehr als zwei Dinge vergleicht:

Geraldine is the older of the two **sisters.**	*Geraldine ist die ältere der zwei Schwestern.*
Geraldine is the oldest of the three **sisters.**	*Geraldine ist die älteste der drei Schwestern.*

Grammatik

Vergleiche mit than

Wenn man einen direkten Vergleich zwischen zwei Dingen herstellt und meint, dass eins mehr von einer Eigenschaft hat als das andere, verwendet man **than**:

Kate is happier than Stephanie.	*Kate ist glücklicher als Stephanie.*
My computer is more powerful than your computer.	*Mein Computer ist leistungsfähiger als dein Computer.*

Dies gilt auch, wenn das erste weniger von der Eigenschaft hat:

The stepsisters were less beautiful than Cinderella.	*Die Stiefschwestern waren nicht so schön wie Aschenputtel.*

Bei dieser Verwendung, wo **than** keinen Nebensatz einleitet, nehmen die Personal Pronouns zumindest in der gesprochenen Sprache die Objektform an:

His brother is much taller than him.	*Sein Bruder ist viel größer als er.*

Than

Sehr üblich sind Äußerungen, in denen man das Subjekt und das entsprechende Hilfsverb nach **than** setzt:

Sarah looks older than Jessica does.	*Sarah sieht älterer aus als Jessica.*
Stephen was less experienced in catching potato bugs than Meredith was.	*Stephen hatte weniger Erfahrung im Fangen von Kartoffelkäfern als Meredith.*

Man kann statt des Hilfsverbs auch ein Vollverb verwenden:

Law is more interesting than it looks.	*Jura ist interessanter als man denkt.*

Grammatik

Vergleiche mit as ... as

Wenn man sagen will, dass zwei Dinge gleich viel von einer Eigenschaft haben, verwendet man **as ... as**, wobei man die Grundform zwischen die beiden **as** schiebt:

My pregnant cousin is as big as a house.	*Meine schwangere Kusine ist so rund wie eine Tonne.*
Gary looks as healthy as his father.	*Gary sieht so gesund aus wie sein Vater.*

Ebenso wie **than** kann das zweite **as** einen Nebensatz einleiten:

The soup tastes just as sweet as the cake does.	*Die Suppe schmeckt genauso süß wie der Kuchen.*
Their children are as fat as they are.	*Ihre Kinder sind genauso dick wie sie.*
Paddy was as pleasant as I had expected him to be.	*Paddy war so liebenswürdig wie ich ihn mir vorgestellt hatte.*

Am meisten

Nach einem Verb kann man das Superlative eines Adjektivs mit oder ohne **the** verwenden:

The old lady was (the) friendliest.	*Die alte Dame war am freundlichsten.*
That building is the most modern.	*Das Gebäude da ist am modernsten.*

Wenn man die Gruppe nennen will, aus der man das Extrembeispiel nimmt, leitet man diese mit **of** ein. In diesem Fall braucht man **the**:

Brady was the stupidest of our students.	*Brady war der dümmste unserer Studenten.*
That story was the funniest of all.	*Diese Geschichte war die witzigste von allen.*

Allgemeine Fragen

Die allgemeinste Frage nach den Eigenschaften einer Sache ist: **What is it like?** (*Wie ist es?*). Natürlich kann man diese Frage je nach Zeit, Modalverb usw. entsprechend umgestalten:

What's the weather been like?	*Wie war das Wetter in letzter Zeit?*
What should the drawing be like?	*Wie soll die Zeichnung aussehen?*

Eine verwandte Frage lautet: **How is it?** (*Wie ist es?*). Damit fragt man mehr nach dem Empfinden des Gesprächspartners. Man erwartet dann eine Beurteilung:

How's the pumpkin salad? | *Wie ist der Kürbissalat?*

Vergleichen Sie folgende Dialoge:

Sprecher A:	
What was the music like?	*Wie war die Musik?*
Sprecher B:	
It was a mixture of jazz and blues.	*Es war eine Mischung aus Jazz und Blues.*

Sprecher A:	
How was the music?	*Wie war die Musik?*
Sprecher B:	
It was too loud, the pianist wasn't very good, but otherwise it was all right.	*Sie war zu laut, der Klavierspieler war nicht sehr gut, aber sonst war sie in Ordnung.*

Wenn man die Frage **How is/are...?** auf Personen bezieht, wird sie zu einer Frage nach deren Gesundheit bzw. deren Wohlbefinden:

How are your parents?	*Wie geht's deinen Eltern?*
Hi! How've you been?	*Hallo! Was treibst du so?*

Grammatik

Wenn man nach der Farbe von etwas fragt, verwendet man **What color** und die richtige Form von **be**:

Sprecher A:	
What color is it?	*Welche Farbe hat es?*
Sprecher B:	
It's blue and green.	*Es ist blau und grün.*

Fragen mit wahrnehmungsbezogenen Verben

Das allgemeine Schema für Fragen mit den in diesem Kapitel aufgeführten wahrnehmungsbezogenen Verben ist: **What ... like?**

What does it look like?	*Wie sieht es aus?*
What did the perfume smell like?	*Wie hat das Parfüm gerochen?*

9 Adverbs | *Umstandswörter*

Der Unterschied zwischen Adjective und Adverb

Im Deutschen sehen Adjectives (Eigenschaftswörter) und Adverbs (Umstandswörter) genau gleich aus. Daher kann es am Anfang schwer sein, sie voneinander zu unterscheiden.

Adjectives beschreiben immer ein Noun oder eine Noun Phrase.

The little mouse was nervous.	*Die kleine Maus war nervös.*

Ein Adverb beschreibt dagegen etwas anderes: ein Verb, ein Adjective, ein anderes Adverb oder den Satz selbst.

Es beschreibt ein *Verb*:	
The jogger ran into the house fast and immediately disappeared into the bathroom.	*Der Jogger lief schnell ins Haus und verschwand sofort ins Bad.*
Es beschreibt ein *Adjective*:	
The rather relieved parents welcomed their extremely tardy son home.	*Die Eltern waren ganz erleichtert und hießen ihren Sohn, der sehr spät nach Hause kam, willkommen.*
Es beschreibt ein *Adverb*:	
You've weeded the garden very thoroughly.	*Du hast den Garten aber sehr gründlich gejätet.*

Die Bildung von Adverbs

Viele (aber nicht alle!) Adverbs werden auf der Grundlage von Adjectives gebildet, in dem man man **-ly** ans Adjective hängt.

Adjective		*Adverb*	*Übersetzung*
probable	▶	probably	*wahrscheinlich*
quick	▶	quickly	*schnell*
horrible	▶	horribly	*schrecklich*

Grammatik

In der Umgangssprache lässt man aber manchmal das **-ly** einfach weg.

He drank real quick.	*Er trank echt schnell.*

Wichtige Ausnahmen

Manche Adverbs haben die gleiche Form wie die entsprechenden Adjectives:

back	*zurück*	**high**	*hoch*
close	*nahe*	**late**	*spät*
deep	*tief*	**left/right**	*links/rechts*
early	*früh*	**long**	*lang*
enough	*genug*	**near**	*nah*
far	*weit*	**right/wrong**	*richtig/falsch*
fast	*schnell*	**straight**	*gerade, direkt*
hard	*kräftig, hart*		

Bei diesen Adjectives und Adverbs muss man natürlich besonders darauf achten, um was es sich handelt:

Adjectives:	
Their service is fast.	*Ihr Service ist schnell.*
But that hotel is too far from the train station.	*Aber das Hotel ist zu weit vom Bahnhof entfernt.*
Who knows the right answer?	*Wer weiß die richtige Antwort?*
Adverbs:	
Our secretary types fast.	*Unsere Sekretärin kann schnell tippen.*
On a clear day you can see far.	*Bei klarem Wetter kann man weit sehen.*
Can't you do anything right?	*Kannst du denn nichts richtig machen?*

Manche dieser Adjectives haben zu dem auch noch eine **-ly** Form, die dann aber eine etwas andere Bedeutung oder Verwendung hat:

hardly	*kaum*	**nearly**	*beinahe, fast*
deeply	*tief*	**closely**	*nah*
lately	*kürzlich, vor kurzem*		

I **hardly** know him!	*Ich kenne ihn kaum.*
They **nearly** missed the train.	*Sie hätten fast den Zug verpasst.*
She's done a lot of charity **lately**.	*Sie hat vor kürzlich bei vielen Wohltätigkeitsaktionen gemacht.*

Well

Well als Adverb bedeutet *gut*. Als Adjective dagegen bedeutet es etwa *gesund*.

Adjective:

He was **well** when I last was there.	*Das letzte Mal als ich dort war, war er gesund.*

Adverb:

They did their work **well**.	*Sie machten ihre Arbeit gut.*

Well kann in der gesprochenen Sprache aber auch ganz anders, in der Art von *nun* oder *ääh* verwendet werden:

Well, sometimes it's hard to see.	*Nun, manchmal ist es schwer zu erkennen.*
Well... can I ask you something?	*Ääh... kann ich Dich was fragen?*

Adjectives mit der Endung -ly

Es gibt auch Adjectives, die mit **-ly** enden: **elderly** (*betagt*), **sickly** (*kränklich*), **kindly** (*liebenswürdig*), **likely** (*wahrscheinlich*) und **friendly** (*freundlich*) können sogar **nur** als Adjectives gebraucht werden:

A nurse takes care of their **sickly** child.	*Eine Krankenschwester pflegt ihr kränkliches Kind.*
A **kindly** woman helped us.	*Eine liebenswürdige Frau hat uns geholfen.*
It was **likely** that they would start fighting again.	*Sehr wahrscheinlich würden sie wieder anfangen miteinander zu streiten.*
There comes that **friendly** man with his dachshund.	*Da kommt dieser freundliche Herr mit seinem Dackel.*

Grammatik

Wenn man ein Adverb mit der Bedeutung *wahrscheinlich* verwenden möchte, greift man am besten auf **probably** zurück. Man kann aber auch **more likely** und **most likely** als gesteigerte Adverbs gebrauchen!

They **probably** went home already.	*Wahrscheinlich sind sie schon nach Hause gegangen.*
Eric **most likely** was after the ice cream.	*Sehr wahrscheinlich hatte es Eric auf das Eis abgesehen.*

Friendly

Friendly hat kein Adverb. Um eine adverbiale Bedeutung zu erzielen, muss man es deshalb umschreiben: Man setzt **friendly** in eine Phrase wie **in a friendly way**, oder formeller, **in a friendly manner**. Beide bedeuten *freundlich*.

Whitney looked up **in a friendly manner**.	*Whitney schaute freundlich auf.*
The business partners shook hands **in a friendly way**.	*Die Geschäftspartner gaben sich freundlich die Hand.*

Home

Alleine verwendet bedeutet das Wort **home** fast immer *nach Hause*:

Ray got fed up and went **home**.	*Ray hatte die Nase voll und ging nach Hause.*
Everybody was driving **home** from vacation on the same day.	*Alle fuhren am selben Tag aus dem Urlaub nach Hause.*

Wenn man **home** nach **be, stay, remain** gebraucht, heißt es *zu Hause*. Wenn man sonst *zu Hause* sagen will, muss man **at home** benutzen:

They **were home** but refused to open the door.	*Sie waren zu Hause, aber wollten nicht aufmachen.*
Many college students live **at home** with their parents.	*Viele Studenten wohnen zu Hause bei ihren Eltern.*

Die Steigerung

Genau wie bei den Adjectives (▶ Adjektive) haben kurze, höchstens zweisilbige Adverbs oft regelmäßig gesteigerte Formen im Comparative und Superlative:

Grundform	Comparative	Superlative	Übersetzung
close	closer	closest	*nahe*
early	earlier	earliest	*früh*
fast	faster	fastest	*schnell*
hard	harder	hardest	*hart, kräftig*
wide	wider	widest	*weit, breit*

Lange Adverbs mit mehr als drei Silben werden in der Regel mit **more** und **most** gesteigert:

Grundform	Comparative	Superlative	Übersetzung
beautifully	more beautifully	most beautifully	*schön*
effectively	more effectively	most effectively	*effektiv, wirkungsvoll*

He sang the most beautifully. | *Er sang am schönsten.*

Natürlich gibt es auch unregelmäßige Steigerungsformen, die man auswendig lernen muss:

Grundform	Comparative	Superlative	Übersetzung
badly	worse	worst	*schlecht*
far	farther, further	farthest, furthest	*weit*
little	less	least	*wenig*
much	more	most	*viel*
well	better	best	*gut*

The sound of jets overhead bothers us **less** than our neighbors' music.	*Der Lärm von Düsenflugzeugen stört uns weniger als die Musik von unseren Nachbarn.*
Who can get there the **fastest**?	*Wer kann am schnellsten dort sein?*

Verb- und satzbeschreibende Adverbs

Während Adverbs, die Adjectives und Adverbs beschreiben, ganz einfach vor diesem Wort stehen, ist die Platzierung im Satz der verb- und satzbeschreibenden Adverbs viel lockerer geregelt.

Adverbs der Art und Weise stehen manchmal vor dem *Verb*:

Dustin had **carefully brushed** his coat.	*Dustin hatte seinen Mantel sorgfältig gebürstet.*
Ruby **cheerfully hummed** a song.	*Ruby summte fröhlich ein Lied.*

Sie können auch nach dem Objekt des Verb stehen. Hat das Verb kein Objekt, dann setzt man das Adverb direkt nach dem Verb:

Dustin had brushed **his coat carefully**.	*Dustin hatte seinen Mantel sorgfältig gebürstet.*
Ruby hummed **a song cheerfully**.	*Ruby summte fröhlich ein Lied.*
The police **appeared quickly**.	*Die Polizei erschien schnell.*

Das Adverb kann aber niemals zwischen Verb und Objekt stehen.

Adverbs der Häufigkeit stehen meistens unmittelbar vor oder nach dem (ersten) Hilfsverb. Wenn kein Hilfsverb da ist, kommt das Adverb zwischen Subjekt und Vollverb:

Jo **would never** do such a thing.	*Jo würde so was nie machen.*
I **sometimes have** seen him there.	*Ich habe ihn manchmal dort gesehen.*
The train **usually arrives** on time.	*Der Zug kommt meistens pünktlich an.*

Die Adverbs **always, usually, often, frequently, sometimes, occasionally** können zur Betonung auch am Satzanfang stehen.

Usually the train arrives on time, but where is it today?	*Meistens kommt der Zug pünktlich an, aber wo bleibt er denn heute?*
Occasionally they visit Mr. McMurtry, but more often they stay home and gossip about him.	*Gelegentlich besuchen sie Mr. McMurtry, aber öfter bleiben sie daheim und tratschen über ihn.*
Evidently they've gone to look for a bar.	*Sie sind offenbar eine Bar suchen gegangen.*
Possibly Ross has frightened off all the clients.	*Ross hat vielleicht alle Klienten abgeschreckt.*

Man kann auch Adverbs mit negativer Bedeutung, wie z.B. **never** (*niemals*), an den Satzanfang stellen (▶ Kapitel Verneinung). Dann vertauschen aber Subjekt und erstes Verb ihre Position, d.h. es kommt zur sogenannten *Inversion*:

Never had I felt so embarrassed!	*Nie habe ich mich so geschämt!*

Das gleiche geschieht oft auch mit Adverbs, die Zeit, Ort oder Richtung eines Ereignisses betonen (z.B. **here, now, down, up, there** usw.):

Here comes the bus.	*Da kommt der Bus.*
Now is the time to say goodbye.	*Jetzt ist es an der Zeit, sich zu verabschieden.*
Down came the rain.	*Da fiel der Regen literweise!*
There stood a confused student.	*Da stand ein verwirrter Schüler.*

10 Coordinating Conjunctions
Bindewörter

Einzelwörter

Die Bindewörter **and** (*und*), **but** (*aber*) und **or** (*oder*) können sowohl zwischen Hauptsätzen als auch zwischen anderen Satzteilen stehen.

Zwischen Hauptsätzen

Carol chose a book on difficult parents, and her mother chose one on difficult children.	*Carol suchte sich ein Buch über schwierige Eltern aus, und ihre Mutter suchte sich eins über schwierige Kinder aus.*
The boy wanted an ice cream cone, but his parents wouldn't buy him one before dinner.	*Der Junge wollte ein Eis, aber seine Eltern weigerten sich, ihm eins vor dem Abendessen zu kaufen.*
Perhaps Jerry was looking for a raccoon, or perhaps he was going to dig holes in the flower garden.	*Vielleicht hat Jerry nach einem Waschbär gesucht, oder vielleicht ist er auch Löcher im Blumengarten graben gegangen.*

Zwischen anderen Satzteilen

We looked for Perry in his room but not under the bed.	*Wir haben Perry in seinem Zimmer gesucht, aber nicht unterm Bett.*
My cat loves strawberries and cream – or at least the cream.	*Meine Katze liebt Erdbeeren mit Sahne – oder zumindest die Sahne.*

Mehrwortbildungen

Es gibt auch noch die komplexeren Bildungen **both ... and, either ... or** und dessen verneinendes Gegenstück **neither ... nor**:

Both our dog **and** our cat love to go for walks.	*Sowohl unser Hund als auch unsere Katze gehen gern spazieren.*
Either Harvey is lying, **or** there's an elephant hiding in the backyard.	*Entweder Harvey lügt, oder ein Elefant hat sich im Hinterhof versteckt.*
The travellers found **neither** an oasis **nor** the promised camels.	*Die Reisenden fanden weder eine Oase noch die versprochenen Kamele vor.*

Wenn man **neither ... nor** in zwei Sätzen benutzen möchte, muss man etwas aufpassen: Im ersten Satz steht **neither** nach dem Subjekt, und im zweiten muss ein Hilfsverb vor dem Subjekt stehen:

Sylvia **neither** intended to get married, **nor** did she approve of living together.	*Sylvia hatte weder vor zu heiraten, noch hielt sie viel vom Zusammenleben.*

11 Sentence Construction | *Satzbau*

Der Aussagesatz

Im Deutschen beginnt ein Hauptsatz meistens mit einer einzigen Phrase, die vor dem (ersten) Verb steht. Diese Phrase kann das Subjekt sein – oder auch nicht. Wenn sie nicht das Subjekt ist, dann steht das Subjekt hinter dem Verb.

Im Englischen ist dies anders. Egal was am Satzanfang steht: man muss das Subjekt vor dem (ersten) Verb platzieren:

After the conference **some of us** went out for a drink.	*Nach der Konferenz sind einige von uns etwas trinken gegangen.*
The chewing gum, **she** liked; the cream pie, **she** didn't like.	*Den Kaugummi mochte sie, die Cremetorte mochte sie nicht.*

Auch wenn der Satz mit einem Nebensatz anfängt, steht das Subjekt des Hauptsatzes vor dem Verb:

Although it was late, **we** didn't go home.	*Obwohl es spät war, sind wir nicht nach Hause gegangen.*

Was nach dem Verb kommt

Eine ganze Reihe von Phrasen kann nach dem Vollverb eines Satzes stehen. Wenn es ein Objekt gibt (eine Noun Phrase), kommt dieses unmittelbar nach dem Verb. Danach stehen Phrasen, die eine enge Verbindung zum Verb haben. Diese haben eine vom Verb verlangte Präposition, wie z.B. die *woher-* und *wohin-*Phrasen. Dahinter setzt man Phrasen, die das bezeichnen, womit die Handlung ausgeführt wird. Erst danach kommen *wo-*Phrasen und als Schlusslicht *wann-*Phrasen. Natürlich enthält nicht jeder Satz alle diese Phrasenarten gleichzeitig, aber in dieser Reihenfolge werden sie geordnet:

Rick ate at the restaurant on Tuesday.	*Rick hat am Dienstag in dem Restaurant gegessen.*
The guru explained yoga to his pupils.	*Der Guru erklärte seinen Schülern Yoga.*
The cook chased the intruders out of the kitchen with a rolling pin that day.	*An jenem Tag jagte die Köchin die Eindringlinge mit einem Nudelholz aus der Küche.*

Ein störender Faktor bei dieser Regel ist die Länge der Phrasen: Lange Phrasen stehen gern hinten. Nebensätze tauchen oft am Satzende auf und nicht da, wo man sie sonst erwarten würde:

I finally found the missing papers yesterday where no one would ever think to look.	*Schließlich habe ich die Papiere dort gefunden, wo es niemandem in den Sinn käme zu schauen.*

Nebensatz-Fragen

Nebensatz-Fragen sind keine direkten Fragen, so wie sie einem immer gestellt werden, sondern Fragen, von denen berichtet wird. Typischerweise werden sie von Hauptsatz-Verben wie **ask, wonder** (*sich etwas fragen*), **learn** (*erfahren*), know, hear usw. eingeleitet. Nebensatz-Fragen lassen sich in zwei Klassen einteilen: ob-Fragen und Fragewort-Fragen:

Ob-Fragen

She asked whether I ski.	*Sie fragte, ob ich Ski fahre.*
He asked his friend whether she had seen that film.	*Er fragte seine Freundin, ob sie den Film schon gesehen hätte.*

Im Englischen gibt es zwei Wörter für *ob* – **if** und **whether**:

They hadn't heard whether Karen was working in town.	*Sie hatten nicht gehört, ob Karen in der Stadt arbeitete.*
I'm not sure if we need cheese for the pizza.	*Ich bin mir nicht sicher, ob wir Käse für die Pizza brauchen.*

Beide Wörter sind grundsätzlich gleich, auch wenn **whether** etwas formeller klingt.

Indirect Speech | *Indirekte Rede*

Zeitanpassung

Es gibt zwei Möglichkeiten davon zu berichten, was jemand gesagt hat: Man kann die Person wörtlich zitieren, oder man kann einfach von dem Inhalt erzählen. Die erste Methode heißt direct speech (direkte Rede) und die zweite indirect speech (indirekte Rede).

Direct Speech:	**She said, "Rover bit the policeman."**
Indirect Speech:	**She said that Rover had bitten the policeman.**

Bei der direct speech hat man am Gesagten natürlich nichts zu ändern.

Bei der indirect speech hingegen passt sich die Zeit des Nebensatzes an die des Hauptsatzes an. Wenn der Hauptsatz in der Gegenwart oder Zukunft steht, kann man die Zeit des Nebensatzes so lassen, wie sie ist. Wenn der Hauptsatz aber in der Vergangenheit steht, so müssen gewöhnlich alle Zeiten in der berichteten Aussage eine Stufe zurückgesetzt werden. Aus der einfachen Gegenwart wird dann die einfache Vergangenheit, aus der einfachen Vergangenheit wird das Past Perfect (die Vorvergangenheit), bei der Zukunft gelten die Regeln für Modalverben:

Hauptsatz in der Gegenwart oder Zukunft	
He **says** that the painting **is finished**.	*Er sagt, dass das Gemälde fertig ist.*
She **will want** to know what you**'ve done**.	*Sie wird wissen wollen, was ihr getan habt.*
They **have** often **told** me that **they plan** to import coconuts.	*Sie haben mir oft gesagt, dass sie vorhaben, Kokosnüsse zu importieren.*

Hauptsatz in der Vergangenheit

- Aus der Gegenwart wird Vergangenheit:

The painting is finished. **He said** that the painting **was** finished. ▶	*Das Gemälde ist fertig.* *Er sagte, dass das Gemälde fertig sei.*

- Aus der Vergangenheit wird Plusquamperfekt (Vorvergangenheit):

France won the game. **She said** that France **had won** the game. ▶	*Frankreich gewann das Spiel.* *Sie sagte, dass Frankreich das Spiel gewonnen hatte.*

Modalverben in der indirekten Rede

Bei der Vergangenheit der indirekten Rede verwendet man die Vergangenheitsformen der Modalverben:

Elliot claimed that he could read minds.	*Elliot behauptete, dass er Gedanken lesen könne.*
We wondered what they would do next.	*Wir haben uns gefragt, was sie wohl als Nächstes tun würden.*

Pronouns | *Fürwörter*

Man muss bei der indirekten Rede darauf achten, dass die Pronouns stimmen. D. h. ein *ich* im direkten Zitat ist nicht immer gleich mit dem *ich*, das jetzt von der Äußerung berichtet: Wenn es in der **direct speech** heisst **I see him** (*Ich sehe ihn*), wie soll man von dieser Aussage berichten? Wenn man es selbst gesagt hat, sagt man natürlich: **I said that I saw him**. Wenn es eine Äußerung des jetzigen Gesprächspartners war, so sagt man: **You said that you saw him.** Oder wenn es jemand anderes, z.B. Anne gesagt hat, sagt man: **She/Anne said that she saw him.**

Adverbiale Nebensätze

Adverbiale Nebensätze sind Sätze, die ungefähr die gleiche Funktion haben wie Adverbien. Solche Nebensätze haben meist die gleiche Wortfolge wie Aussagesätze:

Adverbien

Therefore the glass was empty.	*Deshalb war das Glas leer.*
Something will happen **soon**.	*Bald wird etwas passieren.*

Adverbiale Nebensätze

Because my friend had passed by and seen the wine, the glass was empty.	*Weil mein Freund vorbeigekommen war und den Wein gesehen hatte, war das Glas leer.*
Something will happen **when the monkeys are let out of the cage**.	*Wenn die Affen aus dem Käfig gelassen werden, wird etwas passieren.*

Man sollte sich einprägen, dass zukünftige Ereignisse in Nebensätzen selten mit **will** oder **shall** ausgedrückt werden. Vielmehr verwendet man Gegenwartsbildungen:

As soon as you get home, turn on the heater.	*Sobald du heimkommst, dreh die Heizung auf.*
Before the players take the field, the coach will remind them of the strategy.	*Bevor die Spieler auf das Feld kommen, erinnert sie der Trainer an ihre Strategie.*

Wenn-Sätze

If (*falls*) und **when** (*wenn*) werden leicht verwechselt, weil sie beide oft als *wenn* übersetzt werden. **If** bedeutet *wenn* im Sinne von *falls* oder *wenn es stimmt, dass*; es drückt Möglichkeit aus:

We can go to the zoo if you want.	*Wir können in den Zoo gehen, wenn du willst.*
If it rains today, I'll stay home.	*Wenn es heute regnet, bleibe ich daheim.*

Dagegen ist **when** immer zeitlich zu verstehen:

When you see Gina tonight, give her this book for me.	*Wenn du heute abend Gina siehst, gib ihr dieses Buch von mir.*
I always stay home when it rains.	*Ich bleibe immer zu Hause, wenn es regnet.*

When wird auch mit *als* übersetzt, wenn es Vergangenheitssätze einleitet:

We were glad when they left.	*Wir waren froh, als sie gingen.*
When he started to sing, everyone left the room.	*Als er anfing zu singen, verließen alle den Raum.*

Man sieht deutlich den Unterschied in diesen beiden Sätzen:

When you get up tomorrow, call me up.	*Sobald du morgen aufstehst, ruf mich an.*
If you get up tomorrow, call me up.	*Falls du morgen aufstehst, ruf mich an.*

Verbformen mit if-Sätzen

Im Allgemeinen kann man Gegenwart und Vergangenheit in if-Sätzen wie im Hauptsatz ausdrücken:

If she's tired, let her go to bed.	*Wenn sie müde ist, lass sie ins Bett gehen.*
If they've been doing their homework, why are they covered with dirt?	*Wenn sie gerade ihre Hausaufgaben gemacht haben, warum sind sie dann mit Dreck verschmiert?*
If she was tired, she didn't say so.	*Wenn sie müde war, so hat sie es nicht gesagt.*
If they were sleeping at the time, the telephone surely woke them up.	*Wenn sie um diese Zeit geschlafen haben, so hat sie das Telefon ganz sicher geweckt.*

Wenn es im if-Satz um ein Ereignis in der Zukunft geht, hat der if-Satz meist eine Gegenwartszeit:

If that dog bites me, I'll sue you.	*Falls mich dieser Hund beißt, werde ich Sie verklagen.*
If you go to Russia next year, I will go to the States.	*Wenn Du nächstes Jahr nach Russland fährst, fahre ich in die Staaten.*

Um auszudrücken, dass das Ereignis geplant oder vorhergesagt ist, verwendet man **be going to** (▶ Wie man über die Zukunft spricht):

If they **are going to** tear down that hotel, it must not be doing well.	*Wenn sie vorhaben, das Hotel abzureißen, dann läuft das Geschäft dort wahrscheinlich nicht gut.*
If prices **are going to** rise, we should stock up on chocolate bars.	*Wenn es stimmt, dass die Preise steigen werden, sollten wir uns einen Vorrat an Schokoladenriegeln zulegen.*

Grammatik

Wenn man **will** im if-Satz verwendet, deutet es darauf hin, dass die Subjektsperson einwilligt die Handlung auszuführen – mehr oder weniger, dass sie so nett ist, es zu tun:

If you will just close the window, we can get started.	*Wenn Sie das Fenster zumachen wollen, können wir anfangen.*
If Jasper will do the washing, the others can concentrate on the repairs.	*Wenn Jasper bereit ist die Wäsche zu waschen, können sich die anderen auf die Reparaturen konzentrieren.*

Oft will man mit einem if-Satz eine Situation beschreiben, die eigentlich nicht real ist, die aber – zumindest in der Fantasie – stattgefunden könnte. Dafür braucht man das Past Subjunctive.

If I were an ostrich, I would run 50 km every day.	*Wenn ich ein Strauß wäre, würde ich jeden Tag 50 km laufen.*
If Jackie had more Money, we would buy a yacht.	*Falls Jackie mehr Geld hätte, würden wir eine Jacht kaufen.*

Wenn das Nichtexistierende in der Vergangenheit war, so nimmt man das Past Perfect:

If I had been an ostrich at the time, I would have run 50 km every day.	*Wenn ich damals ein Strauß gewesen wäre, wäre ich jeden Tag 50 km gelaufen.*
If Anne hadn't brought the drinks, we couldn't have held the party.	*Wenn Anne die Getränke nicht gebracht hätte, hätten wir das Fest nicht feiern können.*

Andere adverbiale Nebensätze

- Adverbiale Nebensätze können zeitliche Verhältnisse beschreiben:

After Colin had his coffee, he read the newspaper.	*Nachdem Colin seinen Kaffee getrunken hatte, las er die Zeitung.*
Before Alberta went to work, she called five clients.	*Bevor Alberta zur Arbeit ging, hat sie noch fünf Kunden angerufen.*
As soon as the results are made public, the company will act.	*Sobald die Ergebnisse bekannt gegeben worden sind, wird die Firma handeln.*
Since he's been here, there's been nothing but trouble.	*Seitdem er hier ist, hat's nichts als Ärger gegeben.*
As long as Perry thinks you're here, he won't get suspicious.	*Solange Perry glaubt, dass du hier bist, wird er nicht stutzig werden.*

Es gibt ein allgemeines Wort für *während*, nämlich **while**.

Im britischen Englisch kann man im sehr gehobenen Sprachgebrauch auch **whilst** sagen.

While Naomi was singing in the bathtub, the man left with the contents of her wallet.	*Während Naomi noch in der Badewanne sang, ist der Mann mit dem Inhalt ihrer Brieftasche verschwunden.*
Whilst Moira played the piano, Francis worked in the garden.	*Während Moira Klavier spielte, arbeitete Francis im Garten.*

- Adverbiale Nebensätze die sonstige Umstände (z.B. Gründe, Bedingungen) beschreiben:

Because there was a lot of snow last night, we have to stay indoors today.	*Weil es letzte Nacht viel geschneit hat, müssen wir heute drinnen bleiben.*
Since you think you're so smart, you can finish the work yourself.	*Da du dich für so gescheit hältst, kannst du die Arbeit selber zu Ende machen.*
Although Tim wanted a car, he only bought himself a bike.	*Obwohl Tim ein Auto wollte, kaufte er sich nur ein Fahrrad.*
Unless the weather improves, we'll have to stay indoors.	*Falls das Wetter nicht besser wird, werden wir drinnen bleiben müssen.*
As long as you're here, you can help me with the chores.	*Wenn du sowieso da bist, kannst du mir im Haushalt helfen.*
So long as Patsy and Mark don't try to climb the trees, they can come too.	*Solange Patsy and Mark nicht ver-suchen auf die Bäume zu klettern, dürfen sie auch mitkommen.*

Infinitivsätze

Wo immer man einen **to**-Infinitiv findet, handelt es sich um einen Nebensatz. Aus diesem Grund kann nach **to** entweder ein Vollverb alleine oder ein Hilfsverb(en) + Vollverb stehen.

Unter anderem können bestimmte Verbs (Verben), Adjectives (Eigenschaftswörter) und Nouns (Hauptwörter) einen Infinitivsatz verlangen. Der Infintivsatz beginnt jeweils mit **to**.

We **meant** to send you a card.	*Wir hatten vor, euch eine Karte zu schicken.*
My parents would **be sorry** to have to see you again.	*Meine Eltern würden es bedauern, dich wieder sehen zu müssen.*
Greta Garbo's **desire** to be alone disappointed her fans.	*Greta Garbos Wunsch alleine zu sein, enttäuschte ihre Fans.*
To have danced badly **would have been embarrassing**.	*Schlecht getanzt zu haben wäre peinlich gewesen.*

Grammatik

Bei gewissen Verben kann ein Objekt zwischen dem Verb und dem Infinitivsatz stehen:

I asked the committee **to pay for it.**	*Ich habe das Komitee darum gebeten, es zu bezahlen.*
The owner told the rowdy customers **to get out of the bar.**	*Der Besitzer forderte die randalierenden Gäste auf, seine Bar zu verlassen.*

Ein paar Verben erlauben, dass der Infinitivsatz sein eigenes Subjekt hat. Bei **want** und **need** gibt es übrigens keine andere Möglichkeit, dieses Subjekt auszudrücken: sie vertragen keinen **that**-Satz!

The athletes wanted the spectators **to cheer them up.**	*Die Athleten wollten vom Publikum aufgemuntert werden.*
They expect it **to stop raining tomorrow.**	*Sie nehmen an, dass es morgen aufhört zu regnen.*
I need him **to move furniture for me.**	*Ich hätte gern, dass er für mich Möbel umstellt.*

Wenn das Subjekt des Infinitivsatzes allerdings mit dem Subjekt des Hauptsatzes identisch ist, so erscheint das Subjekt nur im Hauptsatz:

We **wanted to see New York in spring.**	*Wir wollten New York im Frühjahr sehen.*
They **expect to find some buried treasures soon.**	*Sie erwarten, bald vergrabene Schätze zu finden.*
I **need to call the movers.**	*Ich muss die Spedition anrufen.*

Adverbiale Anwendung

Mit einem Infinitivsatz kann man den Sinn und Zweck einer Handlung ausdrücken: Entweder man setzt **to** an den Anfang des Infinitivsatzes, oder man leitet den Satz mit **in order to** ein:

Mrs. Green went to the party **to** keep an eye on her daughters.	*Mrs. Green ist zu der Party gegangen, um ihre Töchter im Auge zu behalten.*
You need to turn on the light **in order to see** properly.	*Du musst das Licht anmachen, um besser sehen zu können.*

ing-Sätze

Man kann die *ing*-Form als Verb eines Nebensatzes verwenden. Dies ist aber sprachlich etwas formell:

Desperately **needing** money, they started a small business.	*Da sie dringend Geld benötigten, gründeten sie ein kleines Geschäft.*
Having lost his car keys, he continued his journey on foot.	*Da er seine Autoschlüssel verloren hatte, setzte er seine Reise zu Fuß fort.*

Man kann einen *ing*-Satz am Ende des Hauptsatzes anhängen um zu zeigen, was das Subjekt gleichzeitig tut, d.h. welche Handlungen gerade ablaufen:

Maurice was at home **eating steaks for breakfast**.	*Maurice war zu Hause und aß zum Frühstück Steaks.*
Sabrina crawled around on the floor **picking up the fallen coins**.	*Sabrina kroch auf dem Boden herum und hob alle Münzen auf, die heruntergefallen waren.*

Grammatik

Before, after, without, while können auch mit einer *ing*-Form als Nebensatz verwendet werden. Dies geht aber nur, wenn sich der Inhalt des Nebensatzes auf das Subjekt des längeren Satzes (d. h. des Hauptsatzes) bezieht:

Clean up **after finishing your work**.	*Räumt auf, wenn ihr mit eurer Arbeit fertig seid.*
Before bathing, he looked at the clock.	*Bevor er badete, schaute er auf die Uhr.*
He put up his feet **without removing his shoes**.	*Er legte seine Füße hoch, ohne seine Schuhe auszuziehen.*
The chef prepared the salad **while flipping pancakes**.	*Der Koch bereitete den Salat zu, während er Pfannkuchen in der Luft herumwirbelte.*

Instead of und **by** müssen mit einer *ing*-Form verwendet werden:

Instead of buying groceries, he spent the money on pinball.	*Anstatt Lebensmittel zu kaufen, gab er das Geld für Flipperspiele aus.*
You could try to fix it **by pressing** that button.	*Du könntest versuchen es zu reparieren, in dem du diesen Knopf drückst.*

Ein *ing*-Satz kann auch als Subjekt eines längeren Satzes dienen:

Climbing mountains can be great fun.	*Auf Berge steigen kann viel Spaß machen.*
Seeing their incompetence drives me crazy.	*Es macht mich wahnsinnig, wenn ich mir ansehen muss, wie unfähig sie sind.*

Verben, nach denen eine ing-Form steht

Nach bestimmten Verben kann oder muss man eine *ing*-Form verwenden:

enjoy	*sehr gern tun, genießen*	**mind**	*etwas ausmachen*
finish	*beenden, aufhören, etwas zu Ende machen*	**miss**	*vermissen*
		practice	*üben*
go	*gehen*	**remember**	*sich an etwas erinnern*
imagine	*sich etwas vorstellen*	**stop**	*aufhören*
keep	*weitermachen*	**try**	*versuchen*
like	*gern tun*	**start**	*anfangen*

They finally **stopped banging** the pans together.	*Endlich hörten sie damit auf, Pfannen zusammenzuknallen.*
I **enjoy swimming** in warm water.	*Ich schwimme sehr gern in warmem Wasser.*
We didn't **mind walking** the ten miles.	*Es machte uns nichts aus, die zehn Meilen zu Fuß zu gehen.*
Let's **go swimming** tomorrow!	*Gehen wir morgen schwimmen!*
Pauline **kept bothering** me.	*Pauline hat mich ständig gestört.*

Vorsicht! Bei **stop** gibt es sowohl eine Ergänzung mit *ing*-Form als auch mit **to**-Infinitiv. Beide haben völlig unterschiedliche Bedeutungen: **stop doing something** heißt *aufhören, etwas zu tun*, **stop to do something** heißt *aufhören, um etwas zu tun*:
They finally **stopped shouting** at me.	*Sie hörten endlich auf, mich anzuschreien.*
They finally **stopped to shout** at me.	*Sie hörten endlich auf, um mich anzuschreien.*

Nach einer Präposition braucht man fast immer einen *ing*-Satz:

be afraid of	*davor Angst haben*	**believe in**	*daran glauben*
be for/against	*dafür/dagegen sein*	**feel like**	*dazu Lust haben*
be good/bad at	*darin gut/schlecht sein*	**insist on**	*darauf bestehen*
be interested in	*daran interessiert sein*	**look forward to**	*sich darauf freuen*
be tired of	*es satt haben*	**think about**	*daran denken, sich überlegen*
be used to	*es gewohnt sein*		

Grammatik

I look forward to hearing from you.	Ich freue mich darauf, von Ihnen zu hören.
I feel like having a swim.	Ich habe Lust zu schwimmen.
I didn't feel like working.	Ich hatte keine Lust zu arbeiten.
My grandmother believes in eating porridge for breakfast every day.	Meine Großmutter ist davon überzeugt, dass man jeden Tag Haferbrei zum Frühstück essen sollte.

Vorsicht: Wenn die scheinbare Präposition **to** ist, gebraucht man oft die Grundform, da es sich eigentlich um das *to* des *to*-Infinitivs handelt:

I was prepared to do anything.	Ich war bereit, alles zu tun.
The group went on to discuss the weather.	Die Gruppe unterhielt sich anschließend über das Wetter.
He used to call me up in the middle of the night.	Früher hat er mich mitten in der Nacht angerufen.

Einige Ergänzungen haben aber tatsächlich die Präposition **to**, die einen *–ing*-Satz fordert:

I have no objection to waiting.	Ich habe nichts dagegen, zu warten.
Next to sleeping, my favorite activity is watching TV.	Neben Schlafen ist Fernsehen meine Lieblingsbeschäftigung.
I'm used to hearing his complaints.	Ich bin es gewohnt, seine Klagen zu hören.

Bei bestimmten Verben und Präpositionen kann man ein Element vor der *ing*-Form einschieben. Dieses Element kann entweder in der Objektform oder in der Possessivform stehen:

appreciate	zu schätzen wissen	remember	sich daran erinnern
excuse	entschuldigen	resent	übel nehmen
mind	etwas dagegen haben	understand	verstehen
miss	vermissen		

I remember him/his burning the photo.	Ich erinnere mich daran, wie er das Foto verbrannte.		
I can understand them/their wanting to be alone.	Ich kann es verstehen, dass sie alleine sein wollen.		
be afraid of	davor Angst haben	hear about	davon hören
be fed up with	die Nase voll von … haben	look forward to	sich darauf freuen
be used to	es gewöhnt sein	object to	etwas dagegen haben
I'm fed up with you/your running around with other women.	Ich habe die Nase voll davon, dass du mit anderen Frauen herumläufst.		
They objected to people('s) sunbathing naked.	Sie hatten etwas dagegen, dass Leute nackt sonnenbaden.		

Lassen

Das deutsche Verb *lassen* bringt oft eine Art „kleinen Satz" mit sich. Wie ein normaler Satz hat auch dieser kleine Satz sein eigenes Verb. Es gibt zwei verschiedene Arten den kleinen Satz zu bilden. Da kommt es darauf an, ob das Verb des kleinen Satzes eine normale Aktivbedeutung oder eher eine Passivbedeutung hat.

Normale Sätze	Kleine Sätze
Die Angestellten gehen.	*Die Chefin lässt die Angestellten früh gehen.*
Der Hund hat die Möbel zerstört.	*Frieda hat den Hund die Möbel zerstören lassen.*
Mein Rock ist gereinigt worden.	*Ich habe meinen Rock reinigen lassen.*

Dieses *lassen* hat zweierlei Bedeutungen: *erlauben, zulassen* und *veranlassen*. Wenn es *erlauben* heißt, übersetzt man es oft mit **let**. Wenn es *veranlassen* heißt, übersetzt man es meist mit **have** oder **make.** Dabei drückt **have** aus, dass man jemanden beauftragt hat, während **make** (bei absichtlichen Handlungen) andeutet, dass man diesen jemanden dazu gezwungen hat – oder zumindest seine Autorität über den anderen ausgeübt hat.

Grammatik

Let | *erlauben, zulassen*

In der Aktivbedeutung bildet man nach **let** einen kleinen Satz. Dieser besteht aus mindestens einem Subjekt und einem Verb im Infinitiv (der Grundform) ohne **to**. Andere Elemente (z. B. Objekt, Adverb) können folgen, je nachdem, was das Verb verlangt und was man sagen will:

Despite the complaints, the police **let** them **sing**.	*Trotz der Beschwerden hat die Polizei sie singen lassen.*
He **let** the sand **run** through his fingers.	*Er hat den Sand durch seine Finger rieseln lassen.*

Man kann nach **let** auch ein Passiv mit dem Passivhilfsverb **be** bilden:

The guards **let** the money **be stolen**.	*Die Wächter haben es zugelassen, dass das Geld gestohlen wurde.*
The injured athlete **let** himself **be carried** off the field.	*Der verletzte Spieler ließ sich vom Feld tragen.*

Have | *veranlassen, in Auftrag geben*

In der Aktivbedeutung verwendet man **have** wie **let**: Man bildet einen kleinen Satz, dessen Verb im Infinitiv (der Grundform) ohne **to** steht:

The Ellisons are **having** the carpenter **make** them a kitchen cabinet.	*Die Ellisons lassen sich vom Schreiner einen Küchenschrank machen.*
Merle **had** her daughter **do** the dishes.	*Merle hat ihre Tochter abspülen lassen.*

In der Passivbedeutung verwendet man keine Infinitivform (Grundform), sondern ein Past Participle (die dritte Form):

The priest has the church bells **rung** before weddings.	*Der Priester lässt die Kirchenglocken vor Hochzeiten läuten.*
I had my suit **cleaned** only last week.	*Ich habe meinen Anzug erst letzte Woche reinigen lassen.*

Make | *veranlassen, zwingen*

Make kann man nur in der Aktivbedeutung verwenden. Wie oben schon erwähnt, enthält es bei absichtlichen Handlungen die Andeutung, dass jemand gezwungen wurde.

Mrs. Grundy **made** her children **give** their teacher a present.	*Mrs. Grundy zwang ihre Kinder, ihrer Lehrerin einen Geschenk zu machen.*
Sherrie always **makes** her little brother **take** out the garbage.	*Sherrie läßt immer ihren kleinen Bruder den Müll nach draußen bringen.*

Make wählt man auch, um auszudrücken, dass ein Gegenstand, Ereignis usw. etwas unabsichtlich verursacht:

Howard's thoughtless remark **made** his listeners **see** red.	*Howards gedankenlose Bemerkung ließ seine Zuhörer rotsehen.*
The loud bang **made** the passers-by **run** away in fright.	*Der laute Knall ließ die Passanten vor Schreck weglaufen.*

12 Questions Words | *Fragewort-Fragen*

Die englischen Fragewörter:

what	was	when	wann
which	welches	where	wo
who	wer, wen, wem	why	warum
whose	wessen	how	wie
whom	wen, wem		

Anwendung

Genau wie im Deutschen verwendet man Fragewörter, um Phrasen zu bilden, mit denen man nach fehlenden Informationen fragen kann. Fragewort-Phrasen stehen meist am Satzanfang:

What do you want?	*Was willst du?*
How much does that gold ring cost?	*Wie viel kostet dieser Goldring?*

Um großes Erstaunen auszudrücken, kann man aber auch die Wortfolge eines Aussagesatzes kopieren und die entsprechende Stelle (meist eine Noun Phrase), die zur Überraschung geführt hat, durch das jeweilige Fragewort ersetzen. Auf gleiche Art kann man auch – relativ unhöflich und umgangssprachlich – nachfragen, wenn man einen einzelnen Satzteil nicht verstanden hat:

Sprecher A:	
Leah's been eating peach sandwiches.	*Leah hat in letzter Zeit Pfirsichbrote gegessen.*
Sprecher B:	
Leah's been eating WHAT?	*Leah hat WAS in letzter Zeit gegessen?*

Man kann sogar das Verb durch die entsprechende Form von **do** und die Noun Phrase durch ein Fragewort ersetzen:

Sprecher A:	
Gonzuela gave Peter the car.	*Gonzuela hat Peter das Auto gegeben.*
Sprecher B:	
Gonzuela did WHAT?	*Gonzuela hat WAS getan?*

Das Fragewort **whom** (*wen, wem*) existiert kaum noch in der gesprochenen Sprache.

Vor allem in den USA ist **whom** fast völlig verschwunden. An seiner Stelle verwendet man *who*:

Who did she see?	*Wen hat sie gesehen?*
Who were you talking to just now?	*Mit wem hast du gerade gesprochen?*

Whom findet man jedoch noch in der formellen Schriftsprache:

Whom did she see?	*Wen hat sie gesehen?*
To whom must one speak about such matters?	*Mit wem muss man über solche Angelegenheiten sprechen?*

Wenn man eine Präposition (**on, by, in, to** usw.) in der Fragekonstruktion braucht, gibt es zwei Möglichkeiten, um diese zu positionieren.

1. In sehr formellen, hauptsächlich schriftlichen Situationen stellt man die Präposition an den Anfang der Fragewort-Phrase:

On which corner was the musician standing?	*An welcher Ecke stand der Musikant?*
To which thief did the docent show the collection?	*Welchem Dieb zeigte die Museumspädagogin die Sammlung?*

Grammatik

Dies ist auch der einzige Fall, wo man gelegentlich noch **whom** hört oder liest:

To whom did you turn then?	*An wen haben Sie sich dann gewandt?*

2. Im normalen Sprachgebrauch aber steht die Präposition am Ende oder in der Mitte des Satzes:

Which corner was the musician standing **on**?	*An welcher Ecke ist der Musikant gestanden?*
Which thief did the docent show the collection **to**?	*Welchem Dieb hat die Museumspädagogin die Sammlung gezeigt?*
Who did you turn **to** then?	*An wen haben Sie sich dann gewandt?*

Fragewort-Fragen im Nebensatz

Fragewort-Fragen im Nebensatz haben normalerweise eine andere Wortfolge als im Hauptsatz. Im Nebensatz nämlich schiebt man kein Hilfsverb zwischen Fragewort-Phrase und Subjekt. Wenn ein Hilfsverb vorhanden ist, steht es nach dem Subjekt, wie in einem Aussagesatz. Wenn von der Bedeutung her kein Hilfsverb notwendig ist, setzt man auch keines hinein.

Fragewort-Fragen im Hauptsatz:	
What did you say?	*Was hast du gesagt?*
How many would you like?	*Wie viele möchten Sie?*
What do we want?	*Was wollen wir?*
Fragewort-Fragen im Nebensatz:	
She asked him **what he'd said**.	*Sie fragte ihn, was er gesagt hatte.*
The salesclerk asked **how many they would like**.	*Die Verkäuferin fragte, wie viele sie möchten.*
Simon and Bonnie don't know **what they want**.	*Simon und Bonnie wissen nicht, was sie wollen.*

13 Relative Clauses | *Relativsätze*

Relativsätze sind Nebensätze, die in der Regel ein Noun (Hauptwort) oder eine Noun Phrase beschreiben:

The girl **who swims fastest** wins a prize.	*Das Mädchen, das am schnellsten schwimmt, gewinnt einen Preis.*
The fish **which jumped out of the water** was a salmon.	*Der Fisch, der aus dem Wasser sprang, war ein Lachs.*

Die Beispielsätze zeigen, dass hier der Relativsatz ein notwendiger Teil des Satzes ist, da er definiert, wer genau gemeint ist. Wenn man den Relativsatz weglassen würde, wüsste man nicht, welche Person einen Preis gewinnt oder welcher Fisch ein Lachs war. Zum Vergleich: in den beiden folgenden Beispielsätzen wäre trotzdem klar, wer oder was gemeint ist: **The fastest one** bzw. **Peter** sagt schon alles, so dass der Relativsatz zwar eine zusätzliche Information bringt, jedoch nicht notwendig zur Identifikation beiträgt.

The fastest one, **who of course wins**, receives a prize.	*Die Schnellste, die natürlich gewinnt, bekommt einen Preis.*
Peter, **who was a bit shy**, kept quiet.	*Peter, der ein bisschen schüchtern war, blieb still.*

Kommaregel für Relativsätze

In der geschriebenen Sprache unterscheidet man zwischen den beiden genannten Relativsatztypen durch die Interpunktion. Wo nämlich der Relativsatz zur Identifikation des gemeinten notwendig ist, benutzt man weder davor noch danach ein Komma. Wo der Relativsatz lediglich zusätzliche Informationen gibt, also nur beschreibt und nicht notwendig ist (und deshalb weggelassen werden kann), benutzt man jeweils vor und nach dem Relativsatz ein Komma:

Those books **which everyone has read** are boring.	*Die Bücher, die jeder gelesen hat, sind langweilig.*
His new book, **which everyone has read**, is boring.	*Sein neues Buch, das jeder gelesen hat, ist langweilig.*

Grammatik

> Wenn die Zeichensetzung im Englischen sonst auch relativ unwichtig ist, so ist die Unterscheidung zwischen den beiden Typen sehr wichtig, da sie zu großen Missverständnissen führen kann:
> **Mary knows few boys who are knitting.** Mary kennt nur wenige Jungs, die häkeln.
> **Mary knows few boys, who are knitting.** Mary kennt nur wenige Jungs, und die Jungs häkeln alle.

In der gesprochenen Sprache muss man sich auf sein Ohr verlassen. Das Komma der geschriebenen Sprache entspricht hier in etwa einer kleinen Pause.

Relative Pronouns | *Relativpronomen*

Die Relativpronomen im Englischen lauten: **who, whom, whose, which, when, where** und **why**.

- **Who**, **whose** und **whom** werden für Menschen und manchmal auch für Haustiere verwendet:

I met a man who can walk on his hands.	*Ich habe einen Mann getroffen, der auf seinen Händen laufen kann.*
A woman who was sweeping the sidewalk gave us directions.	*Eine Frau, die gerade den Gehweg kehrte, erklärte uns den Weg.*
That dog, who did tricks, followed me home.	*Dieser Hund, der Kunststücke machen konnte, folgte mir nach Hause.*

Wie bei den Fragewörtern (▶ Kapitel Fragewort-Fragen) findet **whom** selten Gebrauch in der gesprochenen Sprache. Dafür verwendet man **who**:

The police officer whom you saw.	*Der Polizist, den/Die Polizistin, die du gesehen hast.*
▶ **The police officer who you saw.**	

Im Gegensatz zu **who** und **whom** kann man **whose** auch bei Gegenständen benutzen:

A chest, whose hinges were broken, stood in the corner.	*Eine Kiste, deren Scharniere kaputt waren, stand in der Ecke.*

Die gleichwertige Alternative für Gegenstände ist **of which**, dieses benötigt jedoch manchmal schwierige Satzstellungen:

A chest, the hinges of which were broken, stood in the corner.	*Eine Kiste, deren Scharniere kaputt waren, stand in der Ecke.*

- **Which** verwendet man ausschliesslich für Gegenstände und Lebewesen, zu denen man wenig Bezug hat.

The cookies which I dropped made Fido happy.	*Die Kekse, die mir aus der Hand gefallen sind, machten Fido glücklich.*

In der gesprochenen Sprache lässt man eine Präposition wie bei Fragen am Ende des Relativsatzes:

The businesswoman who Graham was talking to was his aunt.	*Die Geschäftsfrau, mit der Graham gesprochen hat, war seine Tante.*
The vegetables which the chef had asked for were delivered.	*Das Gemüse, um das der Koch gebeten hatte, wurde geliefert.*

Im sehr formellen Sprachgebrauch jedoch kommt die Präposition vor dem Relative Pronoun, das bei Personen dann *whom* lautet:

The businesswoman to whom Graham was talking was his aunt.	*Die Geschäftsfrau, mit der Graham gesprochen hat, war seine Tante.*

Grammatik

- **When, where** und **why**

    When kann man nach verschiedenen Zeitangaben verwenden:

Do you remember the time when Walt scared the neighbors with his trumpet?	*Erinnerst du dich daran, als Walt mit seiner Trompete die Nachbarn erschreckte?*
That was the night when the electricity went out.	*Das war der Abend, an dem der Strom ausgefallen ist.*

    Where kann sowohl für Ortsangaben als auch für andere Dinge verwendet werden:

The city where I left my heart was San Francisco.	*Die Stadt, wo ich mein Herz verlor, war San Francisco.*
I know a restaurant where you get all you can eat for ten dollars.	*Ich kenne ein Restaurant, wo man für zehn Dollar so viel bekommt, wie man essen kann.*
It was a situation where nobody could win.	*Es war so eine Situation, wo keiner gewinnen konnte.*
I was having a day where everything went wrong.	*Ich hatte gerade so einen Tag, wo alles schief geht.*

    Why verwendet man nur als Relativpronomen, um einen gemeinten Grund zu verdeutlichen:

I never understood the reason why he left her.	*Ich habe nie verstanden, warum er sie verlassen hat.*

That

Sehr häufig verzichtet man ganz auf Relativpronomen und verwendet stattdessen das unveränderliche Wort **that**. In der gesprochenen Sprache hört sich **that** viel natürlicher an als das Relativpronomen für Gegenstände, **which**:

The lamp that we bought was very expensive.	*Die Lampe, die wir gekauft haben, war sehr teuer.*
The mouse that lives in my kitchen is quite clever.	*Die Maus, die in meiner Küche lebt, ist ganz schön schlau.*

Präpositionen bleiben bei **that** grundsätzlich am Ende des Relativsatzes:

The chair that Andrew was sitting on collapsed.	*Der Stuhl, auf dem Andrew saß, ist zusammengebrochen.*
The young woman that he was talking about doesn't like us.	*Die junge Frau, von der er geredet hat, mag uns nicht.*

That eignet sich nur für Relativsätze, die unbedingt nötig sind, weil sie etwas näher definieren. Wenn man einen Relativsatz bilden will, der nur zusätzliche Informationen bietet, aber nicht unbedingt nötig ist, muss man ein Relativpronomen verwenden. **That** kann das besitzanzeigende Relativpronomen **whose** nicht ersetzen.

Manchmal braucht man weder ein Relativpronomen noch **that**. Diese Form von Relativsatz ist besonders in der gesprochenen Sprache sehr üblich:

The hotel ___ they took Debbie to had a swimming pool.	*Das Hotel, in das sie Debbie einluden, hatte einen Swimmingpool.*

Grammatik

Es gibt zwei wichtige Regeln, die man beachten muss, wenn man das Relativpronomen bzw. **that** ganz weglassen möchte:

1. Man kann diese Wörter nur bei Relativsätzen weglassen, die unbedingt nötig sind. Ist ein Relativsatz nicht nötig, d.h. er steht zwischen zwei Kommas, dann muss das entsprechende Relativpronomen benutzt werden.
2. Das Relativpronomen bzw. **that** darf nicht als das Subjekt des Relativsatzes fungieren, wenn es ersetzt werden soll.

the man who/that saw the movie star	der Mann, der den Filmstar sah
the man (who/that) the movie star saw	der Mann, den der Filmstar sah
the man (who/that) I saw the movie star with	der Mann, mit dem ich den Filmstar sah
Peter, who saw the movie star, kissed the girl.	Peter, der den Filmstar sah, küsste das Mädchen.

Im ersten Beispielsatz kann man das Relativpronomen bzw. **that** nicht weglassen, weil **who/that** das Subjekt innerhalb des Relativsatzes ist. Im zweiten und dritten Beispiel dagegen kann man das Relativpronomen bzw. **that** weglassen. Im vierten Beispielsatz kann **who** nicht weggelassen werden, da der Relativsatz nur Zusatzinformationen gibt, aber nicht zur Identifikation von Peter notwendig ist.

Free Relatives | *freie Relativsätze*

Ein Free Relative ist eine Art Relativsatz, der eine Noun Phrase nicht ergänzen, sondern alleine eine bilden kann. Mit anderen Worten: diese Relativsätze können selbst als Subjekte, Objekte usw. fungieren.

Subjekt:	
What irritated me so much was their attitude.	*Was mich so ärgerte, war ihre Einstellung.*
Objekt:	
He likes **what he cooks**.	*Er mag, was er kocht.*

Grammatik

In Free Relatives kann man **what, where, when** und manchmal **who** verwenden:

What you need is exercise.	Was du brauchst, ist Bewegung.
I have **what you want**.	Ich habe, was du willst.
It wasn't **where it was supposed to be**.	Es war nicht dort, wo es hätte sein sollen.
They came and went **when they pleased**.	Sie kamen und gingen, wann es ihnen passte.
I'm going to thrash **who did it**.	Ich werde den verprügeln, der es gemacht hat.

Ausserdem kann man diese Fürwörter mit **–ever** ergänzen. Sie bedeuten dann soviel wie *was auch immer* (**whatever**)*, wo auch immer* (**wherever**)*, wann auch immer* (**whenever**) und *wer auch immer* (**whoever**)*.*

Whoever told you that was lying.	Wer immer dir das auch gesagt hat, hat gelogen.
I'll bring **whatever** you need.	Ich bringe dir, was immer du brauchst.
They simply went **wherever** the bus took them.	Sie sind einfach dorthin gefahren, wo der Bus gerade hinfuhr.
We can leave **whenever** you're ready.	Wir können gehen, wann immer du fertig bist.

14 Negation | *Verneinung*

Negative Ausdrücke

Ein paar grammatische Abweichungen kommen hauptsächlich in verneinten Sätzen vor. Dabei zählen nicht nur die offensichtlich verneinenden Ausdrücke (wie z. B. **not, never, no**) als negativ, sondern auch die untenstehenden:

few	*nur wenige*
rarely, seldom	*selten*
hardly, scarcely, barely	*kaum*

Any-Wörter

Das Wort **any** und seine Zusammensetzungen, wie **anyone, anywhere** verwendet man in verneinten Sätzen, wo man in nicht verneinten Sätzen **some** und verwandte Wörter, wie **someone, somewhere** gebraucht. Das entsprechende Wort für die Zeitangabe enthält aber kein **any**, es heißt **ever.**

1. Wenn das Subjekt negativ ist, verwendet man **any**-Wörter hinten im Satz:

No one ever said **anything.**	*Keiner hat jemals etwas gesagt.*
Few sloths went **anywhere.**	*Nur wenige Faultiere sind irgendwohin gegangen.*

2. Wenn man vor dem Verb ein negatives Adverb benutzt, braucht man nach dem Verb anstatt **some**-Wörter **any**-Wörter:

Kerry seldom talked to **anybody.**	*Kerry hat selten mit irgend jemand gesprochen.*
Duncan almost never does **anything.**	*Duncan tut fast nie etwas.*

3. Im Deutschen verwendet man gern negative Objekte, Zeitangaben, usw. Wenn diese im englischen Satz nach dem Verb stehen würden, ist es viel üblicher, **not** plus **any-**Wort zu verwenden:

There weren't any more.	*Es gab keine mehr.*
I couldn't find my gloves anywhere.	*Ich konnte meine Handschuhe nirgendwo finden.*

In Ja-Nein-Fragen sind any-Wörter auch sehr üblich

Has anybody seen my raincoat?	*Hat jemand meinen Regenmantel gesehen?*
Has Toby blabbed the secret to anyone yet?	*Hat Toby das Geheimnis schon irgend jemandem ausgeplaudert?*

15 Glossary | *Glossar*

Active

dt.: Aktiv. Eine Satzform, in der das vom Verb verlangte Subjekt auch tatsächlich als Subjekt dient. Vgl. Passive.

Adjective

dt.: Eigenschaftswort, Adjektiv. Ein Adjective beschreibt ein Noun oder eine Noun Phrase.

Adverb

dt.: Umstandswort, Adverb. Ein Adverb ist ein *Wort*, das ein Verb, ein Adjective, ein anderes Adverb oder einen Satz beschreibt.

Article

dt.: Artikel. Ein Article steht am Anfang einer Noun Phrase und zeigt an, ob diese bestimmt oder unbestimmt ist.

Auxiliary

▶ Hilfsverb.

Full verb

▶ Vollverb.

Hauptsatz

Ein Hauptsatz ist ein Satz, der das Hauptereignis bzw. der Hauptzustand eines Satzes ausdrückt. In **They said that the tree was old** ist **They said** der Hauptsatz, weil der Satz primär ausdrückt, dass jemand etwas gesagt hat.

Hilfsverb

Ein Hilfsverb ist eine Art Verb, welches das Vollverb unterstützt – in der Zeitbildung, der Vervollständigung der Bedeutung (bei manchen Modalverben), oder der Erfüllung grammatischer Bedingungen. Im Englischen stehen die Hilfsverben immer vor dem Vollverb.

Infinitive

dt.: Infinitiv, Grundform des Verbs. Der Infinitive ist die erste Form des Verbs und diejenige, die am wenigsten zeitliche Information enthält.

Modalverb
Die primären englischen Modalverben sind **can, could, will, would, shall, should, may, might** und **must**. **Need**, **dare** und **ought to** verhalten sich ähnlich wie Modalverben. Das englische Modalverb besitzt weder Infinitiv noch Partizipformen und ändert seine Form nicht, um mit dem Subjekt übereinzustimmen.

Nebensatz
Ein Nebensatz ist ein Teilsatz, der einem Hauptsatz beigefügt ist.

Noun
dt.: Hauptwort, Substantiv, Nomen. Ein Noun ist ein Wort, das in der Regel einen Gegenstand, ein Lebewesen oder einen abstrakten Begriff bezeichnet.

Noun Phrase
dt.: Nominalphrase. Eine Noun Phrase ist eine Phrase mit einem Noun als Kern, oder auch ein Pronoun. Sie kann z.B. als Subjekt oder Objekt im Satz fungieren. Vgl. Phrase

Objekt
Ein Objekt ist eine Noun Phrase, die nach dem Verb kommt. Manche Verben lassen zwei Objekte zu: Das erste heißt dann das indirekte Objekt und das zweite das direkte Objekt.

Participle
dt.: Partizip. Ein Participle ist eine Form des Verbs, die zum einen als Verb, zum anderen als Adjective auftreten kann. In ihrer Funktion als Verb können Partizipien im englischen Hauptsatz nur hinter einem Hilfsverb stehen; im Nebensatz können sie allein auftreten. Vgl. Past Participle

Passive
dt.: Passiv. Eine Satzform, bei der das normale Subjekt des Vollverbs seinen Status als Subjekt verliert und entweder nach einer Präposition erscheint (im Englischen **by**) oder sogar verschwindet. Im Deutschen bildet man den Passiv mit dem Hilfsverb *werden*, im Englischen mit **be** oder manchmal mit **get**.

Grammatik

Past Participle

dt.: Partizip Perfekt, dritte Form. Das Past Participle wird bei der Bildung der Perfect Tenses (Hilfsverb: **have**) und des Passivs (Hilfsverb: **be**) verwendet.

Perfect Tenses

dt.: Perfekttempora, „vollendete" Zeiten. Die Perfect Tenses werden mit **have** + Past Participle gebildet. Sie beschreiben, dass ein Ereignis oder Zustand vor einem gegebenen Zeitpunkt geschehen ist bzw. gegolten hat.

Phrase

dt.: Phrase. Eine Phrase ist eine Reihe von Wörtern, die eine bestimmte „Stelle" oder Funktion in der Wortfolge einnehmen können: z. B. die Subjektsfunktion. Eine Phrase kann aus einem Wort bestehen: insbesondere sind alle Fürwörter gleichzeitig auch Phrases. Vgl. Noun Phrase

Possessive

dt.: possessiv, besitzanzeigend. Possessive Formen erklären, wem etwas gehört, zuzuorden ist, usw.

Preposition

dt.: Präposition, Verhältniswort. Eine Preposition gibt in erster Linie an, wo jemand oder eine Sache sich befindet oder in welche Richtung sich etwas oder jemand bewegt bzw. bewegt wird.

Progressive Tenses

dt.: Verlaufsformen. Die Progressive Tenses sind Zeiten, die darauf hinweisen, dass ein Geschehen zu einem bestimmten Zeitpunkt im Gange ist.

Pronoun

dt.: Fürwort. Pronouns sind einzelne Wörter, deren Funktion es ist, ein Noun oder ganze Phrasen zu ersetzen. Vgl. Phrase

Reflexive Pronoun

dt.: Reflexivpronomen, rückbezügliches Fürwort. Ein Reflexive Pronoun ist ein Pronoun, das sich auf dieselbe Person oder dasselbe Ding wie das Subjekt bezieht.

Grammatik

Relative Pronoun

dt.: Relativpronomen. Ein Relative Pronoun steht am Anfang eines Relativsatzes, um diesen mit dem davorstehenden Noun bzw. der Noun Phrase zu verbinden.

Relative Clause

dt.: Relativsatz. Ein Relativsatz ist ein Nebensatz, der ein Noun oder eine Noun Phrase beschreibt. Vgl. Noun, Noun Phrase

Subject

dt.: Subjekt. Das Subjekt ist das Element, um das es im Satz oder Teilsatz geht. Im Deutschen steht das Subjekt fast immer im Nominativ (Werfall) und oft am Satzanfang. Im Englischen steht das Subjekt in der Regel vor dem ersten Verb im Satz, nicht unbedingt direkt am Anfang.

Tense

dt.: Tempus, Zeit. Eine Tense ist eine grammatische Zeit.

Verb

Im Deutschen auch „Tunwort" genannt. Das Verb beschreibt ein Ereignis bzw. einen Zustand oder hilft einem anderen Verb. Vgl. Vollverb, Hilfsverb

Vollverb

Das Vollverb ist das Verb, das die meiste Bedeutung in den Satz bringt. Im Englischen muss jeder vollständige Haupt- bzw. Nebensatz ein Vollverb enthalten, wobei es immer als letztes der Verben auftritt. Vgl. Verb, Hilfsverb

Stichwortregister

adjective 90–99
Adjektiv 90–99
adverb 101–106
Adverb 101–106
adverbiale Nebensätze 114, 118, 121
any 78
any-Wörter 138
article 79–84
Artikel 79–84
as ... as 98
Aussagesatz 110
auxiliary 24

be used to 41
be-Formen 35
bestimmter Artikel 81–83
both 74

conjunction 108
continuous tenses 19
coordinating conjunction 108

demonstrative pronoun 73–78, 83
Demonstrativpronomen 73–78, 83
do-Formen 39

each 75
either 76

Frageanhängsel 28
Fragewort-Fragen 128–130
Fragewörter 128
free relatives 136
freie Relativsätze 136
friendly 104
Futur 17, 22

future 17, 22
future continuous 23

Gerundium 16
get used to 41
get-Formen 40
good/well 96
Groß- und Kleinschreibung 55
have (veranlassen) 126
have-Formen 37
Hilfsverb 24–29
Höflichkeitsformen 35
home 104

if-Sätze 116–117
independent possessive forms 68–70
indirect speech 112
indirekte Rede 112
infinitive 119–120
Infinitivsätze 119–120
ing-Sätze 121–125
intransitive verb 11
intransitives Verb 11

komplexe Präpositionen 50
Konjunktion 108
Kurzantworten 27–28

lassen 125
let 126

make (veranlassen) 127
measurements 87–89
Mehrwortbildungen 109
Mengen- und Maßangaben 87–89
Modalverb 29–34

Nebensatzfragen 111
negation 26, 138
neither 76
nicht zählbare Nomen 60–61
Nomen 55–63
none 77
noun 55–63
noun phrase 51, 52, 53, 54, 94–95

object 11
object pronouns 66
Objekt 11
of-phrase 48
one 76
Ortsangaben 45–46
own 96
pair nouns 61
participle 11
Partikel 51, 52–54
Partizip 11
passive form 17
past continuous 21
past perfect 16–17
perfect tense 16–17
Perfekt 16–17
personal pronouns 64–66
Personalpronomen 64–66
phrasal verbs 51–54
phrase 110
plural 55–57
Plural 55–57
Plusquamperfekt 16–17
possessive 57–59
possessive forms 67–70
Possessivpronomen 67–70
Präposition 42–50
Präsens 12

preposition 42–50
present 12
present continuous 16, 19, 23
present perfect 16, 19
Pronomen 64–78, 113
pronouns 64–78, 113
proper names 62–63

quantities 87–89

reflexive pronouns 70–72
Reflexivpronomen 70–72
relative clause 131
relative pronouns 132–134
Relativpronomen 132–134
Relativsatz 131
Richtungsangabe 47–48

Satzbau 110–127
sentence construction 110–127
simple past 13–15, 20, 21
simple present 13–15, 20, 21
singular 55–57
Singular 55–57
some 77
Steigerungsformen 91, 105–106
subject 110
subject pronouns 64–65
Subjekt 110
Substantiv 55–57

tag questions 28
tenses 12–24
than 97
that 135
there is/there are 37
titles 62–63
transitive verb 11
transitives Verb 11

Grammatik

unbestimmter Artikel 79–81
used to 18

verbs 11–41
Verben 11–41
Vergleiche 97–100
Verneinung 26, 138
Vokal 10
Vollverb 11
vowel 10

well/good 96
Wenn-Sätze 115–116

zählbare Nomen 60–61
Zeitformen 12–24

2 | Verbtabellen

Grammatikbegriffe in der Übersicht

Englisch	Lateinischer Ursprung	Deutsch
active	Aktiv	Tätigkeitsform
auxiliary	Hilfsverb	Hilfszeitwort
conditional present	Konditional I	Bedingungsform I
conditional past	Konditional II	Bedingungsform II
conjugation	Konjugation	Beugung des Zeitworts
continuous form	progressive Form	Verlaufsform
consonant	Konsonant	Mitlaut
future	Futur I	unvollendete Zukunft
future 2 (future perfect)	Futur II	vollendete Zukunft
gerund	Gerundium	Gerundium
imperative	Imperativ	Befehlsform
infinitive	Infinitiv	Grundform des Zeitworts
irregular verb	unregelmäßiges Verb	unregelmäßiges Zeitwort
modal verb	Modalverb	Modalverb
participle	Partizip	Mittelwort
passive	Passiv	Leideform
past	Präteritum	Vergangenheit
past participle	Partizip Perfekt	Mittelwort der Vergangenheit
past perfect	Plusquamperfekt	Vorvergangenheit
plural	Plural	Mehrzahl
present	Präsens	Gegenwart
present perfect	Perfekt	vollendete Gegenwart
pronoun	Pronomen	Fürwort
reflexive verb	reflexives Verb	rückbezügliches Zeitwort
regular verb	regelmäßiges Verb	regelmäßiges Zeitwort
simple form	—	einfache Form
singular	Singular	Einzahl
subject	Subjekt	Satzgegenstand
verb	Verb	Zeitwort
vowel	Vokal	Selbstlaut

AE = amerikanisches Englisch
BE = britisches Englisch

Inhalt

Grammatikbegriffe in der Übersicht 148

Einleitung 150

Orthographische Besonderheiten 152

Aussprache 154

Kurzformen 155

Reflexivpronomen 155

Zeitformen 156

Passiv 161

Konjugationstabellen 162

Unregelmäßige englische Verben 246

Alphabetische Verbliste Deutsch–Englisch 251

Verbtabellen

Einleitung

Sie wollen sich die Formen eines bestimmten Verbs einprägen und dabei auf Besonderheiten und Unregelmäßigkeiten aufmerksam gemacht werden, Sie möchten aber auch eine seltene Verbform rasch und gezielt nachschlagen können.

Das Kapitel Verbtabellen bietet Ihnen übersichtliche Konjugationstabellen in alphabetischer Reihenfolge zu 84 regelmäßigen und unregelmäßigen Musterverben. Diese Konjugationsmuster zeigen Ihnen alle Formen auf einen Blick; auf Besonderheiten wird durch farbige Hervorhebung und praktische Faustregeln hingewiesen.

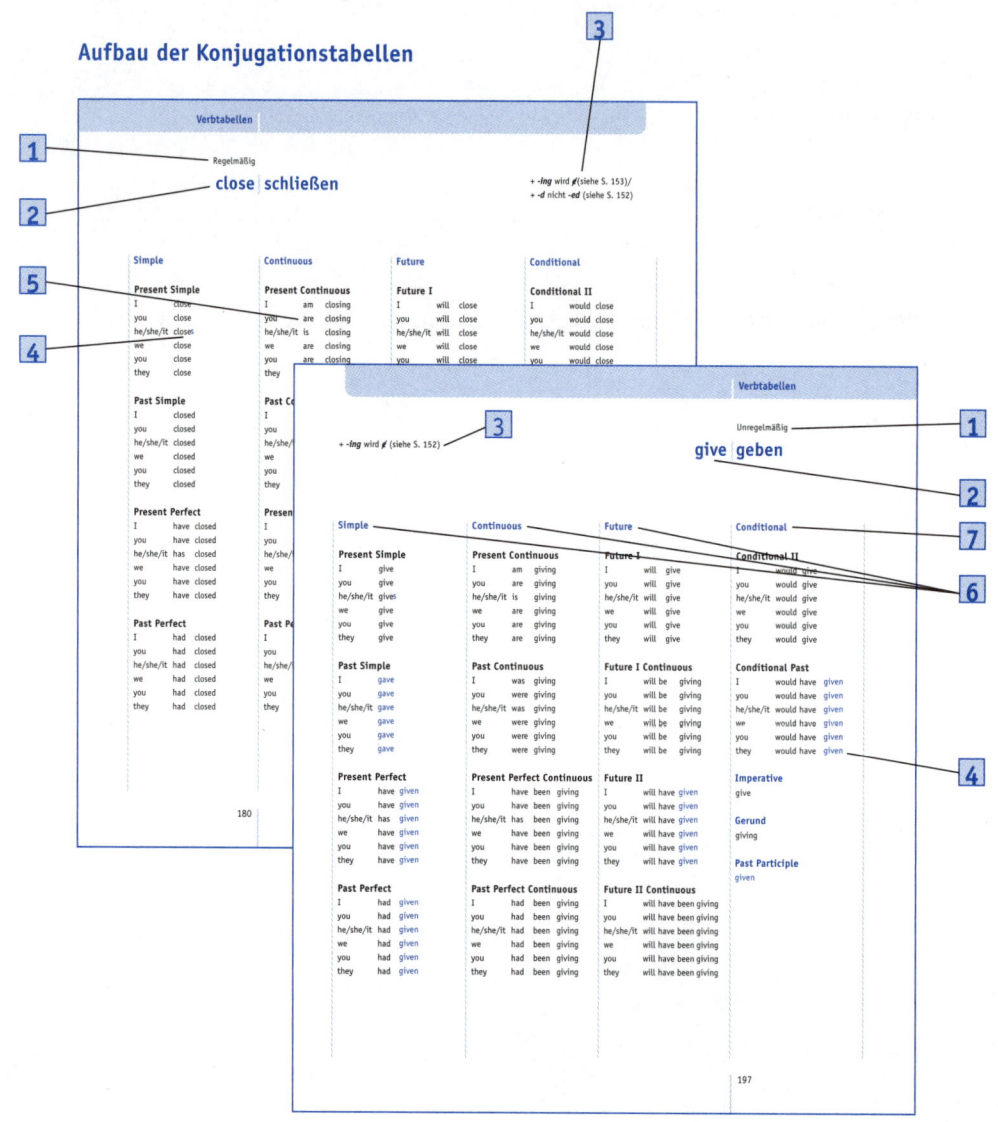

Aufbau der Konjugationstabellen

Verbtabellen

1 Konjugationstyp: Mit diesem Hinweis lassen sich die englischen Verben der regelmäßigen bzw. der unregelmäßigen Konjugation zuordnen.

2 Verb mit Übersetzung: Sie finden in den Konjugationstabellen eine Auswahl englischer Verben, die im täglichen Sprachgebrauch häufige Verwendung finden. Die gängigste deutsche Übersetzung für diese Verben wurde ausgewählt.

3 Kurzcharakteristik: Merksatz zu den Besonderheiten/Unregelmäßigkeiten des Konjugationsmusters.

4 Farbige Hervorhebung: Formen, die vom regelmäßigen Konjugationsschema abweichen bzw. Besonderheiten der englischen Sprache (z. B. 3. Person Singular -s), sind blau hervorgehoben.

5 Vollformen: In den Konjugationstabellen wurde grundsätzlich das Hilfsverb in der ausgeschriebenen Form angegeben. Die Verwendung der Kurzform können Sie auf Seite 155 ersehen.

6 Gliederung der Tabelle: In der ersten Spalte finden Sie die einfachen Formen des Verbs, in der zweiten Spalte die Verlaufsformen und in der dritten Spalte alle Zukunftsformen.

7 Conditional: Da Conditional I und Futur I gleich gebildet werden, wurde bewusst auf die Aufführung von Conditional I verzichtet.

In der Liste der unregelmäßigen Verben am Ende des Kapitels Verbtabellen finden Sie 100 der gebräuchlichsten unregelmäßigen Verben. Im Anschluss daran können Sie in einer alphabetischen deutsch-englischen Verbliste alle in diesem Band konjugierten Verben nachschlagen und erhalten zugleich einen entsprechenden Seitenverweis.

Übrigens: Im Vorspann zu den Konjugationstabellen erhalten Sie wertvolle Informationen. Sie finden auf Seite 152 und 153 einen systematischen Überblick über wichtige orthographische Besonderheiten sowie Angaben zur Aussprache. Auf Seite 155 können Sie die Reflexivpronomen nachschlagen. Kurze, präzise Angaben zum Gebrauch der Zeiten werden ab Seite 156 gemacht.

Viel Erfolg!

Orthographische Besonderheiten

Verben können die folgenden Endungen haben:
1. Verb + -s/-es
2. Verb + -ed/-d/-ied
3. Verb + -ing

Dabei erfahren manche Verben orthographische Änderungen.

1. Verb + -s/-es
für die 3. Person Singular im *Simple Present* – in der einfachen Gegenwart

Verben, die auf -ch, -sh, -ss, -o, -x enden	Anhängen von -es	watch push go	watch**es** push**es** go**es**
Verben, die auf einen Konsonanten + -y enden	Anhängen von -ies Wegfall von -y	study try carry	stud**ies** tr**ies** carr**ies**
Aber: Verben, die auf einen Vokal + -y enden	Anhängen von -s	play buy enjoy	play**s** buy**s** enjoy**s**

2. Verb + -ed/-d/-ied
Die Endung *-ed* wird für regelmäßige Verben im *Simple Past* – in der einfachen Vergangenheit und für das *Past Participle* von regelmäßigen Verben benutzt.

Verben, die auf -e enden	Anhängen von -d	arrive change	arrive**d** change**d**
Verben, die auf einen Konsonanten + -y enden	-y wird zu -ied	carry try study	carr**ied** tr**ied** stud**ied**
Verben, die auf einen Vokal + Konsonant enden	Konsonant wird verdoppelt	stop plan	stop**ped** plan**ned**
Verben mit zwei Silben, die auf einen Konsonant enden	Konsonant wird nur verdoppelt, wenn die letzte Silbe betont wird	prefer *aber* visit offer	prefer**red** visit**ed** offer**ed**
AUSNAHME – Im BE wird ein *-l* am Ende auch bei unbetonter Silbe verdoppelt. Im AE trifft dies nicht zu. Beispielsweise:		travel travel	travelled (BE) traveled (AE)

3. Verb + -ing

Die Endung -ing wird im Partizip Präsens und Gerundium benutzt.

Verben, die auf -e enden	Wegfall von -e Anhängen von -ing	have dance	hav**ing** danc**ing**
Verben, die auf -ee enden	Anhängen von -ing	see	see**ing**
Verben, deren Endkonsonant betont ist und einem Vokal folgt	Konsonant wird verdoppelt	stop plan get begin	stop**ping** plan**ning** get**ting** begin**ning**

AUSNAHME – Im BE wird ein -l am Ende, das einem Vokal folgt, auch bei unbetonter Silbe verdoppelt. Beispielsweise:
    cancel   cancelling (BE)
    cancel   canceling (AE)

Aussprache

Aussprache des -ed im Past Simple und Past Participle
Die Endung -ed wird gesprochen:

nach stimmlosen Konsonanten (nach -p, -f, -ss usw.)	stimmlos (-t)	asked looked stopped	wie t in „Takt" z. B. [ɑːskt]
nach stimmhaften Konsonanten und Vokalen (nach -b, -v, -g usw.)	stimmhaft (-d)	allowed listened opened	wie d in „Ende" z. B. [ˈəʊpənd]
nach -d und -t	silbisch (-id)	needed waited wanted	wie id in „Widder" z. B. [ˈniːdɪd]

Aussprache des -s, in der 3. Person Singular Present Simple
Die Endung -s wird gesprochen:

nach stimmlosen Konsonanten	stimmlos* (-s)	waits gets cuts	wie ss in „nass" z. B. [gets]
nach stimmhaften Konsonanten und Vokalen	stimmhaft* (-z)	runs opens allows	wie s in „Sahne" z. B. [rʌnz]
nach einem Zischlaut, bei Bildung der 3. Person Sing. Present Simple auf -es	silbisch (-iz)	changes watches washes	wie das erste -s in „business" z. B. [ˈwɒʃɪz]

* Es gibt zwei Arten von Konsonanten (Mitlauten) im Englischen:
stimmhafte Konsonanten – Sie fühlen eine Vibration am Kehlkopf.
stimmlose Konsonanten – Sie fühlen keine Vibration am Kehlkopf.

Kurzformen

Kurzformen werden im Allgemeinen in der gesprochenen Sprache benutzt. In der geschriebenen Sprache werden die Vollformen benutzt.

BE			HAVE		
I am	→	I'm	I have	→	I've
you are	→	you're	you have	→	you've
he/she/it is	→	he's/she's/it's	he/she/it has	→	he's/she's/it's
we are	→	we're	we have	→	we've
you are	→	you're	you have	→	you've
they are	→	they're	they have	→	they've

HAD			WILL		
I had	→	I'd	I will	→	I'll
you had	→	you'd	you will	→	you'll
he/she/it had	→	he'd/she'd/it'd	he/she/it will	→	he'll/she'll/it'll
we had	→	we'd	we will	→	we'll
you had	→	you'd	you will	→	you'll
they had	→	they'd	they will	→	they'll

WOULD		
I would	→	I'd
you would	→	you'd
he/she/it would	→	he'd/she'd/it'd
we would	→	we'd
you would	→	you'd
they would	→	they'd

Reflexivpronomen
Rückbezügliche Fürwörter

werden benutzt, wenn man die Handlung auf den Handelnden rückbeziehen kann. Die Reflexivpronomen *myself, yourself, himself* usw. entsprechen dem deutschen mich, dich, sich usw. Vorsicht! Es gibt nicht zu jedem deutschen Reflexivverb ein entsprechendes englisches und umgekehrt – z. B. sich erinnern – *remember*.

I	enjoy	**myself**	we	enjoy	**ourselves**
you	enjoy	**yourself**	you	enjoy	**yourselves**
he	enjoys	**himself**	they	enjoy	**themselves**
she	enjoys	**herself**			
it	enjoys	**itself**			

Zeitformen

Im Englischen gibt es 14 Zeiten. Man unterscheidet zwischen *Simple Form* (einfache Form) und *Continuous Form* (Verlaufsform).

Die **Simple Form** wird verwendet für
- regelmäßige, wiederkehrende Handlungen oder Zustände
- Tatsachen
- Zustände unbegrenzter Dauer.

Die **Continuous Form** wird verwendet für
- eine Handlung, die im Augenblick abläuft
- gerade verlaufende Handlungen, in die eine zweite Handlung eintritt
- zwei parallell verlaufende Handlungen.

Es gibt auch eine Reihe von Verben, die nicht in der Verlaufsform verwendet werden können. Beispielsweise: *like, hope, know, love*.

Present Simple

Das *Present Simple* wird mit der Grundform des Verbs gebildet.
Nur die 3. Person Singular (*he/she/it*) wird verändert, indem ein *-s* angehängt wird.

Aussage		Verneinung			Frage		
I/we/you/they	live.	I/we/you/they	do not (don't)	live.	Do	I/we/you/they	live?
he/she/it	lives.	he/she/it	does not (doesn't)	live.	Does	he/she/it	live?
		Verneinte Sätze werden durch Hinzufügen von don't/doesn't gebildet.			Fragen werden gebildet, indem do/does am Satzanfang hinzugefügt wird. Hier bleibt die Grundform des Verbs erhalten.		

Present Simple Continuous

Das *Present Simple Continuous* wird mit der passenden Form von to be (*is/am/are*) + Anhängen von *-ing* an die Grundform des Verbs gebildet.

Aussage			Verneinung			Frage		
I	am	living.	I	am not ('m not)	living.	Am	I	living?
he/she/it	is	living.	he/she/it	is not ('s not)	living.	Is	he/she/it	living?
we/you/they	are	living.	we/you/they	are not ('re not)	living.	Are	we/you/they	living?
			Verneinte Sätze werden durch Hinzufügen von *not* nach dem Pronomen gebildet.			Bei der Frageform steht *am/is/are* am Anfang des Satzes.		

Verbtabellen

Past Simple

Das *Past Simple* wird gebildet, indem man *-ed* an die Grundform des Verbs anhängt. Eine Liste mit unregelmäßigen Verben befindet sich auf den Seiten 246 bis 250.

Aussage		Verneinung			Frage		
I	lived.	I	did not (didn't)	live.	Did	I	live?
he/she/it		he/she/it				he/she/it	
we/you/they		we/you/they				we/you/they	
		Die Verneinung wird mit *did not* (*didn't*) und der Grundform gebildet.			Fragen werden mit dem Hilfsverb *do* gebildet. *Did* ist die Vergangenheitsform von *do/does* und steht am Anfang des Satzes. Das Verb steht in der Grundform.		

Achtung! Eine der gebräuchlichsten Vergangenheitsformen ist das *Past Simple*. Mit dem *Past Simple* berichtet man über Vorgänge in der Vergangenheit, die keinen direkten Bezug zur Gegenwart haben.

Past Continuous

Das *Past Continuous* wird mit *was/were* + *-ing* Form des Verbs gebildet.

Aussage			Verneinung			Frage		
I/he/she/it	was	living.	I/he/she/it	was not	living.	Was	I/he/she/it	living?
we/you/they	were	living.	we/you/they	were not	living.	Were	we/you/they	living?
			Verneinte Sätze werden durch Hinzufügen von *not* nach *was* bzw. *were* gebildet.			Bei der Frageform steht *was/were* am Anfang des Satzes.		

Present Perfect

Das *Present Perfect* wird mit *have/has* + Partizip Perfekt (dritte Form des Verbs) gebildet. Regelmäßige Formen werden durch Anhängen von *-ed* gebildet. Die unregelmäßigen Formen befinden sich auf den Seiten 246 bis 250.

Aussage			Verneinung			Frage		
I/we/you/they	have	lived.	I/we/you/they	have not (haven't)	lived.	Have	I/we/you/they	lived?
he/she/it	has	lived.	he/she/it	has not (hasn't)	lived.	Has	he/she/it	lived?
			Verneinte Sätze werden durch Hinzufügen von *not* vor dem Partizip Perfekt gebildet.			Bei der Frageform steht *have/has* am Anfang des Satzes.		

Achtung! Das *Present Perfect* ist streng von der *Past Simple* Form zu unterscheiden, da es entgegen der einfachen Vergangenheit einen Bezug zur Gegenwart hat. Das *Present Perfect* bildet eine Brücke zwischen Vergangenheit und Gegenwart.

Present Perfect Continuous

Das *Present Perfect Continuous* wird mit *have/has been* + *-ing* Form des Verbs gebildet.

Aussage			Verneinung			Frage		
I/we/you/they	have	been living.	I/we/you/they	have not (haven't)	been living.	Have	I/we/you/they	been living?
he/she/it	has	been living.	he/she/it	has not (hasn't)	been living.	Has	he/she/it	been living?
			Verneinte Sätze werden durch Hinzufügen von *not* vor dem Verb gebildet.			Bei der Frageform steht *have/has* am Anfang des Satzes.		

Past Perfect

Das *Past Perfect* wird mit *had* + Partizip Perfekt (dritte Form des Verbs) gebildet. Regelmäßige Formen werden durch Anhängen von -ed gebildet. Die unregelmäßigen Formen befinden sich auf den Seiten 246 bis 250.

Aussage			Verneinung			Frage		
I	had	lived.	I	had not (hadn't)	lived.	Had	I	lived?
he/she/it			he/she/it				he/she/it	
we/you/they			we/you/they				we/you/they	
			Verneinte Sätze werden durch Hinzufügen von *not* nach *had* gebildet.			Bei der Frageform steht *had* am Anfang des Satzes.		

Past Perfect Continuous

Das *Past Perfect Continuous* wird mit *had been* + *-ing* Form des Verbs gebildet.

Aussage			Verneinung			Frage		
I	had	been living.	I	had not (hadn't)	been living.	Had	I	been living?
he/she/it			he/she/it				he/she/it	
we/you/they			we/you/they				we/you/they	
			Verneinte Sätze werden durch Hinzufügen von *not* zwischen *had* und *been* gebildet.			Bei der Frageform steht *had* am Anfang des Satzes.		

Verbtabellen

Future I

Das *Future I* wird mit *will* und der Grundform des Verbs gebildet.

Aussage			Verneinung			Frage		
I	will	live.	I	will not (won't)	live.	Will	I	live?
he/she/it			he/she/it				he/she/it	
we/you/they			we/you/they				we/you/they	
			Verneinte Sätze werden durch Hinzufügen von *not* nach *will* gebildet. Achtung! Kurzform → *won't*			Bei der Frageform steht *will* am Anfang des Satzes.		

Future I Continuous

Das *Future I Continuous* wird mit *will be* + *-ing* Form des Verbs gebildet.

Aussage			Verneinung			Frage		
I	will be	living.	I	will not be	living.	Will	I	be living?
he/she/it			he/she/it	(won't)			he/she/it	
we/you/they			we/you/they				we/you/they	
			Verneinte Sätze werden durch Hinzufügen von *not* zwischen *will* und *be* gebildet.			Bei der Frageform steht *will* am Anfang des Satzes.		

Future II

Das *Future II* wird mit *will have* + Partizip Perfekt (dritte Form des Verbs) gebildet.

Aussage			Verneinung			Frage		
I	will	lived.	I	will not have	lived.	Will	I	have lived?
he/she/it	have		he/she/it	(won't)			he/she/it	
we/you/they			we/you/they				we/you/they	
			Verneinte Sätze werden durch Hinzufügen von *not* zwischen *will* und *have* gebildet.			Bei der Frageform steht *will* am Anfang des Satzes.		

Future II Continuous

Das *Future II Continuous* wird mit *will have been* + *-ing* Form des Verbs gebildet.

Aussage			Verneinung			Frage		
I	will	living.	I	will not have	living.	Will	I	have
he/she/it	have		he/she/it	been			he/she/it	been
we/you/they	been		we/you/they	(won't)			we/you/they	living?
			Verneinte Sätze werden durch Hinzufügen von *not* nach *will* gebildet.			Bei der Frageform steht *will* am Anfang des Satzes.		

Conditional II

Das *Conditional II* wird mit *would* + Grundform des Verbs gebildet.

Aussage			Verneinung			Frage		
I	would	live.	I	would not	live.	Would	I	live?
he/she/it			he/she/it	(wouldn't)			he/she/it	
we/you/they			we/you/they				we/you/they	
			Verneinte Sätze werden durch Hinzufügen von *not* nach *would* gebildet.			Bei der Frageform steht *would* am Anfang des Satzes.		

Conditional Past

Das *Conditional Past* wird mit *would have* + Partizip Perfekt gebildet.

Aussage			Verneinung			Frage		
I	would	lived.	I	would not have	lived.	Would	I	have
he/she/it	have		he/she/it	(wouldn't)			he/she/it	lived?
we/you/they			we/you/they				we/you/they	
			Verneinte Sätze werden durch Hinzufügen von *not* nach *would* gebildet.			Bei der Frageform steht *would* am Anfang des Satzes.		

Passiv | Leideform

Das Passiv wird mit dem Hilfsverb *to be* (*is/was/has been* usw.) und dem Partizip Perfekt (*cleaned/done/sold* usw.) gebildet.

Simple

Present Simple
I am taught
you are taught
he/she/it is taught
we are taught
you are taught
they are taught

Past Simple
I was taught
you were taught
he/she/it was taught
we were taught
you were taught
they were taught

Present Perfect
I have been taught
you have been taught
he/she/it has been taught
we have been taught
you have been taught
they have been taught

Past Perfect
I had been taught
you had been taught
he/she/it had been taught
we had been taught
you had been taught
they had been taught

Continuous

Present Continuous
I am being taught
you are being taught
he/she/it is being taught
we are being taught
you are being taught
they are being taught

Past Continuous
I was being taught
you were being taught
he/she/it was being taught
we were being taught
you were being taught
they were being taught

Present Perfect Continuous
I have been being taught
you have been being taught
he/she/it has been being taught
we have been being taught
you have been being taught
they have been being taught

Past Perfect Continuous
I had been being taught
you had been being taught
he/she/it had been being taught
we had been being taught
you had been being taught
they had been being taught

Future

Future I
I will be taught
you will be taught
he/she/it will be taught
we will be taught
you will be taught
they will be taught

Future I Continuous
I will be being taught
you will be being taught
he/she/it will be being taught
we will be being taught
you will be being taught
they will be being taught

Future II
I will have been taught
you will have been taught
he/she/it will have been taught
we will have been taught
you will have been taught
they will have been taught

Future II Continuous
I will have been being taught
you will have been being taught
he/she/it will have been being taught
we will have been being taught
you will have been being taught
they will have been being taught

Conditional

Conditional II
I would be taught
you would be taught
he/she/it would be taught
we would be taught
you would be taught
they would be taught

Conditional Past
I would have been taught
you would have been taught
he/she/it would have been taught
we would have been taught
you would have been taught
they would have been taught

Imperative
be + Past Participle*

Gerund
being taught

Regelmäßig

allow | erlauben

Simple

Present Simple
I	allow
you	allow
he/she/it	allows
we	allow
you	allow
they	allow

Past Simple
I	allowed
you	allowed
he/she/it	allowed
we	allowed
you	allowed
they	allowed

Present Perfect
I	have	allowed
you	have	allowed
he/she/it	has	allowed
we	have	allowed
you	have	allowed
they	have	allowed

Past Perfect
I	had	allowed
you	had	allowed
he/she/it	had	allowed
we	had	allowed
you	had	allowed
they	had	allowed

Continuous

Present Continuous
I	am	allowing
you	are	allowing
he/she/it	is	allowing
we	are	allowing
you	are	allowing
they	are	allowing

Past Continuous
I	was	allowing
you	were	allowing
he/she/it	was	allowing
we	were	allowing
you	were	allowing
they	were	allowing

Present Perfect Continuous
I	have	been	allowing
you	have	been	allowing
he/she/it	has	been	allowing
we	have	been	allowing
you	have	been	allowing
they	have	been	allowing

Past Perfect Continuous
I	had	been	allowing
you	had	been	allowing
he/she/it	had	been	allowing
we	had	been	allowing
you	had	been	allowing
they	had	been	allowing

Future

Future I
I	will	allow
you	will	allow
he/she/it	will	allow
we	will	allow
you	will	allow
they	will	allow

Future I Continuous
I	will be allowing
you	will be allowing
he/she/it	will be allowing
we	will be allowing
you	will be allowing
they	will be allowing

Future II
I	will have allowed
you	will have allowed
he/she/it	will have allowed
we	will have allowed
you	will have allowed
they	will have allowed

Future II Continuous
I	will have been allowing
you	will have been allowing
he/she/it	will have been allowing
we	will have been allowing
you	will have been allowing
they	will have been allowing

Conditional

Conditional II
I	would allow
you	would allow
he/she/it	would allow
we	would allow
you	would allow
they	would allow

Conditional Past
I	would have allowed
you	would have allowed
he/she/it	would have allowed
we	would have allowed
you	would have allowed
they	would have allowed

Imperative
allow

Gerund
allowing

Past Participle
allowed

Regelmäßig

answer | antworten

Simple

Present Simple
I	answer
you	answer
he/she/it	answers
we	answer
you	answer
they	answer

Past Simple
I	answered
you	answered
he/she/it	answered
we	answered
you	answered
they	answered

Present Perfect
I	have	answered
you	have	answered
he/she/it	has	answered
we	have	answered
you	have	answered
they	have	answered

Past Perfect
I	had	answered
you	had	answered
he/she/it	had	answered
we	had	answered
you	had	answered
they	had	answered

Continuous

Present Continuous
I	am	answering
you	are	answering
he/she/it	is	answering
we	are	answering
you	are	answering
they	are	answering

Past Continuous
I	was	answering
you	were	answering
he/she/it	was	answering
we	were	answering
you	were	answering
they	were	answering

Present Perfect Continuous
I	have	been	answering
you	have	been	answering
he/she/it	has	been	answering
we	have	been	answering
you	have	been	answering
they	have	been	answering

Past Perfect Continuous
I	had	been	answering
you	had	been	answering
he/she/it	had	been	answering
we	had	been	answering
you	had	been	answering
they	had	been	answering

Future

Future I
I	will	answer
you	will	answer
he/she/it	will	answer
we	will	answer
you	will	answer
they	will	answer

Future I Continuous
I	will	be	answering
you	will	be	answering
he/she/it	will	be	answering
we	will	be	answering
you	will	be	answering
they	will	be	answering

Future II
I	will	have	answered
you	will	have	answered
he/she/it	will	have	answered
we	will	have	answered
you	will	have	answered
they	will	have	answered

Future II Continuous
I	will have been answering
you	will have been answering
he/she/it	will have been answering
we	will have been answering
you	will have been answering
they	will have been answering

Conditional

Conditional II
I	would	answer
you	would	answer
he/she/it	would	answer
we	would	answer
you	would	answer
they	would	answer

Conditional Past
I	would	have	answered
you	would	have	answered
he/she/it	would	have	answered
we	would	have	answered
you	would	have	answered
they	would	have	answered

Imperative
answer

Gerund
answering

Past Participle
answered

Verbtabellen

Regelmäßig

arrive | ankommen

+ *-ing* wird ∅ (siehe S. 153)/
+ *-d* nicht *-ed* (siehe S. 152)

Simple

Present Simple
I arrive
you arrive
he/she/it arrives
we arrive
you arrive
they arrive

Past Simple
I arrived
you arrived
he/she/it arrived
we arrived
you arrived
they arrived

Present Perfect
I have arrived
you have arrived
he/she/it has arrived
we have arrived
you have arrived
they have arrived

Past Perfect
I had arrived
you had arrived
he/she/it had arrived
we had arrived
you had arrived
they had arrived

Continuous

Present Continuous
I am arriving
you are arriving
he/she/it is arriving
we are arriving
you are arriving
they are arriving

Past Continuous
I was arriving
you were arriving
he/she/it was arriving
we were arriving
you were arriving
they were arriving

Present Perfect Continuous
I have been arriving
you have been arriving
he/she/it has been arriving
we have been arriving
you have been arriving
they have been arriving

Past Perfect Continuous
I had been arriving
you had been arriving
he/she/it had been arriving
we had been arriving
you had been arriving
they had been arriving

Future

Future I
I will arrive
you will arrive
he/she/it will arrive
we will arrive
you will arrive
they will arrive

Future I Continuous
I will be arriving
you will be arriving
he/she/it will be arriving
we will be arriving
you will be arriving
they will be arriving

Future II
I will have arrived
you will have arrived
he/she/it will have arrived
we will have arrived
you will have arrived
they will have arrived

Future II Continuous
I will have been arriving
you will have been arriving
he/she/it will have been arriving
we will have been arriving
you will have been arriving
they will have been arriving

Conditional

Conditional II
I would arrive
you would arrive
he/she/it would arrive
we would arrive
you would arrive
they would arrive

Conditional Past
I would have arrived
you would have arrived
he/she/it would have arrived
we would have arrived
you would have arrived
they would have arrived

Imperative
arrive

Gerund
arriving

Past Participle
arrived

Regelmäßig

ask | fragen

Simple

Present Simple
I ask
you ask
he/she/it asks
we ask
you ask
they ask

Past Simple
I asked
you asked
he/she/it asked
we asked
you asked
they asked

Present Perfect
I have asked
you have asked
he/she/it has asked
we have asked
you have asked
they have asked

Past Perfect
I had asked
you had asked
he/she/it had asked
we had asked
you had asked
they had asked

Continuous

Present Continuous
I am asking
you are asking
he/she/it is asking
we are asking
you are asking
they are asking

Past Continuous
I was asking
you were asking
he/she/it was asking
we were asking
you were asking
they were asking

Present Perfect Continuous
I have been asking
you have been asking
he/she/it has been asking
we have been asking
you have been asking
they have been asking

Past Perfect Continuous
I had been asking
you had been asking
he/she/it had been asking
we had been asking
you had been asking
they had been asking

Future

Future I
I will ask
you will ask
he/she/it will ask
we will ask
you will ask
they will ask

Future I Continuous
I will be asking
you will be asking
he/she/it will be asking
we will be asking
you will be asking
they will be asking

Future II
I will have asked
you will have asked
he/she/it will have asked
we will have asked
you will have asked
they will have asked

Future II Continuous
I will have been asking
you will have been asking
he/she/it will have been asking
we will have been asking
you will have been asking
they will have been asking

Conditional

Conditional II
I would ask
you would ask
he/she/it would ask
we would ask
you would ask
they would ask

Conditional Past
I would have asked
you would have asked
he/she/it would have asked
we would have asked
you would have asked
they would have asked

Imperative
ask

Gerund
asking

Past Participle
asked

Verbtabellen

Unregelmäßig
Voll- und Hilfsverb

be | sein

Die Verlaufsformen von *be* werden für die Bildung des Passivs verwendet.

Simple

Present Simple
I am
you are
he/she/it is
we are
you are
they are

Past Simple
I was
you were
he/she/it was
we were
you were
they were

Present Perfect
I have been
you have been
he/she/it has been
we have been
you have been
they have been

Past Perfect
I had been
you had been
he/she/it had been
we had been
you had been
they had been

Continuous

Present Continuous
I am being
you are being
he/she/it is being
we are being
you are being
they are being

Past Continuous
I was being
you were being
he/she/it was being
we were being
you were being
they were being

Present Perfect Contlimous
I have been being
you have been being
he/she/it has been being
we have been being
you have been being
they have been being

Past Perfect Continuous
I had been being
you had been being
he/she/it had been being
we had been being
you had been being
they had been being

Future

Future I
I will be
you will be
he/she/it will be
we will be
you will be
they will be

Future I Continuous
I will be being
you will be being
he/she/it will be being
we will be being
you will be being
they will be being

Future II
I will have been
you will have been
he/she/it will have been
we will have been
you will have been
they will have been

Future II Continuous
I will have been being
you will have been being
he/she/it will have been being
we will have been being
you will have been being
they will have been being

Conditional

Conditional II
I would be
you would be
he/she/it would be
we would be
you would be
they would be

Conditional Past
I would have been
you would have been
he/she/it would have been
we would have been
you would have been
they would have been

Imperative
be

Gerund
being

Past Participle
been

Verbtabellen

+ *-ing* wird ∅ (siehe S. 153)

Unregelmäßig

become | werden

Simple

Present Simple

I	become
you	become
he/she/it	becomes
we	become
you	become
they	become

Past Simple

I	became
you	became
he/she/it	became
we	became
you	became
they	became

Present Perfect

I	have	become
you	have	become
he/she/it	has	become
we	have	become
you	have	become
they	have	become

Past Perfect

I	had	become
you	had	become
he/she/it	had	become
we	had	become
you	had	become
they	had	become

Continuous

Present Continuous

I	am	becoming
you	are	becoming
he/she/it	is	becoming
we	are	becoming
you	are	becoming
they	are	becoming

Past Continuous

I	was	becoming
you	were	becoming
he/she/it	was	becoming
we	were	becoming
you	were	becoming
they	were	becoming

Present Perfect Continuous

I	have	been	becoming
you	have	been	becoming
he/she/it	has	been	becoming
we	have	been	becoming
you	have	been	becoming
they	have	been	becoming

Past Perfect Continuous

I	had	been	becoming
you	had	been	becoming
he/she/it	had	been	becoming
we	had	been	becoming
you	had	been	becoming
they	had	been	becoming

Future

Future I

I	will	become
you	will	become
he/she/it	will	become
we	will	become
you	will	become
they	will	become

Future I Continuous

I	will be	becoming
you	will be	becoming
he/she/it	will be	becoming
we	will be	becoming
you	will be	becoming
they	will be	becoming

Future II

I	will have	become
you	will have	become
he/she/it	will have	become
we	will have	become
you	will have	become
they	will have	become

Future II Continuous

I	will have been becoming
you	will have been becoming
he/she/it	will have been becoming
we	will have been becoming
you	will have been becoming
they	will have been becoming

Conditional

Conditional II

I	would	become
you	would	become
he/she/it	would	become
we	would	become
you	would	become
they	would	become

Conditional Past

I	would have	become
you	would have	become
he/she/it	would have	become
we	would have	become
you	would have	become
they	would have	become

Imperative

become

Gerund

becoming

Past Participle

become

Verbtabellen

Unregelmäßig

begin | beginnen/anfangen

Konsonantenverdopplung
(siehe S. 152)

Simple

Present Simple
I begin
you begin
he/she/it begins
we begin
you begin
they begin

Past Simple
I began
you began
he/she/it began
we began
you began
they began

Present Perfect
I have begun
you have begun
he/she/it has begun
we have begun
you have begun
they have begun

Past Perfect
I had begun
you had begun
he/she/it had begun
we had begun
you had begun
they had begun

Continuous

Present Continuous
I am beginning
you are beginning
he/she/it is beginning
we are beginning
you are beginning
they are beginning

Past Continuous
I was beginning
you were beginning
he/she/it was beginning
we were beginning
you were beginning
they were beginning

Present Perfect Continuous
I have been beginning
you have been beginning
he/she/it has been beginning
we have been beginning
you have been beginning
they have been beginning

Past Perfect Continuous
I had been beginning
you had been beginning
he/she/it had been beginning
we had been beginning
you had been beginning
they had been beginning

Future

Future I
I will begin
you will begin
he/she/it will begin
we will begin
you will begin
they will begin

Future I Continuous
I will be beginning
you will be beginning
he/she/it will be beginning
we will be beginning
you will be beginning
they will be beginning

Future II
I will have begun
you will have begun
he/she/it will have begun
we will have begun
you will have begun
they will have begun

Future II Continuous
I will have been beginning
you will have been beginning
he/she/it will have been beginning
we will have been beginning
you will have been beginning
they will have been beginning

Conditional

Conditional II
I would begin
you would begin
he/she/it would begin
we would begin
you would begin
they would begin

Conditional Past
I would have begun
you would have begun
he/she/it would have begun
we would have begun
you would have begun
they would have begun

Imperative
begin

Gerund
beginning

Past Participle
begun

Verbtabellen

Regelmäßig

book | buchen

Simple

Present Simple
I book
you book
he/she/it books
we book
you book
they book

Past Simple
I booked
you booked
he/she/it booked
we booked
you booked
they booked

Present Perfect
I have booked
you have booked
he/she/it has booked
we have booked
you have booked
they have booked

Past Perfect
I had booked
you had booked
he/she/it had booked
we had booked
you had booked
they had booked

Continuous

Present Continuous
I am booking
you are booking
he/she/it is booking
we are booking
you are booking
they are booking

Past Continuous
I was booking
you were booking
he/she/it was booking
we were booking
you were booking
they were booking

Present Perfect Continuous
I have been booking
you have been booking
he/she/it has been booking
we have been booking
you have been booking
they have been booking

Past Perfect Continuous
I had been booking
you had been booking
he/she/it had been booking
we had been booking
you had been booking
they had been booking

Future

Future I
I will book
you will book
he/she/it will book
we will book
you will book
they will book

Future I Continuous
I will be booking
you will be booking
he/she/it will be booking
we will be booking
you will be booking
they will be booking

Future II
I will have booked
you will have booked
he/she/it will have booked
we will have booked
you will have booked
they will have booked

Future II Contlimous
I will have been booking
you will have been booking
he/she/it will have been booking
we will have been booking
you will have been booking
they will have been booking

Conditional

Conditional II
I would book
you would book
he/she/it would book
we would book
you would book
they would book

Conditional Past
I would have booked
you would have booked
he/she/it would have booked
we would have booked
you would have booked
they would have booked

Imperative
book

Gerund
booking

Past Participle
booked

Verbtabellen

Unregelmäßig

break | (zer)brechen

Simple

Present Simple
I break
you break
he/she/it breaks
we break
you break
they break

Past Simple
I broke
you broke
he/she/it broke
we broke
you broke
they broke

Present Perfect
I have broken
you have broken
he/she/it has broken
we have broken
you have broken
they have broken

Past Perfect
I had broken
you had broken
he/she/it had broken
we had broken
you had broken
they had broken

Continuous

Present Continuous
I am breaking
you are breaking
he/she/it is breaking
we are breaking
you are breaking
they are breaking

Past Continuous
I was breaking
you were breaking
he/she/it was breaking
we were breaking
you were breaking
they were breaking

Present Perfect Continuous
I have been breaking
you have been breaking
he/she/it has been breaking
we have been breaking
you have been breaking
they have been breaking

Past Perfect Continuous
I had been breaking
you had been breaking
he/she/it had been breaking
we had been breaking
you had been breaking
they had been breaking

Future

Future I
I will break
you will break
he/she/it will break
we will break
you will break
they will break

Future I Continuous
I will be breaking
you will be breaking
he/she/it will be breaking
we will be breaking
you will be breaking
they will be breaking

Future II
I will have broken
you will have broken
he/she/it will have broken
we will have broken
you will have broken
they will have broken

Future II Continuous
I will have been breaking
you will have been breaking
he/she/it will have been breaking
we will have been breaking
you will have been breaking
they will have been breaking

Conditional

Conditional II
I would break
you would break
he/she/it would break
we would break
you would break
they would break

Conditional Past
I would have broken
you would have broken
he/she/it would have broken
we would have broken
you would have broken
they would have broken

Imperative
break

Gerund
breaking

Past Participle
broken

Verbtabellen

Unregelmäßig

bring | (mit)bringen

Simple

Present Simple
I bring
you bring
he/she/it brings
we bring
you bring
they bring

Past Simple
I brought
you brought
he/she/it brought
we brought
you brought
they brought

Present Perfect
I have brought
you have brought
he/she/it has brought
we have brought
you have brought
they have brought

Past Perfect
I had brought
you had brought
he/she/it had brought
we had brought
you had brought
they had brought

Continuous

Present Continuous
I am bringing
you are bringing
he/she/it is bringing
we are bringing
you are bringing
they are bringing

Past Continuous
I was bringing
you were bringing
he/she/it was bringing
we were bringing
you were bringing
they were bringing

Present Perfect Continuous
I have been bringing
you have been bringing
he/she/it has been bringing
we have been bringing
you have been bringing
they have been bringing

Past Perfect Continuous
I had been bringing
you had been bringing
he/she/it had been bringing
we had been bringing
you had been bringing
they had been bringing

Future

Future I
I will bring
you will bring
he/she/it will bring
we will bring
you will bring
they will bring

Future I Continuous
I will be bringing
you will be bringing
he/she/it will be bringing
we will be bringing
you will be bringing
they will be bringing

Future II
I will have brought
you will have brought
he/she/it will have brought
we will have brought
you will have brought
they will have brought

Future II Continuous
I will have been bringing
you will have been bringing
he/she/it will have been bringing
we will have been bringing
you will have been bringing
they will have been bringing

Conditional

Conditional II
I would bring
you would bring
he/she/it would bring
we would bring
you would bring
they would bring

Conditional Past
I would have brought
you would have brought
he/she/it would have brought
we would have brought
you would have brought
they would have brought

Imperative
bring

Gerund
bringing

Past Participle
brought

Verbtabellen

Unregelmäßig

buy | kaufen

Simple

Present Simple
I buy
you buy
he/she/it buys
we buy
you buy
they buy

Past Simple
I bought
you bought
he/she/it bought
we bought
you bought
they bought

Present Perfect
I have bought
you have bought
he/she/it has bought
we have bought
you have bought
they have bought

Past Perfect
I had bought
you had bought
he/she/it had bought
we had bought
you had bought
they had bought

Continuous

Present Continuous
I am buying
you are buying
he/she/it is buying
we are buying
you are buying
they are buying

Past Continuous
I was buying
you were buying
he/she/it was buying
we were buying
you were buying
they were buying

Present Perfect Continuous
I have been buying
you have been buying
he/she/it has been buying
we have been buying
you have been buying
they have been buying

Past Perfect Continuous
I had been buying
you had been buying
he/she/it had been buying
we had been buying
you had been buying
they had been buying

Future

Future I
I will buy
you will buy
he/she/it will buy
we will buy
you will buy
they will buy

Future I Continuous
I will be buying
you will be buying
he/she/it will be buying
we will be buying
you will be buying
they will be buying

Future II
I will have bought
you will have bought
he/she/it will have bought
we will have bought
you will have bought
they will have bought

Future II Continuous
I will have been buying
you will have been buying
he/she/it will have been buying
we will have been buying
you will have been buying
they will have been buying

Conditional

Conditional II
I would buy
you would buy
he/she/it would buy
we would buy
you would buy
they would buy

Conditional Past
I would have bought
you would have bought
he/she/it would have bought
we would have bought
you would have bought
they would have bought

Imperative
buy

Gerund
buying

Past Participle
bought

Verbtabellen

Regelmäßig

call | (an)rufen

Simple

Present Simple
I call
you call
he/she/it calls
we call
you call
they call

Past Simple
I called
you called
he/she/it called
we called
you called
they called

Present Perfect
I have called
you have called
he/she/it has called
we have called
you have called
they have called

Past Perfect
I had called
you had called
he/she/it had called
we had called
you had called
they had called

Continuous

Present Continuous
I am calling
you are calling
he/she/it is calling
we are calling
you are calling
they are calling

Past Continuous
I was calling
you were calling
he/she/it was calling
we were calling
you were calling
they were calling

Present Perfect Continuous
I have been calling
you have been calling
he/she/it has been calling
we have been calling
you have been calling
they have been calling

Past Perfect Continuous
I had been calling
you had been calling
he/she/it had been calling
we had been calling
you had been calling
they had been calling

Future

Future I
I will call
you will call
he/she/it will call
we will call
you will call
they will call

Future I Continuous
I will be calling
you will be calling
he/she/it will be calling
we will be calling
you will be calling
they will be calling

Future II
I will have called
you will have called
he/she/it will have called
we will have called
you will have called
they will have called

Future II Continuous
I will have been calling
you will have been calling
he/she/it will have been calling
we will have been calling
you will have been calling
they will have been calling

Conditional

Conditional II
I would call
you would call
he/she/it would call
we would call
you would call
they would call

Conditional Past
I would have called
you would have called
he/she/it would have called
we would have called
you would have called
they would have called

Imperative
call

Gerund
calling

Past Participle
called

173

Verbtabellen

Unregelmäßig
Modalverb

can/be able to | können

Unvollständiges Modalverb – *Can* bzw. *could* werden nur im *Present Simple* und *Past Simple* verwendet.
Can/could/be able to haben keine Verlaufsform.

Simple

Present Simple
I	can/am	able to
you	can/are	able to
he/she/it	can/is	able to
we	can/are	able to
you	can/are	able to
they	can/are	able to

Past Simple
I	could/was	able to
you	could/were	able to
he/she/it	could/was	able to
we	could/were	able to
you	could/were	able to
they	could/were	able to

Present Perfect
I	have	been	able to
you	have	been	able to
he/she/it	has	been	able to
we	have	been	able to
you	have	been	able to
they	have	been	able to

Past Perfect
I	had	been	able to
you	had	been	able to
he/she/it	had	been	able to
we	had	been	able to
you	had	been	able to
they	had	been	able to

Continuous

Present Continuous

—

Past Continuous

—

Present Perfect Continuous

—

Past Perfect Continuous

—

Future

Future I
I	will	be	able to
you	will	be	able to
he/she/it	will	be	able to
we	will	be	able to
you	will	be	able to
they	will	be	able to

Future I Continuous

—

Future II
I	will have	been	able to
you	will have	been	able to
he/she/it	will have	been	able to
we	will have	been	able to
you	will have	been	able to
they	will have	been	able to

Future II Continuous

—

Conditional

Conditional II
I	would	be	able to
you	would	be	able to
he/she/it	would	be	able to
we	would	be	able to
you	would	be	able to
they	would	be	able to

Conditional Past
I	would have	been	able to
you	would have	been	able to
he/she/it	would have	been	able to
we	would have	been	able to
you	would have	been	able to
they	would have	been	able to

Imperative
be able to

Gerund
being able to

Past Participle
been able to

Verbtabellen

Im AE wird das **-l** nicht verdoppelt.

Regelmäßig

cancel | absagen/stornieren

Simple

Present Simple
I cancel
you cancel
he/she/it cancels
we cancel
you cancel
they cancel

Past Simple
I cancelled
you cancelled
he/she/it cancelled
we cancelled
you cancelled
they cancelled

Present Perfect
I have cancelled
you have cancelled
he/she/it has cancelled
we have cancelled
you have cancelled
they have cancelled

Past Perfect
I had cancelled
you had cancelled
he/she/it had cancelled
we had cancelled
you had cancelled
they had cancelled

Continuous

Present Continuous
I am cancelling
you are cancelling
he/she/it is cancelling
we are cancelling
you are cancelling
they are cancelling

Past Continuous
I was cancelling
you were cancelling
he/she/it was cancelling
we were cancelling
you were cancelling
they were cancelling

Present Perfect Continuous
I have been cancelling
you have been cancelling
he/she/it has been cancelling
we have been cancelling
you have been cancelling
they have been cancelling

Past Perfect Continuous
I had been cancelling
you had been cancelling
he/she/it had been cancelling
we had been cancelling
you had been cancelling
they had been cancelling

Future

Future I
I will cancel
you will cancel
he/she/it will cancel
we will cancel
you will cancel
they will cancel

Future I Continuous
I will be cancelling
you will be cancelling
he/she/it will be cancelling
we will be cancelling
you will be cancelling
they will be cancelling

Future II
I will have cancelled
you will have cancelled
he/she/it will have cancelled
we will have cancelled
you will have cancelled
they will have cancelled

Future II Continuous
I will have been cancelling
you will have been cancelling
he/she/it will have been cancelling
we will have been cancelling
you will have been cancelling
they will have been cancelling

Conditional

Conditional II
I would cancel
you would cancel
he/she/it would cancel
we would cancel
you would cancel
they would cancel

Conditional Past
I would have cancelled
you would have cancelled
he/she/it would have cancelled
we would have cancelled
you would have cancelled
they would have cancelled

Imperative
cancel

Gerund
cancelling

Past Participle
cancelled

Verbtabellen

Regelmäßig

carry | tragen

-y wird *-ie* vor *-s/-y* wird *-i* vor *-ed* (siehe S. 152)

Simple

Present Simple
I carry
you carry
he/she/it carries
we carry
you carry
they carry

Past Simple
I carried
you carried
he/she/it carried
we carried
you carried
they carried

Present Perfect
I have carried
you have carried
he/she/it has carried
we have carried
you have carried
they have carried

Past Perfect
I had carried
you had carried
he/she/it had carried
we had carried
you had carried
they had carried

Continuous

Present Continuous
I am carrying
you are carrying
he/she/it is carrying
we are carrying
you are carrying
they are carrying

Past Continuous
I was carrying
you were carrying
he/she/it was carrying
we were carrying
you were carrying
they were carrying

Present Perfect Continuous
I have been carrying
you have been carrying
he/she/it has been carrying
we have been carrying
you have been carrying
they have been carrying

Past Perfect Continuous
I had been carrying
you had been carrying
he/she/it had been carrying
we had been carrying
you had been carrying
they had been carrying

Future

Future I
I will carry
you will carry
he/she/it will carry
we will carry
you will carry
they will carry

Future I Continuous
I will be carrying
you will be carrying
he/she/it will be carrying
we will be carrying
you will be carrying
they will be carrying

Future II
I will have carried
you will have carried
he/she/it will have carried
we will have carried
you will have carried
they will have carried

Future II Continuous
I will have been carrying
you will have been carrying
he/she/it will have been carrying
we will have been carrying
you will have been carrying
they will have been carrying

Conditional

Conditional II
I would carry
you would carry
he/she/it would carry
we would carry
you would carry
they would carry

Conditional Past
I would have carried
you would have carried
he/she/it would have carried
we would have carried
you would have carried
they would have carried

Imperative
carry

Gerund
carrying

Past Participle
carried

Verbtabellen

+ *-es* in 3. Person Singular
(siehe S. 152)

Unregelmäßig

catch | fangen

Simple

Present Simple
I catch
you catch
he/she/it catches
we catch
you catch
they catch

Past Simple
I caught
you caught
he/she/it caught
we caught
you caught
they caught

Present Perfect
I have caught
you have caught
he/she/it has caught
we have caught
you have caught
they have caught

Past Perfect
I had caught
you had caught
he/she/it had caught
we had caught
you had caught
they had caught

Continuous

Present Continuous
I am catching
you are catching
he/she/it is catching
we are catching
you are catching
they are catching

Past Continuous
I was catching
you were catching
he/she/it was catching
we were catching
you were catching
they were catching

Present Perfect Continuous
I have been catching
you have been catching
he/she/it has been catching
we have been catching
you have been catching
they have been catching

Past Perfect Continuous
I had been catching
you had been catching
he/she/it had been catching
we had been catching
you had been catching
they had been catching

Future

Future I
I will catch
you will catch
he/she/it will catch
we will catch
you will catch
they will catch

Future I Continuous
I will be catching
you will be catching
he/she/it will be catching
we will be catching
you will be catching
they will be catching

Future II
I will have caught
you will have caught
he/she/it will have caught
we will have caught
you will have caught
they will have caught

Future II Continuous
I will have been catching
you will have been catching
he/she/it will have been catching
we will have been catching
you will have been catching
they will have been catching

Conditional

Conditional II
I would catch
you would catch
he/she/it would catch
we would catch
you would catch
they would catch

Conditional Past
I would have caught
you would have caught
he/she/it would have caught
we would have caught
you would have caught
they would have caught

Imperative
catch

Gerund
catching

Past Participle
caught

Verbtabellen

Regelmäßig

change | ändern/wechseln

+ **-ing** wird ø (siehe S. 153)/
+ **-d** nicht **-ed** (siehe S. 152)

Simple

Present Simple
I change
you change
he/she/it changes
we change
you change
they change

Past Simple
I changed
you changed
he/she/it changed
we changed
you changed
they changed

Present Perfect
I have changed
you have changed
he/she/it has changed
we have changed
you have changed
they have changed

Past Perfect
I had changed
you had changed
he/she/it had changed
we had changed
you had changed
they had changed

Continuous

Present Continuous
I am changing
you are changing
he/she/it is changing
we are changing
you are changing
they are changing

Past Continuous
I was changing
you were changing
he/she/it was changing
we were changing
you were changing
they were changing

Present Perfect Continuous
I have been changing
you have been changing
he/she/it has been changing
we have been changing
you have been changing
they have been changing

Past Perfect Continuous
I had been changing
you had been changing
he/she/it had been changing
we had been changing
you had been changing
they had been changing

Future

Future I
I will change
you will change
he/she/it will change
we will change
you will change
they will change

Future I Continuous
I will be changing
you will be changing
he/she/it will be changing
we will be changing
you will be changing
they will be changing

Future II
I will have changed
you will have changed
he/she/it will have changed
we will have changed
you will have changed
they will have changed

Future II Continuous
I will have been changing
you will have been changing
he/she/it will have been changing
we will have been changing
you will have been changing
they will have been changing

Conditional

Conditional II
I would change
you would change
he/she/it would change
we would change
you would change
they would change

Conditional Past
I would have changed
you would have changed
he/she/it would have changed
we would have changed
you would have changed
they would have changed

Imperative
change

Gerund
changing

Past Participle
changed

Verbtabellen

Unregelmäßig

choose | (aus)wählen

+ *-ing* wird ∉ (siehe S. 153)

Simple

Present Simple
I choose
you choose
he/she/it chooses
we choose
you choose
they choose

Past Simple
I chose
you chose
he/she/it chose
we chose
you chose
they chose

Present Perfect
I have chosen
you have chosen
he/she/it has chosen
we have chosen
you have chosen
they have chosen

Past Perfect
I had chosen
you had chosen
he/she/it had chosen
we had chosen
you had chosen
they had chosen

Continuous

Present Continuous
I am choosing
you are choosing
he/she/it is choosing
we are choosing
you are choosing
they are choosing

Past Continuous
I was choosing
you were choosing
he/she/it was choosing
we were choosing
you were choosing
they were choosing

Present Perfect Continuous
I have been choosing
you have been choosing
he/she/it has been choosing
we have been choosing
you have been choosing
they have been choosing

Past Perfect Continuous
I had been choosing
you had been choosing
he/she/it had been choosing
we had been choosing
you had been choosing
they had been choosing

Future

Future I
I will choose
you will choose
he/she/it will choose
we will choose
you will choose
they will choose

Future I Continuous
I will be choosing
you will be choosing
he/she/it will be choosing
we will be choosing
you will be choosing
they will be choosing

Future II
I will have chosen
you will have chosen
he/she/it will have chosen
we will have chosen
you will have chosen
they will have chosen

Future II Continuous
I will have been choosing
you will have been choosing
he/she/it will have been choosing
we will have been choosing
you will have been choosing
they will have been choosing

Conditional

Conditional II
I would choose
you would choose
he/she/it would choose
we would choose
you would choose
they would choose

Conditional Past
I would have chosen
you would have chosen
he/she/it would have chosen
we would have chosen
you would have chosen
they would have chosen

Imperative
choose

Gerund
choosing

Past Participle
chosen

Verbtabellen

Regelmäßig

close | schließen

+ **-ing** wird ∉ (siehe S. 153)/
+ **-d** nicht **-ed** (siehe S. 152)

Simple	**Continuous**	**Future**	**Conditional**
Present Simple	**Present Continuous**	**Future I**	**Conditional II**
I close	I am closing	I will close	I would close
you close	you are closing	you will close	you would close
he/she/it closes	he/she/it is closing	he/she/it will close	he/she/it would close
we close	we are closing	we will close	we would close
you close	you are closing	you will close	you would close
they close	they are closing	they will close	they would close
Past Simple	**Past Continuous**	**Future I Continuous**	**Conditional Past**
I closed	I was closing	I will be closing	I would have closed
you closed	you were closing	you will be closing	you would have closed
he/she/it closed	he/she/it was closing	he/she/it will be closing	he/she/it would have closed
we closed	we were closing	we will be closing	we would have closed
you closed	you were closing	you will be closing	you would have closed
they closed	they were closing	they will be closing	they would have closed
Present Perfect	**Present Perfect Continuous**	**Future II**	**Imperative**
I have closed	I have been closing	I will have closed	close
you have closed	you have been closing	you will have closed	
he/she/it has closed	he/she/it has been closing	he/she/it will have closed	**Gerund**
we have closed	we have been closing	we will have closed	closing
you have closed	you have been closing	you will have closed	
they have closed	they have been closing	they will have closed	**Past Participle**
Past Perfect	**Past Perfect Continuous**	**Future II Continuous**	closed
I had closed	I had been closing	I will have been closing	
you had closed	you had been closing	you will have been closing	
he/she/it had closed	he/she/it had been closing	he/she/it will have been closing	
we had closed	we had been closing	we will have been closing	
you had closed	you had been closing	you will have been closing	
they had closed	they had been closing	they will have been closing	

Verbtabellen

+ *-ing* wird ∅ (siehe S. 153)

Unregelmäßig

come | kommen

Simple

Present Simple
- I come
- you come
- he/she/it comes
- we come
- you come
- they come

Past Simple
- I came
- you came
- he/she/it came
- we came
- you came
- they came

Present Perfect
- I have come
- you have come
- he/she/it has come
- we have come
- you have come
- they have come

Past Perfect
- I had come
- you had come
- he/she/it had come
- we had come
- you had come
- they had come

Continuous

Present Continuous
- I am coming
- you are coming
- he/she/it is coming
- we are coming
- you are coming
- they are coming

Past Continuous
- I was coming
- you were coming
- he/she/it was coming
- we were coming
- you were coming
- they were coming

Present Perfect Continuous
- I have been coming
- you have been coming
- he/she/it has been coming
- we have been coming
- you have been coming
- they have been coming

Past Perfect Continuous
- I had been coming
- you had been coming
- he/she/it had been coming
- we had been coming
- you had been coming
- they had been coming

Future

Future I
- I will come
- you will come
- he/she/it will come
- we will come
- you will come
- they will come

Future I Continuous
- I will be coming
- you will be coming
- he/she/it will be coming
- we will be coming
- you will be coming
- they will be coming

Future II
- I will have come
- you will have come
- he/she/it will have come
- we will have come
- you will have come
- they will have come

Future II Continuous
- I will have been coming
- you will have been coming
- he/she/it will have been coming
- we will have been coming
- you will have been coming
- they will have been coming

Conditional

Conditional II
- I would come
- you would come
- he/she/it would come
- we would come
- you would come
- they would come

Conditional Past
- I would have come
- you would have come
- he/she/it would have come
- we would have come
- you would have come
- they would have come

Imperative
come

Gerund
coming

Past Participle
come

Verbtabellen

Regelmäßig

cook | kochen

Simple

Present Simple
I	cook
you	cook
he/she/it	cooks
we	cook
you	cook
they	cook

Past Simple
I	cooked
you	cooked
he/she/it	cooked
we	cooked
you	cooked
they	cooked

Present Perfect
I	have	cooked
you	have	cooked
he/she/it	has	cooked
we	have	cooked
you	have	cooked
they	have	cooked

Past Perfect
I	had	cooked
you	had	cooked
he/she/it	had	cooked
we	had	cooked
you	had	cooked
they	had	cooked

Continuous

Present Continuous
I	am	cooking
you	are	cooking
he/she/it	is	cooking
we	are	cooking
you	are	cooking
they	are	cooking

Past Continuous
I	was	cooking
you	were	cooking
he/she/it	was	cooking
we	were	cooking
you	were	cooking
they	were	cooking

Present Perfect Continuous
I	have	been	cooking
you	have	been	cooking
he/she/it	has	been	cooking
we	have	been	cooking
you	have	been	cooking
they	have	been	cooking

Past Perfect Continuous
I	had	been	cooking
you	had	been	cooking
he/she/it	had	been	cooking
we	had	been	cooking
you	had	been	cooking
they	had	been	cooking

Future

Future I
I	will	cook
you	will	cook
he/she/it	will	cook
we	will	cook
you	will	cook
they	will	cook

Future I Continuous
I	will be	cooking
you	will be	cooking
he/she/it	will be	cooking
we	will be	cooking
you	will be	cooking
they	will be	cooking

Future II
I	will have	cooked
you	will have	cooked
he/she/it	will have	cooked
we	will have	cooked
you	will have	cooked
they	will have	cooked

Future II Continuous
I	will have been	cooking
you	will have been	cooking
he/she/it	will have been	cooking
we	will have been	cooking
you	will have been	cooking
they	will have been	cooking

Conditional

Conditional II
I	would	cook
you	would	cook
he/she/it	would	cook
we	would	cook
you	would	cook
they	would	cook

Conditional Past
I	would have	cooked
you	would have	cooked
he/she/it	would have	cooked
we	would have	cooked
you	would have	cooked
they	would have	cooked

Imperative
cook

Gerund
cooking

Past Participle
cooked

Verbtabellen

Unregelmäßig

cost | kosten

Simple

Present Simple
I cost
you cost
he/she/it costs
we cost
you cost
they cost

Past Simple
I cost
you cost
he/she/it cost
we cost
you cost
they cost

Present Perfect
I have cost
you have cost
he/she/it has cost
we have cost
you have cost
they have cost

Past Perfect
I had cost
you had cost
he/she/it had cost
we had cost
you had cost
they had cost

Continuous

Present Continuous
I am costing
you are costing
he/she/it is costing
we are costing
you are costing
they are costing

Past Continuous
I was costing
you were costing
he/she/it was costing
we were costing
you were costing
they were costing

Present Perfect Continuous
I have been costing
you have been costing
he/she/it has been costing
we have been costing
you have been costing
they have been costing

Past Perfect Continuous
I had been costing
you had been costing
he/she/it had been costing
we had been costing
you had been costing
they had been costing

Future

Future I
I will cost
you will cost
he/she/it will cost
we will cost
you will cost
they will cost

Future I Continuous
I will be costing
you will be costing
he/she/it will be costing
we will be costing
you will be costing
they will be costing

Future II
I will have cost
you will have cost
he/she/it will have cost
we will have cost
you will have cost
they will have cost

Future II Continuous
I will have been costing
you will have been costing
he/she/it will have been costing
we will have been costing
you will have been costing
they will have been costing

Conditional

Conditional II
I would cost
you would cost
he/she/it would cost
we would cost
you would cost
they would cost

Conditional Past
I would have cost
you would have cost
he/she/it would have cost
we would have cost
you would have cost
they would have cost

Imperative
cost

Gerund
costing

Past Participle
cost

Verbtabellen

Unregelmäßig

cut | schneiden

Konsonantenverdopplung
(siehe S. 152)

Simple

Present Simple

I	cut
you	cut
he/she/it	cuts
we	cut
you	cut
they	cut

Past Simple

I	cut
you	cut
he/she/it	cut
we	cut
you	cut
they	cut

Present Perfect

I	have	cut
you	have	cut
he/she/it	has	cut
we	have	cut
you	have	cut
they	have	cut

Past Perfect

I	had	cut
you	had	cut
he/she/it	had	cut
we	had	cut
you	had	cut
they	had	cut

Continuous

Present Continuous

I	am	cutting
you	are	cutting
he/she/it	is	cutting
we	are	cutting
you	are	cutting
they	are	cutting

Past Continuous

I	was	cutting
you	were	cutting
he/she/it	was	cutting
we	were	cutting
you	were	cutting
they	were	cutting

Present Perfect Continuous

I	have	been	cutting
you	have	been	cutting
he/she/it	has	been	cutting
we	have	been	cutting
you	have	been	cutting
they	have	been	cutting

Past Perfect Continuous

I	had	been	cutting
you	had	been	cutting
he/she/it	had	been	cutting
we	had	been	cutting
you	had	been	cutting
they	had	been	cutting

Future

Future I

I	will	cut
you	will	cut
he/she/it	will	cut
we	will	cut
you	will	cut
they	will	cut

Future I Continuous

I	will	be	cutting
you	will	be	cutting
he/she/it	will	be	cutting
we	will	be	cutting
you	will	be	cutting
they	will	be	cutting

Future II

I	will have	cut
you	will have	cut
he/she/it	will have	cut
we	will have	cut
you	will have	cut
they	will have	cut

Future II Continuous

I	will have been cutting
you	will have been cutting
he/she/it	will have been cutting
we	will have been cutting
you	will have been cutting
they	will have been cutting

Conditional

Conditional II

I	would	cut
you	would	cut
he/she/it	would	cut
we	would	cut
you	would	cut
they	would	cut

Conditional Past

I	would have	cut
you	would have	cut
he/she/it	would have	cut
we	would have	cut
you	would have	cut
they	would have	cut

Imperative

cut

Gerund

cutting

Past Participle

cut

Verbtabellen

+ *-ing* wird ~~e~~ (siehe S. 153)/
+ *-d* nicht *-ed* (siehe S. 152)

Regelmäßig

decide | entscheiden

Simple

Present Simple
I	decide
you	decide
he/she/it	decides
we	decide
you	decide
they	decide

Past Simple
I	decided
you	decided
he/she/it	decided
we	decided
you	decided
they	decided

Present Perfect
I	have	decided
you	have	decided
he/she/it	has	decided
we	have	decided
you	have	decided
they	have	decided

Past Perfect
I	had	decided
you	had	decided
he/she/it	had	decided
we	had	decided
you	had	decided
they	had	decided

Continuous

Present Continuous
I	am	deciding
you	are	deciding
he/she/it	is	deciding
we	are	deciding
you	are	deciding
they	are	deciding

Past Continuous
I	was	deciding
you	were	deciding
he/she/it	was	deciding
we	were	deciding
you	were	deciding
they	were	deciding

Present Perfect Continuous
I	have	been	deciding
you	have	been	deciding
he/she/it	has	been	deciding
we	have	been	deciding
you	have	been	deciding
they	have	been	deciding

Past Perfect Continuous
I	had	been	deciding
you	had	been	deciding
he/she/it	had	been	deciding
we	had	been	deciding
you	had	been	deciding
they	had	been	deciding

Future

Future I
I	will	decide
you	will	decide
he/she/it	will	decide
we	will	decide
you	will	decide
they	will	decide

Future I Continuous
I	will be	deciding
you	will be	deciding
he/she/it	will be	deciding
we	will be	deciding
you	will be	deciding
they	will be	deciding

Future II
I	will have	decided
you	will have	decided
he/she/it	will have	decided
we	will have	decided
you	will have	decided
they	will have	decided

Future II Continuous
I	will have been	deciding
you	will have been	deciding
he/she/it	will have been	deciding
we	will have been	deciding
you	will have been	deciding
they	will have been	deciding

Conditional

Conditional II
I	would	decide
you	would	decide
he/she/it	would	decide
we	would	decide
you	would	decide
they	would	decide

Conditional Past
I	would have	decided
you	would have	decided
he/she/it	would have	decided
we	would have	decided
you	would have	decided
they	would have	decided

Imperative
decide

Gerund
deciding

Past Participle
decided

Verbtabellen

Unregelmäßig

do | tun/machen

+ *-es* in 3. Person Singular (siehe S. 152)

Simple

Present Simple
I do
you do
he/she/it does
we do
you do
they do

Past Simple
I did
you did
he/she/it did
we did
you did
they did

Present Perfect
I have done
you have done
he/she/it has done
we have done
you have done
they have done

Past Perfect
I had done
you had done
he/she/it had done
we had done
you had done
they had done

Continuous

Present Continuous
I am doing
you are doing
he/she/it is doing
we are doing
you are doing
they are doing

Past Continuous
I was doing
you were doing
he/she/it was doing
we were doing
you were doing
they were doing

Present Perfect Continuous
I have been doing
you have been doing
he/she/it has been doing
we have been doing
you have been doing
they have been doing

Past Perfect Continuous
I had been doing
you had been doing
he/she/it had been doing
we had been doing
you had been doing
they had been doing

Future

Future I
I will do
you will do
he/she/it will do
we will do
you will do
they will do

Future I Continuous
I will be doing
you will be doing
he/she/it will be doing
we will be doing
you will be doing
they will be doing

Future II
I will have done
you will have done
he/she/it will have done
we will have done
you will have done
they will have done

Future II Continuous
I will have been doing
you will have been doing
he/she/it will have been doing
we will have been doing
you will have been doing
they will have been doing

Conditional

Conditional II
I would do
you would do
he/she/it would do
we would do
you would do
they would do

Conditional Past
I would have done
you would have done he/she/it would have done
we would have done
you would have done
they would have done

Imperative
do

Gerund
doing

Past Participle
done

Verbtabellen

Unregelmäßig

drink | trinken

Simple

Present Simple
I drink
you drink
he/she/it drinks
we drink
you drink
they drink

Past Simple
I drank
you drank
he/she/it drank
we drank
you drank
they drank

Present Perfect
I have drunk
you have drunk
he/she/it has drunk
we have drunk
you have drunk
they have drunk

Past Perfect
I had drunk
you had drunk
he/she/it had drunk
we had drunk
you had drunk
they had drunk

Continuous

Present Continuous
I am drinking
you are drinking
he/she/it is drinking
we are drinking
you are drinking
they are drinking

Past Continuous
I was drinking
you were drinking
he/she/it was drinking
we were drinking
you were drinking
they were drinking

Present Perfect Continuous
I have been drinking
you have been drinking
he/she/it has been drinking
we have been drinking
you have been drinking
they have been drinking

Past Perfect Continuous
I had been drinking
you had been drinking
he/she/it had been drinking
we had been drinking
you had been drinking
they had been drinking

Future

Future I
I will drink
you will drink
he/she/it will drink
we will drink
you will drink
they will drink

Future I Continuous
I will be drinking
you will be drinking
he/she/it will be drinking
we will be drinking
you will be drinking
they will be drinking

Future II
I will have drunk
you will have drunk
he/she/it will have drunk
we will have drunk
you will have drunk
they will have drunk

Future II Continuous
I will have been drinking
you will have been drinking
he/she/it will have been drinking
we will have been drinking
you will have been drinking
they will have been drinking

Conditional

Conditional II
I would drink
you would drink
he/she/it would drink
we would drink
you would drink
they would drink

Conditional Past
I would have drunk
you would have drunk
he/she/it would have drunk
we would have drunk
you would have drunk
they would have drunk

Imperative
drink

Gerund
drinking

Past Participle
drunk

Verbtabellen

Unregelmäßig

drive | fahren

+ *-ing* wird ∅ (siehe S. 153)

Simple

Present Simple
I drive
you drive
he/she/it drives
we drive
you drive
they drive

Past Simple
I drove
you drove
he/she/it drove
we drove
you drove
they drove

Present Perfect
I have driven
you have driven
he/she/it has driven
we have driven
you have driven
they have driven

Past Perfect
I had driven
you had driven
he/she/it had driven
we had driven
you had driven
they had driven

Continuous

Present Continuous
I am driving
you are driving
he/she/it is driving
we are driving
you are driving
they are driving

Past Continuous
I was driving
you were driving
he/she/it was driving
we were driving
you were driving
they were driving

Present Perfect Continuous
I have been driving
you have been driving
he/she/it has been driving
we have been driving
you have been driving
they have been driving

Past Perfect Continuous
I had been driving
you had been driving
he/she/it had been driving
we had been driving
you had been driving
they had been driving

Future

Future I
I will drive
you will drive
he/she/it will drive
we will drive
you will drive
they will drive

Future I Continuous
I will be driving
you will be driving
he/she/it will be driving
we will be driving
you will be driving
they will be driving

Future II
I will have driven
you will have driven
he/she/it will have driven
we will have driven
you will have driven
they will have driven

Future II Continuous
I will have been driving
you will have been driving
he/she/it will have been driving
we will have been driving
you will have been driving
they will have been driving

Conditional

Conditional II
I would drive
you would drive
he/she/it would drive
we would drive
you would drive
they would drive

Conditional Past
I would have driven
you would have driven
he/she/it would have driven
we would have driven
you would have driven
they would have driven

Imperative
drive

Gerund
driving

Past Participle
driven

Verbtabellen

Unregelmäßig

eat | essen

Simple

Present Simple
I eat
you eat
he/she/it eats
we eat
you eat
they eat

Past Simple
I ate
you ate
he/she/it ate
we ate
you ate
they ate

Present Perfect
I have eaten
you have eaten
he/she/it has eaten
we have eaten
you have eaten
they have eaten

Past Perfect
I had eaten
you had eaten
he/she/it had eaten
we had eaten
you had eaten
they had eaten

Continuous

Present Continuous
I am eating
you are eating
he/she/it is eating
we are eating
you are eating
they are eating

Past Continuous
I was eating
you were eating
he/she/it was eating
we were eating
you were eating
they were eating

Present Perfect Continuous
I have been eating
you have been eating
he/she/it has been eating
we have been eating
you have been eating
they have been eating

Past Perfect Continuous
I had been eating
you had been eating
he/she/it had been eating
we had been eating
you had been eating
they had been eating

Future

Future I
I will eat
you will eat
he/she/it will eat
we will eat
you will eat
they will eat

Future I Continuous
I will be eating
you will be eating
he/she/it will be eating
we will be eating
you will be eating
they will be eating

Future II
I will have eaten
you will have eaten
he/she/it will have eaten
we will have eaten
you will have eaten
they will have eaten

Future II Continuous
I will have been eating
you will have been eating
he/she/it will have been eating
we will have been eating
you will have been eating
they will have been eating

Conditional

Conditional II
I would eat
you would eat
he/she/it would eat
we would eat
you would eat
they would eat

Conditional Past
I would have eaten
you would have eaten
he/she/it would have eaten
we would have eaten
you would have eaten
they would have eaten

Imperative
eat

Gerund
eating

Past Participle
eaten

Verbtabellen

Regelmäßig

enjoy | genießen

Simple

Present Simple

	enjoy
I	enjoy
you	enjoy
he/she/it	enjoys
we	enjoy
you	enjoy
they	enjoy

Past Simple

I	enjoyed
you	enjoyed
he/she/it	enjoyed
we	enjoyed
you	enjoyed
they	enjoyed

Present Perfect

I	have enjoyed
you	have enjoyed
he/she/it	has enjoyed
we	have enjoyed
you	have enjoyed
they	have enjoyed

Past Perfect

I	had enjoyed
you	had enjoyed
he/she/it	had enjoyed
we	had enjoyed
you	had enjoyed
they	had enjoyed

Continuous

Present Continuous

I	am enjoying
you	are enjoying
he/she/it	is enjoying
we	are enjoying
you	are enjoying
they	are enjoying

Past Continuous

I	was enjoying
you	were enjoying
he/she/it	was enjoying
we	were enjoying
you	were enjoying
they	were enjoying

Present Perfect Continuous

I	have been enjoying
you	have been enjoying
he/she/it	has been enjoying
we	have been enjoying
you	have been enjoying
they	have been enjoying

Past Perfect Continuous

I	had been enjoying
you	had been enjoying
he/she/it	had been enjoying
we	had been enjoying
you	had been enjoying
they	had been enjoying

Future

Future I

I	will enjoy
you	will enjoy
he/she/it	will enjoy
we	will enjoy
you	will enjoy
they	will enjoy

Future I Continuous

I	will be enjoying
you	will be enjoying
he/she/it	will be enjoying
we	will be enjoying
you	will be enjoying
they	will be enjoying

Future II

I	will have enjoyed
you	will have enjoyed
he/she/it	will have enjoyed
we	will have enjoyed
you	will have enjoyed
they	will have enjoyed

Future II Continuous

I	will have been enjoying
you	will have been enjoying
he/she/it	will have been enjoying
we	will have been enjoying
you	will have been enjoying
they	will have been enjoying

Conditional

Conditional II

I	would enjoy
you	would enjoy
he/she/it	would enjoy
we	would enjoy
you	would enjoy
they	would enjoy

Conditional Past

I	would have enjoyed
you	would have enjoyed
he/she/it	would have enjoyed
we	would have enjoyed
you	would have enjoyed
they	would have enjoyed

Imperative

enjoy

Gerund

enjoying

Past Participle

enjoyed

Unregelmäßig

fall | fallen/stürzen

Simple

Present Simple
I fall
you fall
he/she/it falls
we fall
you fall
they fall

Past Simple
I fell
you fell
he/she/it fell
we fell
you fell
they fell

Present Perfect
I have fallen
you have fallen
he/she/it has fallen
we have fallen
you have fallen
they have fallen

Past Perfect
I had fallen
you had fallen
he/she/it had fallen
we had fallen
you had fallen
they had fallen

Continuous

Present Continuous
I am falling
you are falling
he/she/it is falling
we are falling
you are falling
they are falling

Past Continuous
I was falling
you were falling
he/she/it was falling
we were falling
you were falling
they were falling

Present Perfect Continuous
I have been falling
you have been falling
he/she/it has been falling
we have been falling
you have been falling
they have been falling

Past Perfect Continuous
I had been falling
you had been falling
he/she/it had been falling
we had been falling
you had been falling
they had been falling

Future

Future I
I will fall
you will fall
he/she/it will fall
we will fall
you will fall
they will fall

Future I Continuous
I will be falling
you will be falling
he/she/it will be falling
we will be falling
you will be falling
they will be falling

Future II
I will have fallen
you will have fallen
he/she/it will have fallen
we will have fallen
you will have fallen
they will have fallen

Future II Continuous
I will have been falling
you will have been falling
he/she/it will have been falling
we will have been falling
you will have been falling
they will have been falling

Conditional

Conditional II
I would fall
you would fall
he/she/it would fall
we would fall
you would fall
they would fall

Conditional Past
I would have fallen
you would have fallen
he/she/it would have fallen
we would have fallen
you would have fallen
they would have fallen

Imperative
fall

Gerund
falling

Past Participle
fallen

Verbtabellen

Unregelmäßig

feel | fühlen

Simple

Present Simple
I feel
you feel
he/she/it feels
we feel
you feel
they feel

Past Simple
I felt
you felt
he/she/it felt
we felt
you felt
they felt

Present Perfect
I have felt
you have felt
he/she/it has felt
we have felt
you have felt
they have felt

Past Perfect
I had felt
you had felt
he/she/it had felt
we had felt
you had felt
they had felt

Continuous

Present Continuous
I am feeling
you are feeling
he/she/it is feeling
we are feeling
you are feeling
they are feeling

Past Continuous
I was feeling
you were feeling
he/she/it was feeling
we were feeling
you were feeling
they were feeling

Present Perfect Continuous
I have been feeling
you have been feeling
he/she/it has been feeling
we have been feeling
you have been feeling
they have been feeling

Past Perfect Continuous
I had been feeling
you had been feeling
he/she/it had been feeling
we had been feeling
you had been feeling
they had been feeling

Future

Future I
I will feel
you will feel
he/she/it will feel
we will feel
you will feel
they will feel

Future I Continuous
I will be feeling
you will be feeling
he/she/it will be feeling
we will be feeling
you will be feeling
they will be feeling

Future II
I will have felt
you will have felt
he/she/it will have felt
we will have felt
you will have felt
they will have felt

Future II Continuous
I will have been feeling
you will have been feeling
he/she/it will have been feeling
we will have been feeling
you will have been feeling
they will have been feeling

Conditional

Conditional II
I would feel
you would feel
he/she/it would feel
we would feel
you would feel
they would feel

Conditional Past
I would have felt
you would have felt
he/she/it would have felt
we would have felt
you would have felt
they would have felt

Imperative
feel

Gerund
feeling

Past Participle
felt

Verbtabellen

Unregelmäßig

find | finden

Simple

Present Simple
I find
you find
he/she/it finds
we find
you find
they find

Past Simple
I found
you found
he/she/it found
we found
you found
they found

Present Perfect
I have found
you have found
he/she/it has found
we have found
you have found
they have found

Past Perfect
I had found
you had found
he/she/it had found
we had found
you had found
they had found

Continuous

Present Continuous
I am finding
you are finding
he/she/it is finding
we are finding
you are finding
they are finding

Past Continuous
I was finding
you were finding
he/she/it was finding
we were finding
you were finding
they were finding

Present Perfect Continuous
I have been finding
you have been finding
he/she/it has been finding
we have been finding
you have been finding
they have been finding

Past Perfect Continuous
I had been finding
you had been finding
he/she/it had been finding
we had been finding
you had been finding
they had been finding

Future

Future I
I will find
you will find
he/she/it will find
we will find
you will find
they will find

Future I Continuous
I will be finding
you will be finding
he/she/it will be finding
we will be finding
you will be finding
they will be finding

Future II
I will have found
you will have found
he/she/it will have found
we will have found
you will have found
they will have found

Future II Continuous
I will have been finding
you will have been finding
he/she/it will have been finding
we will have been finding
you will have been finding
they will have been finding

Conditional

Conditional II
I would find
you would find
he/she/it would find
we would find
you would find
they would find

Conditional Past
I would have found
you would have found
he/she/it would have found
we would have found
you would have found
they would have found

Imperative
find

Gerund
finding

Past Participle
found

193

Verbtabellen

Unregelmäßig

fly | fliegen

-y wird *-ie* vor *-s* (siehe S. 152)

Simple

Present Simple
I fly
you fly
he/she/it flies
we fly
you fly
they fly

Past Simple
I flew
you flew
he/she/it flew
we flew
you flew
they flew

Present Perfect
I have flown
you have flown
he/she/it has flown
we have flown
you have flown
they have flown

Past Perfect
I had flown
you had flown
he/she/it had flown
we had flown
you had flown
they had flown

Continuous

Present Continuous
I am flying
you are flying
he/she/it is flying
we are flying
you are flying
they are flying

Past Continuous
I was flying
you were flying
he/she/it was flying
we were flying
you were flying
they were flying

Present Perfect Continuous
I have been flying
you have been flying
he/she/it has been flying
we have been flying
you have been flying
they have been flying

Past Perfect Continuous
I had been flying
you had been flying
he/she/it had been flying
we had been flying
you had been flying
they had been flying

Future

Future I
I will fly
you will fly
he/she/it will fly
we will fly
you will fly
they will fly

Future I Continuous
I will be flying
you will be flying
he/she/it will be flying
we will be flying
you will be flying
they will be flying

Future II
I will have flown
you will have flown
he/she/it will have flown
we will have flown
you will have flown
they will have flown

Future II Continuous
I will have been flying
you will have been flying
he/she/it will have been flying
we will have been flying
you will have been flying
they will have been flying

Conditional

Conditional II
I would fly
you would fly
he/she/it would fly
we would fly
you would fly
they would fly

Conditional Past
I would have flown
you would have flown
he/she/it would have flown
we would have flown
you would have flown
they would have flown

Imperative
fly

Gerund
flying

Past Participle
flown

Verbtabellen

Konsonantenverdopplung
(siehe S. 152)

Unregelmäßig

forget | vergessen

Simple

Present Simple
I forget
you forget
he/she/it forgets
we forget
you forget
they forget

Past Simple
I forgot
you forgot
he/she/it forgot
we forgot
you forgot
they forgot

Present Perfect
I have forgotten
you have forgotten
he/she/it has forgotten
we have forgotten
you have forgotten
they have forgotten

Past Perfect
I had forgotten
you had forgotten
he/she/it had forgotten
we had forgotten
you had forgotten
they had forgotten

Continuous

Present Continuous
I am forgetting
you are forgetting
he/she/it is forgetting
we are forgetting
you are forgetting
they are forgetting

Past Continuous
I was forgetting
you were forgetting
he/she/it was forgetting
we were forgetting
you were forgetting
they were forgetting

Present Perfect Continuous
I have been forgetting
you have been forgetting
he/she/it has been forgetting
we have been forgetting
you have been forgetting
they have been forgetting

Past Perfect Continuous
I had been forgetting
you had been forgetting
he/she/it had been forgetting
we had been forgetting
you had been forgetting
they had been forgetting

Future

Future I
I will forget
you will forget
he/she/it will forget
we will forget
you will forget
they will forget

Future I Continuous
I will be forgetting
you will be forgetting
he/she/it will be forgetting
we will be forgetting
you will be forgetting
they will be forgetting

Future II
I will have forgotten
you will have forgotten
he/she/it will have forgotten
we will have forgotten
you will have forgotten
they will have forgotten

Future II Continuous
I will have been forgetting
you will have been forgetting
he/she/it will have been forgetting
we will have been forgetting
you will have been forgetting
they will have been forgetting

Conditional

Conditional II
I would forget
you would forget
he/she/it would forget
we would forget
you would forget
they would forget

Conditional Past
I would have forgotten
you would have forgotten
he/she/it would have forgotten
we would have forgotten
you would have forgotten
they would have forgotten

Imperative
forget

Gerund
forgetting

Past Participle
forgotten

Verbtabellen

Unregelmäßig

get | bekommen

Im AE ist das Partizip Perfekt *gotten*.

Simple

Present Simple
I get
you get
he/she/it gets
we get
you get
they get

Past Simple
I got
you got
he/she/it got
we got
you got
they got

Present Perfect
I have got
you have got
he/she/it has got
we have got
you have got
they have got

Past Perfect
I had got
you had got
he/she/it had got
we had got
you had got
they had got,

Continuous

Present Continuous
I am getting
you are getting
he/she/it is getting
we are getting
you are getting
they are getting

Past Continuous
I was getting
you were getting
he/she/it was getting
we were getting
you were getting
they were getting

Present Perfect Continuous
I have been getting
you have been getting
he/she/it has been getting
we have been getting
you have been getting
they have been getting

Past Perfect Continuous
I had been getting
you had been getting
he/she/it had been getting
we had been getting
you had been getting
they had been getting

Future

Future I
I will get
you will get
he/she/it will get
we will get
you will get
they will get

Future I Continuous
I will be getting
you will be getting
he/she/it will be getting
we will be getting
you will be getting
they will be getting

Future II
I will have got
you will have got
he/she/it will have got
we will have got
you will have got
they will have got

Future II Continuous
I will have been getting
you will have been getting
he/she/it will have been getting
we will have been getting
you will have been getting
they will have been getting

Conditional

Conditional II
I would get
you would get
he/she/it would get
we would get
you would get
they would get

Conditional Past
I would have got
you would have got
he/she/it would have got
we would have got
you would have got
they would have got

Imperative
get

Gerund
getting

Past Participle
got/gotten

Verbtabellen

+ *-ing* wird ∅ (siehe S. 152)

Unregelmäßig

give | geben

Simple

Present Simple
I give
you give
he/she/it gives
we give
you give
they give

Past Simple
I gave
you gave
he/she/it gave
we gave
you gave
they gave

Present Perfect
I have given
you have given
he/she/it has given
we have given
you have given
they have given

Past Perfect
I had given
you had given
he/she/it had given
we had given
you had given
they had given

Continuous

Present Continuous
I am giving
you are giving
he/she/it is giving
we are giving
you are giving
they are giving

Past Continuous
I was giving
you were giving
he/she/it was giving
we were giving
you were giving
they were giving

Present Perfect Continuous
I have been giving
you have been giving
he/she/it has been giving
we have been giving
you have been giving
they have been giving

Past Perfect Continuous
I had been giving
you had been giving
he/she/it had been giving
we had been giving
you had been giving
they had been giving

Future

Future I
I will give
you will give
he/she/it will give
we will give
you will give
they will give

Future I Continuous
I will be giving
you will be giving
he/she/it will be giving
we will be giving
you will be giving
they will be giving

Future II
I will have given
you will have given
he/she/it will have given
we will have given
you will have given
they will have given

Future II Continuous
I will have been giving
you will have been giving
he/she/it will have been giving
we will have been giving
you will have been giving
they will have been giving

Conditional

Conditional II
I would give
you would give
he/she/it would give
we would give
you would give
they would give

Conditional Past
I would have given
you would have given
he/she/it would have given
we would have given
you would have given
they would have given

Imperative
give

Gerund
giving

Past Participle
given

Verbtabellen

Unregelmäßig

go | gehen

+ *-es* in 3. Person Singular (siehe S. 152)

Simple

Present Simple
I go
you go
he/she/it goes
we go
you go
they go

Past Simple
I went
you went
he/she/it went
we went
you went
they went

Present Perfect
I have gone
you have gone
he/she/it has gone
we have gone
you have gone
they have gone

Past Perfect
I had gone
you had gone
he/she/it had gone
we had gone
you had gone
they had gone

Continuous

Present Continuous
I am going
you are going
he/she/it is going
we are going
you are going
they are going

Past Continuous
I was going
you were going
he/she/it was going
we were going
you were going
they were going

Present Perfect Continuous
I have been going
you have been going
he/she/it has been going
we have been going
you have been going
they have been going

Past Perfect Continuous
I had been going
you had been going
he/she/it had been going
we had been going
you had been going
they had been going

Future

Future I
I will go
you will go
he/she/it will go
we will go
you will go
they will go

Future I Continuous
I will be going
you will be going
he/she/it will be going
we will be going
you will be going
they will be going

Future II
I will have gone
you will have gone
he/she/it will have gone
we will have gone
you will have gone
they will have gone

Future II Continuous
I will have been going
you will have been going
he/she/it will have been going
we will have been going
you will have been going
they will have been going

Conditional

Conditional II
I would go
you would go
he/she/it would go
we would go
you would go
they would go

Conditional Past
I would have gone
you would have gone he/she/it
we would have gone
you would have gone
they would have gone

Imperative
go

Gerund
going

Past Participle
gone

Verbtabellen

Unregelmäßig
Voll- und Hilfsverb

have | haben

+ *-ing* wird ∅ (siehe S. 152)

Simple

Present Simple
I	have
you	have
he/she/it	has
we	have
you	have
they	have

Past Simple
I	had
you	had
he/she/it	had
we	had
you	had
they	had

Present Perfect
I	have	had
you	have	had
he/she/it	has	had
we	have	had
you	have	had
they	have	had

Past Perfect
I	had	had
you	had	had
he/she/it	had	had
we	had	had
you	had	had
they	had	had

Continuous

Present Continuous
I	am	having
you	are	having
he/she/it	is	having
we	are	having
you	are	having
they	are	having

Past Continuous
I	was	having
you	were	having
he/she/it	was	having
we	were	having
you	were	having
they	were	having

Present Perfect Continuous
I	have been having
you	have been having
he/she/it	has been having
we	have been having
you	have been having
they	have been having

Past Perfect Continuous
I	had been having
you	had been having
he/she/it	had been having
we	had been having
you	had been having
they	had been having

Future

Future I
I	will have
you	will have
he/she/it	will have
we	will have
you	will have
they	will have

Future I Continuous
I	will be having
you	will be having
he/she/it	will be having
we	will be having
you	will be having
they	will be having

Future II
I	will have had
you	will have had
he/she/it	will have had
we	will have had
you	will have had
they	will have had

Future II Continuous
I	will have been having
you	will have been having
he/she/it	will have been having
we	will have been having
you	will have been having
they	will have been having

Conditional

Conditional II
I	would have
you	would have
he/she/it	would have
we	would have
you	would have
they	would have

Conditional Past
I	would have had
you	would have had
he/she/it	would have had
we	would have had
you	would have had
they	would have had

Imperative
have

Gerund
having

Past Participle
had

Verbtabellen

Unregelmäßig

hear | hören

Simple

Present Simple
I	hear
you	hear
he/she/it	hears
we	hear
you	hear
they	hear

Past Simple
I	heard
you	heard
he/she/it	heard
we	heard
you	heard
they	heard

Present Perfect
I	have	heard
you	have	heard
he/she/it	has	heard
we	have	heard
you	have	heard
they	have	heard

Past Perfect
I	had	heard
you	had	heard
he/she/it	had	heard
we	had	heard
you	had	heard
they	had	heard

Continuous

Present Continuous
I	am	hearing
you	are	hearing
he/she/it	is	hearing
we	are	hearing
you	are	hearing
they	are	hearing

Past Continuous
I	was	hearing
you	were	hearing
he/she/it	was	hearing
we	were	hearing
you	were	hearing
they	were	hearing

Present Perfect Continuous
I	have	been	hearing
you	have	been	hearing
he/she/it	has	been	hearing
we	have	been	hearing
you	have	been	hearing
they	have	been	hearing

Past Perfect Continuous
I	had	been	hearing
you	had	been	hearing
he/she/it	had	been	hearing
we	had	been	hearing
you	had	been	hearing
they	had	been	hearing

Future

Future I
I	will	hear
you	will	hear
he/she/it	will	hear
we	will	hear
you	will	hear
they	will	hear

Future I Continuous
I	will	be	hearing
you	will	be	hearing
he/she/it	will	be	hearing
we	will	be	hearing
you	will	be	hearing
they	will	be	hearing

Future II
I	will have	heard
you	will have	heard
he/she/it	will have	heard
we	will have	heard
you	will have	heard
they	will have	heard

Future II Continuous
I	will have been	hearing
you	will have been	hearing
he/she/it	will have been	hearing
we	will have been	hearing
you	will have been	hearing
they	will have been	hearing

Conditional

Conditional II
I	would	hear
you	would	hear
he/she/it	would	hear
we	would	hear
you	would	hear
they	would	hear

Conditional Past
I	would have	heard
you	would have	heard
he/she/it	would have	heard
we	would have	heard
you	would have	heard
they	would have	heard

Imperative

hear

Gerund

hearing

Past Participle

heard

Verbtabellen

Regelmäßig

help | helfen

Simple

Present Simple
I help
you help
he/she/it helps
we help
you help
they help

Past Simple
I helped
you helped
he/she/it helped
we helped
you helped
they helped

Present Perfect
I have helped
you have helped
he/she/it has helped
we have helped
you have helped
they have helped

Past Perfect
I had helped
you had helped
he/she/it had helped
we had helped
you had helped
they had helped

Continuous

Present Continuous
I am helping
you are helping
he/she/it is helping
we are helping
you are helping
they are helping

Past Continuous
I was helping
you were helping
he/she/it was helping
we were helping
you were helping
they were helping

Present Perfect Continuous
I have been helping
you have been helping
he/she/it has been helping
we have been helping
you have been helping
they have been helping

Past Perfect Continuous
I had been helping
you had been helping
he/she/it had been helping
we had been helping
you had been helping
they had been helping

Future

Future I
I will help
you will help
he/she/it will help
we will help
you will help
they will help

Future I Continuous
I will be helping
you will be helping
he/she/it will be helping
we will be helping
you will be helping
they will be helping

Future II
I will have helped
you will have helped
he/she/it will have helped
we will have helped
you will have helped
they will have helped

Future II Continuous
I will have been helping
you will have been helping
he/she/it will have been helping
we will have been helping
you will have been helping
they will have been helping

Conditional

Conditional II
I would help
you would help
he/she/it would help
we would help
you would help
they would help

Conditional Past
I would have helped
you would have helped
he/she/it would have helped
we would have helped
you would have helped
they would have helped

Imperative
help

Gerund
helping

Past Participle
helped

Verbtabellen

Unregelmäßig

hit | schlagen

Konsonantenverdopplung
(siehe S. 152)

Simple

Present Simple
I hit
you hit
he/she/it hits
we hit
you hit
they hit

Past Simple
I hit
you hit
he/she/it hit
we hit
you hit
they hit

Present Perfect
I have hit
you have hit
he/she/it has hit
we have hit
you have hit
they have hit

Past Perfect
I had hit
you had hit
he/she/it had hit
we had hit
you had hit
they had hit

Continuous

Present Continuous
I am hitting
you are hitting
he/she/it is hitting
we are hitting
you are hitting
they are hitting

Past Continuous
I was hitting
you were hitting
he/she/it was hitting
we were hitting
you were hitting
they were hitting

Present Perfect Continuous
I have been hitting
you have been hitting
he/she/it has been hitting
we have been hitting
you have been hitting
they have been hitting

Past Perfect Continuous
I had been hitting
you had been hitting
he/she/it had been hitting
we had been hitting
you had been hitting
they had been hitting

Future

Future I
I will hit
you will hit
he/she/it will hit
we will hit
you will hit
they will hit

Future I Continuous
I will be hitting
you will be hitting
he/she/it will be hitting
we will be hitting
you will be hitting
they will be hitting

Future II
I will have hit
you will have hit
he/she/it will have hit
we will have hit
you will have hit
they will have hit

Future II Continuous
I will have been hitting
you will have been hitting
he/she/it will have been hitting
we will have been hitting
you will have been hitting
they will have been hitting

Conditional

Conditional II
I would hit
you would hit
he/she/it would hit
we would hit
you would hit
they would hit

Conditional Past
I would have hit
you would have hit
he/she/it would have hit
we would have hit
you would have hit
they would have hit

Imperative
hit

Gerund
hitting

Past Participle
hit

Verbtabellen

Unregelmäßig

hurt | wehtun

Simple

Present Simple
I hurt
you hurt
he/she/it hurts
we hurt
you hurt
they hurt

Past Simple
I hurt
you hurt
he/she/it hurt
we hurt
you hurt
they hurt

Present Perfect
I have hurt
you have hurt
he/she/it has hurt
we have hurt
you have hurt
they have hurt

Past Perfect
I had hurt
you had hurt
he/she/it had hurt
we had hurt
you had hurt
they had hurt

Continuous

Present Continuous
I am hurting
you are hurting
he/she/it is hurting
we are hurting
you are hurting
they are hurting

Past Continuous
I was hurting
you were hurting
he/she/it was hurting
we were hurting
you were hurting
they were hurting

Present Perfect Continuous
I have been hurting
you have been hurting
he/she/it has been hurting
we have been hurting
you have been hurting
they have been hurting

Past Perfect Continuous
I had been hurting
you had been hurting
he/she/it had been hurting
we had been hurting
you had been hurting
they had been hurting

Future

Future I
I will hurt
you will hurt
he/she/it will hurt
we will hurt
you will hurt
they will hurt

Future I Continuous
I will be hurting
you will be hurting
he/she/it will be hurting
we will be hurting
you will be hurting
they will be hurting

Future II
I will have hurt
you will have hurt
he/she/it will have hurt
we will have hurt
you will have hurt
they will have hurt

Future II Continuous
I will have been hurting
you will have been hurting
he/she/it will have been hurting
we will have been hurting
you will have been hurting
they will have been hurting

Conditional

Conditional II
I would hurt
you would hurt
he/she/it would hurt
we would hurt
you would hurt
they would hurt

Conditional Past
I would have hurt
you would have hurt
he/she/it would have hurt
we would have hurt
you would have hurt
they would have hurt

Imperative
hurt

Gerund
hurting

Past Participle
hurt

Regelmäßig

invite | einladen

+ *-ing* wird ɇ (siehe S. 153)/
+ *-d* nicht *-ed* (siehe S. 152)

Simple

Present Simple
I invite
you invite
he/she/it invites
we invite
you invite
they invite

Past Simple
I invited
you invited
he/she/it invited
we invited
you invited
they invited

Present Perfect
I have invited
you have invited
he/she/it has invited
we have invited
you have invited
they have invited

Past Perfect
I had invited
you had invited
he/she/it had invited
we had invited
you had invited
they had invited

Continuous

Present Continuous
I am inviting
you are inviting
he/she/it is inviting
we are inviting
you are inviting
they are inviting

Past Continuous
I was inviting
you were inviting
he/she/it was inviting
we were inviting
you were inviting
they were inviting

Present Perfect Continuous
I have been inviting
you have been inviting
he/she/it has been inviting
we have been inviting
you have been inviting
they have been inviting

Past Perfect Continuous
I had been inviting
you had been inviting
he/she/it had been inviting
we had been inviting
you had been inviting
they had been inviting

Future

Future I
I will invite
you will invite
he/she/it will invite
we will invite
you will invite
they will invite

Future I Continuous
I will be inviting
you will be inviting
he/she/it will be inviting
we will be inviting
you will be inviting
they will be inviting

Future II
I will have invited
you will have invited
he/she/it will have invited
we will have invited
you will have invited
they will have invited

Future II Continuous
I will have been inviting
you will have been inviting
he/she/it will have been inviting
we will have been inviting
you will have been inviting
they will have been inviting

Conditional

Conditional II
I would invite
you would invite
he/she/it would invite
we would invite
you would invite
they would invite

Conditional Past
I would have invited
you would have invited
he/she/it would have invited
we would have invited
you would have invited
they would have invited

Imperative
invite

Gerund
inviting

Past Participle
invited

Verbtabellen

Unregelmäßig

know | wissen/kennen

Know hat keine Verlaufsform

Simple

Present Simple
I know
you know
he/she/it knows
we know
you know
they know

Past Simple
I knew
you knew
he/she/it knew
we knew
you knew
they knew

Present Perfect
I have known
you have known
he/she/it has known
we have known
you have known
they have known

Past Perfect
I had known
you had known
he/she/it had known
we had known
you had known
they had known

Continuous

Present Continuous
—

Past Continuous
—

Present Perfect Continuous
—

Past Perfect Continuous
—

Future

Future I
I will know
you will know
he/she/it will know
we will know
you will know
they will know

Future I Continuous
—

Future II
I will have known
you will have known
he/she/it will have known
we will have known
you will have known
they will have known

Future II Continuous
—

Conditional

Conditional II
I would know
you would know
he/she/it would know
we would know
you would know
they would know

Conditional Past
I would have known
you would have known
he/she/it would have known
we would have known
you would have known
they would have known

Imperative
know

Gerund
knowing

Past Participle
known

Unregelmäßig

learn | lernen

Im AE ist das Partizip Perfekt *learned*.

Simple

Present Simple
I	learn
you	learn
he/she/it	learns
we	learn
you	learn
they	learn

Past Simple
I	learnt
you	learnt
he/she/it	learnt
we	learnt
you	learnt
they	learnt

Present Perfect
I	have	learnt
you	have	learnt
he/she/it	has	learnt
we	have	learnt
you	have	learnt
they	have	learnt

Past Perfect
I	had	learnt
you	had	learnt
he/she/it	had	learnt
we	had	learnt
you	had	learnt
they	had	learnt

Continuous

Present Continuous
I	am	learning
you	are	learning
he/she/it	is	learning
we	are	learning
you	are	learning
they	are	learning

Past Continuous
I	was	learning
you	were	learning
he/she/it	was	learning
we	were	learning
you	were	learning
they	were	learning

Present Perfect Continuous
I	have	been	learning
you	have	been	learning
he/she/it	has	been	learning
we	have	been	learning
you	have	been	learning
they	have	been	learning

Past Perfect Continuous
I	had	been	learning
you	had	been	learning
he/she/it	had	been	learning
we	had	been	learning
you	had	been	learning
they	had	been	learning

Future

Future I
I	will	learn
you	will	learn
he/she/it	will	learn
we	will	learn
you	will	learn
they	will	learn

Future I Continuous
I	will	be	learning
you	will	be	learning
he/she/it	will	be	learning
we	will	be	learning
you	will	be	learning
they	will	be	learning

Future II
I	will	have	learnt
you	will	have	learnt
he/she/it	will	have	learnt
we	will	have	learnt
you	will	have	learnt
they	will	have	learnt

Future II Continuous
I	will	have	been	learning
you	will	have	been	learning
he/she/it	will	have	been	learning
we	will	have	been	learning
you	will	have	been	learning
they	will	have	been	learning

Conditional

Conditional II
I	would learn
you	would learn
he/she/it	would learn
we	would learn
you	would learn
they	would learn

Conditional Past
I	would have	learnt
you	would have	learnt
he/she/it	would have	learnt
we	would have	learnt
you	would have	learnt
they	would have	learnt

Imperative

learn

Gerund

learning

Past Participle

learnt/learned

Verbtabellen

Unregelmäßig

leave | verlassen

+ -*ing* wird ∅ (siehe S. 153)

Simple

Present Simple
I leave
you leave
he/she/it leaves
we leave
you leave
they leave

Past Simple
I left
you left
he/she/it left
we left
you left
they left

Present Perfect
I have left
you have left
he/she/it has left
we have left
you have left
they have left

Past Perfect
I had left
you had left
he/she/it had left
we had left
you had left
they had left

Continuous

Present Continuous
I am leaving
you are leaving
he/she/it is leaving
we are leaving
you are leaving
they are leaving

Past Continuous
I was leaving
you were leaving
he/she/it was leaving
we were leaving
you were leaving
they were leaving

Present Perfect Continuous
I have been leaving
you have been leaving
he/she/it has been leaving
we have been leaving
you have been leaving
they have been leaving

Past Perfect Continuous
I had been leaving
you had been leaving
he/she/it had been leaving
we had been leaving
you had been leaving
they had been leaving

Future

Future I
I will leave
you will leave
he/she/it will leave
we will leave
you will leave
they will leave

Future I Continuous
I will be leaving
you will be leaving
he/she/it will be leaving
we will be leaving
you will be leaving
they will be leaving

Future II
I will have left
you will have left
he/she/it will have left
we will have left
you will have left
they will have left

Future II Continuous
I will have been leaving
you will have been leaving
he/she/it will have been leaving
we will have been leaving
you will have been leaving
they will have been leaving

Conditional

Conditional II
I would leave
you would leave
he/she/it would leave
we would leave
you would leave
they would leave

Conditional Past
I would have left
you would have left
he/she/it would have left
we would have left
you would have left
they would have left

Imperative
leave

Gerund
leaving

Past Participle
left

Verbtabellen

Unregelmäßig

lend | (aus)leihen

Simple

Present Simple
I	lend
you	lend
he/she/it	lends
we	lend
you	lend
they	lend

Past Simple
I	lent
you	lent
he/she/it	lent
we	lent
you	lent
they	lent

Present Perfect
I	have	lent
you	have	lent
he/she/it	has	lent
we	have	lent
you	have	lent
they	have	lent

Past Perfect
I	had	lent
you	had	lent
he/she/it	had	lent
we	had	lent
you	had	lent
they	had	lent

Continuous

Present Continuous
I	am	lending
you	are	lending
he/she/it	is	lending
we	are	lending
you	are	lending
they	are	lending

Past Continuous
I	was	lending
you	were	lending
he/she/it	was	lending
we	were	lending
you	were	lending
they	were	lending

Present Perfect Continuous
I	have	been	lending
you	have	been	lending
he/she/it	has	been	lending
we	have	been	lending
you	have	been	lending
they	have	been	lending

Past Perfect Continuous
I	had	been	lending
you	had	been	lending
he/she/it	had	been	lending
we	had	been	lending
you	had	been	lending
they	had	been	lending

Future

Future I
I	will	lend
you	will	lend
he/she/it	will	lend
we	will	lend
you	will	lend
they	will	lend

Future I Continuous
I	will	be	lending
you	will	be	lending
he/she/it	will	be	lending
we	will	be	lending
you	will	be	lending
they	will	be	lending

Future II
I	will	have	lent
you	will	have	lent
he/she/it	will	have	lent
we	will	have	lent
you	will	have	lent
they	will	have	lent

Future II Continuous
I	will have been lending
you	will have been lending
he/she/it	will have been lending
we	will have been lending
you	will have been lending
they	will have been lending

Conditional

Conditional II
I	would lend
you	would lend
he/she/it	would lend
we	would lend
you	would lend
they	would lend

Conditional Past
I	would have	lent
you	would have	lent
he/she/it	would have	lent
we	would have	lent
you	would have	lent
they	would have	lent

Imperative

lend

Gerund

lending

Past Participle

lent

Verbtabellen

Like hat keine Verlaufsform

Regelmäßig

like | mögen

Simple

Present Simple
I like
you like
he/she/it likes
we like
you like
they like

Past Simple
I liked
you liked
he/she/it liked
we liked
you liked
they liked

Present Perfect
I have liked
you have liked
he/she/it has liked
we have liked
you have liked
they have liked

Past Perfect
I had liked
you had liked
he/she/it had liked
we had liked
you had liked
they had liked

Continuous

Present Continuous

—

Past Continuous

—

Present Perfect Continuous

—

Past Perfect Continuous

Future

Future I
I will like
you will like
he/she/it will like
we will like
you will like
they will like

Future I Continuous

—

Future II
I will have liked
you will have liked
he/she/it will have liked
we will have liked
you will have liked
they will have liked

Future II Continuous

—

Conditional

Conditional II
I would like
you would like
he/she/it would like
we would like
you would like
they would like

Conditional Past
I would have liked
you would have liked
he/she/it would have liked
we would have liked
you would have liked
they would have liked

Imperative
like

Gerund
liking

Past Participle
liked

209

Verbtabellen

Regelmäßig

listen | zuhören

Simple

Present Simple
I listen
you listen
he/she/it listens
we listen
you listen
they listen

Past Simple
I listened
you listened
he/she/it listened
we listened
you listened
they listened

Present Perfect
I have listened
you have listened
he/she/it has listened
we have listened
you have listened
they have listened

Past Perfect
I had listened
you had listened
he/she/it had listened
we had listened
you had listened
they had listened

Continuous

Present Continuous
I am listening
you are listening
he/she/it is listening
we are listening
you are listening
they are listening

Past Continuous
I was listening
you were listening
he/she/it was listening
we were listening
you were listening
they were listening

Present Perfect Continuous
I have been listening
you have been listening
he/she/it has been listening
we have been listening
you have been listening
they have been listening

Past Perfect Continuous
I had been listening
you had been listening
he/she/it had been listening
we had been listening
you had been listening
they had been listening

Future

Future I
I will listen
you will listen
he/she/it will listen
we will listen
you will listen
they will listen

Future I Continuous
I will be listening
you will be listening
he/she/it will be listening
we will be listening
you will be listening
they will be listening

Future II
I will have listened
you will have listened
he/she/it will have listened
we will have listened
you will have listened
they will have listened

Future II Continuous
I will have been listening
you will have been listening
he/she/it will have been listening
we will have been listening
you will have been listening
they will have been listening

Conditional

Conditional II
I would listen
you would listen
he/she/it would listen
we would listen
you would listen
they would listen

Conditional Past
I would have listened
you would have listened
he/she/it would have listened
we would have listened
you would have listened
they would have listened

Imperative
listen

Gerund
listening

Past Participle
listened

Verbtabellen

Regelmäßig

+ *-ing* wird ∅ (siehe S. 153)/
+ *-d* statt *-ed* (siehe S. 152)

live | leben/wohnen

Simple

Present Simple
I live
you live
he/she/it live**s**
we live
you live
they live

Past Simple
I lived
you lived
he/she/it lived
we lived
you lived
they lived

Present Perfect
I have lived
you have lived
he/she/it has lived
we have lived
you have lived
they have lived

Past Perfect
I had lived
you had lived
he/she/it had lived
we had lived
you had lived
they had lived

Continuous

Present Continuous
I am living
you are living
he/she/it is living
we are living
you are living
they are living

Past Continuous
I was living
you were living
he/she/it was living
we were living
you were living
they were living

Present Perfect Continuous
I have been living
you have been living
he/she/it has been living
we have been living
you have been living
they have been living

Past Perfect Continuous
I had been living
you had been living
he/she/it had been living
we had been living
you had been living
they had been living

Future

Future I
I will live
you will live
he/she/it will live
we will live
you will live
they will live

Future I Continuous
I will be living
you will be living
he/she/it will be living
we will be living
you will be living
they will be living

Future II
I will have lived
you will have lived
he/she/it will have lived
we will have lived
you will have lived
they will have lived

Future II Continuous
I will have been living
you will have been living
he/she/it will have been living
we will have been living
you will have been living
they will have been living

Conditional

Conditional II
I would live
you would live
he/she/it would live
we would live
you would live
they would live

Conditional Past
I would have lived
you would have lived
he/she/it would have lived
we would have lived
you would have lived
they would have lived

Imperative
live

Gerund
living

Past Participle
lived

Regelmäßig

look | sehen

Simple

Present Simple
I look
you look
he/she/it looks
we look
you look
they look

Past Simple
I looked
you looked
he/she/it looked
we looked
you looked
they looked

Present Perfect
I have looked
you have looked
he/she/it has looked
we have looked
you have looked
they have looked

Past Perfect
I had looked
you had looked
he/she/it had looked
we had looked
you had looked
they had looked

Continuous

Present Continuous
I am looking
you are looking
he/she/it is looking
we are looking
you are looking
they are looking

Past Continuous
I was looking
you were looking
he/she/it was looking
we were looking
you were looking
they were looking

Present Perfect Continuous
I have been looking
you have been looking
he/she/it has been looking
we have been looking
you have been looking
they have been looking

Past Perfect Continuous
I had been looking
you had been looking
he/she/it had been looking
we had been looking
you had been looking
they had been looking

Future

Future I
I will look
you will look
he/she/it will look
we will look
you will look
they will look

Future I Continuous
I will be looking
you will be looking
he/she/it will be looking
we will be looking
you will be looking
they will be looking

Future II
I will have looked
you will have looked
he/she/it will have looked
we will have looked
you will have looked
they will have looked

Future II Continuous
I will have been looking
you will have been looking
he/she/it will have been looking
we will have been looking
you will have been looking
they will have been looking

Conditional

Conditional II
I would look
you would look
he/she/it would look
we would look
you would look
they would look

Conditional Past
I would have looked
you would have looked
he/she/it would have looked
we would have looked
you would have looked
they would have looked

Imperative
look

Gerund
looking

Past Participle
looked

Verbtabellen

+ *-ing* wird ∉(siehe S. 153)

Unregelmäßig

lose | verlieren

Simple

Present Simple
I lose
you lose
he/she/it loses
we lose
you lose
they lose

Past Simple
I lost
you lost
he/she/it lost
we lost
you lost
they lost

Present Perfect
I have lost
you have lost
he/she/it has lost
we have lost
you have lost
they have lost

Past Perfect
I had lost
you had lost
he/she/it had lost
we had lost
you had lost
they had lost

Continuous

Present Continuous
I am losing
you are losing
he/she/it is losing
we are losing
you are losing
they are losing

Past Continuous
I was losing
you were losing
he/she/it was losing
we were losing
you were losing
they were losing

Present Perfect Continuous
I have been losing
you have been losing
he/she/it has been losing
we have been losing
you have been losing
they have been losing

Past Perfect Continuous
I had been losing
you had been losing
he/she/it had been losing
we had been losing
you had been losing
they had been losing

Future

Future I
I will lose
you will lose
he/she/it will lose
we will lose
you will lose
they will lose

Future I Continuous
I will be losing
you will be losing
he/she/it will be losing
we will be losing
you will be losing
they will be losing

Future II
I will have lost
you will have lost
he/she/it will have lost
we will have lost
you will have lost
they will have lost

Future II Continuous
I will have been losing
you will have been losing
he/she/it will have been losing
we will have been losing
you will have been losing
they will have been losing

Conditional

Conditional II
I would lose
you would lose
he/she/it would lose
we would lose
you would lose
they would lose

Conditional Past
I would have lost
you would have lost
he/she/it would have lost
we would have lost
you would have lost
they would have lost

Imperative
lose

Gerund
losing

Past Participle
lost

Verbtabellen

Unregelmäßig

make | machen

+ *-ing* wird ∅ (siehe S. 153)

Simple

Present Simple
I make
you make
he/she/it makes
we make
you make
they make

Past Simple
I made
you made
he/she/it made
we made
you made
they made

Present Perfect
I have made
you have made
he/she/it has made
we have made
you have made
they have made

Past Perfect
I had made
you had made
he/she/it had made
we had made
you had made
they had made

Continuous

Present Continuous
I am making
you are making
he/she/it is making
we are making
you are making
they are making

Past Continuous
I was making
you were making
he/she/it was making
we were making
you were making
they were making

Present Perfect Continuous
I have been making
you have been making
he/she/it has been making
we have been making
you have been making
they have been making

Past Perfect Continuous
I had been making
you had been making
he/she/it had been making
we had been making
you had been making
they had been making

Future

Future I
I will make
you will make
he/she/it will make
we will make
you will make
they will make

Future I Continuous
I will be making
you will be making
he/she/it will be making
we will be making
you will be making
they will be making

Future II
I will have made
you will have made
he/she/it will have made
we will have made
you will have made
they will have made

Future II Continuous
I will have been making
you will have been making
he/she/it will have been making
we will have been making
you will have been making
they will have been making

Conditional

Conditional II
I would make
you would make
he/she/it would make
we would make
you would make
they would make

Conditional Past
I would have made
you would have made
he/she/it would have made
we would have made
you would have made
they would have made

Imperative
make

Gerund
making

Past Participle
made

Verbtabellen

Unregelmäßig

meet | treffen

Simple

Present Simple
I meet
you meet
he/she/it meets
we meet
you meet
they meet

Past Simple
I met
you met
he/she/it met
we met
you met
they met

Present Perfect
I have met
you have met
he/she/it has met
we have met
you have met
they have met

Past Perfect
I had met
you had met
he/she/it had met
we had met
you had met
they had met

Continuous

Present Continuous
I am meeting
you are meeting
he/she/it is meeting
we are meeting
you are meeting
they are meeting

Past Continuous
I was meeting
you were meeting
he/she/it was meeting
we were meeting
you were meeting
they were meeting

Present Perfect Continuous
I have been meeting
you have been meeting
he/she/it has been meeting
we have been meeting
you have been meeting
they have been meeting

Past Perfect Continuous
I had been meeting
you had been meeting
he/she/it had been meeting
we had been meeting
you had been meeting
they had been meeting

Future

Future I
I will meet
you will meet
he/she/it will meet
we will meet
you will meet
they will meet

Future I Continuous
I will be meeting
you will be meeting
he/she/it will be meeting
we will be meeting
you will be meeting
they will be meeting

Future II
I will have met
you will have met
he/she/it will have met
we will have met
you will have met
they will have met

Future II Continuous
I will have been meeting
you will have been meeting
he/she/it will have been meeting
we will have been meeting
you will have been meeting
they will have been meeting

Conditional

Conditional II
I would meet
you would meet
he/she/it would meet
we would meet
you would meet
they would meet

Conditional Past
I would have met
you would have met
he/she/it would have met
we would have met
you would have met
they would have met

Imperative
meet

Gerund
meeting

Past Participle
met

Verbtabellen

Unregelmäßig
Modalverb

must/have to | müssen/sollen

Must kann nur in seiner Grundform gebraucht werden. Ansonsten wird *have to* benutzt. */Have to* im *Present-* und *Past Continuous* wird meistens mit *always* verwendet und drückt ein negatives Empfinden aus.

Simple

Present Simple
I	must/have to
you	must/have to
he/she/it	must/has to
we	must/have to
you	must/have to
they	must/have to

Past Simple
I	had to
you	had to
he/she/it	had to
we	had to
you	had to
they	had to

Present Perfect
I	have	had to
you	have	had to
he/she/it	has	had to
we	have	had to
you	have	had to
they	have	had to

Past Perfect
I	had	had to
you	had	had to
he/she/it	had	had to
we	had	had to
you	had	had to
they	had	had to

Continuous

Present Continuous
I	am	having to
you	are	having to
he/she/it	is	having to
we	are	having to
you	are	having to
they	are	having to

Past Continuous
I	was	having to
you	were	having to
he/she/it	was	having to
we	were	having to
you	were	having to
they	were	having to

Present Perfect Continuous
I	have	been	having to
you	have	been	having to
he/she/it	has	been	having to
we	have	been	having to
you	have	been	having to
they	have	been	having to

Past Perfect Continuous
I	had	been	having to
you	had	been	having to
he/she/it	had	been	having to
we	had	been	having to
you	had	been	having to
they	had	been	having to

Future

Future I
I	will	have	to
you	will	have	to
he/she/it	will	have	to
we	will	have	to
you	will	have	to
they	will	have	to

Future I Continuous
I	will be having to
you	will be having to
he/she/it	will be having to
we	will be having to
you	will be having to
they	will be having to

Future II
I	will have	had to
you	will have	had to
he/she/it	will have	had to
we	will have	had to
you	will have	had to
they	will have	had to

Future II Continuous
I	will have been having to
you	will have been having to
he/she/it	will have been having to
we	will have been having to
you	will have been having to
they	will have been having to

Conditional

Conditional II
I	would have	to
you	would have	to
he/she/it	would have	to
we	would have	to
you	would have	to
they	would have	to

Conditional Past
I	would have	had to
you	would have	had to
he/she/it	would have	had to
we	would have	had to
you	would have	had to
they	would have	had to

Imperative
—

Gerund
having to

Past Participle
had to

Verbtabellen

Regelmäßig

need | brauchen

Simple

Present Simple
I need
you need
he/she/it needs
we need
you need
they need

Past Simple
I needed
you needed
he/she/it needed
we needed
you needed
they needed

Present Perfect
I have needed
you have needed
he/she/it has needed
we have needed
you have needed
they have needed

Past Perfect
I had needed
you had needed
he/she/it had needed
we had needed
you had needed
they had needed

Continuous

Present Continuous
I am needing
you are needing
he/she/it is needing
we are needing
you are needing
they are needing

Past Continuous
I was needing
you were needing
he/she/it was needing
we were needing
you were needing
they were needing

Present Perfect Continuous
I have been needing
you have been needing
he/she/it has been needing
we have been needing
you have been needing
they have been needing

Past Perfect Continuous
I had been needing
you had been needing
he/she/it had been needing
we had been needing
you had been needing
they had been needing

Future

Future I
I will need
you will need
he/she/it will need
we will need
you will need
they will need

Future I Continuous
I will be needing
you will be needing
he/she/it will be needing
we will be needing
you will be needing
they will be needing

Future II
I will have needed
you will have needed
he/she/it will have needed
we will have needed
you will have needed
they will have needed

Future II Contlimous
I will have been needing
you will have been needing
he/she/it will have been needing
we will have been needing
you will have been needing
they will have been needing

Conditional

Conditional II
I would need
you would need
he/she/it would need
we would need
you would need
they would need

Conditional Past
I would have needed
you would have needed
he/she/it would have needed
we would have needed
you would have needed
they would have needed

Imperative
—

Gerund
needing

Past Participle
needed

Verbtabellen

Regelmäßig

open | öffnen

Simple

Present Simple
I open
you open
he/she/it opens
we open
you open
they open

Past Simple
I opened
you opened
he/she/it opened
we opened
you opened
they opened

Present Perfect
I have opened
you have opened
he/she/it has opened
we have opened
you have opened
they have opened

Past Perfect
I had opened
you had opened
he/she/it had opened
we had opened
you had opened
they had opened

Continuous

Present Continuous
I am opening
you are opening
he/she/it is opening
we are opening
you are opening
they are opening

Past Continuous
I was opening
you were opening
he/she/it was opening
we were opening
you were opening
they were opening

Present Perfect Continuous
I have been opening
you have been opening
he/she/it has been opening
we have been opening
you have been opening
they have been opening

Past Perfect Continuous
I had been opening
you had been opening
he/she/it had been opening
we had been opening
you had been opening
they had been opening

Future

Future I
I will open
you will open
he/she/it will open
we will open
you will open
they will open

Future I Continuous
I will be opening
you will be opening
he/she/it will be opening
we will be opening
you will be opening
they will be opening

Future II
I will have opened
you will have opened
he/she/it will have opened
we will have opened
you will have opened
they will have opened

Future II Continuous
I will have been opening
you will have been opening
he/she/it will have been opening
we will have been opening
you will have been opening
they will have been opening

Conditional

Conditional II
I would open
you would open
he/she/it would open
we would open
you would open
they would open

Conditional Past
I would have opened
you would have opened
he/she/it would have opened
we would have opened
you would have opened
they would have opened

Imperative
open

Gerund
opening

Past Participle
opened

Verbtabellen

Unregelmäßig

pay | zahlen

Simple

Present Simple
I pay
you pay
he/she/it pays
we pay
you pay
they pay

Past Simple
I paid
you paid
he/she/it paid
we paid
you paid
they paid

Present Perfect
I have paid
you have paid
he/she/it has paid
we have paid
you have paid
they have paid

Past Perfect
I had paid
you had paid
he/she/it had paid
we had paid
you had paid
they had paid

Continuous

Present Continuous
I am paying
you are paying
he/she/it is paying
we are paying
you are paying
they are paying

Past Continuous
I was paying
you were paying
he/she/it was paying
we were paying
you were paying
they were paying

Present Perfect Continuous
I have been paying
you have been paying
he/she/it has been paying
we have been paying
you have been paying
they have been paying

Past Perfect Continuous
I had been paying
you had been paying
he/she/it had been paying
we had been paying
you had been paying
they had been paying

Future

Future I
I will pay
you will pay
he/she/it will pay
we will pay
you will pay
they will pay

Future I Continuous
I will be paying
you will be paying
he/she/it will be paying
we will be paying
you will be paying
they will be paying

Future II
I will have paid
you will have paid
he/she/it will have paid
we will have paid
you will have paid
they will have paid

Future II Continuous
I will have been paying
you will have been paying
he/she/it will have been paying
we will have been paying
you will have been paying
they will have been paying

Conditional

Conditional II
I would pay
you would pay
he/she/it would pay
we would pay
you would pay
they would pay

Conditional Past
I would have paid
you would have paid
he/she/it would have paid
we would have paid
you would have paid
they would have paid

Imperative
pay

Gerund
paying

Past Participle
paid

Regelmäßig

play | spielen

Simple

Present Simple
I play
you play
he/she/it plays
we play
you play
they play

Past Simple
I played
you played
he/she/it played
we played
you played
they played

Present Perfect
I have played
you have played
he/she/it has played
we have played
you have played
they have played

Past Perfect
I had played
you had played
he/she/it had played
we had played
you had played
they had played

Continuous

Present Continuous
I am playing
you are playing
he/she/it is playing
we are playing
you are playing
they are playing

Past Continuous
I was playing
you were playing
he/she/it was playing
we were playing
you were playing
they were playing

Present Perfect Continuous
I have been playing
you have been playing
he/she/it has been playing
we have been playing
you have been playing
they have been playing

Past Perfect Continuous
I had been playing
you had been playing
he/she/it had been playing
we had been playing
you had been playing
they had been playing

Future

Future I
I will play
you will play
he/she/it will play
we will play
you will play
they will play

Future I Continuous
I will be playing
you will be playing
he/she/it will be playing
we will be playing
you will be playing
they will be playing

Future II
I will have played
you will have played
he/she/it will have played
we will have played
you will have played
they will have played

Future II Continuous
I will have been playing
you will have been playing
he/she/it will have been playing
we will have been playing
you will have been playing
they will have been playing

Conditional

Conditional II
I would play
you would play
he/she/it would play
we would play
you would play
they would play

Conditional Past
I would have played
you would have played
he/she/it would have played
we would have played
you would have played
they would have played

Imperative
play

Gerund
playing

Past Participle
played

Verbtabellen

Konsonantenverdopplung
(siehe S. 152)

Unregelmäßig

put | setzen/stellen/legen

Simple

Present Simple
- I put
- you put
- he/she/it puts
- we put
- you put
- they put

Past Simple
- I put
- you put
- he/she/it put
- we put
- you put
- they put

Present Perfect
- I have put
- you have put
- he/she/it has put
- we have put
- you have put
- they have put

Past Perfect
- I had put
- you had put
- he/she/it had put
- we had put
- you had put
- they had put

Continuous

Present Continuous
- I am putting
- you are putting
- he/she/it is putting
- we are putting
- you are putting
- they are putting

Past Continuous
- I was putting
- you were putting
- he/she/it was putting
- we were putting
- you were putting
- they were putting

Present Perfect Continuous
- I have been putting
- you have been putting
- he/she/it has been putting
- we have been putting
- you have been putting
- they have been putting

Past Perfect Continuous
- I had been putting
- you had been putting
- he/she/it had been putting
- we had been putting
- you had been putting
- they had been putting

Future

Future I
- I will put
- you will put
- he/she/it will put
- we will put
- you will put
- they will put

Future I Continuous
- I will be putting
- you will be putting
- he/she/it will be putting
- we will be putting
- you will be putting
- they will be putting

Future II
- I will have put
- you will have put
- he/she/it will have put
- we will have put
- you will have put
- they will have put

Future II Continuous
- I will have been putting
- you will have been putting
- he/she/it will have been putting
- we will have been putting
- you will have been putting
- they will have been putting

Conditional

Conditional II
- I would put
- you would put
- he/she/it would put
- we would put
- you would put
- they would put

Conditional Past
- I would have put
- you would have put
- he/she/it would have put
- we would have put
- you would have put
- they would have put

Imperative
put

Gerund
putting

Past Participle
put

Verbtabellen

Unregelmäßig

read | lesen

Die *Past simple*-Form und das *Partizip Perfekt* werden wie die Farbe rot – *red* ausgesprochen [red].

Simple

Present Simple
I read
you read
he/she/it reads
we read
you read
they read

Past Simple
I read
you read
he/she/it read
we read
you read
they read

Present Perfect
I have read
you have read
he/she/it has read
we have read
you have read
they have read

Past Perfect
I had read
you had read
he/she/it had read
we had read
you had read
they had read

Continuous

Present Continuous
I am reading
you are reading
he/she/it is reading
we are reading
you are reading
they are reading

Past Continuous
I was reading
you were reading
he/she/it was reading
we were reading
you were reading
they were reading

Present Perfect Continuous
I have been reading
you have been reading
he/she/it has been reading
we have been reading
you have been reading
they have been reading

Past Perfect Continuous
I had been reading
you had been reading
he/she/it had been reading
we had been reading
you had been reading
they had been reading

Future

Future I
I will read
you will read
he/she/it will read
we will read
you will read
they will read

Future I Continuous
I will be reading
you will be reading
he/she/it will be reading
we will be reading
you will be reading
they will be reading

Future II
I will have read
you will have read
he/she/it will have read
we will have read
you will have read
they will have read

Future II Continuous
I will have been reading
you will have been reading
he/she/it will have been reading
we will have been reading
you will have been reading
they will have been reading

Conditional

Conditional II
I would read
you would read
he/she/it would read
we would read
you would read
they would read

Conditional Past
I would have read
you would have read
he/she/it would have read
we would have read
you would have read
they would have read

Imperative
read

Gerund
reading

Past Participle
read

Verbtabellen

Konsonantenverdopplung
(siehe S. 152)

Unregelmäßig

run | laufen/rennen

Simple

Present Simple
I run
you run
he/she/it runs
we run
you run
they run

Past Simple
I ran
you ran
he/she/it ran
we ran
you ran
they ran

Present Perfect
I have run
you have run
he/she/it has run
we have run
you have run
they have run

Past Perfect
I had run
you had run
he/she/it had run
we had run
you had run
they had run

Continuous

Present Continuous
I am running
you are running
he/she/it is running
we are running
you are running
they are running

Past Continuous
I was running
you were running
he/she/it was running
we were running
you were running
they were running

Present Perfect Continuous
I have been running
you have been running
he/she/it has been running
we have been running
you have been running
they have been running

Past Perfect Continuous
I had been running
you had been running
he/she/it had been running
we had been running
you had been running
they had been running

Future

Future I
I will run
you will run
he/she/it will run
we will run
you will run
they will run

Future I Continuous
I will berunning
you will berunning
he/she/it will berunning
we will berunning
you will berunning
they will berunning

Future II
I will have run
you will have run
he/she/it will have run
we will have run
you will have run
they will have run

Future II Contlimous
I will have been running
you will have been running
he/she/it will have been running
we will have been running
you will have been running
they will have been running

Conditional

Conditional II
I would run
you would run
he/she/it would run
we would run
you would run
they would run

Conditional Past
I would have run
you would have run
he/she/it would have run
we would have run
you would have run
they would have run

Imperative
run

Gerund
running

Past Participle
run

Verbtabellen

Unregelmäßig

say | sagen

Die Aussprache von *says* weicht von den restlichen Formen ab. Es wird [sez] ausgesprochen

Simple

Present Simple
I say
you say
he/she/it says
we say
you say
they say

Past Simple
I said
you said
he/she/it said
we said
you said
they said

Present Perfect
I have said
you have said
he/she/it has said
we have said
you have said
they have said

Past Perfect
I had said
you had said
he/she/it had said
we had said
you had said
they had said

Continuous

Present Continuous
I am saying
you are saying
he/she/it is saying
we are saying
you are saying
they are saying

Past Continuous
I was saying
you were saying
he/she/it was saying
we were saying
you were saying
they were saying

Present Perfect Continuous
I have been saying
you have been saying
he/she/it has been saying
we have been saying
you have been saying
they have been saying

Past Perfect Continuous
I had been saying
you had been saying
he/she/it had been saying
we had been saying
you had been saying
they had been saying

Future

Future I
I will say
you will say
he/she/it will say
we will say
you will say
they will say

Future I Continuous
I will be saying
you will be saying
he/she/it will be saying
we will be saying
you will be saying
they will be saying

Future II
I will have said
you will have said
he/she/it will have said
we will have said
you will have said
they will have said

Future II Continuous
I will have been saying
you will have been saying
he/she/it will have been saying
we will have been saying
you will have been saying
they will have been saying

Conditional

Conditional II
I would say
you would say
he/she/it would say
we would say
you would say
they would say

Conditional Past
I would have said
you would have said
he/she/it would have said
we would have said
you would have said
they would have said

Imperative
say

Gerund
saying

Past Participle
said

Verbtabellen

Unregelmäßig

see | sehen

Simple

Present Simple
I see
you see
he/she/it sees
we see
you see
they see

Past Simple
I saw
you saw
he/she/it saw
we saw
you saw
they saw

Present Perfect
I have seen
you have seen
he/she/it has seen
we have seen
you have seen
they have seen

Past Perfect
I had seen
you had seen
he/she/it had seen
we had seen
you had seen
they had seen

Continuous

Present Continuous
I am seeing
you are seeing
he/she/it is seeing
we are seeing
you are seeing
they are seeing

Past Continuous
I was seeing
you were seeing
he/she/it was seeing
we were seeing
you were seeing
they were seeing

Present Perfect Continuous
I have been seeing
you have been seeing
he/she/it has been seeing
we have been seeing
you have been seeing
they have been seeing

Past Perfect Continuous
I had been seeing
you had been seeing
he/she/it had been seeing
we had been seeing
you had been seeing
they had been seeing

Future

Future I
I will see
you will see
he/she/it will see
we will see
you will see
they will see

Future I Continuous
I will be seeing
you will be seeing
he/she/it will be seeing
we will be seeing
you will be seeing
they will be seeing

Future II
I will have seen
you will have seen
he/she/it will have seen
we will have seen
you will have seen
they will have seen

Future II Continuous
I will have been seeing
you will have been seeing
he/she/it will have been seeing
we will have been seeing
you will have been seeing
they will have been seeing

Conditional

Conditional II
I would see
you would see
he/she/it would see
we would see
you would see
they would see

Conditional Past
I would have seen
you would have seen
he/she/it would have seen
we would have seen
you would have seen
they would have seen

Imperative
see

Gerund
seeing

Past Participle
seen

Unregelmäßig

sell | verkaufen

Simple

Present Simple
I sell
you sell
he/she/it sells
we sell
you sell
they sell

Past Simple
I sold
you sold
he/she/it sold
we sold
you sold
they sold

Present Perfect
I have sold
you have sold
he/she/it has sold
we have sold
you have sold
they have sold

Past Perfect
I had sold
you had sold
he/she/it had sold
we had sold
you had sold
they had sold

Continuous

Present Continuous
I am selling
you are selling
he/she/it is selling
we are selling
you are selling
they are selling

Past Continuous
I was selling
you were selling
he/she/it was selling
we were selling
you were selling
they were selling

Present Perfect Continuous
I have been selling
you have been selling
he/she/it has been selling
we have been selling
you have been selling
they have been selling

Past Perfect Continuous
I had been selling
you had been selling
he/she/it had been selling
we had been selling
you had been selling
they had been selling

Future

Future I
I will sell
you will sell
he/she/it will sell
we will sell
you will sell
they will sell

Future I Continuous
I will be selling
you will be selling
he/she/it will be selling
we will be selling
you will be selling
they will be selling

Future II
I will have sold
you will have sold
he/she/it will have sold
we will have sold
you will have sold
they will have sold

Future II Continuous
I will have been selling
you will have been selling
he/she/it will have been selling
we will have been selling
you will have been selling
they will have been selling

Conditional

Conditional II
I would sell
you would sell
he/she/it would sell
we would sell
you would sell
they would sell

Conditional Past
I would have sold
you would have sold
he/she/it would have sold
we would have sold
you would have sold
they would have sold

Imperative
sell

Gerund
selling

Past Participle
sold

Verbtabellen

Unregelmäßig

send | schicken

Simple

Present Simple
I send
you send
he/she/it sends
we send
you send
they send

Past Simple
I sent
you sent
he/she/it sent
we sent
you sent
they sent

Present Perfect
I have sent
you have sent
he/she/it has sent
we have sent
you have sent
they have sent

Past Perfect
I had sent
you had sent
he/she/it had sent
we had sent
you had sent
they had sent

Continuous

Present Continuous
I am sending
you are sending
he/she/it is sending
we are sending
you are sending
they are sending

Past Continuous
I was sending
you were sending
he/she/it was sending
we were sending
you were sending
they were sending

Present Perfect Continuous
I have been sending
you have been sending
he/she/it has been sending
we have been sending
you have been sending
they have been sending

Past Perfect Continuous
I had been sending
you had been sending
he/she/it had been sending
we had been sending
you had been sending
they had been sending

Future

Future I
I will send
you will send
he/she/it will send
we will send
you will send
they will send

Future I Continuous
I will be sending
you will be sending
he/she/it will be sending
we will be sending
you will be sending
they will be sending

Future II
I will have sent
you will have sent
he/she/it will have sent
we will have sent
you will have sent
they will have sent

Future II Continuous
I will have been sending
you will have been sending
he/she/it will have been sending
we will have been sending
you will have been sending
they will have been sending

Conditional

Conditional II
I would send
you would send
he/she/it would send
we would send
you would send
they would send

Conditional Past
I would have sent
you would have sent
he/she/it would have sent
we would have sent
you would have sent
they would have sent

Imperative
send

Gerund
sending

Past Participle
sent

Verbtabellen

Unregelmäßig

shut | schließen

Konsonantenverdopplung
(siehe S. 152)

Simple

Present Simple
I shut
you shut
he/she/it shuts
we shut
you shut
they shut

Past Simple
I shut
you shut
he/she/it shut
we shut
you shut
they shut

Present Perfect
I have shut
you have shut
he/she/it has shut
we have shut
you have shut
they have shut

Past Perfect
I had shut
you had shut
he/she/it had shut
we had shut
you had shut
they had shut

Continuous

Present Continuous
I am shutting
you are shutting
he/she/it is shutting
we are shutting
you are shutting
they are shutting

Past Continuous
I was shutting
you were shutting
he/she/it was shutting
we were shutting
you were shutting
they were shutting

Present Perfect Continuous
I have been shutting
you have been shutting
he/she/it has been shutting
we have been shutting
you have been shutting
they have been shutting

Past Perfect Continuous
I had been shutting
you had been shutting
he/she/it had been shutting
we had been shutting
you had been shutting
they had been shutting

Future

Future I
I will shut
you will shut
he/she/it will shut
we will shut
you will shut
they will shut

Future I Continuous
I will be shutting
you will be shutting
he/she/it will be shutting
we will be shutting
you will be shutting
they will be shutting

Future II
I will have shut
you will have shut
he/she/it will have shut
we will have shut
you will have shut
they will have shut

Future II Continuous
I will have been shutting
you will have been shutting
he/she/it will have been shutting
we will have been shutting
you will have been shutting
they will have been shutting

Conditional

Conditional II
I would shut
you would shut
he/she/it would shut
we would shut
you would shut
they would shut

Conditional Past
I would have shut
you would have shut
he/she/it would have shut
we would have shut
you would have shut
they would have shut

Imperative
shut

Gerund
shutting

Past Participle
shut

Verbtabellen

Konsonantenverdopplung
(siehe S. 152)

Unregelmäßig

sit | sitzen

Simple

Present Simple
I sit
you sit
he/she/it sits
we sit
you sit
they sit

Past Simple
I sat
you sat
he/she/it sat
we sat
you sat
they sat

Present Perfect
I have sat
you have sat
he/she/it has sat
we have sat
you have sat
they have sat

Past Perfect
I had sat
you had sat
he/she/it had sat
we had sat
you had sat
they had sat

Continuous

Present Continuous
I am sitting
you are sitting
he/she/it is sitting
we are sitting
you are sitting
they are sitting

Past Continuous
I was sitting
you were sitting
he/she/it was sitting
we were sitting
you were sitting
they were sitting

Present Perfect Continuous
I have been sitting
you have been sitting
he/she/it has been sitting
we have been sitting
you have been sitting
they have been sitting

Past Perfect Continuous
I had been sitting
you had been sitting
he/she/it had been sitting
we had been sitting
you had been sitting
they had been sitting

Future

Future I
I will sit
you will sit
he/she/it will sit
we will sit
you will sit
they will sit

Future I Continuous
I will be sitting
you will be sitting
he/she/it will be sitting
we will be sitting
you will be sitting
they will be sitting

Future II
I will have sat
you will have sat
he/she/it will have sat
we will have sat
you will have sat
they will have sat

Future II Continuous
I will have been sitting
you will have been sitting
he/she/it will have been sitting
we will have been sitting
you will have been sitting
they will have been sitting

Conditional

Conditional II
I would sit
you would sit
he/she/it would sit
we would sit
you would sit
they would sit

Conditional Past
I would have sat
you would have sat
he/she/it would have sat
we would have sat
you would have sat
they would have sat

Imperative
sit

Gerund
sitting

Past Participle
sat

Verbtabellen

Unregelmäßig

sleep | schlafen

Simple

Present Simple
I sleep
you sleep
he/she/it sleeps
we sleep
you sleep
they sleep

Past Simple
I slept
you slept
he/she/it slept
we slept
you slept
they slept

Present Perfect
I have slept
you have slept
he/she/it has slept
we have slept
you have slept
they have slept

Past Perfect
I had slept
you had slept
he/she/it had slept
we had slept
you had slept
they had slept

Continuous

Present Continuous
I am sleeping
you are sleeping
he/she/it is sleeping
we are sleeping
you are sleeping
they are sleeping

Past Continuous
I was sleeping
you were sleeping
he/she/it was sleeping
we were sleeping
you were sleeping
they were sleeping

Present Perfect Continuous
I have been sleeping
you have been sleeping
he/she/it has been sleeping
we have been sleeping
you have been sleeping
they have been sleeping

Past Perfect Continuous
I had been sleeping
you had been sleeping
he/she/it had been sleeping
we had been sleeping
you had been sleeping
they had been sleeping

Future

Future I
I will sleep
you will sleep
he/she/it will sleep
we will sleep
you will sleep
they will sleep

Future I Continuous
I will be sleeping
you will be sleeping
he/she/it will be sleeping
we will be sleeping
you will be sleeping
they will be sleeping

Future II
I will have slept
you will have slept
he/she/it will have slept
we will have slept
you will have slept
they will have slept

Future II Continuous
I will have been sleeping
you will have been sleeping
he/she/it will have been sleeping
we will have been sleeping
you will have been sleeping
they will have been sleeping

Conditional

Conditional II
I would sleep
you would sleep
he/she/it would sleep
we would sleep
you would sleep
they would sleep

Conditional Past
I would have slept
you would have slept
he/she/it would have slept
we would have slept
you would have slept
they would have slept

Imperative
sleep

Gerund
sleeping

Past Participle
slept

Verbtabellen

Unregelmäßig

speak | sprechen

Simple

Present Simple
I speak
you speak
he/she/it speaks
we speak
you speak
they speak

Past Simple
I spoke
you spoke
he/she/it spoke
we spoke
you spoke
they spoke

Present Perfect
I have spoken
you have spoken
he/she/it has spoken
we have spoken
you have spoken
they have spoken

Past Perfect
I had spoken
you had spoken
he/she/it had spoken
we had spoken
you had spoken
they had spoken

Continuous

Present Continuous
I am speaking
you are speaking
he/she/it is speaking
we are speaking
you are speaking
they are speaking

Past Continuous
I was speaking
you were speaking
he/she/it was speaking
we were speaking
you were speaking
they were speaking

Present Perfect Continuous
I have been speaking
you have been speaking
he/she/it has been speaking
we have been speaking
you have been speaking
they have been speaking

Past Perfect Continuous
I had been speaking
you had been speaking
he/she/it had been speaking
we had been speaking
you had been speaking
they had been speaking

Future

Future I
I will speak
you will speak
he/she/it will speak
we will speak
you will speak
they will speak

Future I Continuous
I will be speaking
you will be speaking
he/she/it will be speaking
we will be speaking
you will be speaking
they will be speaking

Future II
I will have spoken
you will have spoken
he/she/it will have spoken
we will have spoken
you will have spoken
they will have spoken

Future II Continuous
I will have been speaking
you will have been speaking
he/she/it will have been speaking
we will have been speaking
you will have been speaking
they will have been speaking

Conditional

Conditional II
I would speak
you would speak
he/she/it would speak
we would speak
you would speak
they would speak

Conditional Past
I would have spoken
you would have spoken
he/she/it would have spoken
we would have spoken
you would have spoken
they would have spoken

Imperative
speak

Gerund
speaking

Past Participle
spoken

Verbtabellen

Unregelmäßig

spend | ausgeben/verbringen

Simple

Present Simple
I spend
you spend
he/she/it spends
we spend
you spend
they spend

Past Simple
I spent
you spent
he/she/it spent
we spent
you spent
they spent

Present Perfect
I have spent
you have spent
he/she/it has spent
we have spent
you have spent
they have spent

Past Perfect
I had spent
you had spent
he/she/it had spent
we had spent
you had spent
they had spent

Continuous

Present Continuous
I am spending
you are spending
he/she/it is spending
we are spending
you are spending
they are spending

Past Continuous
I was spending
you were spending
he/she/it was spending
we were spending
you were spending
they were spending

Present Perfect Continuous
I have been spending
you have been spending
he/she/it has been spending
we have been spending
you have been spending
they have been spending

Past Perfect Continuous
I had been spending
you had been spending
he/she/it had been spending
we had been spending
you had been spending
they had been spending

Future

Future I
I will spend
you will spend
he/she/it will spend
we will spend
you will spend
they will spend

Future I Continuous
I will be spending
you will be spending
he/she/it will be spending
we will be spending
you will be spending
they will be spending

Future II
I will have spent
you will have spent
he/she/it will have spent
we will have spent
you will have spent
they will have spent

Future II Continuous
I will have been spending
you will have been spending
he/she/it will have been spending
we will have been spending
you will have been spending
they will have been spending

Conditional

Conditional II
I would spend
you would spend
he/she/it would spend
we would spend
you would spend
they would spend

Conditional Past
I would have spent
you would have spent
he/she/it would have spent
we would have spent
you would have spent
they would have spent

Imperative
spend

Gerund
spending

Past Participle
spent

Verbtabellen

Unregelmäßig

stand | stehen

Simple

Present Simple
- I stand
- you stand
- he/she/it stands
- we stand
- you stand
- they stand

Past Simple
- I stood
- you stood
- he/she/it stood
- we stood
- you stood
- they stood

Present Perfect
- I have stood
- you have stood
- he/she/it has stood
- we have stood
- you have stood
- they have stood

Past Perfect
- I had stood
- you had stood
- he/she/it had stood
- we had stood
- you had stood
- they had stood

Continuous

Present Continuous
- I am standing
- you are standing
- he/she/it is standing
- we are standing
- you are standing
- they are standing

Past Continuous
- I was standing
- you were standing
- he/she/it was standing
- we were standing
- you were standing
- they were standing

Present Perfect Continuous
- I have been standing
- you have been standing
- he/she/it has been standing
- we have been standing
- you have been standing
- they have been standing

Past Perfect Continuous
- I had been standing
- you had been standing
- he/she/it had been standing
- we had been standing
- you had been standing
- they had been standing

Future

Future I
- I will stand
- you will stand
- he/she/it will stand
- we will stand
- you will stand
- they will stand

Future I Continuous
- I will be standing
- you will be standing
- he/she/it will be standing
- we will be standing
- you will be standing
- they will be standing

Future II
- I will have stood
- you will have stood
- he/she/it will have stood
- we will have stood
- you will have stood
- they will have stood

Future II Continuous
- I will have been standing
- you will have been standing
- he/she/it will have been standing
- we will have been standing
- you will have been standing
- they will have been standing

Conditional

Conditional II
- I would stand
- you would stand
- he/she/it would stand
- we would stand
- you would stand
- they would stand

Conditional Past
- I would have stood
- you would have stood
- he/she/it would have stood
- we would have stood
- you would have stood
- they would have stood

Imperative
stand

Gerund
standing

Past Participle
stood

Verbtabellen

Regelmäßig

stay | bleiben/übernachten

Simple

Present Simple
I stay
you stay
he/she/it stays
we stay
you stay
they stay

Past Simple
I stayed
you stayed
he/she/it stayed
we stayed
you stayed
they stayed

Present Perfect
I have stayed
you have stayed
he/she/it has stayed
we have stayed
you have stayed
they have stayed

Past Perfect
I had stayed
you had stayed
he/she/it had stayed
we had stayed
you had stayed
they had stayed

Continuous

Present Continuous
I am staying
you are staying
he/she/it is staying
we are staying
you are staying
they are staying

Past Continuous
I was staying
you were staying
he/she/it was staying
we were staying
you were staying
they were staying

Present Perfect Continuous
I have been staying
you have been staying
he/she/it has been staying
we have been staying
you have been staying
they have been staying

Past Perfect Continuous
I had been staying
you had been staying
he/she/it had been staying
we had been staying
you had been staying
they had been staying

Future

Future I
I will stay
you will stay
he/she/it will stay
we will stay
you will stay
they will stay

Future I Continuous
I will be staying
you will be staying
he/she/it will be staying
we will be staying
you will be staying
they will be staying

Future II
I will have stayed
you will have stayed
he/she/it will have stayed
we will have stayed
you will have stayed
they will have stayed

Future II Continuous
I will have been staying
you will have been staying
he/she/it will have been staying
we will have been staying
you will have been staying
they will have been staying

Conditional

Conditional II
I would stay
you would stay
he/she/it would stay
we would stay
you would stay
they would stay

Conditional Past
I would have stayed
you would have stayed
he/she/it would have stayed
we would have stayed
you would have stayed
they would have stayed

Imperative
stay

Gerund
staying

Past Participle
stayed

Verbtabellen

Konsonantenverdopplung
(siehe S. 152)

Unregelmäßig

swim | schwimmen

Simple

Present Simple
I swim
you swim
he/she/it swims
we swim
you swim
they swim

Past Simple
I swam
you swam
he/she/it swam
we swam
you swam
they swam

Present Perfect
I have swum
you have swum
he/she/it has swum
we have swum
you have swum
they have swum

Past Perfect
I had swum
you had swum
he/she/it had swum
we had swum
you had swum
they had swum

Continuous

Present Continuous
I am swimming
you are swimming
he/she/it is swimming
we are swimming
you are swimming
they are swimming

Past Continuous
I was swimming
you were swimming
he/she/it was swimming
we were swimming
you were swimming
they were swimming

Present Perfect Continuous
I have been swimming
you have been swimming
he/she/it has been swimming
we have been swimming
you have been swimming
they have been swimming

Past Perfect Continuous
I had been swimming
you had been swimming
he/she/it had been swimming
we had been swimming
you had been swimming
they had been swimming

Future

Future I
I will swim
you will swim
he/she/it will swim
we will swim
you will swim
they will swim

Future I Continuous
I will be swimming
you will be swimming
he/she/it will be swimming
we will be swimming
you will be swimming
they will be swimming

Future II
I will have swum
you will have swum
he/she/it will have swum
we will have swum
you will have swum
they will have swum

Future II Continuous
I will have been swimming
you will have been swimming
he/she/it will have been swimming
we will have been swimming
you will have been swimming
they will have been swimming

Conditional

Conditional II
I would swim
you would swim
he/she/it would swim
we would swim
you would swim
they would swim

Conditional Past
I would have swum
you would have swum
he/she/it would have swum
we would have swum
you would have swum
they would have swum

Imperative
swim

Gerund
swimming

Past Participle
swum

Verbtabellen

Unregelmäßig

take | nehmen

+ *-ing* wird ∅ (siehe S. 153)

Simple

Present Simple
I take
you take
he/she/it takes
we take
you take
they take

Past Simple
I took
you took
he/she/it took
we took
you took
they took

Present Perfect
I have taken
you have taken
he/she/it has taken
we have taken
you have taken
they have taken

Past Perfect
I had taken
you had taken
he/she/it had taken
we had taken
you had taken
they had taken

Continuous

Present Continuous
I am taking
you are taking
he/she/it is taking
we are taking
you are taking
they are taking

Past Continuous
I was taking
you were taking
he/she/it was taking
we were taking
you were taking
they were taking

Present Perfect Continuous
I have been taking
you have been taking
he/she/it has been taking
we have been taking
you have been taking
they have been taking

Past Perfect Continuous
I had been taking
you had been taking
he/she/it had been taking
we had been taking
you had been taking
they had been taking

Future

Future I
I will take
you will take
he/she/it will take
we will take
you will take
they will take

Future I Continuous
I will be taking
you will be taking
he/she/it will be taking
we will be taking
you will be taking
they will be taking

Future II
I will have taken
you will have taken
he/she/it will have taken
we will have taken
you will have taken
they will have taken

Future II Continuous
I will have been taking
you will have been taking
he/she/it will have been taking
we will have been taking
you will have been taking
they will have been taking

Conditional

Conditional II
I would take
you would take
he/she/it would take
we would take
you would take
they would take

Conditional Past
I would have taken
you would have taken
he/she/it would have taken
we would have taken
you would have taken
they would have taken

Imperative
take

Gerund
taking

Past Participle
taken

Verbtabellen

Unregelmäßig

think | denken

Simple

Present Simple
I think
you think
he/she/it thinks
we think
you think
they think

Past Simple
I thought
you thought
he/she/it thought
we thought
you thought
they thought

Present Perfect
I have thought
you have thought
he/she/it has thought
we have thought
you have thought
they have thought

Past Perfect
I had thought
you had thought
he/she/it had thought
we had thought
you had thought
they had thought

Continuous

Present Continuous
I am thinking
you are thinking
he/she/it is thinking
we are thinking
you are thinking
they are thinking

Past Continuous
I was thinking
you were thinking
he/she/it was thinking
we were thinking
you were thinking
they were thinking

Present Perfect Continuous
I have been thinking
you have been thinking
he/she/it has been thinking
we have been thinking
you have been thinking
they have been thinking

Past Perfect Continuous
I had been thinking
you had been thinking
he/she/it had been thinking
we had been thinking
you had been thinking
they had been thinking

Future

Future I
I will think
you will think
he/she/it will think
we will think
you will think
they will think

Future I Continuous
I will be thinking
you will be thinking
he/she/it will be thinking
we will be thinking
you will be thinking
they will be thinking

Future II
I will have thought
you will have thought
he/she/it will have thought
we will have thought
you will have thought
they will have thought

Future II Continuous
I will have been thinking
you will have been thinking
he/she/it will have been thinking
we will have been thinking
you will have been thinking
they will have been thinking

Conditional

Conditional II
I would think
you would think
he/she/it would think
we would think
you would think
they would think

Conditional Past
I would have thought
you would have thought
he/she/it would have thought
we would have thought
you would have thought
they would have thought

Imperative
think

Gerund
thinking

Past Participle
thought

Verbtabellen

Regelmäßig

travel | reisen

Konsonantenverdopplung im BE (siehe S. 152). Im AE keine Verdopplung.

Simple

Present Simple
I travel
you travel
he/she/it travels
we travel
you travel
they travel

Past Simple
I travelled
you travelled
he/she/it travelled
we travelled
you travelled
they travelled

Present Perfect
I have travelled
you have travelled
he/she/it has travelled
we have travelled
you have travelled
they have travelled

Past Perfect
I had travelled
you had travelled
he/she/it had travelled
we had travelled
you had travelled
they had travelled

Continuous

Present Continuous
I am travelling
you are travelling
he/she/it is travelling
we are travelling
you are travelling
they are travelling

Past Continuous
I was travelling
you were travelling
he/she/it was travelling
we were travelling
you were travelling
they were travelling

Present Perfect Continuous
I have been travelling
you have been travelling
he/she/it has been travelling
we have been travelling
you have been travelling
they have been travelling

Past Perfect Continuous
I had been travelling
you had been travelling
he/she/it had been travelling
we had been travelling
you had been travelling
they had been travelling

Future

Future I
I will travel
you will travel
he/she/it will travel
we will travel
you will travel
they will travel

Future I Continuous
I will be travelling
you will be travelling
he/she/it will be travelling
we will be travelling
you will be travelling
they will be travelling

Future II
I will have travelled
you will have travelled
he/she/it will have travelled
we will have travelled
you will have travelled
they will have travelled

Future II Continuous
I will have been travelling
you will have been travelling
he/she/it will have been travelling
we will have been travelling
you will have been travelling
they will have been travelling

Conditional

Conditional II
I would travel
you would travel
he/she/it would travel
we would travel
you would travel
they would travel

Conditional Past
I would have travelled
you would have travelled
he/she/it would have travelled
we would have travelled
you would have travelled
they would have travelled

Imperative
travel

Gerund
travelling

Past Participle
travelled

Verbtabellen

Regelmäßig

visit | besuchen/besichtigen

Simple

Present Simple
I	visit
you	visit
he/she/it	visits
we	visit
you	visit
they	visit

Past Simple
I	visited
you	visited
he/she/it	visited
we	visited
you	visited
they	visited

Present Perfect
I	have	visited
you	have	visited
he/she/it	has	visited
we	have	visited
you	have	visited
they	have	visited

Past Perfect
I	had	visited
you	had	visited
he/she/it	had	visited
we	had	visited
you	had	visited
they	had	visited

Continuous

Present Continuous
I	am	visiting
you	are	visiting
he/she/it	is	visiting
we	are	visiting
you	are	visiting
they	are	visiting

Past Continuous
I	was	visiting
you	were	visiting
he/she/it	was	visiting
we	were	visiting
you	were	visiting
they	were	visiting

Present Perfect Continuous
I	have	been	visiting
you	have	been	visiting
he/she/it	has	been	visiting
we	have	been	visiting
you	have	been	visiting
they	have	been	visiting

Past Perfect Continuous
I	had	been	visiting
you	had	been	visiting
he/she/it	had	been	visiting
we	had	been	visiting
you	had	been	visiting
they	had	been	visiting

Future

Future I
I	will	visit
you	will	visit
he/she/it	will	visit
we	will	visit
you	will	visit
they	will	visit

Future I Continuous
I	will	be	visiting
you	will	be	visiting
he/she/it	will	be	visiting
we	will	be	visiting
you	will	be	visiting
they	will	be	visiting

Future II
I	will have	visited
you	will have	visited
he/she/it	will have	visited
we	will have	visited
you	will have	visited
they	will have	visited

Future II Contlimous
I	will have been visiting
you	will have been visiting
he/she/it	will have been visiting
we	will have been visiting
you	will have been visiting
they	will have been visiting

Conditional

Conditional II
I	would visit
you	would visit
he/she/it	would visit
we	would visit
you	would visit
they	would visit

Conditional Past
I	would have	visited
you	would have	visited
he/she/it	would have	visited
we	would have	visited
you	would have	visited
they	would have	visited

Imperative

visit

Gerund

visiting

Past Participle

visited

Verbtabellen

Regelmäßig

wait | warten

Simple

Present Simple
I wait
you wait
he/she/it waits
we wait
you wait
they wait

Past Simple
I waited
you waited
he/she/it waited
we waited
you waited
they waited

Present Perfect
I have waited
you have waited
he/she/it has waited
we have waited
you have waited
they have waited

Past Perfect
I had waited
you had waited
he/she/it had waited
we had waited
you had waited
they had waited

Continuous

Present Continuous
I am waiting
you are waiting
he/she/it is waiting
we are waiting
you are waiting
they are waiting

Past Continuous
I was waiting
you were waiting
he/she/it was waiting
we were waiting
you were waiting
they were waiting

Present Perfect Continuous
I have been waiting
you have been waiting
he/she/it has been waiting
we have been waiting
you have been waiting
they have been waiting

Past Perfect Continuous
I had been waiting
you had been waiting
he/she/it had been waiting
we had been waiting
you had been waiting
they had been waiting

Future

Future I
I will wait
you will wait
he/she/it will wait
we will wait
you will wait
they will wait

Future I Continuous
I will be waiting
you will be waiting
he/she/it will be waiting
we will be waiting
you will be waiting
they will be waiting

Future II
I will have waited
you will have waited
he/she/it will have waited
we will have waited
you will have waited
they will have waited

Future II Continuous
I will have been waiting
you will have been waiting
he/she/it will have been waiting
we will have been waiting
you will have been waiting
they will have been waiting

Conditional

Conditional II
I would wait
you would wait
he/she/it would wait
we would wait
you would wait
they would wait

Conditional Past
I would have waited
you would have waited
he/she/it would have waited
we would have waited
you would have waited
they would have waited

Imperative
wait

Gerund
waiting

Past Participle
waited

Verbtabellen

Regelmäßig
Modalverb

want | wollen/mögen

Keine *Present Continuous* Form möglich.

Simple

Present Simple
I want
you want
he/she/it wants
we want
you want
they want

Past Simple
I wanted
you wanted
he/she/it wanted
we wanted
you wanted
they wanted

Present Perfect
I have wanted
you have wanted
he/she/it has wanted
we have wanted
you have wanted
they have wanted

Past Perfect
I had wanted
you had wanted
he/she/it had wanted
we had wanted
you had wanted
they had wanted

Continuous

Present Continuous

—

Past Continuous*
I was wanting
you were wanting
he/she/it was wanting
we were wanting
you were wanting
they were wanting

Present Perfect Continuous
I have been wanting
you have been wanting
he/she/it has been wanting
we have been wanting
you have been wanting
they have been wanting

Past Perfect Continuous
I had been wanting
you had been wanting
he/she/it had been wanting
we had been wanting
you had been wanting
they had been wanting

Future

Future I
I will want
you will want
he/she/it will want
we will want
you will want
they will want

Future I Continuous
I will be wanting
you will be wanting
he/she/it will be wanting
we will be wanting
you will be wanting
they will be wanting

Future II
I will have wanted
you will have wanted
he/she/it will have wanted
we will have wanted
you will have wanted
they will have wanted

Future II Continuous
I will have been wanting
you will have been wanting
he/she/it will have been wanting
we will have been wanting
you will have been wanting
they will have been wanting

Conditional

Conditional II
I would want
you would want
he/she/it would want
we would want
you would want
they would want

Conditional Past
I would have wanted
you would have wanted
he/she/it would have wanted
we would have wanted
you would have wanted
they would have wanted

Imperative
want*

Gerund
wanting

Past Participle
wanted

Verbtabellen

Regelmäßig

wash | waschen

+ *-es* in 3. Person Singular (siehe S. 152, Aussprache siehe S. 154)

Simple

Present Simple
I wash
you wash
he/she/it wash**es**
we wash
you wash
they wash

Past Simple
I washed
you washed
he/she/it washed
we washed
you washed
they washed

Present Perfect
I have washed
you have washed
he/she/it has washed
we have washed
you have washed
they have washed

Past Perfect
I had washed
you had washed
he/she/it had washed
we had washed
you had washed
they had washed

Continuous

Present Continuous
I am washing
you are washing
he/she/it is washing
we are washing
you are washing
they are washing

Past Continuous
I was washing
you were washing
he/she/it was washing
we were washing
you were washing
they were washing

Present Perfect Continuous
I have been washing
you have been washing
he/she/it has been washing
we have been washing
you have been washing
they have been washing

Past Perfect Continuous
I had been washing
you had been washing
he/she/it had been washing
we had been washing
you had been washing
they had been washing

Future

Future I
I will wash
you will wash
he/she/it will wash
we will wash
you will wash
they will wash

Future I Continuous
I will be washing
you will be washing
he/she/it will be washing
we will be washing
you will be washing
they will be washing

Future II
I will have washed
you will have washed
he/she/it will have washed
we will have washed
you will have washed
they will have washed

Future II Continuous
I will have been washing
you will have been washing
he/she/it will have been washing
we will have been washing
you will have been washing
they will have been washing

Conditional

Conditional II
I would wash
you would wash
he/she/it would wash
we would wash
you would wash
they would wash

Conditional Past
I would have washed
you would have washed
he/she/it would have washed
we would have washed
you would have washed
they would have washed

Imperative
wash

Gerund
washing

Past Participle
washed

Verbtabellen

Unregelmäßig

wear | tragen

Simple

Present Simple
I	wear
you	wear
he/she/it	wears
we	wear
you	wear
they	wear

Past Simple
I	wore
you	wore
he/she/it	wore
we	wore
you	wore
they	wore

Present Perfect
I	have	worn
you	have	worn
he/she/it	has	worn
we	have	worn
you	have	worn
they	have	worn

Past Perfect
I	had	worn
you	had	worn
he/she/it	had	worn
we	had	worn
you	had	worn
they	had	worn

Continuous

Present Continuous
I	am	wearing
you	are	wearing
he/she/it	is	wearing
we	are	wearing
you	are	wearing
they	are	wearing

Past Continuous
I	was	wearing
you	were	wearing
he/she/it	was	wearing
we	were	wearing
you	were	wearing
they	were	wearing

Present Perfect Continuous
I	have	been	wearing
you	have	been	wearing
he/she/it	has	been	wearing
we	have	been	wearing
you	have	been	wearing
they	have	been	wearing

Past Perfect Continuous
I	had	been	wearing
you	had	been	wearing
he/she/it	had	been	wearing
we	had	been	wearing
you	had	been	wearing
they	had	been	wearing

Future

Future I
I	will	wear
you	will	wear
he/she/it	will	wear
we	will	wear
you	will	wear
they	will	wear

Future I Continuous
I	will be wearing
you	will be wearing
he/she/it	will be wearing
we	will be wearing
you	will be wearing
they	will be wearing

Future II
I	will have	worn
you	will have	worn
he/she/it	will have	worn
we	will have	worn
you	will have	worn
they	will have	worn

Future II Continuous
I	will have been wearing
you	will have been wearing
he/she/it	will have been wearing
we	will have been wearing
you	will have been wearing
they	will have been wearing

Conditional

Conditional II
I	would wear
you	would wear
he/she/it	would wear
we	would wear
you	would wear
they	would wear

Conditional Past
I	would have	worn
you	would have	worn
he/she/it	would have	worn
we	would have	worn
you	would have	worn
they	would have	worn

Imperative
wear

Gerund
wearing

Past Participle
worn

Verbtabellen

Regelmäßig

work | arbeiten

Simple

Present Simple
I	work
you	work
he/she/it	work**s**
we	work
you	work
they	work

Past Simple
I	worked
you	worked
he/she/it	worked
we	worked
you	worked
they	worked

Present Perfect
I	have	worked
you	have	worked
he/she/it	has	worked
we	have	worked
you	have	worked
they	have	worked

Past Perfect
I	had	worked
you	had	worked
he/she/it	had	worked
we	had	worked
you	had	worked
they	had	worked

Continuous

Present Continuous
I	am	working
you	are	working
he/she/it	is	working
we	are	working
you	are	working
they	are	working

Past Continuous
I	was	working
you	were	working
he/she/it	was	working
we	were	working
you	were	working
they	were	working

Present Perfect Continuous
I	have	been	working
you	have	been	working
he/she/it	has	been	working
we	have	been	working
you	have	been	working
they	have	been	working

Past Perfect Continuous
I	had	been	working
you	had	been	working
he/she/it	had	been	working
we	had	been	working
you	had	been	working
they	had	been	working

Future

Future I
I	will	work
you	will	work
he/she/it	will	work
we	will	work
you	will	work
they	will	work

Future I Continuous
I	will be working
you	will be working
he/she/it	will be working
we	will be working
you	will be working
they	will be working

Future II
I	will have	worked
you	will have	worked
he/she/it	will have	worked
we	will have	worked
you	will have	worked
they	will have	worked

Future II Continuous
I	will have been working
you	will have been working
he/she/it	will have been working
we	will have been working
you	will have been working
they	will have been working

Conditional

Conditional II
I	would work
you	would work
he/she/it	would work
we	would work
you	would work
they	would work

Conditional Past
I	would have	worked
you	would have	worked
he/she/it	would have	worked
we	would have	worked
you	would have	worked
they	would have	worked

Imperative
work

Gerund
working

Past Participle
worked

Verbtabellen

+ *-ing* wird ∅ (siehe S. 153)

Unregelmäßig

write | schreiben

Simple

Present Simple
I write
you write
he/she/it writes
we write
you write
they write

Past Simple
I wrote
you wrote
he/she/it wrote
we wrote
you wrote
they wrote

Present Perfect
I have written
you have written
he/she/it has written
we have written
you have written
they have written

Past Perfect
I had written
you had written
he/she/it had written
we had written
you had written
they had written

Continuous

Present Continuous
I am writing
you are writing
he/she/it is writing
we are writing
you are writing
they are writing

Past Continuous
I was writing
you were writing
he/she/it was writing
we were writing
you were writing
they were writing

Present Perfect Continuous
I have been writing
you have been writing
he/she/it has been writing
we have been writing
you have been writing
they have been writing

Past Perfect Continuous
I had been writing
you had been writing
he/she/it had been writing
we had been writing
you had been writing
they had been writing

Future

Future I
I will write
you will write
he/she/it will write
we will write
you will write
they will write

Future I Continuous
I will be writing
you will be writing
he/she/it will be writing
we will be writing
you will be writing
they will be writing

Future II
I will have written
you will have written
he/she/it will have written
we will have written
you will have written
they will have written

Future II Continuous
I will have been writing
you will have been writing
he/she/it will have been writing
we will have been writing
you will have been writing
they will have been writing

Conditional

Conditional II
I would write
you would write
he/she/it would write
we would write
you would write
they would write

Conditional Past
I would have written
you would have written
he/she/it would have written
we would have written
you would have written
they would have written

Imperative
write

Gerund
writing

Past Participle
written

245

Unregelmäßige englische Verben

Infinitive **Infinitiv**	*Past Simple* **Vergangenheit**	*Past Participle* **Partizip Perfekt**	*German* **Deutsch**
arise	arose	arisen	sich ergeben, entstehen
awake	awoke	awoken	erwachen
be	was/were	been	sein
bear	bore	borne	tragen, ertragen
beat	beat	beaten	schlagen
become	became	become	werden
begin	began	begun	beginnen
bend	bent	bent	beugen, verbiegen
bet	bet, betted	bet, betted	wetten
bind	bound	bound	binden
bleed	bled	bled	bluten
bite	bit	bitten	beißen
blow	blew	blown	blasen
break	broke	broken	(zer)brechen
breed	bred	bred	züchten, brüten
bring	brought	brought	(her)bringen
build	built	built	bauen
burn	burnt	burnt	verbrennen
burst	burst	burst	platzen, aufbrechen
buy	bought	bought	kaufen
can	could	(been able)	können
cast	cast	cast	werfen
catch	caught	caught	fangen
choose	chose	chosen	wählen
come	came	come	kommen
cost	cost	cost	kosten
creep	crept	crept	schleichen, kriechen
cut	cut	cut	schneiden

dig	dug	dug	graben
do	did	done	machen, tun
draw	drew	drawn	zeichnen
dream	dreamt	dreamt	träumen
drink	drank	drunk	trinken
drive	drove	driven	fahren
eat	ate	eaten	essen
fall	fell	fallen	fallen
feed	fed	fed	füttern
feel	felt	felt	(sich) fühlen
fight	fought	fought	kämpfen
find	found	found	finden
flee	fled	fled	fliehen, flüchten
fling	flung	flung	schleudern
fly	flew	flown	fliegen
forbid	forbad, forbade	forbidden	verbieten
forecast	forecast, forecasted	forecast, forecasted	vorhersagen
forget	forgot	forgotten	vergessen
forgive	forgave	forgiven	verzeihen
freeze	froze	frozen	(ge)frieren
get	got	got, AE: gotten	bekommen
give	gave	given	geben
go	went	gone	gehen
grind	ground	ground	(zer)mahlen
grow	grew	grown	wachsen
hang	hung	hung	hängen
have	had	had	haben
hear	heard	heard	hören
hide	hid	hidden	(sich) verstecken
hit	hit	hit	schlagen
hold	held	held	halten
hurt	hurt	hurt	wehtun
keep	kept	kept	behalten
kneel	knelt	knelt	knien
know	knew	known	wissen, kennen

Verbtabellen

lay	laid	laid	legen
lead	led	led	führen
lean	leant, leaned	leant, leaned	lehnen, sich neigen
leap	leapt, leaped	leapt, leaped	springen
learn	learnt, learned	learnt, learned	lernen
leave	left	left	(ver)lassen
lend	lent	lent	(aus)leihen
let	let	let	lassen
lie	lay	lain	liegen
light	lit	lit	anzünden
lose	lost	lost	verlieren
make	made	made	machen
may	might	—	dürfen
mean	meant	meant	bedeuten, meinen
meet	met	met	treffen
mistake	mistook	mistaken	falsch verstehen
must	(had to)	(had to)	müssen
pay	paid	paid	bezahlen
put	put	put	legen, stellen, setzen
quit	quit, quitted	quit, quitted	aufhören
read	read	read	lesen
ride	rode	ridden	reiten, fahren
ring	rang	rung	klingeln
rise	rose	risen	aufstehen, (an)steigen
run	ran	run	rennen
saw	sawed	sawn, sawed	sägen
say	said	said	sagen
see	saw	seen	sehen
seek	sought	sought	suchen, streben
sell	sold	sold	verkaufen
send	sent	sent	schicken
set	set	set	setzen, legen, festsetzen
sew	sewed	sewn	nähen
shake	shook	shaken	schütteln
shine	shone	shone	scheinen

shoot	shot	shot	(er)schießen
show	showed	shown	zeigen
shrink	shrank	shrunk	einlaufen, schrumpfen
shut	shut	shut	schließen
sing	sang	sung	singen
sink	sank	sunk	versenken, sinken
sit	sat	sat	sitzen
sleep	slept	slept	schlafen
slide	slid	slid	rutschen
smell	smelt	smelt	riechen
sow	sowed	sown, sowed	säen
speak	spoke	spoken	sprechen
spell	spelt, spelled	spelt, spelled	buchstabieren
spend	spent	spent	ausgeben, verbringen
spill	spilt, spilled	spilt, spilled	verschütten
spin	spun	spun	spinnen, drehen
spit	spat	spat	spucken
split	split	split	spalten
spoil	spoilt, spoiled	spoilt, spoiled	verderben
spread	spread	spread	ausbreiten, bestreichen
stand	stood	stood	stehen
steal	stole	stolen	stehlen
stick	stuck	stuck	kleben
sting	stung	stung	stechen
stink	stank	stunk	stinken
stride	strode	stridden	schreiten
strike	struck	struck	schlagen
strive	strove	striven	sich bemühen
swear	swore	sworn	schwören
sweep	swept	swept	kehren
swim	swam	swum	schwimmen
swing	swung	swung	schwingen
take	took	taken	nehmen
teach	taught	taught	lehren
tear	tore	torn	zerreißen
tell	told	told	erzählen

Verbtabellen

think	thought	thought	denken
throw	threw	thrown	werfen
understand	understood	understood	verstehen
upset	upset	upset	umstoßen, erschüttern
wake	woke	woken	(auf)wachen
wear	wore	worn	tragen
weave	wove	woven	weben
weep	wept	wept	weinen
win	won	won	gewinnen
wind	wound	wound	wickeln, spulen
wring	wrung	wrung	auswringen
write	wrote	written	schreiben

Alphabetische Verbliste Deutsch – Englisch

A

		Seite
absagen	cancel	175
ändern	change	178
anfangen	begin	168
ankommen	arrive	164
anrufen	call	173
antworten	answer	163
arbeiten	work	244
ausgeben	spend	232
ausleihen	lend	208
auswählen	choose	179

B

beginnen	begin	168
bekommen	get	196
besichtigen	visit	239
besuchen	visit	239
bleiben	stay	234
brauchen	need	217
brechen	break	170
bringen	bring	171
buchen	book	169

D

denken	think	237

E

einladen	invite	204
entscheiden	decide	185
erlauben	allow	162
essen	eat	189

F

fahren	drive	188
fallen	fall	191
fangen	catch	177
finden	find	193
fliegen	fly	194
fragen	ask	165
fühlen	feel	192

G

geben	give	197
gehen	go	198
genießen	enjoy	190

H

haben	have	199
helfen	help	201
hören	hear	200

K

kaufen	buy	172
kennen	know	205
kochen	cook	182
können	can/be able to	174
kommen	come	181
kosten	cost	183

L

laufen	run	223
leben	live	211
legen	put	221
leihen	lend	208
lernen	learn	206
lesen	read	222

M

machen	make	214
mitbringen	bring	171
mögen	like	209
mögen	want	241
müssen	must	216

Verbtabellen

N
nehmen	take	236

O
öffnen	open	218

R
rufen	call	173
reisen	travel	238
rennen	run	223

S
sagen	say	224
schicken	send	227
schlafen	sleep	230
schlagen	hit	202
schließen	close	180
schließen	shut	228
schneiden	cut	184
schreiben	write	245
schwimmen	swim	235
sehen	see	225
sehen	look	212
sein	be	166
setzen	put	221
sitzen	sit	229
sollen	must	216
spielen	play	220
sprechen	speak	231
stehen	stand	233
stellen	put	221
stornieren	cancel	175
stürzen	fall	191

T
tragen	carry	176
tragen	wear	243
treffen	meet	215
trinken	drink	187
tun	do	186

U
übernachten	stay	234

V
verbringen	spend	232
vergessen	forget	195
verkaufen	sell	226
verlassen	leave	207
verlieren	lose	213

W
wählen	choose	179
warten	wait	240
waschen	wash	242
wechseln	change	178
wehtun	hurt	203
werden	become	167
wissen	know	251
wohnen	live	211
wollen	want	241

Z
zahlen	pay	219
zuhören	listen	210

3 | Übungsgrammatik

Inhalt

Modul 1 — 257
Substantive
Groß- und Kleinschreibung
The und **a/an**
Pluralbildung
There is und **there are**
Länder und Sprachen
Test 1 — 265

Modul 2 — 267
Fragen und Antworten
Das **present simple**
Verwendung des **present simple**
Unregelmäßige Verben
Verneinung
Das Verb **be**
Kurzantworten
Test 2 — 275

Modul 3 — 277
Personalpronomen
Have und **have got**
Demonstrativpronomen
Pronomenarten
Test 3 — 285

Modul 4 — 287
Die **ing**-Form
Present continuous
Verneinung und Fragen im **present continuous**
Kurzantworten
Present simple oder **continuous**?
Test 4 — 295

Modul 5 — 297
Die Zukunft
Das **will future**
Fragen und Kurzantworten
Das **will future** mit **if**
Will future oder **present continuous**
Test 5 — 305

Modul 6 — 307
Das **past simple**
Unregelmäßige Verben im **past simple**
Zeitangaben und das **past simple**
Fragen und Verneinung
Das Verb **be** im **past simple**
Be oder **do**?
Verbformen im **past simple**
Kurzantworten
Test 6 — 315

Modul 7 — 317
Adjektive
Steigerung von Adjektiven
More und **most**
Unregelmäßige Adjektive
Dinge vergleichen
Adverbien der Art und Weise
Unregelmäßige Adverbien
Test 7 — 325

Modul 8 — 327
Have to
Must
Die modalen Hilfsverben **should** und **can**
Can oder **be able to**?
Would, **may** und **might**
Der Imperativ
Test 8 — 335

Modul 9	337	**Modul 12**	367
Arten von Substantiven		Das **past participle**	
Much, **many** und **a lot of**		Das **present perfect**	
Little und **few**		Verneinung, Fragen, Kurzantworten	
Some und **any**		Unregelmäßige Verben	
Someone, **no one** und **anyone**		Gebrauch des **present perfect**	
Test 9	345	**For** oder **since**?	
		Present perfect – past simple	
Modul 10	347	**Test 12**	375
Präpositionen der Zeit			
At und **by**		Lösungen	377
Zeiträume			
Präpositionen des Ortes		Wortverzeichnis	397
Präpositionen der Richtung			
Over, **under**, **in front of**		Trackliste	411
Test 10	355		
Modul 11	357		
Possessivbegleiter			
Possessivpronomen			
Der **'s** Genetiv			
Reflexivpronomen			
Test 11	365		

So ist die Übungsgrammatik aufgebaut

Die Übungsgrammatik besteht aus 12 Modulen und 12 Tests. Jedes Modul beginnt mit einer leichten Einführung zu den jeweiligen Themen. Im Anschluss erhalten Sie genaue Erklärungen und haben die Möglichkeit, in zahlreichen Übungen das Gelernte anzuwenden. Nach jedem Modul können Sie einen Test machen um zu überprüfen, ob Sie die Inhalte auch sicher beherrschen.

Die Übungsgrammatik wird durch eine **Audio CD** ergänzt. Viele der Übungen und Texte finden Sie auch hier, wodurch Sie zusätzlich ihr Hörverstehen und ihre Aussprache üben können.

Bildsymbole

TR. 01 Dieses Bildsymbol zeigt Ihnen, dass Sie die Übung auch auf der Audio CD hören können. Die Tracknummer gibt Ihnen an, wo Sie die Übung auf der CD finden.

Für eine Übung mit diesem Symbol brauchen Sie einen Stift, um etwas zu schreiben oder einzutragen.

Auch für diese Übungen brauchen Sie einen Stift, diesmal um etwas anzukreuzen oder zu verbinden.

Bei diesem Symbol werden Sie aufgefordert ein zusätzliches Blatt zu verwenden, um die Übung zu machen.

Mit diesem Symbol werden Sie darauf hingewiesen, dass Sie die Inhalte besonders aufmerksam lesen sollten.

Nice to know
Im gesprochenen Englisch sagt man sehr oft **I guess** an Stelle von **I think**.

In der Box erhalten Sie nützliche und interessante Hinweise zur englischen Sprache und landesüblichen Besonderheiten.

book – *Buch*
kiss – *Kuss*
knive – *Messer*
half – *Hälfte*

Das Wortschatzfeld enthält Wörter und Wendungen, die für die jeweiligen Übungen hilfreich sind.

Lerntipp!
Oft müssen Sie sich noch unbekannte Wörter selbst erschließen. Stellen Sie sich dabei z.B. folgende Frage: Kenne ich ein deutsches Wort, das ähnlich ist?

In dieser Box finden Sie Tipps, die Ihnen das Lernen erleichtern können.

Lösungen: In diesem Teil finden Sie die Lösungen zu allen Übungen.
Wortverzeichnis: In diesem alphabetisch sortierten Wortverzeichnis finden Sie schnell alle verwendeten Wörter mit deren Übersetzungen.

1 Übungsgrammatik

Die Einkaufsliste / Englische Substantive

1

Die Familie Smith, Paul, seine Frau Kate und ihre beiden Kinder Ben und Jane leben in Manchester. Montags gehen Paul und Kate immer einkaufen. Kate ist gerade dabei, die Einkaufsliste zu schreiben.
Lesen Sie den Dialog und markieren Sie im Text die Pluralformen (Mehrzahl) der Substantive (Hauptwörter).
Sie können den Dialog auch auf der CD hören.

Kate: What do we need?
Paul: Oranges, apples, pears and bananas.
Kate: There are apples in the fruit bowl.
Paul: Yes, I know, but I prefer green apples. Oh, and we definitely need a bottle of milk and a piece of butter.
Kate: Do we have salad?
Paul: No, we don't. Write it down, please. What about Ben's birthday present? Does he need new trousers?
Kate: Hmm ... We can buy him tickets for the Manchester United football match. There's a ticket-office near the supermarket.
Paul: That's a good idea. How about for dinner tonight?
Kate: We can buy a bottle of wine for us and an apple pie for dessert for the children.
Paul: Why only for the children? I love apple pie with vanilla ice cream.

> **need** – *brauchen*
> **apple** – *Apfel*
> **pear** – *Birne*
> **banana** – *Banane*
> **fruit bowl** – *Obstschale*
> **know** – *wissen*
> **prefer** – *bevorzugen*
> **definitely** – *unbedingt*
> **bottle** – *Flasche*
> **milk** – *Milch*
> **piece** – *Stück*
> **birthday present** – *Geburtstagsgeschenk*
> **trousers** – *Hose*
> **near** – *in der Nähe von*
> **office** – *Büro*
> **idea** – *Idee*
> **wine** – *Wein*
> **apple pie** – *Apfelkuchen*
> **dessert** – *Nachtisch*
> **children** – *Kinder*
> **vanilla ice cream** – *Vanilleeis*

2

Hier sehen Sie englische Substantive mit dem bestimmten Artikel **the**.
Sprechen Sie die Wörter laut aus. Wenn Sie möchten, können Sie sich die Begriffe auf der CD anhören. Achten Sie dabei auf die unterschiedliche Aussprache des Artikels.

1. the apple   2. the pear   3. the trousers
4. the office   5. the children

Übungsgrammatik

Groß- und Kleinschreibung

3

Groß- und **Kleinschreibung**
Im Gegensatz zum Deutschen werden Substantive im Englischen meist kleingeschrieben: **bus**, **love**, **child**, **dog**.

Es gibt aber auch Substantive, die immer großgeschrieben werden.
Hierzu gehören
- die Wochentage: **Monday**, **Tuesday**, **Wednesday**, **Thursday**, **Friday**, **Saturday**, **Sunday**

- die Monate: **January**, **February**, **March**, **April**, **May**, **June**, **July**, **August**, **September**, **October**, **November**, **December**

- Länder, Sprachen und Nationalitäten:

England	**English**
France	**French**
the United States of America	**American**
Germany	**German**

- sowie Eigennamen: z.B. **Paul Smith**, **the Beatles** oder **Top Line Software Company**.

> **Nice to know**
>
> Das Wort für Sprache und Nationalität ist im Englischen oft gleich.
> **I'm English.**
> *Ich bin Engländer.*
> **She speaks English.**
> *Sie spricht Englisch.*

4

Schreiben Sie die englischen Übersetzungen der Wörter in die Lücken.
Achten Sie besonders auf die Groß- und Kleinschreibung.

1. *Nachtisch* _____

2. *Hose* _____

3. *französisch* _____

4. *Hund* _____

5. *März* _____

6. *Samstag* _____

7. *Kinder* _____

8. *Freitag* _____

9. *Abendessen* _____

10. *Spanien* _____

1 Übungsgrammatik

The und *a/an*

5 TR. 03

Die Artikel
Im Englischen gibt es nur einen bestimmten Artikel: **the**.

the computer	*der Computer*
the door	*die Tür*
the car	*das Auto*

Die Aussprache stellt dabei eine Besonderheit dar:
Beginnt das nachfolgende Substantiv mit einem Vokal (a, e, i, o, u), so wird der Artikel **the** mit **i** ausgesprochen. Folgt ein Substantiv, das mit einem Konsonanten (b, m, t, r, w, s, etc.) beginnt, so bleibt die Aussprache von **the** so wie Sie sie bereits kennen.
Wenn Sie möchten, finden Sie hierzu auf Ihrer CD Hörbeispiele, die Sie nachsprechen können.

TR. 04

Der unbestimmte Artikel (*ein, eine*) heißt **a** oder **an**.
Beginnt das nachfolgende Wort mit einem Konsonanten, verwendet man **a**, wie in **a pear**.
Beginnt das nachfolgende Wort mit einem Vokal, verwendet man **an**, wie in **an apple**. Auch diese Beispiele finden Sie auf der CD.

> **Nice to know**
> Bei Wörtern, die mit **h** beginnen, wird **a** zu **an**, wenn das **h** nicht gesprochen wird.
> Man sagt **a house**, aber **an hour**.

6

Welcher unbestimmte Artikel ist hier richtig? Schreiben Sie **a** oder **an** in die Lücken.

1. _____ office
2. _____ bottle
3. _____ dog
4. _____ ice cream
5. _____ hour
6. _____ minute
7. _____ orange
8. _____ computer
9. _____ idea
10. _____ banana
11. _____ office
12. _____ pear

> ◀ **dog** – *Hund*
> **hour** – *Stunde*
> **minute** – *Minute*
> **orange** – *Orange*

Übungsgrammatik 1

Pluralbildung

7

Die Bildung des Plural
Der Plural (Mehrzahl) von Substantiven wird gebildet, indem man einfach ein **-s** an die Singularform anhängt: **book – books**.

Bei Wörtern, die auf einen Zischlaut enden, **-s**, **-ss**, **-sh**, **-ch**, **-x** oder **-z**, wird im Plural ein **-es** als Endung angehängt: **kiss – kisses**.

Endet ein Wort auf einen **Konsonanten + -y**, fällt das **y** weg und es wird **-ies** angehängt: **family – families**.
Endet das Wort jedoch auf einen **Vokal + -y**, wird nur ein **-s** angehängt:
     day – days.

Bei Substantiven, die auf **-f** oder **-fe** enden, ändert sich das **f** zu **v** und es wird **-ves** angehängt.
     knife – knives
     half – halves
Es gibt allerdings einige Ausnahmen, die den Plural regelmäßig bilden wie zum Beispiel **roof – roofs**.

Die häufigsten unregelmäßigen Pluralformen lauten:

child	children	Kinder
man	men	Männer
woman	women	Frauen
foot	feet	Füße
tooth	teeth	Zähne
mouse	mice	Mäuse
tomato	tomatoes	Tomaten
fish	fish	Fische

book – *Buch*
kiss – *Kuss*
knive – *Messer*
half – *Hälfte*
roof – *Dach*

Nice to know
Es gibt auch Substantive, die nur im Plural gebraucht werden.
glasses   *Brille*
trousers   *Hose*
news   *Nachrichten*

8 TR. 05

Verbinden Sie die Wörter links jeweils mit der richtigen Pluralform rechts.
Die Aussprache der Vokabeln können Sie sich auf der CD anhören.

1. knife
2. woman
3. orange
4. house
5. child

a. houses
b. children
c. knives
d. oranges
e. women

house – *Haus*

1 Übungsgrammatik

Plural / Zählbare und nicht zählbare Substantive

9

Schreiben Sie die Pluralformen der folgenden Wörter in die Lücken.

1. **book** _____   6. **knife** _____
2. **city** _____   7. **ticket** _____
3. **tomato** _____   8. **kiss** _____
4. **fish** _____   9. **mouse** _____
5. **present** _____ 10. **roof** _____

10

Zählbar oder **nicht zählbar**?
Im Englischen wird zwischen zählbaren (**apple**, **car** etc.) und nicht zählbaren (**love**, **milk** etc.) Substantiven unterschieden.

Zählbare Substantive haben sowohl eine Plural- als auch eine Singularform und können mit **a/an** oder einer Zahl verwendet werden:
That's a good idea. We need four bananas.

Nicht zählbare Substantive haben nur eine Form. **A** oder **an** können nie direkt vor dem betreffenden Wort stehen.
   Too much coffee isn't good for you.
   Zu viel Kaffee ist nicht gut für dich.
   Music helps me to relax. *Musik hilft mir zu entspannen.*

Durch **a ... of ...** können nicht zählbare Dinge eine zählbare Form bekommen.

a cup of coffee	*eine Tasse Kaffee*
a slice of toast	*eine Scheibe Toast*
a packet of rice	*eine Packung Reis*
a piece of cake	*ein Stück Kuchen*
a bottle of coke	*eine Flasche Cola*

Übungsgrammatik | **1**

Zählbar oder nicht zählbar?

11 ✎

Kreuzen Sie jeweils das Wort an, das **nicht** zählbar ist.

1. ☐ a. office
   ☐ b. child
   ☐ c. coffee
   ☐ d. supermarket

2. ☐ a. music
   ☐ b. house
   ☐ c. woman
   ☐ d. banana

3. ☐ a. bottle
   ☐ b. butter
   ☐ c. ticket
   ☐ d. knife

4. ☐ a. present
   ☐ b. party
   ☐ c. football
   ☐ d. love

12 ✎

Schauen Sie sich die Bilder an und schreiben Sie das fehlende Wort in die Lücken.

cheese – *Käse* ▶
wine – *Wein*
hot chocolate
 – *heiße Schokolade*
bread – *Brot*
sugar – *Zucker*

1. a _____ of cheese
2. a _____ of wine
3. a _____ of hot chocolate
4. a _____ of bread
5. a _____ of sugar

Übungsgrammatik

There is und *there are*

13

There is und **there are**
There is und **there are** entsprechen etwa den deutschen Konstruktionen *es gibt* und *es ist/sind*.

Steht das Substantiv, auf das Bezug genommen wird, im Singular (Einzahl), verwendet man **there is** oder abgekürzt **there's**.

> **There's a ticket-office near the supermarket.**
> *Es gibt ein Kartenbüro in der Nähe des Supermarktes.*

Auch mit nicht zählbaren Substantiven wird **there is** gebraucht.

> **There's live music at the party.**
> *Es gibt Live-Musik auf dem Fest.*

Steht das Substantiv, auf das Bezug genommen wird, im Plural (Mehrzahl), verwendet man **there are**.

> **There are apples in the fruit bowl.**
> *Es sind Äpfel in der Obstschale.*

14

Nach dem Besuch im Supermarkt ist der Kühlschrank von Kate und Paul wieder gut gefüllt. Was ist im Kühlschrank?
Schreiben Sie **There is** oder **There are** in die Lücken.

1. _____ an apple pie.
2. _____ a bottle of wine.
3. _____ oranges.
4. _____ a piece of butter.
5. _____ two bottles of milk.
6. _____ green apples.

Übungsgrammatik 1

Plural / Länder und Sprachen

15

1	2	3	4
5	6	7	8
9	10	11	12

A	C	T	O	M	A	T	O	E	S
K	C	P	W	F	I	S	H	T	B
I	N	E	B	G	E	P	U	W	O
C	H	I	L	D	R	E	N	O	T
A	M	N	V	G	L	A	T	M	T
K	M	I	C	E	P	R	Z	E	L
E	B	O	O	K	S	S	T	N	E
S	K	T	R	O	U	S	E	R	S

Finden Sie die Pluralformen, die diese Bilder darstellen, im Buchstaben-gitter. Die Wörter können senkrecht, waagerecht und diagonal im Gitter versteckt sein.

16

Ordnen Sie jedem Land die Landessprache zu, indem Sie den richtigen Buchstaben in das jeweilige Kästchen eintragen.

1. ☐ England
2. ☐ Germany
3. ☐ France
4. ☐ Norway
5. ☐ Sweden
6. ☐ Portugal

a. Swedish
b. French
c. German
d. English
e. Norwegian
f. Portuguese

Test **1** **Übungsgrammatik**

Groß oder klein? / Nicht zählbare

1

Ergänzen Sie die fehlenden Anfangsbuchstaben der Wörter. Achten Sie dabei auf die Groß- und Kleinschreibung.

1. ___erman
2. ___ootball
3. ___anchester ___nited
4. ___arch
5. ___uesday
6. ___inner
7. ___nglish
8. ___anana

2

Kreuzen Sie jeweils das passende Wort an.

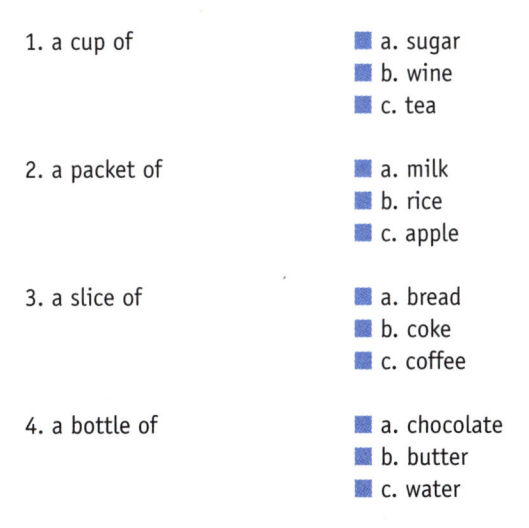

1. a cup of
   - a. sugar
   - b. wine
   - c. tea

2. a packet of
   - a. milk
   - b. rice
   - c. apple

3. a slice of
   - a. bread
   - b. coke
   - c. coffee

4. a bottle of
   - a. chocolate
   - b. butter
   - c. water

265

Übungsgrammatik — **1** Test

*Substantive **A** oder **an**? / Substantive im Plural*

3 ✎

Schreiben Sie **a** oder **an** in die Lücke vor dem Substantiv.

1. _____ kiss
2. _____ idea
3. _____ hour
4. _____ house
5. _____ match
6. _____ apple pie

4 ✎

Schreiben Sie die Pluralformen der abgebildeten Gegenstände in die Lücken.

1. _____

2. _____

3. _____

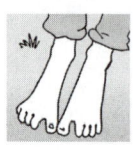

4. _____

5. _____

6. _____

266

2 Übungsgrammatik

Ein ganz normaler Tag / Fragen und Antworten

1 TR. 06

Diese Sätze schildern einen typischen Tag im Leben von Paul und Kate aus Manchester. Ordnen Sie den Sätzen die dazugehörenden Bilder zu.
Wenn Sie möchten, können Sie sich den Text auch auf der CD anhören.

a   b   c   d
e   f   g   h

1. Paul and Kate get up at seven o'clock.
2. They have breakfast together with their children, Ben and Jane.
3. Paul leaves the house at eight o'clock.
4. Ben and Jane take the bus to school.
5. Kate goes to work at half past nine.
6. The children come home from school at half past four.
7. At six o'clock, they have dinner together.
8. They all go to bed at eleven o'clock.

◀ **get up** – *aufstehen*
at – *um*
o'clock – *Uhr*
breakfast – *Frühstück*
leave – *verlassen*
take – *nehmen*
half past nine – *halb neun*
work – *Arbeit*
finish – *beenden/fertig sein mit*
come – *kommen*
home – *nach Hause*
together – *zusammen*
evening – *Abend*
watch TV – *fernsehen*
go to bed – *ins Bett gehen*

2

Verbinden Sie die Fragen auf der linken Seite mit den jeweils korrekten Antworten auf der rechten Seite.

1. Does Paul live in London?
2. Do Paul and Kate have two children?
3. Are the Beatles from Manchester?
4. Is Edinburgh in England?

a. No, they aren't. They are from Liverpool.
b. Yes, they do. The children are called Ben and Jane.
c. No, it isn't. It's in Scotland.
d. No, he doesn't. He lives in Manchester.

◀ **live** – *wohnen, leben*
be called – *heißen*

Übungsgrammatik 2

*Das **present simple** / Unregelmäßige Verben*

3

Bildung des present simple
Die Bildung des englischen **present simple** (einfache Gegenwart) ist sehr einfach, da es bei **regelmäßigen** Verben nur zwei Formen aufweist. Man benutzt für alle Personen die Grundform des Verbs, ausgenommen die 3. Person Singular (**he**, **she**, **it**), bei der ein **-s** an das Verb angehängt wird.

> **Nice to know**
>
> Merken Sie sich als Faustregel für das **present simple** einfach den folgenden Reim:
> „Bei **he**, **she**, **it** - das **s** muss mit!"

They get up at seven o'clock.   **Jane gets up at seven o'clock.**
Sie stehen um sieben Uhr auf.   *Jane steht um sieben Uhr auf.*
The children leave the house at a quarter past eight.
Die Kinder verlassen um Viertel nach acht das Haus.
Paul leaves the house at eight o'clock.
Paul verlässt um acht Uhr das Haus.

4

Schreiben Sie die fehlenden Verben in die Lücken.

> gets up   live   works
>   loves   take

1. We _____ in Manchester.
2. Ben and Jane _____ the bus to school.
3. Paul _____ at seven o'clock.
4. Kate _____ in a shop.
5. She _____ shopping.

5

Unregelmäßige Verben
Einige Verben haben eine **unregelmäßige** Form im **present simple**. Dies sind vor allem die Hilfsverben **do** (*tun*), **be** (*sein*), **have** (*haben*) sowie das Verb **go** (*gehen*). Sehen Sie sich dazu die Tabelle links an.

Unregelmäßige Verben:	
I	am
	have
	do
	go
you	are
	have
	do
	go
he/she/it	is
	has
	does
	goes
we	are
	have
	do
	go
you	are
	have
	do
	go
they	are
	have
	do
	go

Ben and Jane go to school.   **Paul goes to work.**
Ben und Jane gehen in die Schule.   *Paul geht zur Arbeit.*
Paul and Kate have two children.   **Ben has a little sister.**
Paul und Kate haben zwei Kinder.   *Ben hat eine kleine Schwester.*

2 Übungsgrammatik

Verwendung des present simple

6

Diese Bilder zeigen einen typischen Montag im Leben von Jane.
Sehen Sie sich die Bilder an und schreiben Sie dann in der dritten Person
(z.B. **She gets up.**) in die Lücken, was Jane auf den Bildern macht.
Auf der CD können Sie hören, was Jane Ihnen über ihren Montag erzählt.

> I have breakfast at home.
>
> Then I go to school by bus.
>
> In the morning, I have maths.
>
> In the break, I go to the library.
>
> After lunch, I have sports.

1. Jane _____
2. Then she _____
3. _____
4. _____
5. _____

Lerntipp!
Viele der Übungen, die Ihnen etwas schwerer gefallen sind als andere, können Sie bei Gelegenheit wiederholen, wenn Sie möchten. Sie lernen so schneller und es kostet Sie nur ein paar Minuten.

◀ **maths** – *Mathe*
break – *Pause*
library – *Bibliothek/Bücherei*
lunch – *Mittagessen*

7

Verwendung des present simple
Das **present simple** wird für allgemein gültige Aussagen oder Feststellungen in der Gegenwart benutzt. Man kann damit generelle Informationen über Personen oder Dinge geben, die sich normalerweise nicht ständig verändern.

    Kate works in a shop.   *Kate arbeitet in einem Laden.*
    Paul drives to work every day. *Paul fährt jeden Tag zur Arbeit.*

Man kann das **present simple** auch benutzen, um Gewohnheiten oder sich regelmäßig wiederholende Handlungen zu beschreiben, wobei oftmals Signalwörter wie **usually** (*normalerweise*), **always** (*immer*), **every day** (*jeden Tag*) oder **never** (*nie*) vorkommen. Achtung! Hierbei steht das Signalwort immer vor dem Verb, nicht danach!

    She always drinks coffee on Sundays.
    Sie trinkt sonntags immer Kaffee.
    Kate usually goes shopping on Mondays.
    Normalerweise geht Kate montags einkaufen.

Übungsgrammatik 2

Present simple / *Kate trifft eine Freundin*

8

Sehen Sie sich die Bilder an. Schreiben Sie dann ein passendes Verb aus der Box im **present simple** in der richtigen Form in die Lücken.

watch – *ansehen, schauen*
drive – *fahren*
clean – *saubermachen, putzen*
dishes – *Geschirr*
cycle – *Fahrrad fahren*

1. We _____ TV every evening.
2. He _____ to work every day.
3. She _____ the dishes every day.
4. They _____ home every evening.

9

Beim Einkaufen trifft Kate eine alte Schulfreundin. Lesen Sie den Dialog und versuchen Sie, so viel wie möglich zu verstehen. Sie können sich das Gespräch auch auf der CD anhören.

believe – *glauben*
fine – *gut/prima*
still – *noch/immer noch*
remember – *sich erinnern*
really – *wirklich*
married – *verheiratet*
primary school – *Grundschule*
visit – *Besuch*
as – *als*
sister – *Schwester*
wedding – *Hochzeit*
listen – *zuhören*
a lot of – *viel*
meet – *treffen*
sure – *sicher*
maybe – *vielleicht*
station – *Bahnhof*
by – *an/bei*
there – *dorthin*
often – *oft*
nice – *nett/schön*
see you – *bis bald*

Kate: Louise? Is that you?
Louise: Kate? Oh, I don't believe it! It's you! How are you?
Kate: I'm fine. How are you?
Louise: Fine, fine. Do you still live here in Manchester?
Kate: Yes, I still live here. Do you remember Paul?
Louise: Yes, I do. Does he still live here?
Kate: Yes, he does. We're married now. Paul works in a bank. But what about you? Are you here on a visit?
Louise: Yes, I am. It's my sister's wedding on Saturday, so I'm here for that. I now live in Edinburgh.
Kate: Oh, really? And what do you do there?
Louise: I work as a teacher in a primary school. And you? What do you do?
Kate: I work in a shop.
Louise: Listen, I don't have a lot of time now. Can we meet for a coffee tomorrow?
Kate: Yes, sure. What time?
Louise: Two o'clock, maybe?
Kate: That's OK. Two o'clock at the coffee bar by the station? I often go there. It's a nice place.
Louise: Fine. See you tomorrow!
Kate: Bye!

10

Verneinung
Man kann Sätze im **present simple** verneinen, indem man dem Hauptverb **do not**/**don't** bzw. **does not**/**doesn't** voranstellt. Hierbei wechselt in der 3. Person Singular das **-s** vom Hauptverb zum Hilfsverb (**does**). Das Hauptverb bleibt für alle Personen immer unverändert.

Kate lives in Manchester.	*Kate wohnt in Manchester.*
Kate doesn't live in London.	*Kate wohnt nicht in London.*
I remember Paul.	*Ich erinnere mich an Paul.*
I don't remember John.	*Ich erinnere mich nicht an John.*

11

Als Paul noch keine Familie hatte, hatte er viel mehr Zeit für seine Hobbys. Lesen Sie, was Paul jetzt alles nicht mehr (**not any more**) macht, und unterstreichen Sie die korrekte Form der Verneinung.
Sie können Ihre Lösungen auch überprüfen, indem Sie die CD hören.

1. Well, I have a family, so I *don't have / haven't / not have* so much time for myself any more.
2. I *go not / don't go / isn't go* to the pub with my mates any more. Well, not so often, anyway.
3. And I *go not / 'm not go / don't go* swimming so often, either.
4. I *never / isn't / always* go out during the week. I'm always at home.
5. But the good thing is, I *isn't / don't / not* work so much overtime either!

> **well** – *nun/na ja*
> **any more** – *nicht mehr*
> **much** – *viel*
> **myself** – *mich/mich selbst*
> **pub** – *Kneipe*
> **mate** – *Kumpel/Freund*
> **anyway** – *jedenfalls*
> **either** – *auch nicht*
> **during** – *während*
> **week** – *Woche*
> **overtime** – *Überstunden*

12

Fragen
Zur Bildung von **Fragen** benötigt man, wie bei der Verneinung, ebenfalls das Hilfsverb **do** bzw. **does**. Dieses stellt man einfach an den Anfang des Fragesatzes.

Do you still **live** here?	*Wohnst du immer noch hier?*
Does Louise **work** in a school?	*Arbeitet Louise in einer Schule?*

Auch bei Fragen steht das Hauptverb immer in der Grundform, d.h. ohne **s**-Endung in der dritten Person Singular.

Übungsgrammatik

Das Verb be / Fragen

13

Das Verb be

Wir haben bereits gesehen, dass das Verb **be** (*sein*) im **present simple** unregelmäßig ist. Die Formen von **be** sind:

I	am (*bin*)	we	are (*sind*)
you	are (*bist*)	you	are (*seid/sind*)
he/she/it	is (*ist*)	they	are (*sind*)

Aus den Personalpronomen (**I**, **you**, **he**, etc.) und dem Verb **be** im **present simple** wird sehr häufig eine verkürzte Form gebildet. Der erste Buchstabe des Verbs wird weggelassen und durch einen Apostroph ersetzt.

I'm	we're
you're	you're
he's/she's/it's	they're

Wenn man **be** verneinen oder Fragen damit bilden möchte, braucht man das Hilfsverb **do** nicht.

Bei **Verneinungen** wird einfach nur **not** hinter das Verb gestellt.

I'm not stupid.   **He's not** the best.
Ich bin nicht blöd.   *Er ist nicht der Beste.*

In **Fragen** werden Subjekt und Objekt vertauscht.

Are you not cold?   **Is he** still in Manchester?
Ist dir nicht kalt?   *Ist er immer noch in Manchester?*

Nice to know

In verneinten Sätzen gibt es zwei Formen der Verkürzung:
He's not German.
oder
He isn't German.
You're not Italian.
oder
You aren't Italian.
They're not late.
oder
They aren't late.
We're not angry.
oder
We aren't angry.

14

Bringen Sie diese Fragen und Sätze in die richtige Reihenfolge und schreiben Sie sie in die Lücken.

1. John / you / Do / know / ?   _____
2. he / Is / Japanese / ?   _____
3. at / Jane / school / isn't / .   _____
4. not / happy / We're / very / .   _____
5. read / she / a / book / Does / ?   _____
6. tired / you / Are / ?   _____

2 Übungsgrammatik

Kurzantworten

15

Kurzantworten
Auf Fragen, die mit **Ja** oder **Nein** beantwortet werden können, reagiert man im Englischen häufig mit einer so genannten **Kurzantwort**. Hierzu wird das Hilfsverb aus der Frage wieder aufgenommen und in der entsprechenden Form in der Antwort wiederholt. Wird die Frage verneint, hängt man einfach **not** an das Verb an.

Do you like Manchester? *Mögen sie Manchester?*
Yes, I do.   **No, I don't.**
Ja, (das tu ich).   *Nein, (das tu ich nicht).*

Does Ben like chocolate? *Mag Ben Schokolade?*
Yes, he does.   **No, he doesn't.**
Ja, (das tut er).   *Nein, (das tut er nicht).*

Is London beautiful? *Ist London schön?*
Yes, it is.   **No, it isn't.**
Ja, (das ist es).   *Nein, (das ist es nicht).*

Are you tired? *Bist du müde?*
Yes, I am.   **No, I'm not.**
Ja, (das bin ich).   *Nein, (das bin ich nicht).*

> **Nice to know**
> Im Englischen klingt es oft sehr direkt und unhöflich, wenn man Fragen nur mit **Yes** oder **No** beantwortet. Benutzen Sie immer die entsprechende Kurzantwort und Sie werden gleich viel freundlicher klingen!

16

Sehen Sie sich die Bilder an und beantworten Sie dann die Fragen, indem Sie die passende Kurzantwort in die Lücke schreiben
(z.B. **Is he tired? Yes, he is. / No, he isn't.**).

Is he fat?
_____

Are they thin?
_____

Does he cycle?
_____

Do they play football?
_____

Is she angry?
_____

> **fat** – *dick, fett*
> **thin** – *dünn*
> **cycle** – *Fahrrad fahren*
> **angry** – *wütend, verärgert*

Übungsgrammatik | **2**

Present simple

17 ✏

Sehen Sie sich die Sätze an und schreiben Sie das jeweils fehlende Wort in das Gitter. Achtung! Auch Apostrophe (') benötigen ein eigenes Kästchen!

1. Kate … from London.
2. Does Paul work in a bank? Yes, he … .
3. Ben's … a football player.
4. Louise … in a school.
5. Are you tired? Yes, I … .
6. Are Kate and Paul married? Yes, they … .
7. Does Louise work in a bank? No, she … .
8. Jane … a book.
9. Ben … Jane's brother.
10. Do you remember John? Yes, I … .

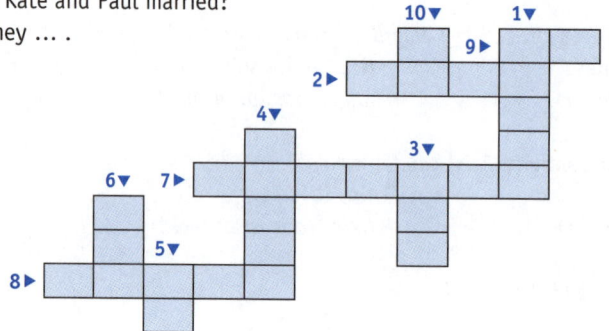

18 ✏

> **great aunt** – *Groß-tante*
> **wear** – *tragen*
> **tie** – *Krawatte*
> **jumper** – *Pullover*
> **skirt** – *Rock*
> **brother** – *Bruder*

Großtante Hermione ist zu Besuch und fragt Jane über ihren Schulalltag aus. Die Zeiten haben sich geändert, seit sie selbst einmal zur Schule ging. Ergänzen Sie das Gespräch, indem Sie die fehlenden Wörter in die Lücken schreiben.

| does | do | wear | don't | wear | don't | does |

1. **Great Aunt:** So, Jane, _____ you _____ a tie to school?

2. **Jane:** No, we _____. We _____ a uniform, but it's a jumper and skirt.

3. **Great Aunt:** I see. What about your brother, _____ he wear a tie?

4. **Jane:** Yes, he _____. Boys wear ties in our school, and girls _____.

5. **Great Aunt:** No ties for girls … I see … Very modern.

> **Nice to know**
>
> Im Englischen sagt man oft **I see.** um auszudrücken, dass man etwas zwar versteht, es darum aber noch lange nicht gutheißt!

Test **2** **Übungsgrammatik**

*3. Person **present simple** / Verneinung*

1

Wandeln Sie diese Sätze in die dritte Person Singular (**he**) um
(z.B. **I walk home. - He walks home**.).

1. I drive to work. _____

2. I like swimming. _____

3. I don't go to work by bus. _____

4. I don't read many books. _____

5. I'm very thin. _____

6. I'm not angry. _____

2

Verneinen Sie diese Sätze, indem Sie die Verben in der entsprechenden Form
in die Lücken schreiben (z.B. Hermione **lives** in Manchester. - Hermione **doesn't
live** in Manchester.)

1. Paul is Japanese. Paul _____ Japanese.

2. Kate reads books. Kate _____ books.

3. Ben and Jane like bananas. Ben and Jane _____ bananas.

4. We watch TV every evening. We _____ TV every evening.

5. I'm very angry. I _____ very angry.

6. They play football. They _____ football.

7. The apples are green. The apples _____ green.

Übungsgrammatik **2 Test**

Kurzantworten

3

Lesen Sie die Fragen und wählen Sie durch Ankreuzen die korrekte Antwort aus.

1. Do you like chocolate?
   - ☐ a. No, I'm not.
   - ☐ b. Yes, I do.
   - ☐ c. Yes, I doesn't.

2. Does Ben like swimming?
   - ☐ a. No, he doesn't.
   - ☐ b. Yes, he is.
   - ☐ c. No, he don't.

3. Do you go to work by bus?
   - ☐ a. No, I do.
   - ☐ b. Yes, I do.
   - ☐ c. Yes, I does.

4. Is Kate a teacher?
   - ☐ a. No, she aren't.
   - ☐ b. No, she isn't.
   - ☐ c. No, she doesn't.

5. Are you a teacher?
   - ☐ a. Yes, I'm not.
   - ☐ b. Yes, I do.
   - ☐ c. Yes, I am.

4 TR. 10

Bilden Sie Fragen, indem Sie die korrekte Wortgruppe unterstreichen und wählen Sie dann die passende Antwort aus.
Sie können Ihre Lösungen auch überprüfen, indem Sie sich die CD anhören.

1. *Know you / Do you know / You know* Kate? _____

2. *Does Kate / Kate does / Is Kate* smoke? _____

3. *Jane is / Is Jane / Does Jane* from Birmingham? _____

4. *You are / Do you / Are you* cold? _____

smoke – *rauchen*

Yes, I do.   No, she isn't.   Yes, I am.   No, she doesn't.

3 Übungsgrammatik

Paul und seine Familie / Nur halbe Sätze

1 TR. 11

Auf diesem Bild sehen Sie Pauls Familie. Lesen Sie, was Paul über seine Familienmitglieder zu sagen hat, oder hören Sie es sich, wenn Sie möchten, auf der CD an. Ordnen Sie dann die Sätze den richtigen Personen zu, indem Sie die entsprechende Ziffer in die Kästchen schreiben.

◀ **mother** – *Mutter*
father – *Vater*
homework – *Hausaufgaben*
visit – *besuchen*

- [ ] a. These are my kids. I help them with their homework.
- [ ] b. This is my sister. She often visits us.
- [ ] c. This is my mother. I like her very much.
- [ ] d. This is my father. He comes to see me every day.
- [ ] e. That is my brother. I often play tennis with him.

2 TR. 12

Können Sie die Satzanfänge auf der linken Seite mit den passenden Enden auf der rechten Seite verbinden? Die Lösung können Sie auch auf der CD überprüfen.

1. Ben's got
2. He has to
3. My daughter's always
4. She's
5. Do you want to

a. out. I never see her.
b. see them?
c. his exams this year.
d. fifteen years old.
e. study a lot.

◀ **have got** – *haben*
have to – *müssen*
daughter – *Tochter*
want – *wollen*
out – *aus/weg*
her – *sie/ihr*
them – *sie/ihnen*
his – *sein/seine*
exam – *Prüfung*
year – *Jahr*
study – *studieren/lernen*
a lot – *viel*

Personalpronomen

3

Personalpronomen

Wenn man die handelnde Person (das Subjekt) in einem Satz nicht immer wiederholen möchte, kann man sie durch ein **Personalpronomen** (**he**, **she**, **it**, ...) ersetzen.

Paul arrives at the bank.	**He** arrives at the bank.
Paul kommt in der Bank an.	*Er kommt in der Bank an.*
Ben and Jane go to school.	**They** go to school.
Ben und Jane gehen in die Schule.	*Sie gehen in die Schule.*

Die Form des **Personalpronomens** kann sich ändern, wenn es nicht die handelnde Person (das Subjekt), sondern das Objekt im Satz ersetzt.

Paul speaks to **Kate**.	Paul speaks to **her**.
Paul spricht mit Kate.	*Paul spricht mit ihr.*
Kate speaks to **Paul**.	Kate speaks to **him**.
Kate spricht mit Paul.	*Kate spricht mit ihm.*

Subjektpronomen

I (*ich*)	I go home.
you (*du/Sie*)	You are very nice.
he (*er*)	He plays tennis.
she (*sie*)	She reads.
it (*es*)	It is very nice.
we (*wir*)	We are a family.
you (*ihr/Sie*)	You are wonderful.
they (*sie*)	They go home.

Objektpronomen

me (*mir/mich*)	He likes me.
you (*dir/dich*)	He likes you.
him (*ihm/ihn*)	I like him.
her (*ihr/sie*)	I like her.
it (*ihm/es*)	I like it.
us (*uns*)	He likes us.
you (*euch/Sie*)	He likes you.
them (*ihnen/sie*)	He likes them.

> **Nice to know**
>
> Wortschatz
> Im Englischen gibt es keinen Unterschied zwischen **du**, **ihr** und **Sie**. Und auch nicht zwischen **dich**, **dir**, **euch** und **Ihnen**. Es bleibt immer bei **you**.

Übungsgrammatik

Im Café / Personalpronomen

4

Kate und Louise sitzen zusammen im Café. Sie haben sich wirklich lange nicht mehr gesehen und tauschen nun Neuigkeiten aus.
Lesen Sie den Dialog oder hören Sie sich ihn auf Ihrer CD an.
Markieren Sie dann alle **Personalpronomen** im Text.

Louise: Kate, it's so good to see you! And you're married to Paul, that's wonderful!
Kate: Yes, I'm married to him. And we've got two teenage kids.
Louise: Really? Oh, tell me all about them!
Kate: Well, Ben's sixteen now and Jane's fourteen. They're both at school, and they're out a lot. We don't see them much.
Louise: Yeah, I know all about that. I've got a daughter, you know. She's fifteen. She's always out, too. I never see her at all.
Kate: Well, at that age they really have their own life ...
Louise: That's true.
Kate: Well, what can we do? Anyway, Ben's got his exams this year, so he has to be at home more to study.
Louise: Oh, yes, school exams ... Do you remember when we ...?
Kate: Yes, of course. Wait, I've got some pictures here from last year, with some people you know. Do you want to see them?
Louise: Oh yes, please.

tell – sagen/erzählen
both – beide
too – auch
at all – überhaupt
age – Alter
own – eigener/eigen/eigenes
life – Leben
true – wahr
when – wenn/als
wait – warten
some – einige, ein paar
picture – Bild, Foto
last – letzter/letzte/letztes
people – Leute

5

Entziffern Sie diese Sätze und schreiben Sie sie auf ein Blatt Papier (z.B. **I s e e t h e m . – I see them.**).

1. S h e o f t e n s e e s h e r .
2. I n e v e r p l a y t e n n i s w i t h h i m .
3. T h e y a l w a y s v i s i t u s .
4. S h e v i s i t s h e r i n t h e e v e n i n g .
5. S h e n e v e r t a l k s a b o u t t h e m .
6. W e p l a y f o o t b a l l o n S a t u r d a y s .
7. D o y o u r e m e m b e r h e r ?

Lerntipp!

Oft müssen Sie sich noch unbekannte Wörter selbst erschließen. Stellen Sie sich dabei z.B. folgende Frage: Kenne ich ein deutsches Wort, das ähnlich ist?
Manchmal kennt man auch schon eine Vokabel, die denselben Wortstamm hat. Wenn Sie z.B. wissen, was **know** heißt, können Sie sicher auch erraten was **knowledge** bedeutet. Und zu guter Letzt lassen sich viele Wörter auch aus dem Zusammenhang erschließen.

Übungsgrammatik | **3**

Personalpronomen

6 ✎

Lesen Sie die Sätze und schreiben Sie dann die Sätze mit den korrekten Personalpronomen in die Lücken.

> He meets him.   They talk about him.
> We see them.   She meets her.
> He talks about them.   She sees her.

1. Jane and I see Ben and Paul. _____
2. Kate sees Jane. _____
3. Paul meets Ben. _____
4. Kate meets Louise. _____
5. Ben and Jane talk about Paul. _____
6. Paul talks about his children. _____

7 ✎

Zur Familie gehört auch Hermione, Kates Tante.
Lesen Sie den Text über Hermione und schreiben Sie jeweils das passende **Personalpronomen** in die Lücken.

nearly – *fast*
visit – *besuchen*
enjoy – *genießen*
talk – *sich unterhalten/sprechen*
however – *jedoch/wie auch immer*
say – *sagen*
think – *denken/glauben*
question – *Frage*
ask – *fragen*
should – *sollten*

Hermione is Kate's aunt. 1. _____ is nearly 80 years old and lives near Kate and Paul. 2. _____ often visits 3. _____. Kate really likes 4. _____ and enjoys 5. _____ visits. 6. _____ drink tea and talk. Ben and Jane, however, are not so happy. Ben says: "7. _____ don't think my great aunt likes 8. _____. 9. _____ always asks 10. _____ stupid questions about school. 11. _____ should listen to 12. _____!" And Aunt Hermione says: "Kate's children are wonderful. Ben really likes 13. _____. He enjoys talking about his school so much. And Paul, I really like 14. _____, too."

Übungsgrammatik

Have und *have got*

8

Have und **have got**
Im britischen Englisch wird anstatt **have** oft die Form **have got** benutzt. In der gesprochenen Sprache wird **have** dann meist zu **'ve** und **has** zu **'s** verkürzt.

Sehen Sie sich noch einmal diese Beispiele aus dem Dialog an bzw. hören Sie sie sich auf der CD an:
  We've got two kids.   *Wir haben zwei Kinder.*
  I've got some pictures.   *Ich habe ein paar Fotos.*

Wenn man **have got** verneint, braucht man das Hilfsverb **do** nicht. Nach **have** wird einfach **not** eingefügt, wobei dann oft zu **haven't** bzw. **hasn't** verkürzt wird.
  Kate **hasn't got** three children.
  Kate hat keine drei Kinder.
  Paul and Kate **haven't got** a big house.
  Paul und Kate haben kein großes Haus.

Bei Fragen wird **have**/**has** an den Anfang der Frage gestellt und **got** steht direkt nach dem Subjekt (der handelnden Person).
  Has Kate **got** three children?   *Hat Kate drei Kinder?*
  Have we **got** apples?   *Haben wir Äpfel?*

Nice to know
Im amerikanischen Englisch wird **have got** nicht benutzt. Man sagt dort nur **have**:
He has a lot of money.
I don't have a lot of time.

9

Sehen Sie sich die Bilder an. Schreiben Sie dann die jeweils korrekte Form von **have got** in die Lücke.

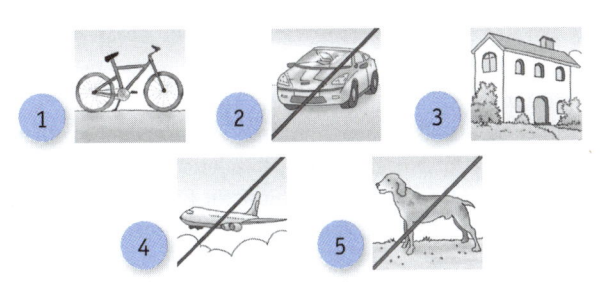

1. Ben _____ a bicycle.
2. I _____ a car.
3. We _____ a house.
4. They _____ an airplane.
5. He _____ a dog.

Lerntipp!
Sicherlich haben Sie schon bemerkt, dass das britische und das amerikanische Englisch sich nicht nur in der Aussprache unterscheiden, sondern dass manche Vokabeln auch ganz verschieden sind oder unterschiedlich geschrieben werden. In diesem Kurs lernen Sie britisches Englisch, im Wortverzeichnis finden Sie jedoch auch amerikanische Varianten.

◀ **bicycle** – *Fahrrad*
  airplane – *Flugzeug*

Übungsgrammatik 3

Im Café / Demonstrativpronomen

10

Hier sehen Sie den zweiten Teil des Gesprächs zwischen Kate und Louise im Café. Lesen Sie den Dialog oder hören Sie sich ihn auf Ihrer CD an.
Der Text enthält viele der englischen Demonstrativpronomen **this**, **that**, **these** und **those**. Markieren Sie alle Demonstrativpronomen, die Sie finden können.

> **recognize** – *erkennen*
> **let** – *lassen*
> **where** – *wo*
> **look** – *schauen/ aussehen*
> **different** – *anders*
> **my goodness** – *meine Güte*
> **same** – *gleich*
> **who** – *wer*
> **next to** – *neben*
> **those** – *jene*
> **hope** – *hoffen*

Kate: Let me see, where have I got them? Ah, here they are. Look, do you recognize these people?
Louise: No, I don't. Oh, wait, is that Julia?
Kate: Yes, that's right. That is Julia. She looks very different now!
Louise: Yes, totally. And this? Is this Paul?
Kate: Yes, it is.
Louise: My goodness, he still looks just the same. And here, next to him? Who's that?
Kate: That's Keith. Do you remember him? The best in our class at school? He now works at the airport. And those two are his children.
Louise: We really are old now. Everyone's got teenage children.
Kate: I know. Listen, have you got some time on Sunday? We could have a barbecue in the garden.
Louise: Sounds good. Can I bring my daughter?
Kate: Yes, sure. Let's hope for good weather!

> **Lerntipp!**
>
> Das Markieren von Textstellen oder Wörtern kann sehr hilfreich sein. Nehmen Sie sich ab und an die Zeit, einen Text aus einer englischen Zeitung oder eine Passage aus einem Buch nach Ihren eigenen Vorgaben zu bearbeiten. So können Sie zum Beispiel eine Zeitform, die Sie gerade gelernt haben, im Text markieren und in den unterschiedlichen Zusammenhängen lernen. Oder Sie können Wörter, die Ihnen nicht geläufig sind, hervorheben und gezielt üben. Ihren eigenen Ideen sind da keine Grenzen gesetzt.

11

Demonstrativpronomen
Wenn man etwas besonders herausheben möchte, benutzt man die **Demonstrativpronomen** **this** und **that** für einzelne Personen oder Objekte, oder **these** und **those** für mehrere. Dabei stehen **this** und **these** immer für Personen oder Sachen, die dem Betrachter näher sind, und **that** und **those** für Personen oder Sachen, die weiter entfernt sind.

3 Übungsgrammatik

Demonstrativpronomen

12

Sehen Sie sich die Bildpaare an. Lesen Sie den Satz bzw. hören Sie ihn sich an und entscheiden Sie, zu welchem Bild er besser passt, indem Sie den entsprechenden Buchstaben in das Kästchen eintragen.

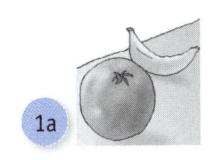

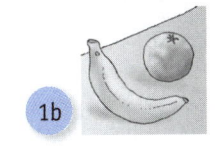

1a 1b

This is a banana and that's an orange. ☐

2a 2b

This is Kate and that's Paul. ☐

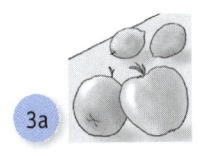

3a 3b

These are apples and those are lemons. ☐

◀ **lemon** – *Zitrone*

4a 4b

These are Ben and Jane,
and those are Paul and Kate. ☐

13

Unterstreichen Sie das Wort, das den Satz korrekt ergänzt.

1. *These / That / This* are bananas.
2. *These / This / Those* is an apple.
3. *That / Those / These* is Paul.
4. *Those / These / This* is a dog.

Übungsgrammatik 3

Have got / *Pronomen raten*

14

Schreiben Sie das passende Wort aus dem Kasten in die Lücken.
Aber Vorsicht! Wenn sie alle Wörter richtig in die Lücken eingetragen und dann im Kasten durchgestrichen haben, bleiben zwei Wörter übrig.
Welcher Satz lässt sich daraus bilden?

> they   Have   got   This   fun   him
> her   them   Has   Those

1. Ben's _____ a bicycle.
2. _____ are tomatoes.
3. Louise? Oh, yes, Kate knows _____.
4. The family? Yes, _____ 've got a garden.
5. _____ here is my car.
6. _____ Jane got a bicycle?
7. Ben and Jane? Yes, we know _____.
8. Paul? Do you know _____?

15

Unterstreichen Sie jeweils das Pronomen, das nicht zu den anderen passt.

1. this	that	those	him
2. he	me	she	it
3. those	that	these	her
4. that	him	her	you
5. we	they	us	it
6. he	she	it	him
7. them	she	it	he
8. us	we	you	those
9. him	her	it	I
10. this	that	you	those
11. them	us	me	he
12. him	she	I	we
13. she	her	I	they
14. them	we	he	she
15. it	she	he	that

Test **3** **Übungsgrammatik**

*Personalpronomen / **Have got***

1

Ersetzen Sie die in Klammern angegebenen Personen durch das passende Personalpronomen.

1. Jane likes _____ (Ben and I).

2. _____ (Paul and Ben) often play football.

3. _____ (Louise and I) like shopping.

4. Kate goes to visit _____ (Louise).

5. Paul speaks to _____ (Ben).

6. We all like _____ (Paul and Kate).

2 TR. 17

Welcher Satz passt zum Bild? Markieren Sie die passende Aussage durch Ankreuzen. Wenn Sie möchten, können Sie sich die Sätze auch auf Ihrer CD anhören.

1.
- a. Ben's got two bicycles.
- b. Ben's got a bicycle.
- c. Ben's got a car.

2.
- a. Jane's got a book.
- b. Jane's not got a book.
- c. Jane's got two books.

3.
- a. Paul and Kate have got a house.
- b. Paul and Kate haven't got a house.
- c. Jane's got a house.

4.
- a. Ben hasn't got a car.
- b. Ben's got two cars.
- c. Ben hasn't got a dog.

5.
- a. Jane hasn't got two dogs.
- b. Jane's got two dogs.
- c. Jane hasn't got a dog.

285

Pronomen

3

Unterstreichen Sie das richtige Demonstrativpronomen.

1. Those / This / These is my sister Kate.
2. That / These / Those is a dog.
3. This / These / That are Ben and Jane.
4. This / That / These are bananas.
5. Those / That / This are apples.

4

Schreiben Sie ein passendes Demonstrativpronomen (**this that**, **these** oder **those**) in die Lücken.

1 _____ are apples.

2 _____ are apples.

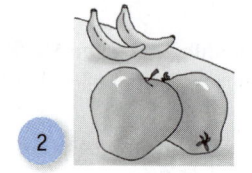

3 _____ is a car.

4 _____ is a car.

5

Bringen Sie die Wörter in diesen kurzen Sätzen wieder in die richtige Reihenfolge und schreiben Sie sie auf ein Blatt Papier.

1. Sunday / her / He / every / visits / .
2. bring / They / us / cakes / often / .
3. many / We / together / do / things / .
4. much / very / like / you / I / .
5. café / You / go / the / me / to / with / .
6. We / play / with / never / him / football / .

4 Übungsgrammatik

Die ing-Form / Zu Hause

1

Verbinden Sie die Beispielsätze auf der linken Seite mit einem passenden Verb auf der rechten Seite. Sie können sich die Sätze auch auf Ihrer CD anhören.

1. Ben's riding a bicycle.
2. Jane's playing the piano.
3. We're watching TV.
4. Paul's driving home.
5. Are they going to the theatre?

a. watch
b. go
c. drive
d. ride
e. play

Nice to know

Im Englischen gibt es zwei Möglichkeiten *Fahrrad fahren* auszudrücken: Man kann sagen **cycle** oder **ride a bike** – man fährt also nicht Fahrrad, sondern man reitet es!

2

Es ist Samstagnachmittag bei Kate und Paul. Sehen Sie sich an, was die Familienmitglieder gerade tun. Lesen Sie dann die Sätze und schreiben Sie die entsprechenden Verben in die Lücken.
Ihre Lösungen können Sie auch überprüfen, indem Sie sich Ihre CD anhören.

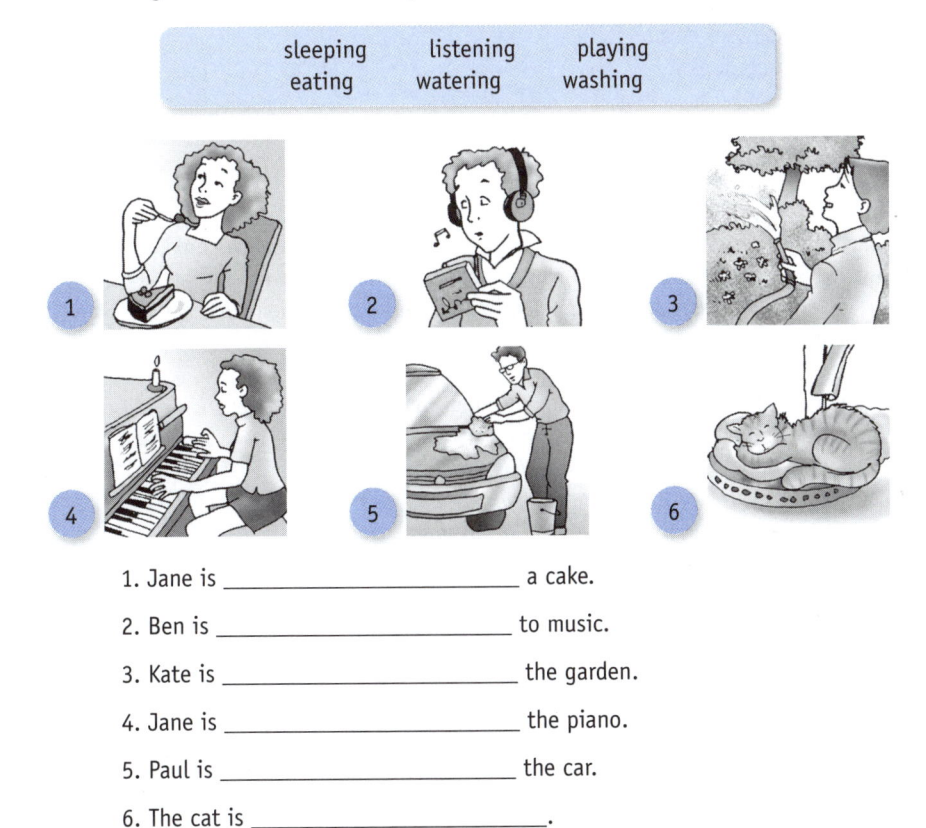

sleeping   listening   playing
eating   watering   washing

1. Jane is _____ a cake.

2. Ben is _____ to music.

3. Kate is _____ the garden.

4. Jane is _____ the piano.

5. Paul is _____ the car.

6. The cat is _____ .

eat – *essen*
water – *gießen*
cat – *Katze*
sleep – *schlafen*

287

Übungsgrammatik

We're having a barbecue! / Present continuous

3

Lesen Sie den Text bzw. hören Sie sich den Dialog auf Ihrer CD an.
Markieren Sie alle **ing-Formen** (**present continuous**) im Text.

Kate: Hi everyone. I'm back!
Paul: Hi, how was the coffee with Louise?
Kate: Really nice. What on earth are you doing?
Paul: We're cooking dinner!
Ben: We're making a roast dinner for tonight …
Paul: … and you're not helping us! We're doing everything ourselves!
Kate: OK, fantastic! By the way, Louise and her daughter are coming here on Saturday.
Paul: Really? Good, we can have a barbecue then. But you know I'm playing tennis with Michael in the early afternoon.
Kate: Yes, sure, I know. Louise is coming at six. I hope that's not too early for you?
Paul: Oh, that's no problem. We usually finish at four o'clock. Are you making your famous egg salad?
Ben: Yes, please, Mum!
Kate: Well, perhaps …

> **was** – *war*
> **on earth** – *auf Erden*
> **roast dinner** – *Bratengericht*
> **everything** – *alles*
> **ourselves** – *selbst*
> **by the way** – *übrigens*
> **early** – *früh*
> **afternoon** – *Nachmittag*
> **no problem** – *kein Problem*
> **famous** – *berühmt*
> **egg salad** – *Eiersalat*
> **perhaps** – *vielleicht*

Nice to know
Ein typisches englisches **roast dinner** besteht aus **meat** (*Fleisch*), **roast potatoes** (*Röstkartoffeln*), **vegetables** (*Gemüse*) und **gravy** (*Bratensoße*). Manchmal gibt es auch **Yorkshire puddings** (ähnlich wie herzhafte Windbeutel) dazu.

4

Formen des present continuous
Eine weitere englische Form der Gegenwart ist das so genannte **present continuous**. Es wird gebildet, indem man an die Grundform des Verbs **-ing** anhängt. Diese Verbform wird immer in Kombination mit einer passenden Form des Hilfsverbs **be** benutzt.

Einige Verben haben bei der Bildung der **ing-Form** Besonderheiten.
Endet ein Verb auf **–e**, so fällt dieser Buchstabe weg:

mak**e**	mak**ing**	We'**re making** a cake.
		Wir machen einen Kuchen.
tak**e**	tak**ing**	I'**m taking** an aspirin.
		Ich nehme ein Aspirin.

Endet ein Verb auf einen Vokal + einen Konsonant, so wird der letzte Konsonant verdoppelt:

sit	si**tt**ing	They'**re sitting** in the garden.
		Sie sitzen im Garten.
shop	sho**pp**ing	Kate'**s shopping** in the supermarket.
		Kate kauft im Supermarkt ein.

4 | Übungsgrammatik

Present continuous

5

Gebrauch des present continuous
Das **present continuous** wird verwendet, wenn:
- etwas genau im Moment des Sprechens geschieht,
    It's four o'clock. Ben and Paul are making dinner.
    Es ist vier Uhr. Ben und Paul machen gerade das Abendessen.

- etwas im Moment gültig ist, aber nicht notwendigerweise genau zum Zeitpunkt des Sprechens geschieht,
    Paul is very tired. He's working too much at the moment.
    Paul ist sehr müde. Er arbeitet im Moment zu viel.

- etwas in naher Zukunft geschehen wird und schon so fest geplant ist, dass es sich aller Voraussicht nach nicht mehr ändern wird.
    Louise is coming to visit.   *Louise kommt zu Besuch.*

Für routinemäßige Abläufe und sich regelmäßig wiederholende Handlungen verwendet man dagegen das **present simple**.
Man benutzt das **present continuous** daher auch oft, um etwas, das im Moment geschieht, mit etwas zu vergleichen, das normalerweise geschieht.
    Kate usually cooks on Saturdays.
    Normalerweise kocht Kate samstags.
    This Saturday, Paul and Ben are cooking.
    Diesen Samstag kochen Paul und Ben.

> **Nice to know**
> Wenn Sie im Deutschen *momentan*, *im Moment*, oder *gerade* sagen würden, dann können Sie im Englischen das **present continuous** benutzen!

> **Nice to know**
> **Study** kann im Englischen sowohl *lernen* als auch *studieren* bedeuten. Sehr junge Schüler bezeichnet man als **pupils**, ab 16 Jahren ist aber jeder Schüler ein **student**.

6

Lesen Sie, worüber Ben sich beschwert, und ergänzen Sie die fehlenden Verben im **present continuous**.

| do | work | do | learn | give | study | write | be |

Well, this year is really horrible. We 1. _____ so hard, I don't believe it. The teachers 2. _____ us so much homework that we 3. _____ until late in the evening. Today I 4. _____ two essays for English, one for history, and then I 5. _____ my maths homework as well! Jane's lucky, she 6. _____ nothing at all! She plays with the cat all afternoon and then she comes and asks me: "7. _____ you _____ again?"

◀ **horrible** – *fürchterlich/schrecklich*
homework – *Hausaufgaben*
late – *spät*
until – *bis*
essay – *Aufsatz*
as well – *auch noch*
nothing – *nichts*
history – *Geschichte*
be lucky – *Glück haben*
again – *wieder*

Übungsgrammatik 4

*Verneinung und Fragen im **present continuous***

7

Verneinung

Sätze im **present continuous** verneint man, indem man dem Hilfsverb **be** ein **not** nachstellt. Dabei wird die Form von **be** oft verkürzt und entweder mit dem Subjekt oder mit **not** zusammengezogen:

You're not helping us!	**You aren't helping us!**
Du hilfst uns nicht!	*Du hilfst uns nicht!*
Jane's not riding a bicycle.	**Jane isn't riding a bicycle.**
Jane fährt nicht Fahrrad.	*Jane fährt nicht Fahrrad.*

8

Schreiben Sie die fehlenden Wörter in die Lücken.

| isn't | 'm not | not | aren't |

1. We _____ playing golf.
2. She's _____ a good swimmer.
3. He _____ a fast driver.
4. I _____ tired.

tired – *müde*

9

Fragen

Zur Bildung von Fragen wird einfach das Subjekt mit der Form von **be** vertauscht.

You are making egg salad.	**Are you making egg salad?**
Du machst Eiersalat.	*Machst du Eiersalat?*
Louise is staying for dinner.	**Is Louise staying for dinner?**
Louise bleibt zum Abendessen.	*Bleibt Louise zum Abendessen?*

10

Unterstreichen Sie die korrekte Form der Fragebildung.

1. *Is you / you are / Are you* staying for dinner?
2. *Paul is / Is Paul / Paul has* playing tennis with Michael?
3. *Are they / they are / Is they* riding a bicycle?
4. *She is / Are she / Is she* a good cook?

11

Kurzantworten

Auf Fragen im **present continuous**, die mit **ja** oder **nein** beantwortet werden können, kann man oft kurz antworten, indem man ein **Personalpronomen** und das Verb **be** in der passenden Form wiederholt.

Is Kate cooking dinner?   **Are** you learning English?
Yes, she **is**.   Yes, I **am**.
No, she **isn't**./No, she**'s not**.   No, I**'m not**.

Lerntipp!

Kurzantworten können mit allen englischen Zeitformen gebildet werden. Schauen Sie sich daher ruhig noch einmal die Bildung der Kurzantworten im **present simple** im Modul 2 an. Je öfter Sie ein Thema wiederholen oder es mit einem neuen Thema vergleichen, umso besser können Sie es sich merken und das Gelernte auch anwenden.

12

Kreuzen Sie die korrekte Antwort auf die Frage an.

1. Are you watching TV?
   - a. No, I'm not.
   - b. No, I don't.
   - c. No, I isn't.

2. Is Paul drinking a beer?
   - a. Yes, he are.
   - b. Yes, he does.
   - c. Yes, he is.

3. Are the children sleeping?
   - a. Yes, they aren't.
   - b. No, they don't.
   - c. No, they aren't.

4. Are you tired?
   - a. No, I not.
   - b. Yes, I am.
   - c. Yes, I do.

13 TR. 21

Sehen Sie sich die Bilder an und beantworten Sie dann die Fragen mit einer passenden Kurzantwort (z. B. **Yes, he is. / No, they aren't.**).
Wenn Sie möchten, können Sie sich die Fragen auf Ihrer CD anhören.

1. Is he playing football? _____
2. Are they dancing? _____
3. Are they cleaning their room? _____
4. Is he doing his homework? _____

Nice to know

Vorsicht Falle! Im Englischen heißt es **I'm doing my homework** (nicht **making**!).

Übungsgrammatik 4

Present simple oder *continuous?*

14

Present simple oder **continuous**?
Im Englischen gibt es zwei Zeitformen, um die Gegenwart auszudrücken: das **present continuous** und das **present simple**.

Sie haben gelernt, dass das **present continuous** dann benutzt wird, wenn etwas im Moment des Sprechens geschieht oder gültig ist oder wenn etwas für die Zukunft fest geplant ist.

Im Gegensatz dazu wird das **present simple** nur dann benutzt, wenn man eine allgemein gültige Aussage oder Feststellung macht oder um eine Gewohnheit oder regelmäßig wiederkehrende Handlung auszudrücken.

Je nachdem, welche Zeitform man benutzt, kann ein Satz also eine andere Bedeutung bekommen.

> I don't **drink** coffee.
> bedeutet, dass ich nie Kaffee trinke.
> I'm not **drinking** coffee.
> bedeutet, dass ich im Moment keinen Kaffee trinke, sondern etwas anderes.

> **Nice to know**
>
> Im Deutschen werden **present simple** und **present continuous** genau gleich übersetzt:
> **Kate cooks every day.**
> *Kate kocht jeden Tag.*
> **Kate is cooking today.**
> *Kate kocht heute.*

15

Schreiben Sie die Verben in die passende Lücke. Achten Sie dabei darauf, ob Sie das **present continuous** oder das **present simple** benötigen.

> is reading   reads   Are … going   go
> works   isn't working   plays   is playing

1. Paul _____ tennis this Saturday. He always _____ tennis on Saturdays.

2. It's nine o'clock and Kate _____ a book. She often _____ in the evening.

3. It's Sunday and Louise _____. She never _____ on Sundays.

4. _____ you _____ home now? Yes, I usually _____ home at five o'clock.

Present continuous

16

Entscheiden Sie bei jedem Satz, ob er etwas beschreibt, das die Person normalerweise (**usually**) macht, oder ob er etwas beschreibt, dass die Person nur im Moment (**at the moment**) tut. Schreiben Sie dann **A** für **usually** bzw. **B** für **at the moment** in das Kästchen daneben. Die Lösung können Sie sich auch auf Ihrer CD anhören. Erst werden alle Sätze im **present simple**, dann die im **present continuous** gesprochen.

1. I go swimming once a week. ☐
   I'm going swimming a lot. ☐
2. Paul is taking the train. ☐
   Paul drives to work. ☐
3. Ben plays football on Mondays. ☐
   Ben's playing in a big match! ☐
4. She's not working late today. ☐
   Kate works late. ☐

Nice to know
Im Englischen sagt man oft **go + -ing**:
I go swimming.
Ich gehe schwimmen.
I go jogging.
Ich gehen joggen.

Im **present continuous** sagt man dann **going + -ing**:
I'm going swimming.
I'm going jogging.

◀ **once** – *einmal*
complain – *sich beschweren*

Nice to know
Anstatt *Ich freue mich wahnsinnig!* sagt man mit typisch britischer Untertreibung oft **I'm not complaining.** (*Ich beschwere mich nicht.*), wenn man über etwas glücklich ist.

17

Im folgenden Text spricht Kate über die Sommerferien der Familie. Ergänzen Sie die Verben in der korrekten Form - manchmal benötigen Sie das **present continuous**, manchmal das **present simple**. Als Hilfestellung sind die Grundformen der benötigten Verben in Klammern angegeben!

Well, normally we 1. _____ (spend) our holidays in the South of England. We 2. _____ (rent) a small cottage by the sea and 3. _____ (relax) on the beach. We 4. _____ (cook) in the evenings and we 5. _____ (play) games together. But this year, we 6. _____ (go) to France. We 7. _____ (drive) there and we 8. _____ (stay) on a camping site in Southern France. It'll be a wonderful holiday, so I 9. _____ (not complain)!

◀ **normally** – *normalerweise*
spend – *verbringen*
holiday – *Ferien/Urlaub*
South of England – *Südengland*
rent – *mieten*
small – *klein*
cottage – *Hütte/kleines Haus*
sea – *Meer*
beach – *Strand*
game – *Spiel*
camping site – *Campingplatz*
Southern France – *Südfrankreich*

Übungsgrammatik 4

Ing-Formen

18

Die **ing-Formen** folgender Verben sind im Gitter versteckt (waagerecht, senkrecht oder diagonal). Können Sie alle Verben finden?

1. look	7. listen	13. take
2. dance	8. drive	14. make
3. feed	9. drink	15. need
4. be	10. speak	16. work
5. have	11. live	17. leave
6. learn	12. write	

J	Z	O	P	L	O	O	K	I	N	G	B	O	O	S
U	U	E	J	I	D	U	K	Y	E	A	E	P	K	J
L	Q	K	O	L	J	X	F	E	E	D	I	N	G	P
J	I	L	U	E	A	L	G		D	P	N	W	S	K
W	P	V	L	A	W	O	R	K	I	N	G	P	U	U
R	U	J	I	R	E	A	D	I	N	G	H	A	Y	T
I	P	U	S	N	D	P	R	R	G	U	G	J	J	T
T	D	Q	T	I	G	U	I	J	I	O	I	J	N	W
I	A	J	E	N	B	H	N	P	D	V	V	L	M	A
N	N	K	N	G	M	A	K	I	N	G	I	D	E	U
G	C	J	I	J	N	V	I	L	Z	A	N	N	P	J
U	I	U	N	N	M	I	N	J	J	E	G	Q	G	Q
J	N	O	G	L	G	N	G	Z	Q	F	O	J	L	K
Z	G	L	X	U	Z	G	S	P	E	A	K	I	N	G
L	E	A	V	I	N	G	H	N	O	E	J	C	H	E

19

Nun sind Sie fast fertig mit dem Modul. **Very good!**
Schreiben Sie nun noch diese Sätze in ihrer richtigen Reihenfolge auf.

1. garden / watering / We / the / 're / .
2. He / book / a / reading / 's / .
3. driving / 's / a / car / He / .
4. 's / She / armchair / in / sitting / an / .
5. We / dinner / 're / making / .

Test 4 | Übungsgrammatik

*Verben im **present continuous***

1

Finden Sie zu jedem Bild einen passenden Satz und schreiben Sie die entsprechende Ziffer in das Kästchen.

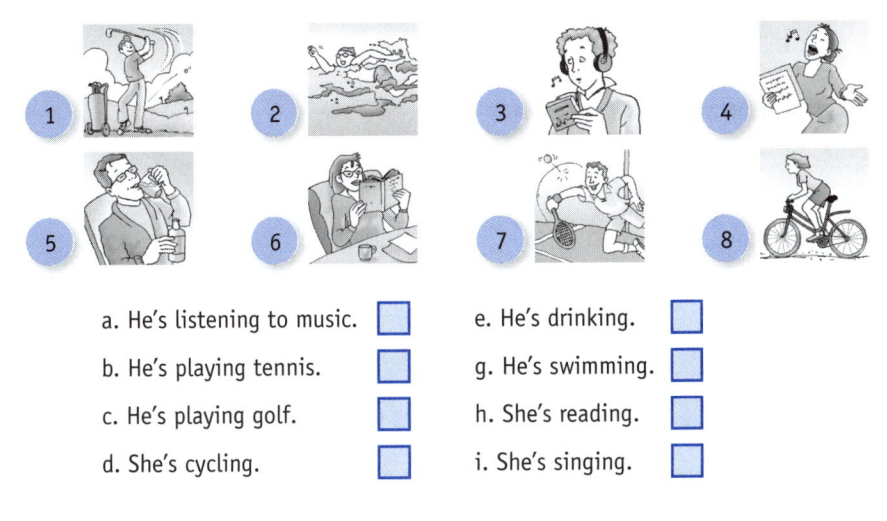

a. He's listening to music. ☐
b. He's playing tennis. ☐
c. He's playing golf. ☐
d. She's cycling. ☐
e. He's drinking. ☐
g. He's swimming. ☐
h. She's reading. ☐
i. She's singing. ☐

2

Was tun die Leute auf den Bildern? Ergänzen Sie die Sätze mit einem passenden Verb im present continuous.

1. They _____ football.

2. The cat _____.

3. He _____.

4. She _____ dinner.

295

*Verneinung / Fragen und Antworten / **Present simple** oder **continuous**?*

3

Ergänzen Sie jeden Satz mit der korrekten Form, indem Sie diese unterstreichen.

1. She *not going / isn't going / isn't go* there.
2. I *not being / be not / 'm not* leaving.
3. *Is you / Are you / You're* working?
4. *She are / Are she / Is she* coming?

4

Lesen Sie die Frage und wählen Sie dann die korrekte Antwort aus.

1. Is he sleeping? Yes, he is. / No, he is. / No, he doesn't.
2. Does she drive? No, she don't. / No, she isn't. / No, she doesn't.
3. Are you going jogging? No, I am. / Yes, I am. / Yes, I'm.
4. Are they leaving? No, they're not. / Yes, they aren't. / No, they don't.

5

Schreiben Sie die fehlenden Verben in der korrekten Form (**present simple** oder **present continuous**) in die Lücken!
Die Grundform der Verben, die Sie benötigen, ist jeweils in Klammern angegeben.

1. I usually _____ (read) a book in the evening.
2. Today, I _____ (drive) to work. I need the car there.
3. She often _____ (prepare) dinner for the family.
4. Today, she _____ (prepare) a roast dinner.
5. They never _____ (leave) the house before seven in the morning.
6. I always _____ (eat) breakfast.

5 Übungsgrammatik

So viele Pläne! / Die Zukunft

1

Ben und Jane haben große Pläne, was sie in der Zukunft alles machen möchten – und sie sind sehr überzeugt davon, dass sie das alles auch schaffen werden! Diese Sätze, die Sie sich auch auf Ihrer CD anhören können, beschreiben die Pläne von Ben und Jane. Verbinden Sie sie mit dem jeweils passenden Bild.

a. I'll drive a big car!
b. I'll become a doctor!
c. I'll go to university and study law!
d. I'll earn a lot of money!
e. I won't drive a big car!

Nice to know

Vorsicht! **Become** heißt auf Deutsch *werden*, nicht, wie man vermuten könnte, *bekommen*! Stellen Sie sich einmal folgendes Gespräch vor:
Tourist:
Waiter, when will I become my steak?
Waiter:
I hope never, sir.

◀ **law** – Jura/Recht
earn – verdienen
will – werden
won't – nicht werden
waiter – Kellner

2

Auch Kate hat Pläne für Ben und Jane - diese befassen sich aber mehr mit der direkten Zukunft ihrer Kinder.
Lesen Sie die Sätze laut bzw. hören Sie auf Ihrer CD, was Kates Pläne für ihre Kinder sind. Sprechen Sie dann die Sätze laut nach.

1. Ben will go to college next year.
2. Jane will learn to dance.
3. Ben will take his driving test next year.
4. Jane won't learn French any more.
5. Ben won't have time to play football.

◀ **driving test** – Führerscheinprüfung

Nice to know

Auf Englisch *nimmt* man eine Prüfung, man *macht* sie nicht:
Ben will take his driving test next year.

297

Übungsgrammatik 5

*Das **will future** / Vorbereitungen fürs Grillfest*

3

Bildung des will future
Das **will future** wird aus dem Hilfsverb **will** und der Grundform des Vollverbs gebildet. Hierbei steht **will** immer vor dem Verb und wird oft zu **'ll** verkürzt. Verneinte Sätze bildet man, indem man nach dem **will** ein **not** einfügt. Dies wird dann meist verkürzt zu **won't**.

> I**'ll** prepare the steaks.
> I **won't** put garlic in the salad.

Bei der Bildung des **will future** muss man nicht auf das **-s** in der 3. Person Singular achten. Die Form ist für alle Personen gleich.

Nice to know
Im Deutschen kann man das **will future** auf zwei Arten übersetzen:
Ben will take his driving test next year.
Ben wird nächstes Jahr seine Führerscheinprüfung machen.
oder
Ben macht nächstes Jahr seine Führerscheinprüfung.

---

need – *müssen, brauchen*
set up – *aufstellen*
barbecue – *Grill*
kitchen – *Küche*
manage – *schaffen*
fridge – *Kühlschrank*
garlic – *Knoblauch*
use – *benutzen*
enough – *genug*
break – *zerbrechen /kaputtmachen*
if – *wenn/falls*
careful – *vorsichtig*
already – *schon*
soon – *bald*

4

Es ist Samstagnachmittag und heute kommen Louise und ihre Tochter zum Grillen. Paul und Kate sind in der Küche und bereiten das Essen vor.
Lesen Sie den Dialog oder hören Sie ihn sich auf der CD an.

Paul: OK then, what do we need to do?
Kate: Well, I'm making the salad now, and then I think, I'll prepare the steaks.
Paul: I'll set up the barbecue, then. Will you need me in the kitchen later?
Kate: Let me think ... No, I won't. I'll manage.
Paul: All right. I'll look after the drinks. I'll put some white wine in the fridge.
Kate: Fine. Now, the salad. I won't put garlic in it, is that all right?
Paul: Yes, sure. Oh, and we won't use the good glasses, I think.
Kate: Why not? The children are old enough, they won't break them if they are careful.
Paul: OK, we'll use them, then. Oh, it's five o'clock already! They'll be here soon.

Entscheiden Sie nun, ob die Sätze falsch (Kreuz) oder richtig (Häkchen) sind.

1. Kate will prepare the steaks. ■
2. Paul will put some beer in the fridge. ■
3. Kate won't put garlic in the salad. ■
4. They will use the good glasses. ■

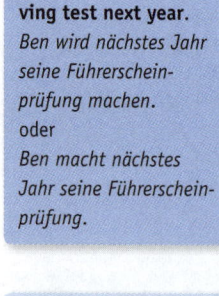

Das will future / Urlaubspläne

5

Gebrauch des will future
Das **will future** wird benutzt, um über zukünftige Ereignisse zu sprechen.
Man kann damit:
- Vorhersagen machen,
  I think it'll rain tomorrow. *Ich denke, es wird morgen regnen.*

- spontane Entscheidungen ausdrücken,
  I won't put garlic in the salad. *Ich werde keinen Knoblauch in den Salat tun.*

- über die Zukunft nachdenken
  Maybe I'll go to the cinema tomorrow. *Vielleicht werde ich morgen ins Kino gehen.*

- und Dinge zusagen oder absagen.
  I'll set up the barbecue. *Ich werde den Grill aufstellen.*
  I won't need you in the kitchen later. *Ich werde dich später nicht in der Küche brauchen.*

> **Nice to know**
> Das **will future** können Sie auch im Restaurant benutzen, wenn Sie Ihr Essen bestellen. Sagen Sie einfach **I'll have** + das Gericht, welches Sie bestellen möchten.
> **Waiter:** What can I get you?
> **Customer:** I'll have a steak, please.

6

Paul und Kate besprechen den geplanten Urlaub in Südfrankreich.
Schreiben Sie die fehlenden Verben im **will future** in die Lücken. Die Verben, die Sie benötigen, stehen in ihrer Grundform in Klammern neben der Lücke. Manchmal brauchen Sie die **positive**, manchmal die **negative** Form.

Kate: We 1. _____ (leave) the house at 8 in the morning, so we 2. _____ (arrive) in Dover at about 4 in the afternoon.

Paul: Oh, no, it 3. _____ (take) us that long. I think the drive 4. _____ (take) 5 hours at most.

Kate: OK, so we 5. _____ (have) extra time in Dover.

Paul: Yes, we 6. _____ (need) that because I 7. _____ (want) to go duty-free shopping!

> leave – *verlassen*
> arrive – *ankommen*
> about – *ungefähr*
> drive – *Fahrt*
> it takes us – *wir brauchen (Zeit)*
> hour – *Stunde*
> at most – *höchstens*
> that long – *so lange*
> because – *weil*
> duty-free – *zollfrei*

Übungsgrammatik 5

Fragen und Kurzantworten

7

> **Nice to know**
>
> Negative Fragen werden oft benutzt, um Überraschung auszudrücken. Wenn jemand Sie fragt: **Won't you be here tomorrow?**, dann erwartet er/sie eigentlich, dass Sie da sein werden.

Fragen und Kurzantworten

Fragen im **will future** bildet man, indem man das Subjekt und **will** vertauscht.
Auf Fragen im **will future**, die mit *ja* oder *nein* beantwortet werden können, kann man eine Kurzantwort geben, indem man nach **yes** oder **no** das Personalpronomen und die passende Form von **will** anhängt.
Negative Fragen bildet man, indem man **will** durch **won't** ersetzt oder indem man nach dem Subjekt ein **not** einfügt:

Won't you come tomorrow? *Wirst du morgen nicht kommen?*
Will you **not** come tomorrow? *Wirst du morgen nicht kommen?*

8

Die folgenden Fragen im **will future** sind durcheinander gepurzelt!
Schreiben Sie sie in ihrer richtigen Reihenfolge auf.

1. come / Will / tomorrow / they / here / ?
2. his / Ben / take / driving test / Won't / ?
3. you / Will / him / later / phone / ?
4. Won't / the / cake / he / bring / ?
5. you / way / find / the / Will / ?
6. go / Jane / university / Will / to / ?

9

Lesen Sie die Fragen oder hören Sie sie sich auf der CD an.
Kreuzen Sie dann die grammatikalisch richtigen Antworten an.
Es können auch mehrere Antworten richtig sein!

> **Nice to know**
>
> Pommes heißen nur in Großbritannien **chips**. In Nordamerika heißen sie **French fries**.

1. Will you go home early today?
- ☐ a. Yes, I will.
- ☐ b. No, I won't.
- ☐ c. Yes, I'll.
- ☐ d. Yes, I do.

2. Will they buy the apples?
- ☐ a. No, they will.
- ☐ b. No, they won't.
- ☐ c. No, they don't.
- ☐ d. No, they aren't.

3. Will Kate make chips?
- ☐ a. Yes, she will.
- ☐ b. No, she willn't.
- ☐ c. No, she want.
- ☐ d. No, she woesn't.

4. Will he drive to work?
- ☐ a. Yes, he will.
- ☐ b. No, he won't.
- ☐ c. He'll.
- ☐ d. No, she won't.

*Das **will future** mit **if***

10

Das will future mit if
Wenn man Bedingungen in der Zukunft ausdrücken will, benutzt man im Hauptsatz das **will future** und im Nebensatz mit **if** (*wenn/falls*) das **present simple**.
    I'll make a salad **if** you **help** me.
    Ich mache einen Salat, wenn Du mir hilfst.

Die Stellung von Haupt- und Nebensatz kann dabei ohne Bedeutungsunterschied vertauscht werden. Man muss aber beachten, dass im Englischen nur dann ein Komma gesetzt wird, wenn der if-Satz zuerst kommt.
    I won't go swimming **if** it **rains** tomorrow.
    Ich werde nicht schwimmen gehen, wenn es morgen regnet.
    If it **rains** tomorrow, I **won't go** swimming.
    Wenn es morgen regnet, werde ich nicht schwimmen gehen.

> **Lerntipp!**
> Es ist sinnvoll, sich die Grammatikregeln immer wieder zu vergegenwärtigen. Vor allem, wenn Sie sich bei einem bestimmten Thema unsicher sind.
> In diesem Buch finden Sie eine Zusammenfassung aller Grammatikthemen, die behandelt werden. Schlagen Sie am besten alles nach, was Ihnen beim Lösen der Übungen Schwierigkeiten bereitet.

11

Entziffern Sie diese Sätze! Schreiben Sie sie richtig auf.

1. I'llbebackearlyifthereisn'tsomuchtraffic.
2. PaulwillsetupthebarbecueifKatepreparesthesteaks.
3. Theywillphoneusiftheycan'tfindtheway.

> ◀ **traffic** – *Verkehr*
> **phone** – *anrufen/telefonieren*

12

Unterstreichen Sie zu den Satzanfängen das jeweils richtige Ende. Denken Sie dabei daran, dass man das **will future** nur in den Nebensätzen mit **if** benutzt.

1. I won't go to the park tomorrow if *it rains. / it will rain. / it is raining.*
2. She'll go to university if *she will work hard. / she works hard. / she is working hard.*
3. If I finish my work, *I'll go home early. / I go home early. / I going home early.*
4. If he gets the job, *he is very happy. / he be very happy. / he will be very happy.*

> **Tipp zur Lösung!**
> In if-Sätzen, die Bedingungen in der Zukunft ausdrücken, verwendet man im Hauptsatz das **will future** und im Nebensatz mit **if** das **present simple**.

Übungsgrammatik 5

Will future oder *present continuous*?

13

Will future oder nicht?
Wenn man über feste Pläne und Vereinbarungen spricht, die sich aller Voraussicht nach nicht mehr ändern werden, benutzt man nicht das **will future**, sondern das **present continuous**.

Paul and Kate are going on holiday to Southern France.
heißt, dass sie diese Entscheidung bereits in der Vergangenheit getroffen haben, dass die Reise gebucht und geplant ist und aller Voraussicht nach nicht mehr abgesagt wird.

Paul and Kate will go on holiday to Southern France.
heißt, dass sie diese Entscheidung jetzt gerade treffen oder dass es sich bis jetzt nur um eine Idee handelt, die sich noch ändern kann.

Wenn man über die Zukunft spricht, benutzt man oft Ausdrücke wie **I think** (*ich denke*), **I hope** (*ich hoffe*), **I fear** (*ich fürchte*), **I suppose** (*ich nehme an*). Nach diesen Ausdrücken benutzt man immer das **will future**.

> **Nice to know**
> Wenn man über das englische Lieblingsthema Wetter diskutieren will, nimmt man immer das **will future** – denn das kann man ja nie 100%ig vorhersagen!

14 TR. 27

Lesen Sie die Sätze oder hören Sie sie sich auf Ihrer CD an. Entscheiden Sie jeweils, ob das **present continuous** oder das **will-future** vorliegt, und geben Sie dann die Zeitform in der Lücke an
(**pc = present continuous**, **wf = will-future**).

1. Will you come back later? _____
2. Are you leaving? _____
3. Paul isn't preparing the barbecue. _____
4. He won't come. _____
5. We're going on holiday. _____
6. I think it'll rain soon. _____

5 Übungsgrammatik

Will future oder *present continuous*?

15

Unterstreichen Sie die korrekten Formen.

1. Kate and Paul *are having / will have / have* a barbecue tonight.
2. I *'m going / 'll go / go* on holiday tomorrow.
3. I think I *'ll phone / phone / 'm phoning* you later.
4. Jane hopes she *studies / is studying / will study* law when she is older.

16

Ergänzen Sie die Sätze mit dem angegebenen Verb im **present continuous** oder **will future**.

1. I think it _____ (rain) soon. There are many clouds in the sky.
2. I _____ (go) to the cinema tonight. I have the tickets.
3. Maybe I _____ (phone) him later.
4. We _____ (have) a barbecue tomorrow. We already have the food.
5. Paul _____ (come). He is ill.
6. I hope he _____ (be) back soon.
7. I think I _____ (do) my homework now.
8. Paul _____ (drive) us back. He knows he has to do that.

Nice to know

Wenn man über feste Pläne und Vereinbarungen spricht, die sich aller Voraussicht nach nicht mehr ändern werden, benutzt man das **present continuous**.

Das **will future** benutzt man hingegen, wenn man eine spontane Entscheidung trifft oder wenn man von Ideen oder Ereignissen spricht, die sich noch ändern können.

Nach Ausdrücken wie **I think**, **I hope**, **I fear** oder **I suppose** benutzt man immer das **will future**.

◀ **cloud** – *Wolke*
   sky – *Himmel*
   ill – *krank*

Übungsgrammatik 5

*Rätselspaß mit dem **will future***

17

Bringen Sie diese Sätze in die richtige Reihenfolge.

1. year / Ben / next / go / will / to / college / .
2. French / will / learn / not / any / more / Jane / .
3. up / I'll / barbecue / the / set / .
4. put / I / the / garlic / won't / in / salad / .

18

Lösen Sie das Kreuzworträtsel, indem Sie die Sätze mit einem jeweils passenden Verb ergänzen.

1. Louise won't ... the flowers.
2. Jane will ... the piano.
3. Kate will ... the steaks.
4. Jane will ... to university.
5. Paul will ... a book.
6. Paul will ... the car home.
7. We'll ... at the table and eat.
8. I'm very tired. I'll ... very well.
9. I'll ... him later. I want to speak to him.
10. Ben will ... a doctor.
11. Louise and Kate will ... in a café.
12. I'll ... the bus.
13. They're having a baby, and they'll ... her Emma.
14. I'll ... a lot of English if I practise.

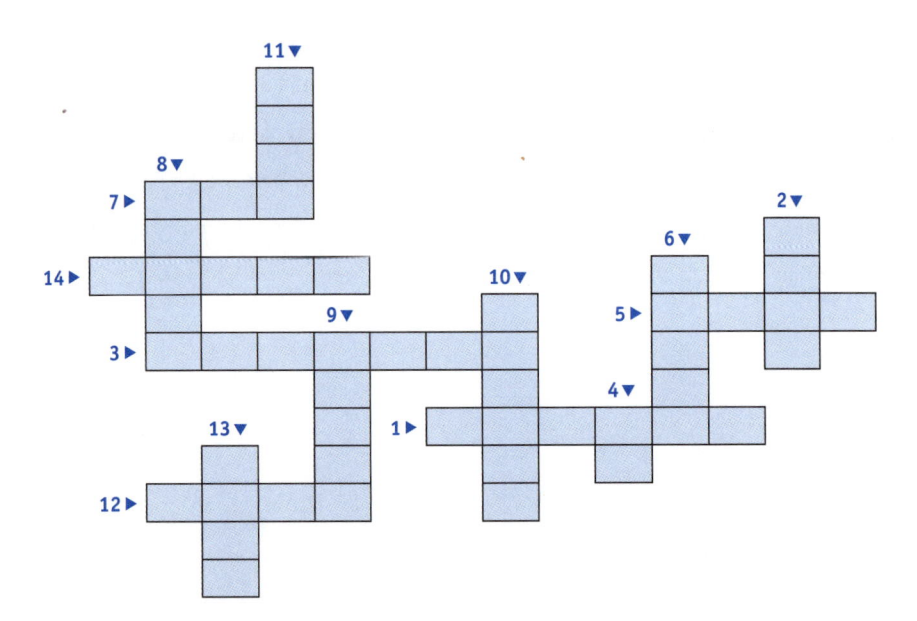

practise – *üben*

Test 5   **Übungsgrammatik**

*Verben im **will future***

1

Unterstreichen Sie die für den Satz passende Verbform.

1. Paul and Jane *will goes / will go / is going* on holiday next year.
2. Jane *will go / will going / are go* to university.
3. Ben *not will become / won't become / will becoming* a doctor.
4. Next year, Kate *will learning / will learns / will learn* Spanish.
5. Paul *won't works / won't work / won't working* more next year.
6. Kate *'ll come / 'll comes / does coming* home early today.
7. Ben *will finishes / is finishing / will finish* the work tomorrow.
8. Jane *will studies / 'll study / not will study* law.

2

Setzen Sie in den folgenden Text die fehlenden Verben im **will future** ein! Die deutsche Übersetzung der gesuchten Verben steht in Klammern hinter der Lücke.

They 1. _____ (*verlassen*) the house at 8 in the morning, and they 2. _____ (*ankommen*) in Dover at about 1 in the afternoon. The drive 3. _____ (*sein*) about 5 hours, so they 4. _____ (*haben*) extra time in Dover. They 5. _____ (*brauchen*) that because Paul 6. _____ (*wollen*) to go duty-free shopping.

305

Übungsgrammatik   **5**   **Test**

*Kurzantworten / Sätze mit **if***

3

Lesen Sie die Fragen oder hören Sie sie sich auf Ihrer CD an. Unterstreichen Sie dann jeweils die passende Antwort.

1. Will they be here soon?   Yes, they will. / Yes, they are. / Yes, they do.
2. Will it rain tomorrow?   No, it doesn't. / No, it won't. / No, it isn't.
3. Will you phone me?   Yes, I will. / Yes, I won't. / No, I want.
4. Will she bring the cake?   No, she isn't. / No, she doesn't. / No, she won't.
5. Will you drive?   Yes, I will. / Yes, I. / No, I will.

4

Lesen Sie die Satzanfänge und kreuzen Sie jeweils das korrekte Ende an.

1. I'll go home early if
   - a. I'll finish my work.
   - b. I am finishing my work.
   - c. I finish my work.

2. She won't go out if
   - a. it rains.
   - b. it is raining.
   - c. it'll rain.

3. If you buy the bananas,
   - a. I'll buy the apples.
   - b. I buy the apples.
   - c. I'm buying the apples.

4. If they arrive early,
   - a. we'll have more time.
   - b. we're having more time.
   - c. we have more time.

5

Schreiben Sie diese Sätze in ihrer richtigen Reihenfolge auf.

1. to / Kate / isn't / cinema / coming / the / .
2. now / I / I / 'll / my / think / homework / finish / .
3. I / it / hope / won't / tonight / rain / .
4. phone / Maybe / will / us / Paul / later / .
5. Ben / Next / test / year, / will / his / driving / take / .

6 Übungsgrammatik

*Was war am Nachmittag? / Das **past simple***

1

Erinnern Sie sich, was die Familie Smith diesen Samstagnachmittag gemacht hat?
Ordnen Sie den Sätzen die richtigen Bilder zu.
Die Sätze können Sie sich auch auf Ihrer CD anhören.

a   b   c

d   e

1. Kate prepared dinner. ☐
2. Jane ate a piece of cake. ☐
3. Paul drank a beer. ☐
4. Jane cleaned her room. ☐
5. Jane played the piano. ☐

◀ **ate** – aß/aßt/aßen
drank – trank/trankst/tranken/trankt

2

Können Sie die Fragen auf der linken Seite mit den passenden Antworten auf der rechten Seite verbinden?
Ihre Lösung können Sie auch überprüfen, indem Sie sich die CD anhören.

1. Did she go swimming?   a. Yes, he did.
2. Did he take his test?   b. No, it didn't.
3. Did they buy the apples?   c. No, we didn't.
4. Did you find the way?   d. No, she didn't.
5. Did it rain yesterday?   e. Yes, I did.
6. Did Paul and you know that? f. Yes, they did.

◀ **find** – finden
yesterday – gestern

307

Übungsgrammatik | **6**

*Erinnerungen / Das **past simple***

3

Es ist Samstagabend und Louise und ihre Tochter sind zum Grillen gekommen. Jetzt werden Erinnerungen ausgetauscht.
Lesen Sie den Dialog bzw. hören Sie sich ihn auf der CD an und versuchen Sie, so viel wie möglich zu verstehen.

> **delicious** – *lecker*
> **recipe** – *Kochrezept*
> **remind** – *jemanden erinnern*
> **decide** – *sich entscheiden*
> **apply** – *sich bewerben*
> **fellow student** – *Kommilitone/Studienkollege*

Louise: Mmh, this salad is delicious! Did you make it?
Kate: Yes, I did. I got the recipe from Suzanne. Do you remember her?
Louise: Yes, I do. Didn't she go to the USA to study?
Kate: Yes, she did, but she wasn't there for very long. She now lives just outside Manchester.
Louise: Oh, really? I must contact her. Have you got her number?
Kate: Yes, remind me later and I'll give it to you. But what about you? What did you do after you left Manchester?
Louise: Well, I went to university in Exeter and studied teaching. When I finished I got a job in Edinburgh so I decided to move up there.
Kate: Didn't you apply for jobs around Manchester?
Louise: Well – no, I didn't. You see, I fell in love with a fellow student. James was from Edinburgh and he really wanted to go back there. He didn't like the South at all, so I followed him to Scotland.
Kate: And do you like it there?
Louise: Yes, it's great. There is so much to do ...

> **Nice to know**
> Ein **recipe** gibt es nur im Kochbuch! Der Zettel, den Sie beim Arzt bekommen, heißt im Englischen **prescription**. Beim Einkaufen oder im Restaurant bekommen Sie auch oft ein **receipt** – eine Quittung.

4

Bildung des past simple

Zur Bildung des **past simple** - der einfachen Vergangenheit - hängt man bei regelmäßigen Verben an die Grundform des Verbs (**work**, **listen**, **play**) die Endung **-ed** an.

> Jane **played** the piano.
> Louise **decided** to move up to Edinburgh.

Endet die Grundform des Verbs auf **-e**, so hängt man nur **-d** an.

> Louise **moved** to Edinburgh.
> Kate **arrived** home late from work.

Endet die Grundform des Verbs auf einen Konsonanten + **y**, so wird das **-y** weggelassen und **-ied** angehängt:

> Suzanne **studied** in the USA.

Die **past simple** Form der Verben ist für alle Personen gleich.

6 Übungsgrammatik

Unregelmäßige Verben im past simple

5

Unregelmäßige Verben
Viele der häufig gebrauchten englischen Verben haben eine unregelmäßige **past simple**-Form.

Kate had no time yesterday. von **have**	
Kate got the recipe from Suzanne. von **get**	
Kate made the salad. von **make**	
Louise went to university in Exeter. von **go**	

Eine Liste aller unregelmäßigen Verben, die bis Modul 6 in diesem Kurs vorgekommen sind, finden Sie rechts am Rand.

6

Diese **past simple**-Formen sind durcheinander geraten! Schreiben Sie die Verben in die Lücken.

1. wtoer _____
2. ovred _____
3. ubogth _____
4. gttuhho _____
5. akdrn _____
6. pesok _____
7. nwek _____
8. tem _____

7

Finden Sie heraus, was Tante Hermione zu erzählen hat. Schreiben Sie die angegebenen Verben im **past simple** in die Lücken.

Well, when I 1. _____ (be) young, life 2. _____ (be) very different. I 3. _____ (have) four sisters, and we all 4. _____ (go) to the same school. We 5. _____ (walk) there, and it 6. _____ (take) us an hour. Nobody 7. _____ (drive) cars then. Sometimes we 8. _____ (buy) sweets in a little shop. At school, I 9. _____ (learn) a lot. Our teachers 10. _____ (ask) us so many questions! We 11. _____ (read) Shakespeare and we 12. _____ (sit) still all day. We 13. _____ (think) our teachers 14. _____ (know) everything!

Infinitiv	past simple
write	wrote
have	had
go	went
speak	spoke
do	did
be	was, were
make	made
read	read
drive	drove
know	knew
buy	bought
drink	drank
see	saw
tell	told
leave	left
say	said
think	thought
swim	swam
ride	rode
sleep	slept
sit	sat
feed	fed
sing	sang
meet	met
take	took
eat	ate
fall	fell
wear	wore
drink	drank
get	got

◀ **young** – *jung*
nobody – *niemand*
sweets – *Süßigkeiten*
little – *klein*
all day – *den ganzen Tag*

Übungsgrammatik 6

Zeitangaben und das past simple

8

Verwendung des past simple
Man benutzt das **past simple**, um über abgeschlossene Handlungen oder Ereignisse in der Vergangenheit zu sprechen.

> **Kate went to school with Louise.**
> *Kate ging mit Louise zur Schule.*
> **Paul and Kate got married.**
> *Paul und Kate haben geheiratet.*

Zusammen mit dem **past simple** werden oft Zeitangaben benutzt, die sich auf die Vergangenheit beziehen, wie z.B. **yesterday** (*gestern*), **last week** (*letzte Woche*), **a year ago** (*vor einem Jahr*) oder **in 1989** (*1989*).

Diese Zeitangaben können entweder am Anfang eines Satzes stehen oder an dessen Ende. Stehen Sie am Anfang, dann steht nach der Zeitangabe ein Komma.

> **Paul and Kate got married in 1987.**
> **In 1987**, Paul and Kate got married.

> **Nice to know**
>
> Im Deutschen können Sie das **past simple** auf zwei Arten übersetzen:
> **Kate went to school with Louise.**
> *Kate ging mit Louise in die Schule.*
> *Kate ist mit Louise in die Schule gegangen.*

9

Unterstreichen Sie das passende Verb.

1. Kate *drank / made / wrote* the salad.
2. Paul *spoke / left / was* to Louise.
3. Kate *said / thought / bought* a dress.
4. Jane *met / learned / saw* French.

10

Schreiben Sie das passende Verb im **past simple** in die Lücken.
Die Lösung können Sie sich auch auf Ihrer CD anhören.

sit	leave	meet	buy

1. Kate _____ Louise in a café last Thursday.
2. Aunt Hermione _____ on a chair all evening.
3. Kate _____ a new dress.
4. Paul _____ the office late.

> **Nice to know**
>
> **Meet** ist im Englischen nicht reflexiv. Man sagt immer **We met** und niemals **We met us**.
> **We met in a café.**
> *Wir trafen uns in einem Café.*

Fragen und Verneinung

11

Fragen
Bei Fragen im **past simple** benutzt man **did** (**past simple** von **do**) und die Grundform des Vollverbs.

> **What did you do after you left Manchester?**
> *Was hast du gemacht, nachdem du aus Manchester weggegangen bist?*

Man kann auch negative Fragen bilden, indem man **didn't** (**did not**) und das Vollverb benutzt.

> **Didn't she go to the USA to study?**
> *Ist sie nicht in die USA gegangen, um zu studieren?*

Auf Fragen, die mit *ja* oder *nein* beantwortet werden können, gibt man oft Kurzantworten, indem man **did/didn't** mit einem passenden Personalpronomen verwendet.

> **Nice to know**
>
> **Did you?** Wird im Englischen sehr oft gebraucht, um auf eine Aussage zu reagieren:
> **I went to Australia last year.**
> **Oh, did you? What did you do there?**

12

Jane interessiert sich immer sehr für alles, was Tante Hermione zu erzählen hat, und sie stellt ihr viele Fragen. Lesen Sie Janes Fragen und kreuzen Sie die richtigen Antworten an.

1. Did you have a bicycle?
   - a. No, I didn't.
   - b. No, I hadn't.
   - c. No, I do not.

2. Did you always wear dresses?
   - a. Yes, I wore.
   - b. Yes, I did.
   - c. Yes, I do.

3. Did you go to school all day?
   - a. Yes, we do.
   - b. No, we don'tid.
   - c. Yes, we did.

4. Did you go dancing on Saturdays?
   - a. Yes, we danced.
   - b. Yes, we did.
   - c. Yes, we dance.

13

Verneinung
Möchte man Sätze verneinen, benutzt man **didn't/did not** und die Grundform des Vollverbs.

> **James didn't like the South at all.**
> **Kate didn't study teaching.**

*Das Verb **be** im past simple*

14

Das Verb be im past simple

Das Verb **be** funktioniert im **past simple** nicht wie andere Vollverben.

Zunächst hat es zwei Vergangenheitsformen: **was** und **were**. Schauen Sie sich die Tabelle rechts an.

Bei Verneinungen, Fragen und Kurzantworten mit **be** benutzt man nicht **did**, sondern nur **was** oder **were**.

> I was
> you were
> he/she/it was
>
> we were
> you were
> they were

Paul was at work yesterday. — Paul war gestern bei der Arbeit.
Louise wasn't in London. — Louise war nicht in London.
Were you at home last night? — Yes, I was. No, I wasn't.
Warst du gestern Abend zu Hause? — Ja. Nein.

Nice to know

Benutzen Sie die kurze Form **wasn't/weren't**, wenn Sie neutral klingen möchten, und die lange Form **was not/were not**, wenn Sie das **not** besonders betonen möchten.
I wasn't here.
I was not here!

15

Unterstreichen Sie die korrekte Form.

1. Louise *wasn't / were / weren't* at university in Manchester.
2. *Were / Was / Did* you at the theatre last Saturday?
3. Were you at home yesterday? Yes, I *did / was / were*.
4. Paul and Kate *was / were / did* at the pub yesterday.

16

Schreiben Sie die folgenden Sätze im **past simple** in die Lücken.

1. I don't go to school. _____
2. I buy cakes. _____
3. I am happy. _____
4. I'm not fat. _____
5. You're ready. _____
6. You're not angry. _____
7. Paul is at work. _____
8. Louise is tired. _____

Be oder *do*? / Tante Hermione erzählt

17

Wählen Sie die richtige Verbform aus. Sie können dann Ihre CD anhören und auch so kontrollieren, ob Sie alles richtig gemacht haben.

1. We *listened not / didn't listened / didn't listen* to the radio.
2. They *did be / were / was* on holiday.
3. Louise *was / didn't / were* at university.
4. *Did you made / You made / Did you make* the salad?
5. Paul *did work / worked / was work* a lot.
6. He *didn't drove / didn't drive / didn't drived* home.
7. We *wasn't / didn't be / weren't* angry.
8. I *wasn't / weren't / didn't* tired.

18

Tante Hermione hat noch mehr zu erzählen.
Ergänzen Sie ihre Erzählung, indem Sie die Verben in der richtigen Form des **past simple** (positiv oder negativ) in die Lücken schreiben.

walk	think	stay	be	be	be
	not be	live		not work	
work	not go	eat	work		not have

Well, we 1. _____ a car, and in the summer we

2. _____ on holiday, we 3. _____

at home. The summers in England 4. _____ beautiful then,

and we 5. _____ unhappy at all. We

6. _____ ice cream in the evenings and 7. _____

in the fields. We 8. _____ in the country, and we

9. _____ it 10. _____ wonderful.

We 11. _____ very hard, oh no! We only

12. _____ hard at school, and our teachers

13. _____ very strict!

◀ **summer** – *Sommer*
unhappy – *unglücklich*
field – *Feld*
country – *Land*
hard – *hart*
strict – *streng*

Übungsgrammatik | **6**

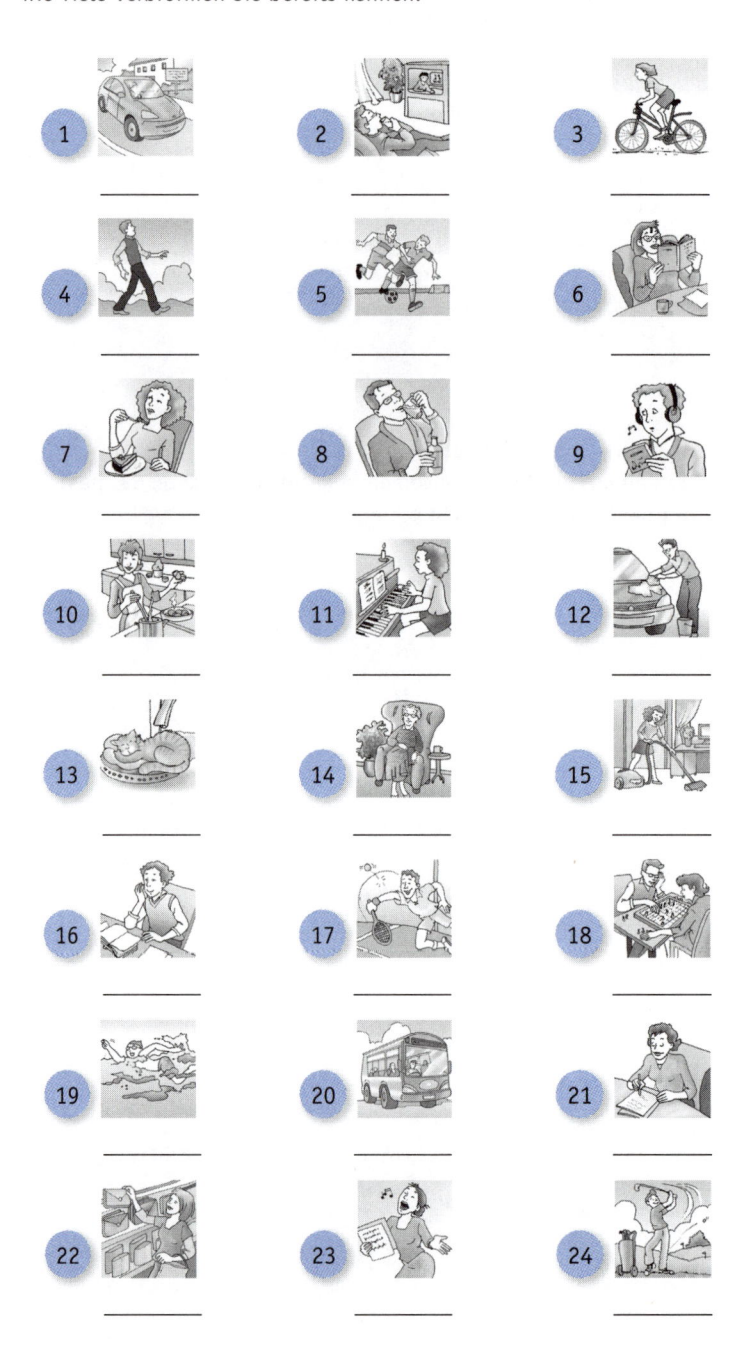

Verbformen im past simple

19 ✏

Schreiben Sie das passende Verb im **past simple** unter das Bild! Sie werden sehen, wie viele Verbformen Sie bereits kennen.

Test **6** Übungsgrammatik

*Verben im **past simple***

1

Diese unregelmäßigen **past simple**-Formen sind durcheinander gepurzelt!
Schreiben Sie sie in die Lücken.
Die Bilder helfen Ihnen herauszufinden, welche Verben gesucht sind.

1. ewotr

_____

2. roved

_____

3. dkrna

_____

4. amsw

_____

5. epslt

_____

6. nags

_____

2

Ergänzen Sie die Sätze mit der richtigen Verbform im **past simple**, indem Sie diese unterstreichen.

1. I *am not going / didn't went / didn't* go to school.
2. She *didn't study / didn't studied / study* law.
3. Did you *know / knew / knows* him?
4. She *plays / was playing / played* the piano.
5. She *didn't go / isn't going / goes* home early.

315

Übungsgrammatik   **6**   **Test**

*Was haben sie gestern getan? / **Be** im **past simple** / Kurzantworten*

3 ✏️

Beschreiben Sie mit einem Verb im **past simple**, was die Person im Bild gestern gemacht hat.

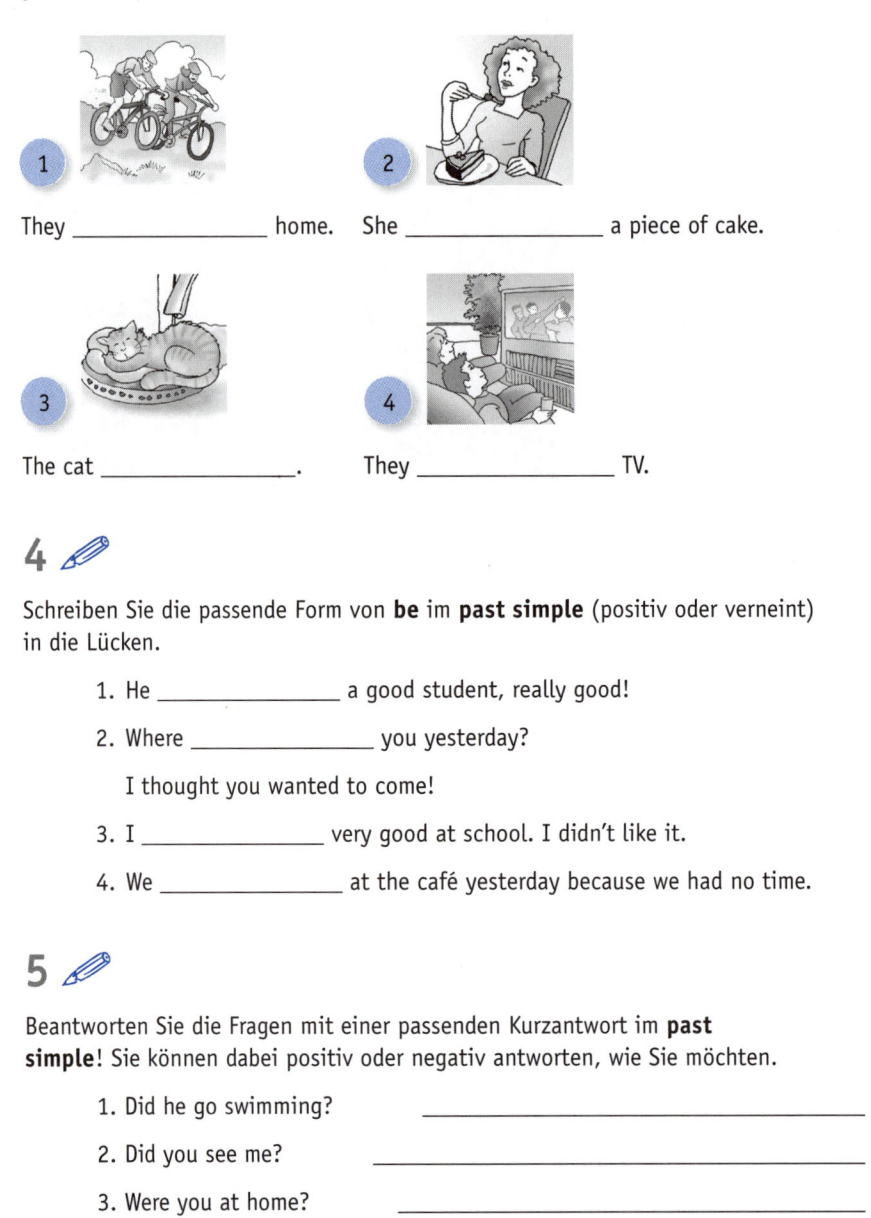

1 They _____ home.   **2** She _____ a piece of cake.

3 The cat _____.   **4** They _____ TV.

4 ✏️

Schreiben Sie die passende Form von **be** im **past simple** (positiv oder verneint) in die Lücken.

1. He _____ a good student, really good!
2. Where _____ you yesterday?
   I thought you wanted to come!
3. I _____ very good at school. I didn't like it.
4. We _____ at the café yesterday because we had no time.

5 ✏️

Beantworten Sie die Fragen mit einer passenden Kurzantwort im **past simple**! Sie können dabei positiv oder negativ antworten, wie Sie möchten.

1. Did he go swimming? _____
2. Did you see me? _____
3. Were you at home? _____
4. Was he there? _____

7 Übungsgrammatik

Bens Zimmer / Landeskunde

1

In Bens Zimmer herrscht Chaos. Betrachen Sie das Bild und ordnen Sie den darunter stehenden Sätzen jeweils den entsprechenden Bildausschnitt zu, indem Sie den korrekten Buchstaben notieren.

1. This is a big poster. ☐
2. This is a nice bag. ☐
3. These are black trousers. ☐
4. This is an open wardrobe. ☐
5. This is an untidy desk. ☐

> **bag** – *Tasche*
> **nice** – *schön*
> **trousers** – *Hosen*
> **black** – *schwarz*
> **white** – *weiß*
> **wardrobe** – *Kleiderschrank*
> **desk** – *Schreibtisch*
> **untidy** – *unordentlich*

> **Nice to know**
> *Hosen* (**trousers**) sind im Englischen immer Plural. Man sagt auch oft *ein Paar Hosen* (**a pair of trousers**).

2

Testen Sie Ihre Kenntnisse der britischen Landeskunde und verbinden Sie die Satzanfänge auf der linken Seite mit einem passenden Ende auf der rechten Seite.

1. London is
2. Ben Nevis is
3. Scotland is
4. Ireland is as large as
5. Oxford has got
6. Big Ben is
7. The London Underground has got
8. The Thames is

a. larger than Wales.
b. the Serengeti in East Africa.
c. the UK's most famous bell.
d. the biggest city in the UK.
e. the world's longest escalators.
f. the UK's oldest university.
g. much smaller than the Rhine.
h. the highest mountain in the UK.

> **city** – *Großstadt*
> **mountain** – *Berg*
> **bell** – *Glocke*
> **escalator** – *Rolltreppe*

Übungsgrammatik 7

Shopping for the summer holiday / Adjektive

3

Kate und Jane sind im Kaufhaus, um einige Sachen für den Urlaub einzukaufen. Lesen bzw. hören Sie den Dialog und sehen Sie sich die Bilder an. Können Sie alles verstehen?

> **Nice to know**
>
> Es gibt im Englischen keinen Unterschied zwischen *rosa* und *pink*. **Pink** bedeutet beides. Oft sagt man **light pink**, wenn man *rosa* meint, und **bright pink**, wenn man *pink* meint.

Kate: Jane, what about this T-shirt? Do you like it?
Jane: Mum, you know I don't like blue. This red one here is much nicer!
Kate: Yes, you're right, but it's more expensive. How about this one? It's red, too, but it's a bit cheaper.
Jane: Hmm, that one's OK. Ooooh, look at this pink one! It's nicer than all the others!
Kate: That's the most expensive T-shirt in the shop!
Jane: Yes, but it's also the nicest. I love pink, and it'll go nicely with my new trousers!
Kate: Well, if you want that one, you can only have one T-shirt. That one's as expensive as two others!
Jane: Thanks! Can I try it on? 
Kate: Go ahead, the changing room's over there.
Jane: It's too big! I need a smaller size.
Kate: What size have you got there?
Jane: A ten.
Kate: I'll get you a size eight, then …

> **more** – *mehr*
> **most** – *am meisten*
> **go with** – *passen zu*
> **than** – *als*
> **as … as** – *so … wie*
> **try on** – *anprobieren*
> **go ahead!** – *tu das!*
> **changing room** – *Umkleidekabine*

4

Ein **Adjektiv** beschreibt, wie jemand oder etwas ist.
Adjektive sind im Englischen unveränderlich und stehen normalerweise direkt vor dem Wort, das sie beschreiben.

        two brown bags   *zwei braune Taschen*
        an untidy desk   *ein unordentlicher Schreibtisch*

In manchen Fällen steht das Adjektiv aber auch nicht direkt vor dem Substantiv, sondern wird dem Verb **be** im Satz nachgestellt.
        The bags we bought are brown.
        Die Taschen, die wir gekauft haben, sind braun.

5

Steigerung von Adjektiven
Adjektive können gesteigert werden.
Von einsilbigen Adjektiven bildet man den **Komparativ** – die erste Steigerungsform – indem man einfach **-er** an das Adjektiv anhängt.
Um den **Superlativ** – die zweite Steigerungsform – zu bilden, wird **-est** an das Adjektiv angehängt.

cheap	**cheaper**	**cheapest**
billig	*billiger*	*am billigsten*
high	**higher**	**highest**
hoch	*höher*	*am höchsten*

Auch einige zweisilbige Adjektive bilden so den Komparativ und den Superlativ.

clever	**cleverer**	**cleverest**
klug	*klüger*	*am klügsten*

Es gibt aber auch einige Besonderheiten:
Bei Adjektiven, die auf **-e** enden, wird nur **-r** oder **-st** angehängt:
    nice   **nicer**   **nicest**

Bei zweisilbigen Adjektiven, die auf **-y** enden, fällt das **-y** weg, und es wird **-ier** oder **-iest** angehängt:
    happy   **happier**   **happiest**

Besteht ein Adjektiv aus der Kombination Konsonant – Vokal – Konsonant, so wird der letzte Konsonant verdoppelt:
    big   **bigger**   **biggest**

6

Schreiben Sie die passenden Adjektive in die Lücken.

> highest   cheaper   oldest   bigger

1. Russia is _____ than the UK.
2. A T-shirt is _____ than a winter coat.
3. Mount Kilimanjaro is the _____ mountain in Africa.
4. Ben is Paul and Kate's _____ child.

Übungsgrammatik 7

More und *most* / Unregelmäßige Adjektive

7

More und most

Sehen und hören Sie sich, wenn möglich, die folgenden Sätze an.

A winter coat is more expensive than a T-shirt.
Ein Wintermantel ist teurer als ein T-Shirt.
Jane buys the most expensive T-shirt in the shop.
Jane kauft das teuerste T-Shirt im Laden.
This book is more interesting than the author's other books.
Dieses Buch ist interessanter als die anderen Bücher dieses Autors.
This book is the most interesting one by this author.
Dieses Buch ist das Interessanteste von diesem Autor.

Können Sie jetzt die folgenden Regeln vervollständigen?

1. Mehrsilbige Adjektive bilden den **Komparativ** mit	2. Den **Superlativ** bilden mehrsilbige Adjektive mit
☐ a. **more** + Grundform.	☐ a. **over** + Grundform.
☐ b. **over** + Grundform.	☐ b. Grundform + **-er**.
☐ c. Grundform + **-er**.	☐ c. **most** + Grundform.

> **Nice to know**
>
> Im Englischen müssen Adjektive immer zusammen mit einem Substantiv stehen. Daher sagt man zum Beispiel für *das Interessanteste* entweder **the most interesting one** oder **the most interesting thing**.

> **Nice to know**
>
> Von sehr vielen Adjektiven gibt es eine Form auf **-ing**, die eine Sache beschreibt, und eine Form auf **-ed**, die das Gefühl einer Person beschreibt:
> **The film was boring.**
> *Der Film war langweilig.*
> **I was bored.**
> *Ich war gelangweilt.*

boring – *langweilig*
exciting – *spannend, aufregend*
frustrating – *frustrierend*

8

Bilden diese Adjektive den Komparativ und Superlativ mit **-er/-est** oder mit **more/most**? Bilden Sie zwei Gruppen.

> big   expensive   boring   quiet   clever   hot   tired
> slow   frustrating   interesting   exciting   heavy

-er / -est	more / most

9

Folgende Adjektive haben eine unregelmäßige Steigerung:

good (*gut*)	**better** (*besser*)	**best** (*am besten*)
bad (*schlecht*)	**worse** (*schlechter*)	**worst** (*am schlechtesten*)
much/many (*viel*)	**more** (*mehr*)	**most** (*am meisten*)
little (*wenig*)	**less** (*weniger*)	**least** (*am wenigsten*)
far (*weit*)	**further** (*weiter*)	**furthest** (*am weitesten*)

Früher und heute / Dinge vergleichen

10 ✏️

Paul hat es manchmal nicht leicht mit Tante Hermione, die so gern von früher erzählt. Lesen Sie, was er zu sagen hat, und ergänzen Sie die fehlenden Adjektive in der richtigen Form (**Grundform** oder **Komparativ**). Die Grundform ist jeweils in Klammern angegeben.

Well, Aunt Hermione is very 1. _____ (old). She thinks everything was 2. _____ (good) when she was 3. _____ (young). For her, everything is 4. _____ (bad) now. Life was 5. _____ (slow), she says, and that is probably 6. _____ (true). People walked 7. _____ (much) and used cars 8. _____ (little). She also thinks people were 9. _____ (nice) and 10. _____ (happy). And, of course, she thinks that everything is 11. _____ (expensive) today than it was. Well, she's right! But I think life is much 12. _____ (exciting) now than when she was young, and, of course, many things are much 13. _____ (easy)!

> **Nice to know**
>
> Im Englischen hat man nicht Recht, man ist es:
> *Du hast Recht!*
> **You're right!**
> *Sie hat Recht.*
> **She's right.**

11 👓

Um Personen oder Dinge miteinander zu vergleichen, verwendet man den **Komparativ + than** (als), oder man benutzt eine Konstruktion mit **not as** + Adjektiv + **as** (nicht so ... wie).

> **Scotland is larger than Wales.**
> *Schottland ist größer als Wales.*
> **Wales is not as large as Scotland.**
> *Wales ist nicht so groß wie Schottland.*

Um auszudrücken, dass zwei Dinge gleich sind, benutzt man **as** + Adjektiv + **as** (so ... wie).

> **Paul is as old as Kate.**   *Paul ist so alt wie Kate.*

Möchte man sagen, dass etwas am besten, schnellsten etc. ist, benutzt man den **Superlativ**. Vor dem Superlativ steht oft **the**.

> **Big Ben is the most famous bell in the UK.**
> *Big Ben ist die berühmteste Glocke in Großbritannien.*

> **Nice to know**
>
> Der eigentliche **Big Ben** ist nicht der Uhrturm am Londoner Parlamentsgebäude, sondern nur die Glocke!

Übungsgrammatik 7

Vergleiche / Adverbien der Art und Weise

12 ✏️

Sehen Sie sich die Bilder an und schreiben Sie die fehlenden Wörter in die Lücken (**as ... as**, **not as ... as**, **than**).

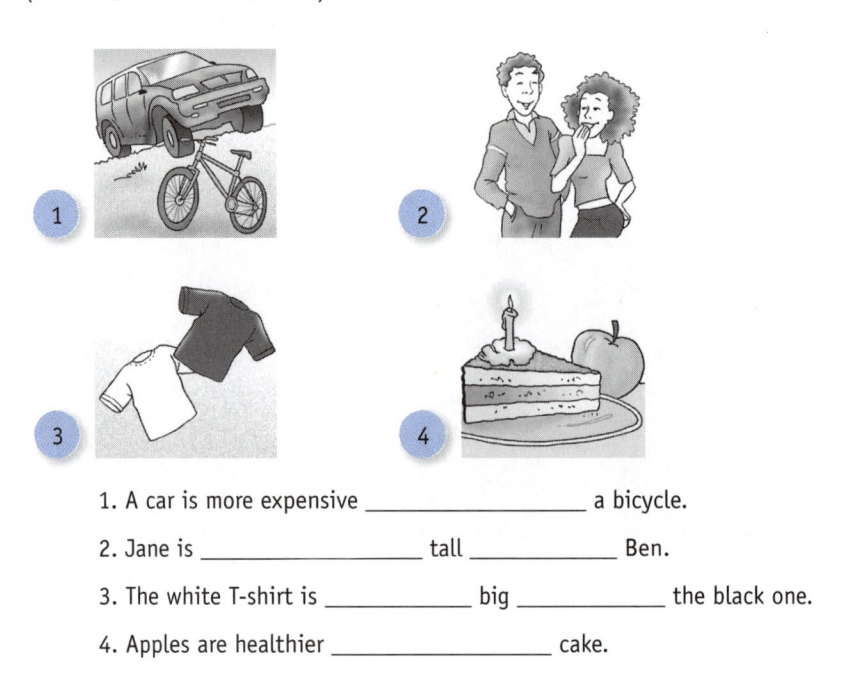

1.
2.
3.
4.

1. A car is more expensive _____ a bicycle.
2. Jane is _____ tall _____ Ben.
3. The white T-shirt is _____ big _____ the black one.
4. Apples are healthier _____ cake.

healthy – *gesund* ▶

13 👓

Adjektive beschreiben Dinge oder Personen. **Adverbien** der Art und Weise beschreiben Verben. Sie werden dazu benutzt, näher zu schildern, wie man etwas macht oder wie etwas geschieht.

    It's raining heavily.   **He drives slowly.**
    Es regnet stark.   *Er fährt langsam.*

Viele **Adverbien** der Art und Weise werden gebildet, indem man einfach **-ly** an das entsprechende Adjektiv anhängt.

    slow   My car is very **slow**.   *Mein Auto ist sehr langsam.*
    slow**ly**   He walks **slowly**.   *Er geht langsam.*

Endet das Adjektiv in **-y**, so fällt das **-y** weg und es wird **-ily** angehängt.
    heav**y**   heav**ily**
    happ**y**   happ**ily**

7 Übungsgrammatik

Unregelmäßige Adjektive und Adverbien

14

Leider gibt es auch hier viele Ausnahmen und nicht aus jedem Adjektiv kann ein Adverb gebildet werden. So ist das Adverb zu **good** beispielsweise **well** und manchmal sind Adverb und Adjektiv auch gleich.

She's a good student.
Sie ist eine gute Schülerin.
It's a hard job.
Es ist eine harte Arbeit.

She plays the piano well.
Sie spielt gut Klavier.
He works hard.
Er arbeitet hart.

> **Nice to know**
>
> Vorsicht! **Hardly** gibt es im Englischen zwar auch, aber es bedeutet *kaum*! Vergleichen Sie:
> **I work hard.**
> *Ich arbeite hart.*
> **I hardly work.**
> *Ich arbeite kaum.*

15

Lesen Sie die Sätze und schauen Sie sich die darin enthaltenen Adjektive an. Suchen Sie dann das passende Adverb in der Buchstabenschlange und unterstreichen Sie es!

1. He is a bad singer.   fdgebadlyfggsingzuasjnvx
2. She is a happy woman.   saddffrguhappilyvcghappy
3. He is a fast driver.   drivefhfastghfhfastlyfgh
4. He is a good football player.   dfghikfflwelljkfgstzhzb
5. This is a hard job.   dfgjdkgvbharddfgbjhardlydfj

> **Nice to know**
>
> **Heavy** bedeutet im Englischen wirklich nur *schwer* im Sinne von „es wiegt viel". Eine schwere Zeit ist **a hard time** oder **a difficult time**!

16

In diesen Sätzen, die Sie sich auch auf der CD anhören können, fehlt entweder das Adverb oder das Adjektiv. Schreiben Sie das fehlende Wort in die Lücke.

1   2   3   4

| gut   schwer   glücklich   schlecht |

1. He drives _____.
2. She sings very _____.
3. The desk is _____.
4. The child is _____.

323

Übungsgrammatik 7

Rätselspaß mit Adjektiven

17

Finden Sie die **Grundform** von Adjektiven im Buchstabengitter. Das Adjektiv kann senkrecht, waagerecht oder diagonal versteckt sein.

C	L	E	A	N	B	K	L	S	S
E	X	P	E	N	S	I	V	E	H
K	Y	A	Y	O	U	N	G	T	O
J	P	F	L	I	T	T	L	E	R
W	M	A	N	I	C	E	S	R	T
L	A	R	G	E	K	R	B	L	P
O	S	M	O	C	H	E	A	P	E
N	L	M	U	C	H	S	D	P	H
G	O	Q	U	I	E	T	P	S	D
U	W	L	E	Q	U	I	C	K	O
P	K	W	M	E	D	N	R	L	L
T	I	D	Y	U	W	G	O	O	D

18

Unterstreichen Sie jeweils das Wort, das nicht zu den anderen passt.

1. red / brown / black / longer
2. quickly / slow / nice / hot
3. more expensive / more interesting / more careful / slower
4. cleanest / tidiest / short / nicest
5. slow / fast / quickly / well
6. easier / happy / heavier / sunnier
7. nicest / longer / hottest / tidiest
8. bigger / hotter / young / older
9. quietly / cheaply / expensively / good
10. large / small / big / well
11. largest / brown / smallest / reddest
12. black / well / quickly / shortly
13. worse / better / less / worst
14. least / most / more / furthest
15. less / least / most

Test **7** | **Übungsgrammatik**

Vergleiche

1

Sehen Sie sich das Bild an, und entscheiden Sie, welche Sätze falsch (Kreuz) und welche richtig (Häkchen) sind.

1. Paul's mother is smaller than his father. ■
2. Jane is taller than Ben. ■
3. Paul's sister is younger than Paul. ■
4. Ben is taller than Jane. ■
5. Paul is smaller than his mother. ■

2

Bringen Sie die folgenden Sätze in die richtige Reihenfolge.

1. is / This / very / big / house / .
2. the / The / than / garden / larger / is / house / .
3. The / is / happy / woman / .
4. book / heavy / The / is / not / as / the / bag / as / .
5. shirt / is / The / T- / as / trousers / as / the / bright / .

3

Sehen Sie sich die Bilder an und schreiben Sie die richtige Form des Adjektivs in Klammern in die Lücke.

1. A house is _____ (expensive) than a car.

2. The cat is not as _____ (big) as the dog.

3. Bananas are _____ (healthy) than chocolate.

4. The glass is not as _____ (tall) as the fruit bowl.

325

Übungsgrammatik 7 Test

Welches Bild passt? / Adverbien / Superlativea

4

Sehen Sie sich die Bilder an und lesen bzw. hören Sie die Sätze. Tragen Sie die Zahl des Bildes ein, zu dem der Satz am besten passt.

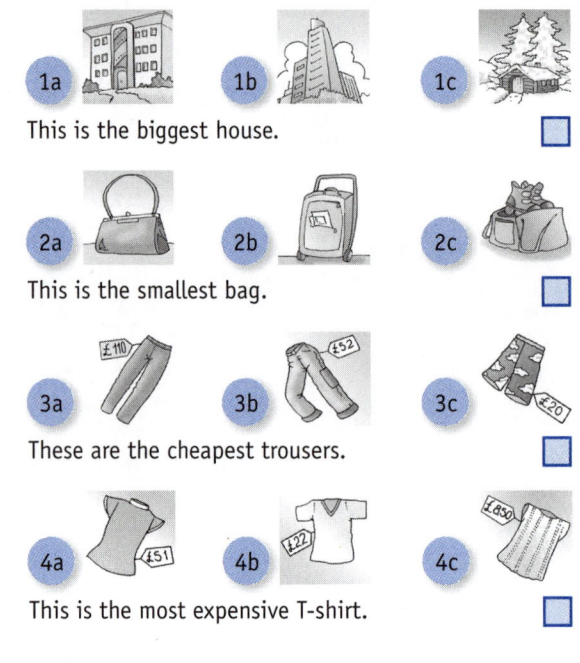

This is the biggest house.

This is the smallest bag.

These are the cheapest trousers.

This is the most expensive T-shirt.

5

Unterstreichen Sie die korrekte Form des Adverbs.

1. He speaks French *good / well / goodly*.
2. He drives *fast / slow / fastly*.
3. They sing *beautiful / beautifully / beautifly*.
4. He works very *hard / hardly / harder*.

6

Schreiben Sie den dazugehörigen Superlativ in die Lücke.

1. bad   worse   _____
2. big   bigger   _____
3. good   better   _____
4. little   less   _____

8 | Übungsgrammatik

Hausarbeit / Was können wir im Urlaub tun?

1

Paul und Kate haben sich die Hausarbeit aufgeteilt. Paul erzählt hier, was seine Aufgaben sind und was nicht.
Betrachen Sie die Bilder und lesen bzw. hören Sie sich die Sätze auf der CD an.
Was muss er tun (**has to do**), was muss er nicht tun (**doesn't have to do**) und was darf er nicht vergessen (**mustn't forget to do**)?
Ordnen Sie den Sätzen die richtigen Bilder zu.

◀ **do not have to/ don't have to** – *nicht müssen*
must – *müssen*
must not/mustn't – *nicht dürfen*

a 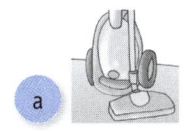   b    c    d

1. I sometimes have to cook. ☐
2. I have to wash the car. ☐
3. I don't have to clean the windows. ☐
4. I mustn't forget to hoover the house. ☐

Nice to know

Im Englischen benutzt man manchmal bekannte Produktnamen für alltägliche Aktivitäten. *Staubsaugen* kann sowohl **vacuum clean** als auch **hoover** heißen.

2

Paul und Kate sind dabei, sich zu überlegen, was sie im Urlaub in Südfrankreich alles tun könnten oder tun sollten.
Verbinden Sie die Sätze mit dem passenden Bild.

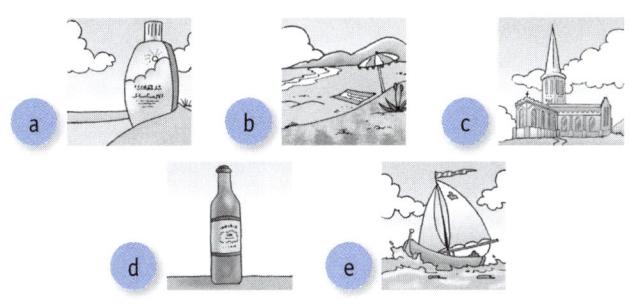

a   b   c

d   e

1. We might buy some wine. ☐
2. We may go sailing for a day. ☐
3. We'll be able to relax on the beach. ☐
4. We should take a lot of suntan lotion. ☐
5. We could visit some old churches. ☐

◀ **suntan lotion** – *Sonnencreme*
be able to – *können*
might – *könnten*
may – *könnten*

327

Übungsgrammatik | **8**

Don't forget the suntan lotion! / Have to

3

Lesen bzw. hören Sie jetzt Paul und Kate zu, wie sie ihren Urlaub planen.

Kate: We may have the time to visit some vineyards. I would love to see how they make wine!
Paul: Yes, good idea, and we might buy some wine there, too.
Kate: Sure, and we could also go sailing for a day. What do you think?
Paul: That would be fantastic! I'm really beginning to look forward to this holiday! The sunshine, the beach …
Kate: That reminds me … we really must buy some more suntan lotion! I think we should take a lot with us.
Paul: Yes, but we don't have to buy it here. Everything is cheaper in France.
Kate: True. Oh, and we have to ask the neighbours if they can look after the cat.
Paul: Yes, we mustn't forget that. I'll do it tonight, don't let me forget!
Kate: I won't. Let's look at the map and plan our route!

4

Unterstreichen Sie jeweils das Wort, das den Satz richtig ergänzt.

1. They may visit some *churches. / vineyards. / boutiques.*
2. They might buy some *wine. / souvenirs. / postcards.*
3. They must buy some more *suntan lotion. / towels. / sleeping bags.*
4. They mustn't forget to ask *their parents. / Louise. / the neighbours.*

5

Have to
Um ganz allgemein auszudrücken, dass man etwas *tun muss*, benutzt man im Englischen **have to**.
   I **have to** wash the car.
   Ich muss das Auto waschen.

Verneint wird **have to** mit **don't** bzw. **doesn't**.
   We **don't have to** buy the suntan lotion here.
   Wir müssen die Sonnencreme nicht hier kaufen.
   He **doesn't have to** work on Sundays.
   Er muss Sonntags nicht arbeiten.

Nice to know

Im Englischen gibt es zwei Worte für *erinnern*:
remember = *sich erinnern*
I can't remember the name of the hotel.
remind = *jemanden erinnern*
Remind me to buy some suntan lotion.

---

vineyard – *Weingut/ Weinberg*
would – *wäre*
look forward to – *sich freuen auf*
neighbour – *Nachbar*
if – *ob*
map – *Karte*
towel – *Handtuch*
sleeping bag – *Schlafsack*
ferry – *Fähre*

Nice to know

Die Bedeutung von **look** verändert sich mit der Präposition, die darauf folgt:
look at – *anschauen*
look after – *sich kümmern um*
look forward to – *sich freuen auf*

6

Must
Um zu betonen, dass etwas unbedingt notwendig ist, benutzt man statt **have to** oft auch **must**. **Must** kann allerdings nur in der Gegenwart verwendet werden. Im **will-future** und im **past simple** bleibt es bei **have to**.

> **I really must go to bed early tonight. I am so tired!**
> *Ich muss heute wirklich früh ins Bett gehen. Ich bin so müde!*
> **I really had to go to bed early. I was so tired!**
> *Ich musste wirklich früh ins Bett gehen. Ich war so müde!*

Vorsicht! **Must not/mustn't** bedeutet nicht, wie man vermuten könnte, *nicht müssen*, sondern *nicht dürfen*.

> **You mustn't smoke in the kitchen.**
> *Man darf in der Küche nicht rauchen.*

Lerntipp!
Im Englischen gibt es Wörter, die den deutschen sehr ähnlich sehen, aber eine völlig andere Bedeutung haben. Man nennt diese Wörter **false friends** – *falsche Freunde*. So heißt **mustn't** beispielsweise *nicht dürfen*, und eben nicht, wie man meinen könnte, *nicht müssen*. Sie sollten versuchen, sich diese ‚falschen Freunde' besonders gut einzuprägen, da sie leicht zu Verwechslungen und Missverständnissen führen.

7

Kate und Paul denken weiter über das nach, was sie noch tun bzw. nicht tun müssen. Lesen Sie den Dialog und schreiben Sie die Wörter im Kasten in die passende Lücke.

> has to   have to   didn't have to   'll have to
> do we have to   don't have to   have to

Kate: Well, we 1. _____ give the neighbours a key to the house.
Paul: No, we 2. _____ . I think they've still got one.
Kate: Really? I'll ask them later. We also 3. _____ cancel the newspaper.
Paul: Do we? We 4. _____ do that last year.
Kate: Well, I think we just forgot … What else 5. _____ do?
Paul: I'm not sure. Oh, Jane 6. _____ take her French books, so she can translate for us.
Kate: Yes, but we 7. _____ speak a little French, too!

◀ **cancel** – *abbestellen*
translate – *übersetzen*
else – *sonst noch*

Übungsgrammatik | 8

*Die modalen Hilfsverben **should** und **can***

8

Should

Das Hilfsverb **should** wird benutzt, um auszudrücken, dass man etwas tun sollte oder dass es ratsam ist, etwas zu tun.

You shouldn't eat so much chocolate.

In Fragen wird es benutzt, um jemanden um Rat zu bitten.

What do you think he should do?

Man kann **should** auch verwenden, um Vermutungen zu äußern:

Louise should be here soon. *Louise sollte bald hier sein.*

Should bleibt im Präsens für alle Personen gleich, das heißt, bei **he**/**she**/**it** wird kein **-s** angehängt.

9

Ergänzen Sie die Sätze mit **should** oder **shouldn't**.
Die Lösung können Sie auch auf der CD überprüfen.

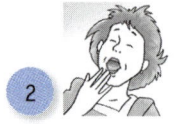

dentist – *Zahnarzt*
stay up – *aufbleiben*

1. He _____ go to the dentist.
2. She _____ stay up so late.
3. He _____ go home.

10

Can

Can drückt aus, dass man fähig oder bereit ist, etwas zu tun.

Jane can play the piano. *Jane kann Klavier spielen.*

Can bleibt für alle Personen gleich. In der Verneinung wird **can** zu **can't** oder **cannot**.

Man kann **can** auch benutzen, um eine Erlaubnis zu erteilen oder jemanden um etwas zu bitten.

Mum, can I go to the cinema? Yes, sure, you can.
Mama, kann ich ins Kino gehen? Ja, sicher kannst du das.

Can oder *be able to*?

11

Could
Can existiert nur im **present simple** und im **past simple**.
Die **past simple** Form von **can** ist **could**.

In anderen Zeitformen als dem **present simple** und dem **past simple** (z.B. im **will-future**) existiert **can/could** nicht. Hier benutzt man **be able to**, um eine Fähigkeit oder Bereitschaft auszudrücken:

> **Jane will be able to play the piano very well if she practises a lot.**
> *Jane wird sehr gut Klavier spielen können, wenn sie viel übt.*

Um sehr höflich um etwas zu bitten, benutzt man statt **can** oft auch **could**.

> **Can I have an apple, please?**
> *Kann ich bitte einen Apfel haben?*
> **Could I have an apple, please?**
> *Könnte ich bitte einen Apfel haben?*

Nice to know
Merken Sie sich, dass **could** sowohl *konnte* als auch *könnte* bedeuten kann!

12

Manchmal sinniert Paul darüber nach, was er als Student alles tun konnte und was er tun können wird, wenn er in Rente geht.
Ergänzen Sie den Text mit einer passenden Form – positiv oder negativ und in der richtigen Zeitform – von **can** oder **be able to**.

When I was a student, I (1.) _____ sleep late during the week, but I (2.) _____ go on holiday, because I didn't have any money. Well, I (3.) _____ go on holiday now, but I (4.) _____ sleep late in the mornings. Oh, and I (5.) _____ stay out as long as I wanted to, it was great! At the moment, I (6.) _____ read many books, because I haven't got the time. I (7.) _____ do that when I retire, I guess. Oh, and then I (8.) _____ go on holiday for as long as I want.

Nice to know
Im gesprochenen Englisch sagt man sehr oft **I guess** an Stelle von **I think**.

◀ **retire** – *in Rente gehen*
guess – *raten/denken*
not any – *kein/keine*

Would, *may* und *might*

13

Would, may und **might**

Mit **would** kann man Angebote machen, Ratschläge erteilen oder hypothetische Situationen ausdrücken.

> **Would you like an apple?** *Möchtest du einen Apfel?*
> **I wouldn't talk to him.** *Ich würde nicht mit ihm sprechen.*
> **That would be great.** *Das wäre großartig.*
> **I'd like to go home now.** *Ich würde jetzt gerne nach Hause gehen.*

May und **might** benutzt man, um die Zukunft betreffende Vermutungen auszudrücken, wobei **may** eine etwas höhere Wahrscheinlichkeit ausdrückt als **might**.

> **We may have the time to visit some vineyards.**
> *Wir werden vielleicht die Zeit haben, um ein paar Weingüter zu besuchen.*
> **We might buy some wine.**
> *Wir könnten vielleicht etwas Wein kaufen.*

Wenn man um Erlaubnis bitten oder eine Erlaubnis erteilen möchte, kann man ebenfalls **may** benutzen.

> **May I leave now?** *Darf ich jetzt gehen?*
> **You may leave now.** *Du darfst jetzt gehen.*

> **Nice to know**
>
> Für *vielleicht* können Sie im Englischen auch **perhaps** sagen. Aber **We might buy some wine.** klingt eleganter als **Perhaps we'll buy some wine.**

14

Von den folgenden Sätzen passt jeweils einer nicht zu den anderen, weil er entweder eine andere Situation beschreibt oder in einer anderen Zeitform steht. Können Sie ihn finden? Dann unterstreichen Sie ihn!

1. I may go. / I might go. / Perhaps I'll go. / I can't go.
2. He really should go. / He must go. / He has to go. / He doesn't have to go.
3. She may see us. / She can't see us. / Perhaps she'll see us. / She might see us.
4. I could work. / I mustn't work. / I can work. / I may work.
5. They played. / They had to play. / They were able to play. / They might play.
6. I must buy food. / I have to buy food. / She must buy food. / She could buy food.

Der Imperativ

15

Let's und Imperativ
Der **Imperativ** (Befehlsform) entspricht im Englischen immer der Grundform eines Verbs, und man verneint ihn mit **don't**. Man kann ihn benutzen, um direkte Aufforderungen auszusprechen.

Go home!	*Geh nach Hause!*
Don't let me forget that!	*Lass mich das nicht vergessen!*

Der Imperativ kann oft direkt und unhöflich klingen. Wenn Sie möchten, dass Ihre Aufforderung mehr wie eine Bitte als wie ein Befehl klingt, benutzen Sie stattdessen lieber **Could you …?**

Tell him I called!
Sagen Sie ihm, dass ich angerufen habe!
Could you tell him I called?
Könnten Sie ihm sagen, dass ich angerufen habe?

Möchte man jemanden auffordern, etwas gemeinsam zu tun, benutzt man im Englischen **let's** (die Kurzform von **let us**) + den **Imperativ**. Diese Form wird verneint durch das Einfügen von **not** nach **let's**.

Let's look at the map and plan our route!
Lass uns auf die Karte schauen und unsere Route planen!
Let's not forget that!
Lass uns das nicht vergessen!

> **Nice to know**
> Man kann den Imperativ auch benutzen, um gute Wünsche oder Aufforderungen auszudrücken:
> **Take care!**
> *Pass auf dich auf!*
> **Get better soon!**
> *Gute Besserung!*
> **Have a nice day!**
> *Einen schönen Tag!*

16

Wenn man jemanden auffordert, etwas zu tun, dann hat man meist einen Grund dafür.
Ordnen Sie jedem Grund eine passende Aufforderung zu.

1. I'm cold.
2. I'm hungry.
3. I'm tired.
4. I've got too much work.
5. I like tennis.
6. I like music.

a. Go and speak to your boss!
b. Close the window!
c. Don't stay up so late!
d. Let's go to a concert.
e. Let's have lunch!
f. Let's go and play!

> **cold** – *kalt*
> **close** – *schließen*
> **window** – *Fenster*
> **hungry** – *hungrig*
> **boss** – *Chef*
> **concert** – *Konzert*

Übungsgrammatik 8

Hilfsverben gesucht! / Endlich Urlaub!

17

Schreiben Sie das fehlende Wort in das Kreuzworträtsel.

1. Jane ... study law. She is not sure, but she wants to.
2. Ben ... go to university. He is really not sure.
3. I don't ... to go to work on Sundays. I can stay at home.
4. ... you like a cup of tea?
5. I was not ... to come earlier.
6. Louise ... be here soon.
7. You ... forget to clean the house!
8. I ... help you, I have no time.
9. ... you help me, please?

18

Erinnern Sie sich noch an die Urlaubspläne von Paul und Kate? Hier sind Sätze gesucht, die ihren Urlaub betreffen. Schreiben Sie sie in der richtigen Reihenfolge auf.

1. beach / able / be / They / to / relax / the / on / 'll / .
2. They / buy / may / wine / some / .
3. could / They / sailing / go / .
4. would / fantastic / be / Sailing / .
5. should / They / take / lotion / suntan / .
6. take / should / books / They / .
7. Jane / French / have / to / will / speak / .
8. the / forget / They / cat / mustn't / .
9. many / England / don't / have / They / to / buy / in / things / .
10. 'll / They / able / to / buy / be / a / in / France / lot / .

Test **8** Übungsgrammatik

Must oder *have to*?

1

Sehen Sie sich diese Schilder (**signs**) an, und ergänzen Sie die Sätze mit **have to** oder **mustn't**!

◀ **mph** – *Meilen in der Stunde*

1. You _____ smoke here!
2. You _____ drive faster than 30 mph here!
3. You _____ be very quiet here!
4. You _____ take this road!

Nice to know

In England werden Distanzen und Geschwindigkeiten in Meilen angegeben. 1 Meile entspricht ca. 1,6 km und 30 mph entsprechen ca. 50km/h.

2

Sehen Sie sich die Bilder an, und ergänzen Sie die Sätze mit **must** oder **have to** in der richtigen Zeitform.

1. Yesterday I _____ work very late.
2. I really _____ go to the dentist!
3. Ben will _____ tidy up his room soon or Kate will get very angry!
4. The Smith family _____ feed their cat every day.

3

Unterstreichen Sie die passende Form.

1. You *don't have to / didn't have to / mustn't* smoke here!
   Can't you see the sign?
2. Paul *doesn't have to / mustn't / have to* work on Sundays.
3. I *don't have to / mustn't / have to* forget to feed the cat.
4. You *mustn't / must / don't have to* finish today.
   Tomorrow will be early enough.

335

Übungsgrammatik | **8 Test**

Can oder *be able to*? / *Should*, *would*, *could* und *might* / *Imperative*

4

Schreiben Sie die vorgegeben Sätze im **present simple** in die Lücken. Benutzen Sie entweder **can** oder **be able to**.

1. I'll be able to swim. _____
2. I couldn't dance. _____
3. I won't be able to drive. _____
4. I was able to read. _____

5

Sehen Sie sich die Bilder an, und ergänzen Sie die Sätze mit **should**, **would**, **could** oder **might**.
Benutzen Sie jedes dieser Hilfsverben genau einmal.

1. I _____ like a cup of tea, please.
2. It _____ rain soon.
3. You _____ go home!
4. _____ you help me, please?

6

Die folgenden Sätze sind durcheinander gepurzelt! Bringen Sie sie auf einem Blatt Papier wieder in die richtige Reihenfolge.

1. let / to / cat / me / the / forget / Don't / feed / !
2. stay / too / Don't / late / out / !
3. him / Tell / called / I / !
4. some / and / milk / Go / buy / !
5. have / Let's / a / next / Saturday / party / !
6. Let's / tomorrow / tennis / play / together / !

9 | Übungsgrammatik

Der Zeitschriftenladen / Was nehmen wir mit?

1 TR. 43

Der Zeitschriftenladen (**corner shop**) in der Straße der Smiths verkauft viele verschiedene Dinge, die Sie sich auch auf Ihrer CD anhören können. Betrachten Sie das Bild und ordnen Sie den darunter stehenden Sätzen jeweils den entsprechenden Bildausschnitt zu, indem Sie den korrekten Buchstaben notieren.

Nice to know

Neben den vielen **corner shops** gibt es in England auch so genannte **off-licences**. Diese haben ein ähnliches Sortiment wie **corner shops**, dürfen aber auch alkoholische Getränke verkaufen.

1. They sell many magazines. ☐
2. They sell a lot of chocolate. ☐
3. They don't sell much milk. ☐
4. They sell some newspapers. ☐
5. They sell little mineral water. ☐
6. They sell a lot of cigarettes. ☐
7. They don't sell many birthday cards. ☐
8. They sell a few stamps. ☐

◀ **sell** – *verkaufen*
stamp – *Briefmarke*
a few – *ein paar*
off-licence – *Wein- und Spirituosengeschäft*

2 TR. 44

Der Sommerurlaub der Familie Smith steht kurz bevor. Da sie zelten wollen, müssen Sie sich sehr genau überlegen, was sie mitnehmen und was nicht. Ordnen Sie den Sätzen, die Sie sich auch anhören können, die richtigen Bilder zu.

Nice to know

Handys gibt es im Englischen nicht. Mobiltelefone heißen in Großbritannien **mobile** (**phone**) und in Nordamerika **cellphone**.

a    b    c    d

1. They're taking a tent. ☐
2. Paul's not taking his mobile phone. ☐
3. They're taking some travel guides. ☐
4. They're not taking any wine. ☐

◀ **tent** – *Zelt*
travel guide – *Reiseführer*

Übungsgrammatik | **9**

Die Packliste / Arten von Substantiven

3

Paul und Kate sind dabei, eine detaillierte Packliste für ihren Urlaub zusammenzustellen. Lesen Sie den Dialog. Wenn Sie möchten, können Sie diesen auch auf der CD hören.

Paul: How many bags will we need?
Kate: Oh, one large bag per person, I think – and we'll need some plastic bags for shoes.
Paul: Are we taking raincoats for everybody?
Kate: Well, I think we should. We should also take some food. It's easier to organise that here, and I don't want to do too much shopping in France – nobody will speak English!
Paul: I think we should take very little food. We'll be able to buy a lot of things there.
Kate: But we should take a few things – just for the first few days.
Paul: All right, but don't forget we're already taking so many other things.
Kate: Well, I just hope we'll be able to get everything in the car!
Paul: Oh, and we must pack a bag with some medicine.
Kate: Yes, we mustn't forget. Let's just hope nobody will need it!

> **large** – *groß*
> **raincoat** – *Regenjacke*
> **get in** – *hineinbekommen*
> **few** – *wenige*
> **medicine** – *Medikamente*

4

Die meisten Substantive im Englischen sind zählbar und besitzen eine Pluralform: **house – houses**   **mouse – mice**
Es gibt aber auch Substantive, die nicht zählbar sind. Diese bilden keine Pluralform und werden ohne unbestimmten Artikel gebraucht.
Einige der wichtigsten nicht zählbaren Substantive, denen Sie immer wieder begegnen werden und die sie sich deshalb gut einprägen sollten, sind:

work (*Arbeit*) — I have a lot of work.
information (*Information*) — I've got no information.
advice (*Rat*) — He gave me some advice.
time (*Zeit*) — I haven't got a lot of time.

> **Nice to know**
>
> Auch das englische Wort **money** ist nicht zählbar. Man kann nur Währungen wie **euros** oder **pounds** zählen.

5

Sind die folgenden Wörter zählbar oder nicht?
Bilden Sie zwei Gruppen.

zählbar	nicht zählbar

water   cheese   apple   money   glass   dog   advice
euro   information   wine   child   towel

338

Much, *many* und *a lot of*

6

Much, **many** und **a lot of**
Zählbare Substantive werden im Englischen oft mit **many** (*viele*) oder **a lot of** (*viele*) benutzt.

> **We are taking so many other things.**
> *Wir nehmen so viele andere Dinge mit.*
> **Are we taking a lot of towels?**
> *Nehmen wir viele Handtücher mit?*

Nicht zählbare Substantive benutzt man mit **much** (*viel*), normalerweise aber nur in Fragen und negativen Sätzen. In positiven Sätzen bleibt es bei **a lot of** (*viel*).

> **I don't want to do much shopping in France.**
> *Ich will in Frankreich nicht viel einkaufen gehen.*
> **We'll need a lot of time to drive to France.**
> *Wir werden viel Zeit brauchen, um nach Frankreich zu fahren.*

Wenn Sie sich unsicher sind, können Sie immer **a lot of** benutzen. Diese Form ist nie falsch.

Lerntipp!
Wenn Sie in einem Modul auf ein Thema stoßen, das Sie zwar schon einmal behandelt haben, an das Sie sich aber nicht mehr genau erinnern, sollten Sie noch einmal zurückblättern in den entsprechenden Modulen. Je öfter Sie ein Thema wiederholen, um so besser beherrschen Sie es. Wenn Sie sich also unsicher sind, wie der Unterschied zwischen zählbaren und nicht zählbaren Substantiven war, dann schauen Sie sich dazu erneut die Erklärungen in Modul 1 an.

7

Benutzt man diese Wörter mit **much** oder mit **many**?
Bilden Sie zwei Gruppen.

much	many

bottle   wine   advice   computer   flower   house
butter   time   car   money   information   apple

8

Lesen Sie die Sätze und unterstreichen Sie dann das Wort, das den Satz richtig ergänzt.

1. I don't have *many / a / much* time.
2. We're taking *much / many / a* bags.
3. They're not taking *much / many / a* food.
4. He's got *much / a / many* friends.

Nice to know
Ein einfacher Weg herauszubekommen, ob Sie **much** oder **many** benutzen müssen, ist die Übersetzung. Sagt man im Deutschen *viel* ist es im Englischen **much**, sagt man *viele* ist es **many**.

339

| Übungsgrammatik | 9 |

Little und *few*

9

Nice to know

Little wird mit **less** und **least** gesteigert.
I have less time than you.
Ich habe weniger Zeit als Du.
She has the least time.
Sie hat am wenigsten Zeit.

Little und **few**
Wenn man ausdrücken will, dass man von einer Sache wenig oder wenige hat, so tut man dies bei zählbaren Substantiven mit **few** und bei nicht zählbaren Substantiven mit **little**.

> There's **little** milk in the bottle.
> *Es ist wenig Milch in der Flasche.*
> There are very **few** flowers in the garden.
> *Es sind wenige Äpfel in der Schale.*

10

Lesen Sie die Sätze bzw. hören Sie sie sich an und entscheiden Sie, welches der Bilder am besten zu dem Satz passt.

Nice to know

Vorsicht! **A few** heißt *einige* oder *ein paar*, und **few** heißt *wenig/e*.
There were a few children at the party.
Es waren ein paar Kinder auf dem Fest.
There were few children at the party.
Es waren wenig Kinder auf dem Fest.

1a 1b 2a 2b

3a 3b 4a 4b

1. There's a lot of water in the glass. ☐
2. There's little milk in the bottle. ☐
3. There are many apples in the bowl. ☐
4. There are very few flowers in the garden. ☐

11

Verwandeln Sie die vorgegeben Sätze jeweils in ihr Gegenteil, indem Sie diese mit **few** oder **little** schreiben (z.B. **There are many people.** / **There are few people.**).

1. There are many apples. _____
2. There is a lot of milk. _____
3. I have a lot of time. _____
4. He has many friends. _____

Some und *any*

12

Some und any
Das Wort **some** (*einige, etwas*) benutzt man sowohl mit zählbaren als auch mit nicht zählbaren Substantiven. Es wird meist in positiven Aussagesätzen verwendet und in Fragen, auf die man eine positive Antwort erwartet.
   We should take some food.
   Did you meet some friends?
   Would you like some tea?

Any, welches man ebenfalls sowohl mit zählbaren als auch mit nicht zählbaren Substantiven benutzen kann, hat in negativen Sätzen die Bedeutung *kein/keine*.
   I don't have any time!   Ich habe keine Zeit!

In positiven Sätzen und Fragen bedeutet **any** *irgendein/e* oder *irgendwelche*.
   I can come at any time.   Ich kann jederzeit kommen.
   Are there any questions?   Gibt es irgendwelche Fragen?

Some bezeichnet immer einen Teil aus der Gesamtheit dessen, was möglich wäre.
   I like some cheese. heißt, dass *ich manchen Käse mag*.

Any bezeichnet hingegen immer alle oder alles.
   I like any cheese. heißt, dass *ich allen/jeden Käse mag*.

> **Nice to know**
>
> Das Wörtchen **some** wird im Deutschen oft gar nicht übersetzt.
> **He took some pictures.**
> *Er hat Fotos gemacht.*

13

Ergänzen Sie die Sätze mit **some** oder **any**.

1. Would you like _____ tea?
2. I would like _____ milk, please.
3. I don't have _____ time now. I'm sorry.
4. Can you help Kate? She's got _____ problems with the computer.
5. I need new furniture for my house! I haven't got _____ at the moment.
6. Paul and Kate haven't got _____ vegetables in the house.

◀ **furniture** – *Möbel*
left – *übrig*

Übungsgrammatik 9

Someone, *no one* und *anyone*

14

Someone, **no one** und **anyone**
Die folgenden Wörter können im Englischen in beliebiger Kombination zusammengesetzt werden.

every (*jede/r/s*)	**thing** (*Ding, Sache*)
any (*irgendein/e/er/es*)	**body** (*Körper, Person*)
some (*einige*)	**one** (*eine/r/s*)
no (*keine/r/s*)	**where** (*wo*)

Entsprechend erhält man:

everything	**Do we have everything?**
alle	*Haben wir alles?*
everybody/everyone	**Everyone knows that!**
jeder	*Das weiß doch jeder!*
everywhere	**He walks everywhere.**
überall	*Er geht überall zu Fuß hin.*

> **Nice to know**
> Im Englischen besteht kein Unterschied zwischen **no one** und **nobody**, **everyone** und **everybody**, **someone** und **somebody** und **anyone** und **anybody**.

Folgende Sätze verdeutlichen Kombinationen im Englischen mit **any**, **some** und **no**:

Would you like **anything** to drink?	*irgendetwas*
I don't know **anybody** here.	*niemanden*
We can go **anywhere** we like.	*überall*
I would like **something** to drink, please.	*etwas*
Somebody told me that.	*jemand*
I left my bag **somewhere**.	*irgendwo*
I know **nothing** about that!	*nichts*
Let's hope **nobody**'ll need the medicine.	*niemand*
I can find him **nowhere**!	*nirgendwo*

Vorsicht! **Everybody** bedeutet *jeder* im Sinne von *alle zusammen*, und **anybody** bedeutet *jeder* im Sinne von *irgendein beliebiger*.

Everybody knows that.	*Jeder weiß das.*
	(Wir alle wissen das.)
Anybody could do that.	*Jeder könnte das tun.*
	(Jeder Beliebige könnte das tun.)

In Fragen hat **anything** die Bedeutung von *irgendetwas*, in der Verneinung bedeutet es *nichts*.

Do you know **anything**?	*Weißt du irgendetwas?*
I don't know **anything**.	*Ich weiß nichts.*

Ebenso verhält es sich mit **anybody**, **anyone** und **anywhere**.

9 **Übungsgrammatik**

Die kennt doch jeder! / Wir hatten so wenig ...

15

Lesen Sie die Sätze und schreiben Sie die Wörter im Kasten in die passenden Lücken.

> everywhere   somewhere
> anybody   everybody   something

1. Margaret Thatcher? Well, _____ knows her!
   She was the prime minister of the UK!
2. Where are my keys? They must be _____ in the house!
3. Does _____ know where I can buy chocolate here?
4. We are going to Louise's tomorrow, and we need _____ _____ to take!
5. Kate likes walking. She walks _____.

◀ **prime minister** – *Premierminister/ Premierministerin*

16

Lesen Sie, was Tante Hermione erzählt, und ergänzen Sie den Text mit **few**, **little**, **much**, **many**, **a lot of**, **some** oder **any**.

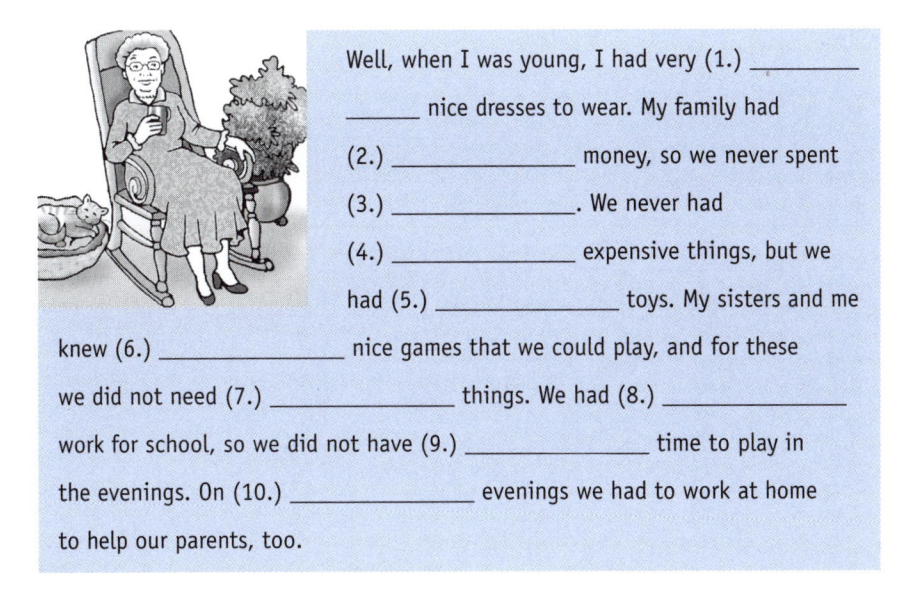

Well, when I was young, I had very (1.) _____ nice dresses to wear. My family had (2.) _____ money, so we never spent (3.) _____. We never had (4.) _____ expensive things, but we had (5.) _____ toys. My sisters and me knew (6.) _____ nice games that we could play, and for these we did not need (7.) _____ things. We had (8.) _____ work for school, so we did not have (9.) _____ time to play in the evenings. On (10.) _____ evenings we had to work at home to help our parents, too.

◀ **spend** – *ausgeben*
toy – *Spielzeug*

Übungsgrammatik | **9**

Gegensätze / Wörter suchen

17 ✎

Schreiben Sie jeweils das Gegenteil in die Lücken.

1. everybody   _____
2. everywhere   _____
3. everything   _____
4. few people   _____
5. only some families _____
6. little time   _____
7. no teacher   _____
8. a lot of dishes   _____
9. only here   _____
10. only now   _____

18 ✎

In diesem Buchstabengitter sind zehn Wörter versteckt, die Sie in dieser Lektion gelernt haben.
Welche sind es?

K	M	U	C	H	Z	K	X	H	G	L	P
P	X	A	P	A	K	P	Z	X	P	I	X
F	P	P	N	N	N	N	K	H	P	T	K
E	V	E	R	Y	B	O	D	Y	E	T	W
W	P	U	P	W	S	B	T	A	X	L	T
P	U	X	C	H	P	O	P	H	Q	E	P
Q	K	X	M	E	X	D	M	B	I	W	K
Q	A	Z	E	R	K	Y	X	E	K	N	K
Z	A	K	L	E	S	S	O	P	P	T	G

Test **9** Übungsgrammatik

Much, many oder *a lot of*? / *Few* oder *little*? / Gegenteile

1

Ergänzen Sie die Sätze mit **much**, **many** oder **a lot of**.

1. There is _____ cheese in the fridge.

2. There are _____ towels in the bag.

3. There isn't _____ milk in the bottle.

4. Are there _____ apples?

2

Ergänzen Sie die folgenden Sätze mit **few** oder **little**.

1. There are _____ children at school today.

2. They have _____ milk left in the fridge.

3. I have _____ books at home.

4. She has _____ time to play.

3

Schreiben Sie die Wörter aus dem Kasten neben den Begriff, der ihr Gegenteil ausdrückt.

| not anybody   few things   nowhere |
| no one   nowhere |

1. everywhere   _____

2. somebody   _____

3. everyone   _____

4. many things   _____

5. somewhere   _____

345

9 Test

Welches Bild passt? / Sätze ordnen

4

Welches Bild passt am besten zu dem Satz?
Die Sätze können Sie sich auch auf der CD anhören.

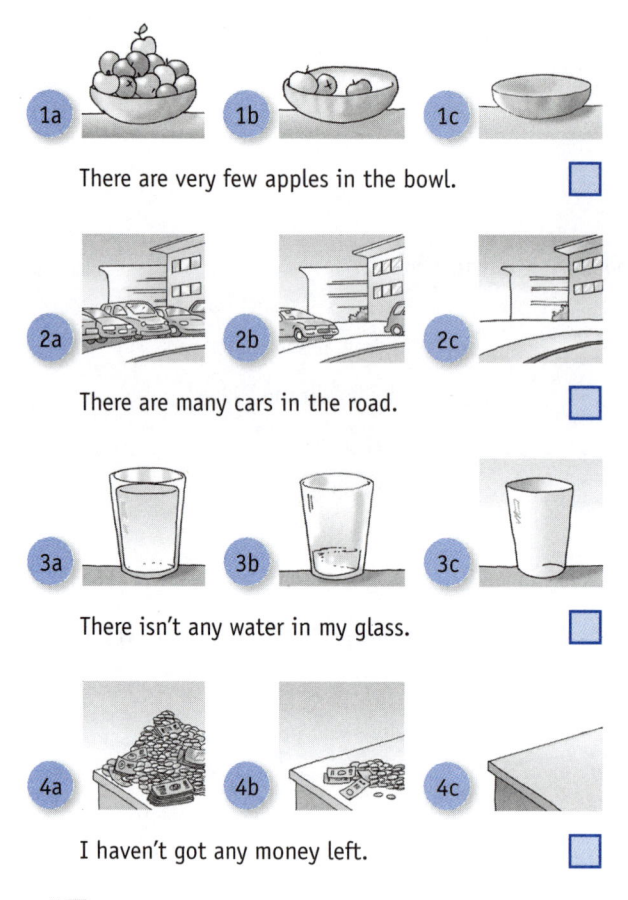

There are very few apples in the bowl.

There are many cars in the road.

There isn't any water in my glass.

I haven't got any money left.

5

Bringen Sie die folgenden Sätze wieder in die richtige Reihenfolge.

1. do / I / time / not / any / have / .
2. him / knows / Nobody / well / very / .
3. much / did / money / not / They / have / .
4. problems / few / had / They / .
5. did / problems / They / not / many / have / .

Übungsgrammatik

Wann war das? / Wo schläft Oscar?

1

Verbinden Sie die Satzanfänge auf der linken Seite mit einem passenden Ende auf der rechten Seite.

1. Paul went to university
2. On Mondays, Paul and
3. The family usually watch TV
4. Ben and Jane come home from school
5. Kate went to school
6. The family go for long walks

a. for 12 years. She didn't go to university.
b. Kate go shopping.
c. at 4:30. They take the school bus.
d. 20 years ago, when he was 19 years old.
e. at the weekend. They enjoy walking very much.
f. in the evening.

◀ **from** – *von*
between – *zwischen*
flat – *Wohnung*
ago – *vor*
in the evening – *abends*

2

Oscar, die Katze der Familie Smith, legt sich gerne an den verschiedensten Orten im Haus zum Schlafen hin. Wo befindet sich Oscar gerade?
Ordnen Sie den Sätzen das jeweils passende Bild zu, indem Sie den korrekten Buchstaben notieren.

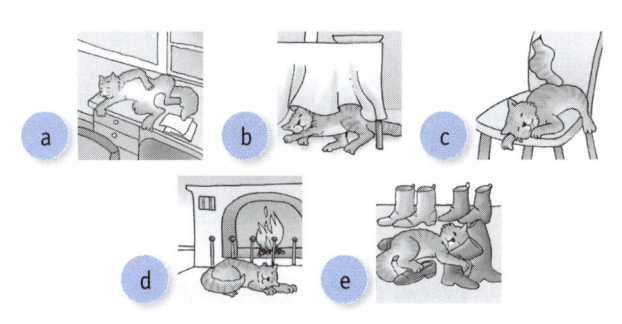

a   b   c
d   e

1. Oscar is sleeping under the dining table. ☐
2. Oscar is sleeping between the shoes. ☐
3. Oscar is sleeping on the desk. ☐
4. Oscar is sleeping in front of the fireplace. ☐
5. Oscar is sleeping on a chair. ☐

◀ **dining table** – *Esstisch*
under – *unter*
in front of – *vor*

Nice to know

Die meisten englischen Häuser haben zwar Zentralheizung, besitzen aber zusätzlich auch noch einen offenen Kamin (**fireplace**). Allerdings wird dieser heute oft elektrisch betrieben.

Breakfast on the way / Präpositionen der Zeit

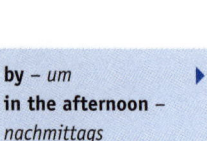

3

by – *um*	
in the afternoon – *nachmittags*	
in the morning – *morgens*	
mean – *meinen/heißen/bedeuten*	
before – *vorher*	
out of – *heraus/hinaus*	
into – *hinein/herein*	
on the way – *unterwegs*	
stuff – *Zeug/Sachen*	
be used to – *an etwas gewöhnt sein*	
down – *herunter/hinunter*	
around – *um ... herum*	
along – *entlang*	
straight – *geradeaus/direkt*	
towards – *in Richtung*	

Lesen Sie den Dialog bzw. hören Sie ihn sich auf der CD an. Achten Sie dabei besonders auf die Präpositionen **on**, **at** und **in**.

Paul: Let's see ... The ferry leaves Dover at six o'clock, so we'll have to be there by five.
Kate: Earlier, I'd say. Let's plan to be there early in the afternoon.
Paul: OK. That means we'll have to leave here early in the morning.
Kate: Yes, but that's no problem. I'll pack us a picnic basket the night before and then we can be out of bed and into the car at seven. We'll have breakfast on the way.
Paul: Good idea. We'll have to take all the picnic stuff anyway, because we'll need it in France.
Kate: Yes, and during the drive, the basket can sit on the back seat between the children. They are used to that.
Paul: Good. Let's plan our route now. We'll take the M6 down to Birmingham and then go along the M1 and around London, then straight towards Dover.
Kate: I'm not looking forward to going around London. Let's hope the traffic isn't too bad.
Paul: True. But we're going on a Sunday, and we're also going in the middle of the school holidays. So I don't think we'll have too many problems.

4

Präpositionen der Zeit
Bei **Zeitangaben** werden am häufigsten die Präpositionen **on**, **at** und **in** verwendet.
On verwendet man, wenn man über einen Wochentag oder ein Datum spricht.

We're going **on** a Sunday.	an einem Sonntag
We're going **on** the 14th of July.	am 14. Juli

At wird mit Uhrzeiten oder auch Mahlzeiten verwendet.

The ferry leaves Dover **at** six o'clock.	um sechs Uhr
I'll see you **at** lunch.	beim Mittagessen

In wird mit Jahreszeiten, Jahren, Monaten und Tageszeiten verwendet.

Let's plan to be there **in** the afternoon.	nachmittags
They go on holiday **in** the summer.	im Sommer
Their holiday is **in** June.	im Juni

At und **by** / Paul im Stress

5

Es gibt einige Zeitangaben, die mit **at** benutzt werden, ohne dass es sich dabei um Uhrzeiten handelt.

at the weekend	am Wochenende
at the moment	im Moment, jetzt gerade
at night	in der Nacht, nachts
at Christmas	an Weihnachten
at the end	am Ende

6

Um auszudrücken, dass etwas bis zu einem bestimmten Zeitpunkt geschehen sein muss, benutzt man die Präposition **by**.

We'll have to be in Dover by five o'clock. *bis/um fünf Uhr*

Zeitangaben wie **tonight** (*heute Abend*), **tomorrow** (*morgen*) oder **this afternoon** (*heute Nachmittag*) benötigen keine Präposition.

7

Lesen Sie, was Paul vor dem Urlaub noch alles erledigen und bis wann er damit fertig sein muss. Schreiben Sie dann passende Präpositionen in die Lücken. Wenn Sie meinen, dass die Lücke leer bleiben muss, schreiben sie einen Bindestrich (-) in die Lücke.

We're leaving (1.) _____ tomorrow morning (2.) _____ seven o'clock. We have to finish all our packing (3.) _____ this evening, so that we'll be able to leave as early as we can (4.) _____ the morning. (5.) _____ five o'clock (6.) _____ this afternoon, I have to pick Kate up from work. Later (7.) _____ the evening, I have to pick Jane up from her friend. (8.) _____ seven, we're seeing the neighbours. Oh, and I also have to phone my brother (9.) _____ tonight, because it's his birthday. I'm just glad that we're going (10.) _____ a Sunday. There won't be so much traffic!

> **Tipp zur Lösung!**
>
> **On** verwendet man, wenn man über einen Wochentag oder ein Datum spricht.
> **At** wird mit Uhrzeiten oder auch Mahlzeiten verwendet.
> **In** wird mit Jahreszeiten, Jahren, Monaten und Tageszeiten verwendet.
> Zeitangaben wie **tonight**, **tomorrow** oder **this afternoon** benötigen keine Präposition.

Zeiträume

8

Zeiträume
Um auszudrücken, wie lange ein Ereignis dauert, gedauert hat oder dauern wird, benutzt man die Präposition **for**.

Louise is in Manchester for two weeks.
Louise ist zwei Wochen lang in Manchester.
Paul went to university for three years.
Paul ging drei Jahre lang zur Universität.

Wenn man von einem zukünftigen Ereignis spricht und sagen möchte, wie lange es noch dauert, bis es passiert, benutzt man die Präposition **in**.

The ferry leaves in ten minutes.
Die Fähre fährt in 10 Minuten ab.
Ben will finish school in two years.
Ben wird in zwei Jahren mit der Schule fertig sein.

Die Präposition **ago** wird mit der Vergangenheit benutzt, um auszudrücken, wie lange etwas her ist. Vorsicht! **Ago** steht immer nach der Zeitangabe.

Kate finished school 19 years ago.
Kate beendete vor 19 Jahren die Schule.
I saw him 10 minutes ago.
Ich habe ihn vor 10 Minuten gesehen.

9

Lesen Sie die Sätze und unterstreichen Sie die passende Präposition.

1. Don't worry. He'll be here *in / for / ago* ten minutes.
2. I moved to London six years *for / in / ago*.
3. Ben usually studies *in / for / ago* three hours every day.
4. He went to school 19 years *for / ago / in*.
5. They will be here *in / ago / for* ten minutes.
6. Louise is staying in Manchester *ago / for / in* two weeks.
7. They went on holiday three years *in / for / ago*.
8. I'll be there *for / in / ago* half an hour. I'll stay all evening if you like.

10 | Übungsgrammatik

Präpositionen des Ortes / Wo ist der Ball?

10 TR. 50

Präpositionen des Ortes

Im Englischen benutzt man verschiedene Präpositionen, um die Position von Dingen und Personen relativ zueinander zu beschreiben.

Die folgenden Sätze, die Sie sich auch auf Ihrer CD anhören können, illustrieren einige dieser Präpositionen.

Können Sie die beschriebenen Objekte und deren Position auf den Illustrationen identifizieren?

Paul is sitting at the desk.
Paul sitzt am Schreibtisch.
The bin is under the desk.
Der Papierkorb ist unter dem Schreibtisch.
The lamp is on the desk.
Die Lampe ist auf dem Schreibtisch.
There is some paper in the drawer.
Da ist etwas Papier in der Schublade.

Ben is standing next to Jane.
Ben steht neben Jane.
Kate is standing behind Jane.
Kate steht hinter Jane.
Ben is standing in front of Paul.
Ben steht vor Paul.
Oscar is sitting between Ben and Jane.
Oscar sitzt zwischen Ben und Jane.

11

Sehen Sie sich die Zeichnungen an und schreiben Sie dann die Präposition aus Übung 10 in die Lücke, die am besten beschreibt, wo sich der Ball gerade befindet.

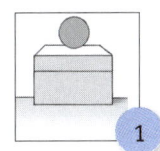

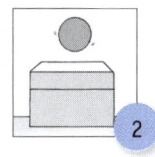

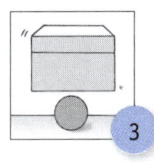

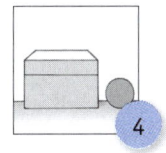

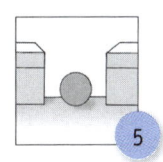

◀ **above** – *über*

351

Übungsgrammatik | 10

Tante Hermiones Wohnung / Ort und Richtung

12

Bei Tante Hermione ist immer alles an seinem angestammten Platz. Sehen Sie sich die Bilder an und vervollständigen Sie die Sätze mit einer passenden Präposition.

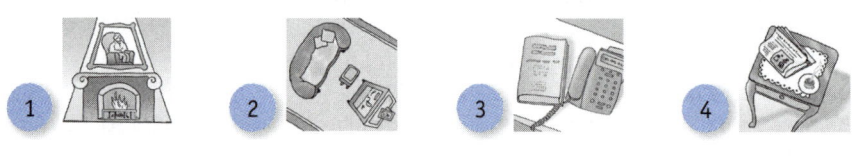

1. The picture is _____ the fireplace.
2. The sofa is _____ the TV.
3. The phone book is _____ the phone.
4. The newspaper is _____ the coffee table.

13

Lesen Sie die Sätze bzw. hören Sie sie sich auf der CD an.
Zwei der verwendeten Präpositionen drücken eine Bewegungsrichtung aus. Können Sie diese durch Ankreuzen identifizieren?

> **Nice to know**
>
> **Between** heißt zwischen zwei genau definierten Objekten, und **among** heißt *irgendwo mittendrin*:
> **between the sofa and the table**
> *zwischen dem Sofa und dem Tisch*
> **among the people**
> *zwischen/unter den Leuten*

> **opposite** – *gegenüber*
> **hairdresser's** – *Friseurgeschäft*
> **below** – *unter*
> **among** – *zwischen/ inmitten/unter*
> **through** – *durch*

1. The post office is **opposite** the bank. ▪
2. The hairdresser's is **above** the post office. ▪
3. The post office is **below** the hairdresser's. ▪
4. The children are playing **in the middle** of the road. ▪
5. The car is parked **near** the corner. ▪
6. The cat is sitting **among** the flowers. ▪
7. The man is walking **through** the post office door. ▪
8. The woman is walking **back** to her car. ▪

10 Übungsgrammatik

Präpositionen der Richtung / Die Reiseroute

14

Präpositionen der Richtung
Sehen Sie sich die Bilder an und schreiben Sie die korrekte Präposition in die Lücke. Als Hilfe können Sie sich die Sätze auch auf Ihrer CD anhören.

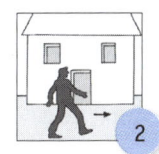

1. He is walking _____ the hill.
2. He is walking _____ the house.
3. He is walking _____ the corner.
4. He is walking _____ the street.
5. Oh no! He's falling _____ the cliff!

round
off
up
across
past

◀ **across** – *über*
up – *hinauf*
past – *an ... vorbei*
round – *um ... herum*
off – *herab/herunter*

15

Paul und Kate gehen noch einmal zusammen ihre Reiseroute durch. Lesen Sie den Text und schreiben Sie die fehlenden Präpositionen in die Lücken.

We'll take the M6 (1.) _____ (*hinunter*) to Birmingham and then go (2.) _____ (*entlang*) the M1 and (3.) _____ (*um ... herum*) London, then straight (4.) _____ (*in Richtung*) Dover. We're taking the ferry, so we're not going (5.) _____ (*durch*) the Channel Tunnel. Then we'll drive (6.) _____ (*heraus*) Calais and follow the motorway (7.) _____ (*bis*) Paris. We'll go (8.) _____ (*an ... vorbei*) Paris and follow the motorway (9.) _____ (*in ... hinein*) the Provence. We'll get (10.) _____ (*herunter*) the motorway (11.) _____ (*in der Nähe von*) Avignon.

Nice to know

Merken Sie sich das Wort **past** am besten als *vorbei*. Das **past simple** ist vorbei (schon geschehen), **past the shop** heißt *am Laden vorbei*, und **half past four** heißt, dass vier Uhr seit einer halben Stunde vorbei ist.

Übungsgrammatik   **10**

Over, under, in front of

16

Schreiben Sie die richtige Präposition in die Lücken. Ihre Lösung können Sie auch überprüfen, indem Sie sich die CD anhören.

> across   for   through   along   at   ago   on
> over   in   in front of   to   among

1. I'm staying here _____ two weeks.
2. The cat usually comes in _____ the window.
3. Paul often plays tennis _____ the weekend.
4. I met him three years _____ .
5. _____ Mondays, they often go shopping.
6. They watch TV _____ the evening.
7. The cat is sleeping _____ the fireplace.
8. They walk _____ school.
9. He is going _____ the street.
10. He is driving _____ the street.
11. There is a plane flying _____ the house.
12. The cat is sitting _____ the flowers.

17

Wohin fährt das Auto? Sehen Sie sich die Bilder genau an und ergänzen Sie die Sätze mit einer passenden Präposition.

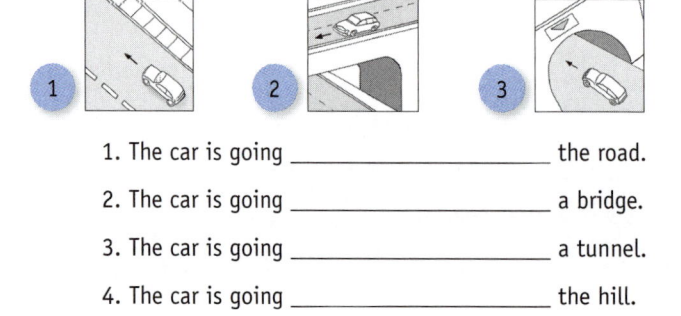

1. The car is going _____ the road.
2. The car is going _____ a bridge.
3. The car is going _____ a tunnel.
4. The car is going _____ the hill.

Test 10 **Übungsgrammatik**

*Wann war das? / **For**, **in** oder **ago**? / Wo ist die Katze?*

1 ✏️

Schreiben Sie die passenden Präpositionen in die Lücken.

1. _____ Monday
2. _____ June
3. _____ the evening
4. _____ six o'clock
5. _____ Christmas
6. _____ night
7. _____ the morning
8. _____ the 14th of December

2 ✏️

Ergänzen Sie die Sätze mit **for**, **in** oder **ago**.

1. She will be here _____ ten minutes.
2. They are staying _____ one week.
3. He finished school two years _____.
4. He'll be back _____ two hours.
5. They're staying _____ two days.

3 ✏️

Wo ist die Katze?
Schreiben Sie eine passende Präposition in die Lücke.

1. _____ the shoes

2. _____ the desk

1. _____ the table

2. _____ the fireplace

355

Übungsgrammatik — 10 Test

Präpositionen des Ortes / Welche Präposition ist richtig?

4

Sehen Sie sich die Bilder an und lesen bzw. hören Sie die Sätze. Kreuzen Sie dann den Satz an, der am besten zum Bild passt.

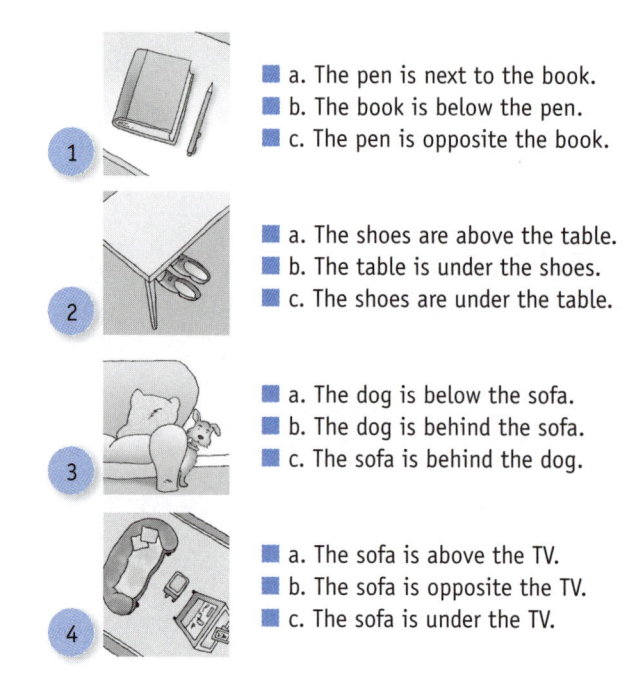

1
- a. The pen is next to the book.
- b. The book is below the pen.
- c. The pen is opposite the book.

2
- a. The shoes are above the table.
- b. The table is under the shoes.
- c. The shoes are under the table.

3
- a. The dog is below the sofa.
- b. The dog is behind the sofa.
- c. The sofa is behind the dog.

4
- a. The sofa is above the TV.
- b. The sofa is opposite the TV.
- c. The sofa is under the TV.

5

Ordnen Sie den Bildern die richtigen Präpositionen zu, indem Sie sie in die Lücken schreiben.

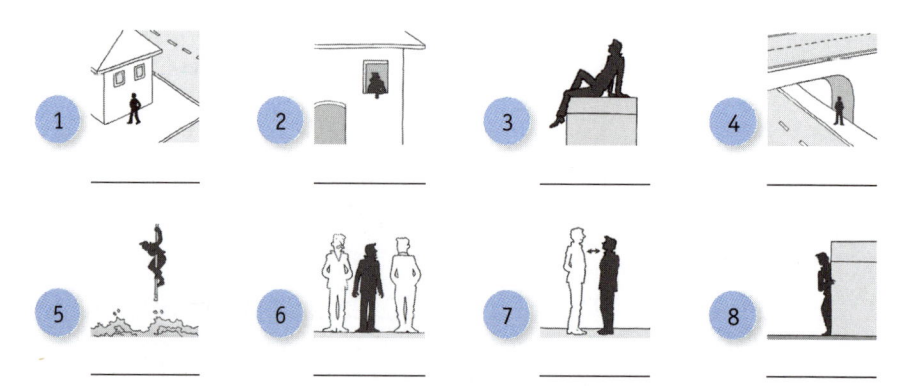

1 _____   2 _____   3 _____   4 _____

5 _____   6 _____   7 _____   8 _____

11 Übungsgrammatik

Es ist meins – es gehört mir! / Ich kann das selbst!

1

Verbinden Sie die Sätze auf der linken Seite jeweils mit einem Satz auf der rechten Seite, der genau das Gleiche ausdrückt.

1. This is my book.
2. This is your camera.
3. This is his bag.
4. This is her pen.
5. This is our computer.
6. This is their living room.

a. This living room is theirs.
b. This book is mine.
c. This bag is his.
d. This pen is hers.
e. This camera is yours.
f. This computer is ours.

◀ **mine** – *meiner/meine/meins*
yours – *deiner/deine/deins*
his – *seiner/seine/seins*
hers – *ihrer/ihre/ihres*
ours – *unserer/unsere/unseres*
theirs – *ihrer/ihre/ihres*

2 TR. 55

Lesen Sie die Fragen und ordnen Sie ihnen dann die richtigen Antworten zu. Sie können sich die Antworten auch auf Ihrer CD anhören. Achten Sie dabei besonders auf die Betonung des letzten Wortes.

1. Can I help you with your bag?
2. Should I help Jane with her homework?
3. Do you and Kate need help with the tent?
4. Should we help Ben and Jane with dinner?
5. Do you need the pump for the air mattress?

a. No, thanks. I can carry it myself!
b. No, I think it inflates itself.
c. No, I think they can do that themselves.
d. No, she should really do it herself!
e. No, thanks. We can put it up ourselves.

◀ **put up** – *aufstellen*
air mattress – *Luftmatratze*
inflate – *aufpumpen/aufblasen*
myself – *selbst*
herself – *selbst*
ourselves – *selbst*
themselves – *selbst*
itself – *selbst*

Übungsgrammatik | 11

Oh dear, where's our mattress? / Possessivbegleiter

3

Die Familie Smith ist in Südfrankreich angekommen, sie haben ihre Zelte aufgestellt und richten sich ein. Dabei geht es etwas chaotisch zu.
Lesen Sie den Dialog. Wenn Sie möchten, können Sie diesen auch auf der CD hören.

Paul: Whose trousers are these?
Jane: I don't know. They're not mine. I think they're Ben's.
Paul: Ben? Are these your trousers? Could you put them away, please?
Ben: All right.
Jane: Does anybody know where my air mattress is?
Paul: Oh, I think it's in our tent. I'll get it for you.
Jane: No, it's all right, Dad. I'll get it myself.
Paul: Right. Now where's ours? I know we've got it. Kate packed it herself. Ben? Do you know where our air mattress is?
Ben: No idea.
Jane: I've got mine!
Paul: Let's see ... It's not in the car, it's not out here ... Oh dear, I hope we packed it. Kate? Kate?
Ben & Jane: Typical!
Jane: They always tell us not to forget anything and then they forget everything themselves!

> whose – wessen
> put away – wegtun/wegpacken
> right – also
> no idea – keine Ahnung
> typical – typisch

4

Diese Sätze sind durcheinander gepurzelt.
Bringen Sie sie wieder in die richtige Reihenfolge.

1. These / trousers / Ben's / are / .
2. her / air mattress / is / This / .
3. is / air mattress / our / Where / ?
4. Paul / forget / and / themselves / everything / Kate / .
5. mine / I / got / 've / !
6. it / herself / packed / Kate / .

11 Übungsgrammatik

Possessivbegleiter / Mein Buch – dein Buch

5

Possessivbegleiter
Um Besitz oder Zugehörigkeit auszudrücken, benutzt man im Englischen die folgenden **Possessivbegleiter**:

my (*mein / meine*)	Where's my air mattress?
your (*dein / deine / ihr / ihre*)	Ben? Are these your trousers?
his (*sein / seine*)	These are his trousers.
her (*ihr / ihre*)	This is her air mattress.
its (*sein / seine*)	The dog ate its food.
our (*unser / unsere*)	I can't find our tent!
their (*ihr / ihre*)	This is their problem.
your (*euer / eure*)	Ben and Jane? Is this your cat?

Nice to know
Vorsicht! Der Possessivbegleiter **its** (*sein / seine*) wird oft mit **it's** (*es ist*) verwechselt.

Die englischen **Possessivbegleiter** stehen immer vor einem Substantiv und bleiben unveränderlich, egal ob dieses im Plural oder im Singular steht.

6

Unterstreichen Sie für jeden Satz den Possessivbegleiter, der sich auf die Person oder Personen bezieht, die vorher im Satz genannt worden sind.

1. Paul forgot to pack *his / her / its* air mattress.
2. Ben and Jane have got *its / our / their* mattresses.
3. Kate has got *our / her / his* sleeping bag.
4. We can't find *your / our / my* bag!

7

Ergänzen Sie die Sätze mit einem passenden Possessivbegleiter (**my**, **your**, **his**, etc.).

1. This book belongs to me. It's _____ book.
2. This car belongs to Paul. It's _____ car.
3. This pen belongs to you. It's _____ pen.
4. This house belongs to Paul and Kate. It's _____ house.
5. This basket belongs to the cat. It's _____ basket.

Übungsgrammatik | **11**

Possessivpronomen / Das ist meins

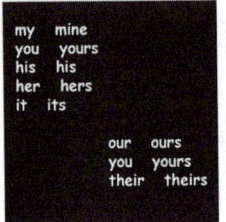

8

my	mine
you	yours
his	his
her	hers
it	its
our	ours
you	yours
their	theirs

Possessivpronomen
Ist bereits klar, von welcher Person oder Sache die Rede ist, wird diese ausgespart und statt einem Possessivbegleiter ein **Possessivpronomen** verwendet.

Nice to know

Die Konstruktion **... of mine/yours** etc. ist sehr häufig.
a friend of mine
ein Freund von mir
a sister of hers
eine Schwester von ihr

Whose trousers are these?
Wessen Hose ist das?
Is this their house?
Ist das ihr Haus?
What's your phone number?
Wie ist deine Telefonnummer?

They're mine.
Das ist meine.
No, theirs is over there.
Nein, ihres ist dort drüben.
576345. What's yours?
576345. Wie ist deine?

Schauen Sie sich in der Abbildung noch einmal alle Possessivbegleiter und die entsprechenden Possessivpronomen an und prägen sie sich ein.

9

Schreiben Sie neben die Possessivbegleiter das entsprechende Possessivpronomen in die Lücke (zum Beispiel: **my - mine**)

1. our _____
2. his _____
3. their _____
4. your _____

10

Formen Sie die Sätze so um, dass sie anstatt des Possessivbegleiters ein Possessivpronomen enthalten (zum Beispiel: **This is my book. – This book is mine.**).

1. This is our house. _____
2. These are my shoes. _____
3. This is your umbrella. _____
4. These are their photos. _____
5. This is his car. _____
6. These are her trousers. _____

11 | Übungsgrammatik

Der 's-Genitiv / Kates Katze

11

Der 's-Genitiv

Der **'s-Genitiv** wird verwendet, um aufzuzeigen, wem etwas gehört. Hierzu wird bei Personen, Tieren oder Ländern im Singular ein **'s** an das Substantiv angehängt. Werden zwei Personen zusammen genannt, so wird das **'s** nur an die letztgenannte Person angehängt.

Paul's car — *Pauls Auto*
Paul and Kate's house — *Paul und Kates Haus*

Endet ein Wort **im Plural** auf **-s**, bekommt es nur ein Apostroph.
the parents' bedroom — *das Schlafzimmer der Eltern*

Bei Substantiven, deren Pluralformen nicht auf **-s** enden, wird **'s** angehängt.
the children's bikes — *die Fahrräder der Kinder*

Statt **'s** wird oft auch eine Konstruktion mit **of** benutzt:
Paul and Kate's house — **the house of Paul and Kate**

> **Nice to know**
> Der **'s-Genitiv** wird auch oft so verwendet, dass er dem deutschen *beim* entspricht:
> **at the doctor's**
> *beim Arzt*
> **at the hairdresser's**
> *beim Friseur*

12

Lesen Sie, wem die abgebildeten Dinge gehören (**belong to**). Formen Sie dann den Satz so um, dass sie den 's-Genitiv benutzen können (zum Beispiel **This cat belongs to Kate. - This is Kate's cat.**).
Die Lösung können Sie auch überprüfen, indem Sie sich die CD anhören.

1. This car belongs to Paul.
_____

2. This bike belongs to Kate
_____

3. This tent belongs to the children.
_____

4. This bedroom belongs to the parents.
_____

Übungsgrammatik | **11**

Wo sind meine Sandalen? / Reflexivpronomen

13 ✎

hang on – *warte mal* ▶	Im Urlaub der Familie Smith geht es manchmal etwas drunter und drüber. Lesen Sie den Dialog und ergänzen Sie die fehlenden **Possessivbegleiter**, **Genitiv-'s** oder **Possessivpronomen**.
have a look – *nachsehen*	
tidy away – *wegräumen*	

Kate: Does anyone know where 1. _____ sandals are?

Paul: No idea. 2. _____ are here. Hang on, are these 3. _____?

Kate: No, I think they're Jane 4. _____. Jane? Are these sandals 5. _____?

Jane: No, they're Ben 6. _____.

Kate: Hmm, I'll have another look in 7. _____ tent ... What's this? Jane, what's 8. _____ swimming costume doing in 9. _____ tent?

Jane: Thanks, Mum! Oh, and 10. _____ sandals are here!

Paul: I wish these kids would tidy 11. _____ things away a bit better!

Nice to know

I wish ... + would ... wird häufig benutzt, um unrealistische Wünsche zu äußern.
I wish I would win the first prize.
Ich wünschte ich würde den ersten Preis gewinnen.

Nice to know

Vorsicht!
I can do it myself. heißt *Ich kann das selbst machen.*
I can do it by myself. heißt *Ich kann das allein machen.*

14 👓

Reflexivpronomen

Im Englischen gibt es die folgenden **Reflexivpronomen**:

myself	mich / mir	**itself**	sich
yourself	dich / dir	**yourselves**	euch
himself	sich	**themselves**	sich
herself	sich	**ourselves**	uns

Diese werden verwendet, wenn sich das Verb im Satz auf die Person bezieht, welche die Handlung auch ausführt. Das heißt, wenn **Subjekt** und **Objekt** identisch sind.

I bought myself a new car.
Ich habe mir ein neues Auto gekauft.
They wash themselves every morning.
Sie waschen sich jeden Morgen.

Sie werden aber auch benutzt, um zu betonen, von wem etwas getan wird. Im Deutschen verwendet man dann das Wort *selbst*.

They forget everything themselves!
Sie vergessen selbst alles!

11 | Übungsgrammatik

Welches Pronomen ist es? / Selbst gemachte Kuchen

15 ✎

Die Buchstaben dieser Reflexivpronomen sind durcheinander gepurzelt. Können Sie sie wieder in die richtige Reihenfolge bringen?

1. ymfels   _____
2. soyurlfe   _____
3. mhfiels   _____
4. hfeselr   _____
5. ilseft   _____

16 ✎

Schreiben Sie ein passendes Reflexivpronomen in die Lücke.

1. Did you make that cake _____?
2. We did everything _____.
3. They did all the work _____.

17 ✎

Wenn Menschen etwas ohne fremde Hilfe geleistet haben, sind sie oft stolz darauf und möchten diese Tatsache besonders betonen.
Lesen Sie die Fragen. Schreiben Sie dann eine positive Antwort, die ein Reflexivpronomen enthält, in die Lücken. Es soll betont werden, dass die genannte Person die Sache *selbst* gemacht hat (z.B. **Did you make the cake yourself? – Yes, I made it myself.**).

1. Did you make the dress yourself?
   _____

2. Did Jane do her homework herself?
   _____

3. Did Paul and Kate do the garden themselves?
   _____

4. Did you and Louise make the cake yourselves?
   _____

Übungsgrammatik | 11

Ordnen Sie die Sätze! / Finden Sie die Pronomen?

18

In diesen Sätzen sind die Wörter durcheinander geraten.
Schreiben Sie sie in der richtigen Reihenfolge auf.

1. bought / five / They / ago / their / years / house / .
2. can / that / I / myself / do / !
3. prepared / He / himself / everything / .
4. The / car / is / red / theirs / .
5. family / much / likes / He / his / very / .
6. opened / himself / the / door / He / .
7. That / Ben's / is / bicycle / .
8. Kate's / is / Paul / and / house / That / .

19

In diesem Buchstabengitter sind zehn Wörter versteckt, die Sie in dieser Lektion gelernt haben.
Welche sind es?

K	Z	D	P	M	W	H	M	W	K	I	O
G	P	B	H	I	S	E	Y	J	K	T	U
J	C	D	A	N	B	R	S	D	A	S	R
D	A	T	H	E	M	S	E	L	V	E	S
A	Z	H	I	M	S	E	L	F	Z	L	B
Y	O	U	R	S	E	L	F	C	A	F	G
P	B	Y	O	U	R	S	E	L	V	E	S

1. _____   6. _____
2. _____   7. _____
3. _____   8. _____
4. _____   9. _____
5. _____   10. _____

Test 11 **Übungsgrammatik**

Possessivbegleiter / Meins und deins / Welches Wort passt nicht?

1

Unterstreichen Sie jeweils den korrekten Possessivbegleiter.

1. This car belongs to you and me. It is *our / their / ours* car.
2. This bike belongs to Ben. It is *her / hers / his* bike.
3. This bag belongs to you. It is *his / yours / your* bag.
4. This house belongs to Paul and Kate. It is *their / theirs / her* house.
5. This book belongs to me. This is *its / my / mine* book.

2

Schreiben Sie die passenden Possessivpronomen neben die entsprechenden Possessivbegleiter.

1. my _____
2. your _____
3. his _____
4. her _____
5. its _____
6. our _____
7. their _____

3

Unterstreichen Sie jeweils das Wort, das nicht zu den anderen in der Gruppe passt. Achten Sie darauf, ob es sich bei den Wörtern um Possessivpronomen, Possessivbegleiter oder Reflexivpronomen handelt.

1. mine / your / yours / his
2. myself / yourselves / our / ourselves
3. our / his / her / yours
4. theirs / their / yours / his
5. ours / ourselves / myself / himself

Übungsgrammatik | 11 Test

Wem gehört das? / Reflexivpronomen

4 ✏️

Wem gehören diese Dinge? Schreiben Sie beispielsweise Jane's T-shirt in die Lücke, wenn Jane mit einem T-Shirt abgebildet ist.

1. _____

2. _____

3. _____

4. _____

5. _____

5 ✏️

Ergänzen Sie die Sätze mit dem jeweils passenden Reflexivpronomen.

1. I can do that _____.

2. You can do that _____.

3. You and Paul, you can do that _____.

4. They can do that _____.

5. We can do that _____.

12 Übungsgrammatik

*Im Urlaub / Das **past participle***

1

Die Familie Smith ist jetzt mitten in ihrem Sommerurlaub in Südfrankreich. Schauen Sie sich an, was sie zu diesem Zeitpunkt schon unternommen haben und was sie noch vorhaben. Wenn Sie möchten, können Sie sich die Sätze auf Ihrer CD anhören. Ordnen Sie dann den Sätzen das passende Bild zu.

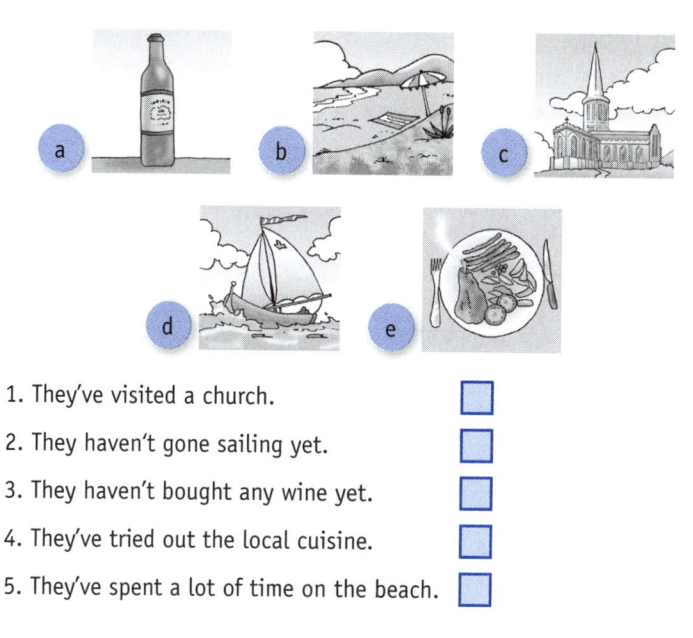

> **Nice to know**
>
> Für das deutsche Wort *Küche* gibt es im Englischen zwei Entsprechungen: **kitchen** ist der Ort, an dem gekocht wird, und **cuisine** sind die typischen Gerichte einer Region.

a   b   c

d   e

1. They've visited a church. ☐
2. They haven't gone sailing yet. ☐
3. They haven't bought any wine yet. ☐
4. They've tried out the local cuisine. ☐
5. They've spent a lot of time on the beach. ☐

> **not ... yet** – *noch nicht*
> **gone** – *gegangen*
> **try out** – *ausprobieren*

2

Die unregelmäßigen Verben unten kennen Sie bereits. Hier sind deren Infinitiv und **past simple**-Form angegeben. Verbinden Sie diese nun mit der passenden dritten Form im Kasten.

a. given	d. done	g. been	i. driven
b. had	e. written	h. eaten	j. made
c. gone	f. seen		

1. be, was / were ☐
2. go, went ☐
3. make, made ☐
4. do, did ☐
5. see, saw ☐
6. have, had ☐
7. drive, drove ☐
8. give, gave ☐
9. write, wrote ☐
10. eat, ate ☐

> **done** – *getan*
> **written** – *geschrieben*
> **seen** – *gesehen*
> **been** – *gewesen*
> **eaten** – *gegessen*
> **driven** – *gefahren*
> **made** – *gemacht*

*Have you written to Louise? / Das **present perfect***

3

Der Urlaub von Kate und Paul neigt sich dem Ende zu. Bevor Sie zurückfahren, schreiben Sie noch einen ganzen Stapel Postkarten. Lesen Sie den Dialog oder hören Sie ihn sich auf der CD an.

> **just** – *gerade*
> **send** – *schicken*
> **either** – *auch nicht*
> **sign** – *unterschreiben*

Paul: Hang on, here's the list. We've written to my parents ...
Kate: Yes, and I've just written to mine, too. Here's the postcard.
Paul: Great. Have we written the card to Louise?
Kate: No, we haven't. I'll do that next.
Paul: OK. What about Stephen and Sue? We should write them a card, too.
Kate: We've never written them postcards, I think. They never send us postcards, either.
Paul: They wrote to us last year, I think. Do you remember they went to Bali?
Kate: You're right. Let's write them a card, too.
Paul: OK. Have you written to Elizabeth?
Kate: Yes, and I've already written to James, too. Here's the card, if you want to sign it.
Paul: Sure. Oooh, hang on, have we written to Aunt Hermione?
Kate: Erm... no, we haven't. Let's do that now, we really mustn't forget!

4

Bildung des **present perfect**
Das **present perfect** wird aus **have/has** und der dritten Form (dem **past participle**) des Hauptverbs gebildet. **Have/has** wird dabei oft abgekürzt zu **'ve/'s**.

Bei regelmäßigen Verben wird das **past participle** gebildet, indem man **-ed** an die Grundform des Verbs anhängt. Endet das Hauptverb auf **-y**, so wird dieses zu **-ied**.

> They**'ve visited** a church.
> *Sie haben eine Kirche besichtigt.*
> They**'ve tried** out the local cuisine.
> *Sie haben die lokale Küche ausprobiert.*

Übungsgrammatik 12

Verneinung, Fragen, Kurzantworten / Unregelmäßige Verben I

5

In der Verneinung wird **not** zwischen **have/has** und dem **past participle** eingefügt. Hierbei wird besonders in der gesprochenen Sprache auf zwei Weisen verkürzt.

They **haven't visited** Marseille.
They**'ve not watched** a lot of TV.

Zur Bildung von Fragen vertauscht man die Position von **have** und dem Subjekt.

Have they watched a lot of TV?

Kurzantworten werden mit **have/has** gebildet.

Has he watched a lot of TV?	No, he **hasn't**.
Hat er viel ferngesehen?	*Nein, hat er nicht.*
Have they visited Marseille?	Yes, they **have**.
Haben sie Marseille besucht?	*Ja, haben sie.*

6

Sie sehen hier Verben, deren **past participle** unregelmäßig ist. Lesen Sie die Beispielsätze laut bzw. hören Sie sie sich an und sprechen Sie diese laut nach. Versuchen Sie, sich die unregelmäßigen Verben samt **past participle** einzuprägen.

be, was/were, **been**	He's been to France.
go, went, **gone**	He's gone home.
make, made, **made**	They've made a mistake.
do, did, **done**	I've done my homework.
see, saw, **seen**	I've seen her!
have, had, **had**	We haven't had enough time.
drive, drove, **driven**	Have you driven him home?
give, gave, **given**	Have you given her the present?
write, wrote, **written**	Have you written to Louise?
eat, ate, **eaten**	You've eaten all the cake!
speak, spoke, **spoken**	She's spoken to me.
tell, told, **told**	Have you told him about the problem?
buy, bought, **bought**	Have you bought everything we need?
think, thought, **thought**	He hasn't thought of that.
sleep, slept, **slept**	I've slept really well.

Unregelmäßige Verben II / Welche Verbform passt?

7

Viele der häufig gebrauchten Verben im Englischen sind unregelmäßig. Es führt kein Weg daran vorbei, sich diese Verben einzeln einzuprägen. In Übung 6 sowie in diesem Kasten finden Sie alle wichtigen unregelmäßigen Verben dieses Kurses.

> **Nice to know**
>
> Vorsicht!
> **He's drunk the wine.**
> heißt *Er hat den Wein getrunken.*
> **He's drunk.** heißt aber *Er ist betrunken.*

begin	began	begun
build	built	built
drink	drank	drunk
fall	fell	fallen
feed	fed	fed
find	found	found
forget	forgot	forgotten
get	got	got/gotten
know	knew	known
leave	left	left
meant	meant	meant
meet	met	met
put	put	put
read	read	read
ride	rode	ridden
say	said	said
sell	sold	sold
send	sent	sent
sing	sang	sung
sit	sat	sat
spend	spent	spent
stand	stood	stood
swim	swam	swum
take	took	taken
wear	wore	worn

8

Lesen Sie die Fragen oder hören Sie sie, wenn Sie möchten, und unterstreichen Sie die Form, welche die Antwort korrekt ergänzt.

1. Have you spoken to Kate? Yes, I've just *speak / spoken / spoke* to her.
2. Has Jane been to France before? No, she's never *been / was / is* there.
3. Do we have any food left? No, the children've *eat / eaten / eating* it all.
4. Does Paul know the way? Yes, he's *drives / drove / driven* there many times.

*Gebrauch des **present perfect** / Los geht's an den Strand!*

9

Das **present perfect** wird verwendet, wenn man von etwas spricht, das in der Vergangenheit begonnen hat und bis in die Gegenwart reicht. Das heißt, wenn man von Handlungen spricht, die noch nicht abgeschlossen sind.

Paul and Kate have gone on holiday.
bedeutet, dass sie immer noch im Urlaub sind.

Man benutzt das **present perfect** auch dann, wenn eine Handlung zwar abgeschlossen ist, aber nur deren Ergebnis wichtig ist.

Have we written the card to Louise?
Hier ist es wichtig, ob die Karte geschrieben wurde, nicht wann.

Man findet im **present perfect** auch oft **not ... yet** (*noch nicht*) oder **never** (*noch nie*).

They haven't bought any wine yet.
They've never been to France.

Fragen werden oft mit **ever** (*jemals*) oder **yet** (*schon*) gestellt.

Have we written to Aunt Hermione yet?
Have you ever been to France?

10

Die Familie Smith bereitet einen Strandtag vor. Lesen Sie den Dialog und ergänzen Sie die fehlenden **past participle** Formen.

> **Kate:** Has anyone (1.) _____ (see) the big towels?
>
> **Paul:** Yes, I've (2.) _____ (put) them in the car.
>   Do we have suntan lotion?
>
> **Kate:** Yes, I've (3.) _____ (buy) some. I've (4.) _____ (leave) it in the car.
>
> **Paul:** Good. Oh, and have we (5.) _____ (pack) some books?
>
> **Kate:** I've (6.) _____ (read) all the ones we brought.
>
> **Paul:** Have you really? I haven't even (7.) _____ (finish) the first one. Oh my goodness!

*Zeitpunkt oder Zeitraum? / **For** oder **since**?*

11

Das **present perfect** wird oft in Verbindung mit **since** (*seit*), **for** (*seit*) oder **how long** verwendet. Es entspricht dann der deutschen Gegenwartsform mit *schon*.

Kate has worked in a shop for ten years.
Kate arbeitet seit zehn Jahren in einem Laden.
Kate has worked in a shop since 1993.
Kate arbeitet seit 1993 in einem Laden.

For steht immer für eine **Zeitdauer**. Es zeigt an, **wie lange** etwas geschieht oder geschehen ist. **Since** bezieht sich auf einen **Zeitpunkt**. Es zeigt an, **seit wann** etwas geschieht oder geschehen ist. Im **present perfect** werden beide Präpositionen mit *seit* übersetzt. Deshalb ist es hier besonders wichtig, darauf zu achten, ob es sich um einen **Zeitpunkt** (**since**) oder um eine **Zeitdauer** (**for**) handelt.

Hier einige Beispiele:
For wird mit Zeitbestimmungen verwendet, die einen **Zeitraum** beschreiben:

two hours	*zwei Stunden*	**a week**	*eine Woche*
20 minutes	*20 Minuten*	**40 years**	*40 Jahre*
six months	*sechs Monate*		

Since wird mit Zeitbestimmungen verwendet, die einen **Zeitpunkt** angeben:

9 o'clock	*9 Uhr*	**Monday**	*Montag*
yesterday	*gestern*	**December**	*Dezember*
Christmas	*(seit) Weihnachten*		

12

Ergänzen Sie die Sätze mit **for** oder **since**.

1. He's lived in this house _____ 10 years.
2. He's lived in this house _____ 1994.
3. She's been out _____ two o'clock.
4. She's been out _____ two hours.
5. Paul has worked at the bank _____ 15 years.
6. Paul has worked at the bank _____ last summer.

Present perfect – past simple / Eine Postkarte an Louise

13

Present perfect – past simple
Das **past simple** wird dann verwendet, wenn man über eine abgeschlossene Handlung oder ein Ereignis in der Vergangenheit redet. Oft findet man Zeitbestimmungen wie **yesterday**, **a year ago**, **last August** oder in **1977**, die eindeutig auf einen Zeitpunkt in der Vergangenheit hinweisen.
    They wrote to us last year.

Das **present perfect** wird hingegen verwendet, wenn ein Bezug zur Gegenwart besteht. Zeitbestimmungen, die häufig im **present perfect** verwendet werden, sind **ever** (*jemals*), **never** (*nie*), **yet** (*schon*), **not ... yet** (*noch nicht*), **just** (*gerade*), **since** (*seit*), **so far** (*bis jetzt*) oder **this week/year** (*diese Woche/dieses Jahr*).
    I've just written to my parents.
    Ich habe gerade meinen Eltern geschrieben.

Im Deutschen werden beide Vergangenheitsformen meist ohne Bedeutungsunterschied benutzt. Im Englischen aber kann sich mit der Vergangenheitsform auch die Bedeutung des Satzes ändern.
    They've gone on holiday. heißt, dass sie noch im Urlaub sind.
    They went on holiday. heißt, dass sie bereits zurück sind.

> **Lerntipp!**
> Indem Sie sich alte Module, Übungen und Erklärungen immer mal wieder anschauen, festigen Sie Ihre englischen Grammatikkenntnisse.
> Schauen Sie doch einfach mal im Inhaltsverzeichnis nach und wiederholen Sie ein Modul, das ein Pensum behandelt, das noch einmal vertieft werden könnte. Oder lesen Sie sich einige Paragraphen, bei denen Sie sich unsicher sind, in Ihrer Grammatik durch.

14

Kate schreibt Louise gerade eine Karte. Ergänzen Sie die Verben in Klammern im **present perfect** oder **past simple**.

Dear Louise,
We're having a fantastic time in France, and we (1.) _____ (be) very active. We (2.) _____ (not go) sailing yet, but we're planning to do that soon. Yesterday we (3.) _____ (go) to a local market and (4.) _____ (buy) some fish. Then we (5.) _____ (grill) the fish on the barbecue – it (6.) _____ (be) delicious! (7.) _____ you ever _____ (try) barbecued fish? The weather (8.) _____ (be) fantastic so far, and we (9.) _____ (spend) a lot of time on the beach. See you soon, Kate and family

Übungsgrammatik | 12

Welches Verb ist das? / Unregelmäßige Verben gesucht!

15 ✏

Bei den folgenden unregelmäßigen **past participle**-Formen sind die Buchstaben durcheinander geraten. Bringen Sie sie wieder in die richtige Reihenfolge. Die Bilder helfen Ihnen herauszufinden, welches Verb gemeint ist.

1	2	3	4
tewnitr	rnkud	tanee	dera
_____	_____	_____	_____

16 ✏

Schreiben Sie das fehlende Verb in der korrekten Zeitform in das Kreuzworträtsel.

1. We know the place. We've ... there before.
2. Have you ... all the postcards yet?
3. I'm sorry, there is no more coffee. I've ... it all.
4. I've never ... those trousers before.
5. Yes, he knows that. I ... him.
6. John's never ... here before. He always sits over there.
7. I've ... to her. She's coming at 7 o'clock.
8. Have you ... that book? It's very good.
9. Where's all the cake? I'm sorry, I've ... it.
10. Yes, I know the way. I've ... there many times.

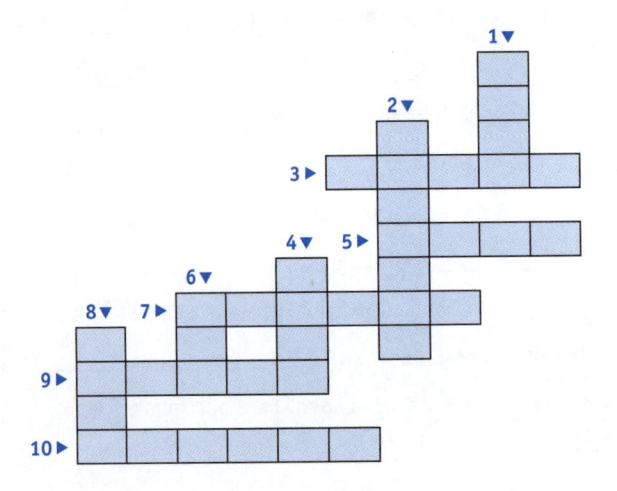

Test **12** | **Übungsgrammatik**

Past participle – Formen / Das *present perfect*

1

Sehen Sie sich das Bild an und ergänzen Sie die Sätze mit der **past participle** Form eines passenden Verbs.

1. She's _____ a letter.
2. Somebody's _____ all the cake!
3. I've _____ the book.
4. You've _____ the dishes.
5. Have you _____ well?

2

Wandeln Sie die folgenden Sätze ins **present perfect** um und schreiben Sie diese in die Lücken.

1. We go shopping.
   _____

2. She is speaking to her friend.
   _____

3. He drives home.
   _____

4. She buys apples.
   _____

5. They take pictures.
   _____

375

Übungsgrammatik — 12 Test

For oder *since*? / Zeitangaben / Verbformen

3

Werden diese Zeitangaben im **present perfect** mit **for** oder mit **since** verwendet? Schreiben Sie die passende Präposition in die Lücken.

1. _____ two years
2. _____ last year
3. _____ one hour
4. _____ 2001
5. _____ one week

4

Unter den folgenden Gruppen von Wörtern ist jeweils ein Wort, das nicht mit dem **present perfect** benutzt werden kann. Können Sie es identifizieren? Kreuzen Sie es an.

1. ☐ a. ever
   ☐ b. yet
   ☐ c. last year
   ☐ d. already

2. ☐ a. never
   ☐ b. two hours ago
   ☐ c. for
   ☐ d. so far

3. ☐ a. yet
   ☐ b. already
   ☐ c. in 1999
   ☐ d. since

4. ☐ a. for
   ☐ b. ago
   ☐ c. since
   ☐ d. just

5

Unterstreichen Sie die Verbform, die den Satz korrekt ergänzt.

1. Yesterday, I *am walking / walked / have walked* home from work.
2. This morning, I *have worked / worked / work* a lot.
3. He *has lived / lives / lived* in this house for ten years, and he likes it very much.
4. Paul *knows / has known / knew* Kate since they went to school together.
5. They *have bought / bought / buy* a new kitchen last year.

Lösungen | Übungsgrammatik

Modul 1

1

Übung 1
oranges, apples, pears, bananas, trousers, tickets, children

Übung 4
1. dessert; 2. trousers; 3. French; 4. dog; 5. March; 6. Saturday; 7. children / kids; 8. Friday; 9. dinner; 10. Spain

Übung 6
1. an; 2. a; 3. a; 4. an; 5. an; 6. a; 7. an; 8. a; 9. an; 10. a; 11. an; 12. a

Übung 8
1. c; 2. e; 3. d; 4. a; 5. b

Übung 9
1. books; 2. cities; 3. tomatoes; 4. fish; 5. presents; 6. knives; 7. tickets; 8. kisses; 9. mice; 10. roofs

Übung 11
1. c; 2. a; 3. b; 4. d

Übung 12
1. piece; 2. bottle; 3. cup; 4. slice; 5. packet

Übung 14
1. There is / There's; 2. There is / There's; 3. There are; 4. There is / There's; 5. There are; 6. There are

Übung 15

A	C	T	O	M	A	T	O	E	S
K	C	P	W	F	I	S	H	T	B
I	N	E	B	G	E	P	U	W	O
C	H	I	L	D	R	E	N	O	T
A	M	N	V	G	L	A	T	M	T
K	M	I	C	E	P	R	Z	E	L
E	B	O	O	K	S	S	T	N	E
S	K	T	R	O	U	S	E	R	S

Übung 16
1. d; 2. c; 3. b; 4. e; 5. a; 6. f

Test 1

Übung 1
1. G; 2. f; 3. M,U; 4. M; 5. T; 6. d; 7. E; 8. b

Module 1 bis 2

Übung 2
1. c; 2. b; 3. a; 4. c

Übung 3
1. a; 2. an; 3. an; 4. a; 5. a; 6. an

Übung 4
1. women; 2. mice; 3. books; 4. feet; 5. bottles; 6. knives

2

Übung 1
1. b; 2. f; 3. g; 4. c; 5. h; 6. e; 7. d; 8. a

Übung 2
1. d; 2. b; 3. a; 4. c

Übung 4
1. live; 2. take; 3. gets up; 4. works; 5. loves

Übung 6
1. Jane has breakfast at home. / Jane has breakfast. / She has breakfast.; 2. She goes to school by bus. / Jane goes to school by bus. / She goes to school. / Jane goes to school.; 3. In the morning, she has maths. / In the morning, Jane has maths. / Jane has maths. / She has maths. / Jane has maths in the morning. / She has maths in the morning.; 4. In the break, she goes to the library. / In the break, Jane goes to the library. / Jane goes to the library in the break. / She goes to the library in the break. / She goes to the library. / Jane goes to the library.; 5. After lunch, she has sports. / After lunch, Jane has sports. / Jane has sports after lunch. / She has sports after lunch. / Jane has sports. / She has sports.

Übung 8
1. watch; 2. drives; 3. cleans / washes; 4. cycle

Übung 11
1. don't have; 2. don't go; 3. don't go; 4. never; 5. don't

Übung 14
1. Do you know John?; 2. Is he Japanese?; 3. Jane isn't at school today. ; 4. We're not very happy. 5. Does she read a book?; 6. Are you tired?

Übung 16
1. Yes, he is.; 2. Yes, they are.; 3. No, he doesn't. / No, he does not.; 4. Yes, they do.; 5. Yes, she is.

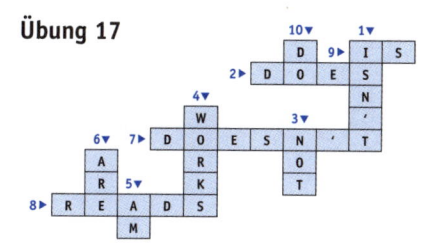

Übung 17

(Crossword puzzle)
- 1↓ IS
- 2→ DOES
- 3↓ NOT
- 4↓ WORK
- 5↓ EADS (READS)
- 6↓ ARM
- 7→ DOESN'T
- 8→ READS
- 9→ IS
- 10↓ D

Übung 18
1. do, wear; 2. don't, wear; 3. does; 4. does, don't

Test 2

Übung 1
1. He drives to work. 2. He likes swimming. 3. He doesn't go to work by bus. / He does not go to work by bus. 4. He doesn't read many books. / He does not read many books. 5. He's very thin. / He is very thin. 6. He's not angry. / He isn't angry. / He is not angry.

Übung 2
1. isn't / is not; 2. doesn't read / does not read; 3. don't like / do not like; 4. don't watch / do not watch; 5. 'm not / am not; 6. don't play / do not play; 7. aren't / are not

Übung 3
1. b; 2. a; 3. b; 4. b; 5. c

Übung 4
1. Do you know Kate? Yes, I do. 2. Does Kate smoke? No, she doesn't. 3. Is Jane from Birmingham? No, she isn't. 4. Are you cold? Yes, I am.

3

Übung 1
a. 3; b. 4; c. 1; d. 2; e. 5

Übung 2
1. c; 2. e; 3. a; 4. d

Übung 4
It, you, you, I, him, we, me, them, they, they, we, them, I, I, you, she, she, I, her, they, we, he, you, we, I, you, you, them

Modul 3

Übung 5
1. She often sees her.
2. I never play tennis with him.
3. They always visit us.
4. She visits her in the evening.
5. She never talks about them.
6. We play football on Saturdays.
7. Do you remember her?

Übung 6
1. We see them.
2. She sees her.
3. He meets him.
4. She meets her.
5. They talk about him.
6. He talks about them.

Übung 7
1. She; 2. She; 3. them; 4. her; 5. her; 6. They; 7. I; 8. us / me; 9. She; 10. us / me; 11. You; 12. her; 13. me; 14. him

Übung 9
1. 's got / has got; 2. haven't got / 've not got / have not got; 3. 've got / have got; 4. haven't got / 've not got / have not got; 5. hasn't got / 's not got / has not got

Übung 10
these, that, that, that, this, this, that, that, those,

Übung 12
1. b; 2. b; 3. a; 4. a

Übung 13
1. These are bananas.
2. This is an apple.
3. That's Paul.
4. This is a dog.

Übung 14
1. got; 2. Those; 3. her; 4. they; 5. This; 6. Has; 7. them; 8. him; Satz: Have fun!

Übung 15
1. him; 2. me; 3. her; 4. that; 5. us; 6. him; 7. them; 8. those; 9. I; 10. you; 11. he; 12. him; 13. her; 14. them; 15. that

Module 3 bis 4

Test 3

Übung 1
1. us; 2. They / they; 3. We / we; 4. her; 5. him; 6. them

Übung 2
1. b; 2. a; 3. a; 4. a; 5. c

Übung 3
1. This; 2. That; 3. These; 4. These; 5. Those

Übung 4
1. Those / those; 2. These / these; 3. This / this; 4. That / that

Übung 5
1. He visits her every Sunday.
2. They often bring us cakes.
3. We do many things together.
4. I like you very much.
5. You go to the café with me.
6. We never play football with him.

4

Übung 1
1. d; 2. e; 3. a; 4. c; 5. b

Übung 2
1. Jane is eating a cake.
2. Ben is listening to music.
3. Kate is watering the garden.
4. Jane is playing the piano.
5. Paul is washing the car.
6. The cat is sleeping.

Übung 3
doing, cooking, making, doing, coming, playing, coming, making

Übung 6
1. 're working / are working; 2. are giving / 're giving; 3. 're studying / are studying;
4. 'm writing / am writing; 5. 'm doing / am doing; 6. 's doing / is doing;
7. Are … learning / studying

Übung 8
1. aren't; 2. not; 3. isn't; 4. 'm not

Modul 4

Übung 10
1. Are you; 2. Is Paul; 3. Are they; 4. Is she

Übung 12
1. a; 2. c; 3. c; 4. b

Übung 13
1. No, he isn't. / No, he's not. / No, he is not. 2. Yes, they are. 3. No, they aren't. / No, they're not. / No, they are not. 4. Yes, he is.

Übung 15
1. is playing, plays; 2. is reading, reads; 3. isn't working, works; 4. Are, going, go

Übung 16
1. a, b; 2. b, a; 3. a, b; 4. b, a

Übung 17
1. spend; 2. rent; 3. relax; 4. cook; 5. play; 6. 're going / are going; 7. 're driving / are driving; 8. 're staying / are staying; 9. 'm not complaining / am not complaining

Übung 18

J	Z	O	P	L	O	O	K	I	N	G	B	O	O	S
U	U	E	J	I	D	U	K	Y	E	A	E	P	K	J
L	Q	K	O	L	J	X	F	E	E	D	I	N	G	P
J	I	L	U	E	A	L	G		D	P	N	W	S	K
W	P	V	L	A	W	O	R	K	I	N	G	P	U	U
R	U	J	I	R	E	A	D	I	N	G	H	A	Y	T
I	P	U	S	N	D	P	R	R	G	U	G	J	J	T
T	D	Q	T	I	G	U	I	J	I	O	I	J	N	W
I	A	J	E	N	B	H	N	P	D	V	V	L	M	A
N	N	K	N	G	M	A	K	I	N	G	I	D	E	U
G	C	J	I	J	N	V	I	L	Z	A	N	N	P	J
U	I	U	N	N	M	I	N	J	J	E	G	Q	G	Q
J	N	O	G	L	G	N	G	Z	Q	F	O	J	L	K
Z	G	L	X	U	Z	G	S	P	E	A	K	I	N	G
L	E	A	V	I	N	G	H	N	O	E	J	C	H	E

Übung 19
1. We're watering the garden.
2. He's reading a book.
3. He's driving a car.
4. She's sitting in an armchair.
5. We're making dinner.

Module 4 bis 5

Test 4

Übung 1
a. 3; b. 7; c. 1; d. 8; e. 5; f. 2; g. 6; h. 4

Übung 2
1. 're playing / are playing; 2. 's sleeping / is sleeping; 3. 's walking / is walking;
4. 's making / is making / 's preparing / is preparing

Übung 3
1. She isn't going there. 2. I'm not leaving. 3. Are you working? 4. Is she coming?

Übung 4
1. Yes, he is. 2. No, she doesn't. 3. Yes, I am. 4. No, they're not.

Übung 5
1. read; 2. 'm driving / am driving; 3. prepares; 4. 's preparing / is preparing;
5. leave; 6. eat

5

Übung 1
1. c; 2. d; 3. a; 4. e; 5. b

Übung 4
1. richtig; 2. falsch; 3. richtig; 4. richtig

Übung 6
1. 'll leave / will leave; 2. 'll arrive / will arrive; 3. won't take / will not take;
4. 'll be / will be / 'll take / will take; 5. 'll have / will have; 6. 'll need / will need;
7. 'll want / will want

Übung 8
1. Will they come here tomorrow?
2. Won't Ben take his driving test?
3. Will you phone him later?
4. Won't he bring the cake?
5. Will you find the way?
6. Will Jane go to university?

Übung 9
1. a, b; 2. b; 3. a; 4. a; b

Modul 5

Übung 11
1. I'll be back early if there isn't so much traffic.
2. Paul will set up the barbecue if Kate prepares the steaks.
3. They will phone us if they can't find the way.

Übung 12
1. it rains; 2. she works hard; 3. I'll go home early; 4. he will be very happy

Übung 14
1. wf; 2. pc; 3. pc; 4. wf; 5. pc; 6. wf

Übung 15
1. are having; 2. 'm going; 3. 'll phone; 4. will study

Übung 16
1. will rain / 'll rain; 2. 'm going / am going; 3. 'll phone / will phone; 4. 're having / are having; 5. isn't coming. / is not coming; 6. 'll be / will be; 7. 'll do / will do; 8. 's driving / is driving

Übung 17
1. Ben will go to college next year.
2. Jane will not learn French any more.
3. I'll set up the barbecue.
4. I won't put garlic in the salad.

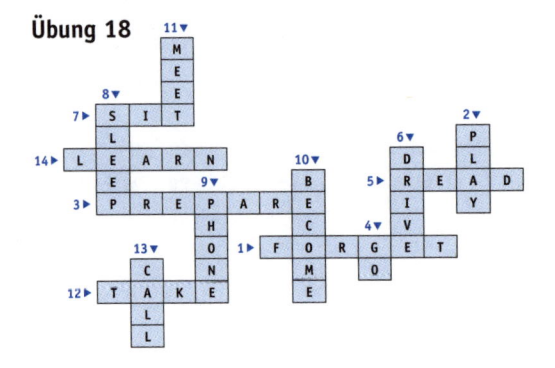

Übung 18

Crossword solution:
- 7► SIT
- 14► LEARN
- 3► PREPARE
- 1► FORGET
- 12► TAKE
- 5► READ
- 8▼ SLEEP
- 11▼ MEET
- 9▼ BCHON
- 10▼ DRIVE
- 6▼ DIY
- 2▼ PLAY
- 4▼ VOMET
- 13▼ COLL

Test 5

Übung 1
1. will go; 2. will go; 3. won't become; 4. will learn; 5. won't work; 6. 'll come; 7. will finish; 8. 'll study

Übung 2
1. 'll leave / will leave; 2. 'll arrive / will arrive; 3. 'll be / will be; 4. 'll have / will have; 5. 'll need / will need; 6. 'll want / will want

Übung 3
1. Yes, they will. 2. No, it won't. 3. Yes, I will. 4. No, she won't. 5. Yes, I will

Übung 4
1. c; 2. a; 3. a; 4. a

Übung 5
1. Kate isn't coming to the cinema.
2. I think I 'll finish my homework now.
3. I hope it won't rain tonight.
4. Maybe Paul will phone us later.
5. Next year, Ben will take his driving test.

6

Übung 1
1. a; 2. e; 3. b; 4. d; 5. c

Übung 2
1. d; 2. a; 3. f; 4. e; 5. b; 6. c

Übung 6
1. wrote   5. drank
2. drove   6. spoke
3. bought   7. knew
4. thought   8. met

Übung 7
1. was; 2. was; 3. had; 4. went; 5. walked; 6. took; 7. drove; 8. bought; 9. learned; 10. asked; 11. read; 12. sat; 13. thought; 14. knew

Übung 9
1. made; 2. spoke; 3. bought; 4. learned

Übung 10
1. met; 2. sat; 3. bought; 4. left

Übung 12
1. a; 2. b; 3. c; 4. b

Übung 15
1. wasn't; 2. Were; 3. was; 4. were

Modul 6

Übung 16
1. I didn't go to school. / I did not go to school.
2. I bought cakes.
3. I was happy.
4. I wasn't fat. / I was not fat.
5. You were ready.
6. You weren't angry. / You were not angry.
7. Paul was at work.
8. Louise was tired.

Übung 17
1. didn't listen; 2. were; 3. was; 4. Did you make; 5. worked; 6. didn't drive; weren't; 8. wasn't

Übung 18
1. didn't have / did not have; 2. didn't go / did not go; 3. stayed / were; 4. were; 5. weren't / were not; 6. ate; 7. walked; 8. lived; 9. thought; 10. was; 11. didn't work / did not work; 12. worked; 13. were

Übung 19
1. drove; 2. watched (TV); 3. cycled; 4. walked; 5. played (football); 6. read; 7. ate; 8. drank; 9. listened (to music); 10. cooked; 11. played (the piano); 12. washed (the car); 13. slept; 14. sat; 15. cleaned (the room); 16. studied; 17. played (tennis); 18. played (chess); 19. swam; 20. took (the bus); 21. wrote; 22. shopped; 23. sang; 24. played (golf)

Test 6

Übung 1
1. wrote; 2. drove; 3. drank; 4. swam; 5. slept; 6. sang

Übung 2
1. didn't go; 2. didn't study; 3. know; 4. played; 5. didn't go

Übung 3
1. cycled; 2. ate; 3. slept; 4. watched

Übung 4
1. was; 2. were; 3. wasn't / was not; 4. weren't / were not

Übung 5
1. Yes, he did. / No, he didn't. / No, he did not.
2. Yes, I did. / No, I didn't. / No, I did not.
3. Yes, I was. / No, I wasn't. / No, I was not.
4. Yes, he was. / No, he wasn't. / No, he was not.

7

Übung 1
1. c; 2. d; 3. a; 4. e; 5. b

Übung 2
1. d; 2. h; 3. a; 4. b; 5. f; 6. c; 7. e; 8. g

Übung 6
1. bigger; 2. cheaper; 3. highest; 4. oldest

Übung 7
1. a. Mehrsilbige Adjektive bilden den Komparativ mit **more** + Grundform.
2. c. Den Superlativ bilden mehrsilbige Adjektive mit **most** + Grundform.

Übung 8
Gruppe 1: -er / -est
big, heavy, clever, quiet, hot, slow

Gruppe 2: more / most
expensive, interesting, boring, exciting, tired, frustrating

Übung 10
1. old; 2. better; 3. young; 4. worse; 5. slower; 6. true; 7. more; 8. less; 9. nicer; 10. happier; 11. more expensive; 12. more exciting; 13. easier

Übung 12
1. than; 2. not as … as; 3. as … as; 4. than

Übung 15
1. badly; 2. happily; 3. fast; 4. well; 5. hard

Übung 16
1. badly; 2. well; 3. heavy; 4. happy

Übung 17

C	L	E	A	N	B	K	L	S	S
E	X	P	E	N	S	I	V	E	H
K	Y	A	Y	O	U	N	G	T	O
J	P	F	L	I	T	T	L	E	R
W	M	A	N	I	C	E	S	R	T
L	A	R	G	E	K	R	B	L	P
O	S	M	O	C	H	E	A	P	E
N	L	M	U	C	H	S	D	P	H
G	O	Q	U	I	E	T	P	S	D
U	W	L	E	Q	U	I	C	K	O
P	K	W	M	E	D	N	R	L	L
T	I	D	Y	U	W	G	O	O	D

Modul 7 bis 8

Übung 18
1. longer; 2. quickly; 3. slower; 4. short; 5. slow; 6. happy; 7. longer; 8. young; 9. good; 10. well; 11. brown; 12. black; 13. worst; 14. more; 15. less

Test 7

Übung 1
1. richtig; 2. falsch; 3. richtig; 4. richtig; 5. falsch

Übung 2
1. This house is very big.
2. The garden is larger than the house. / The house is larger than the garden.
3. The woman is happy.
4. The book is not as heavy as the bag. / The bag is not as heavy as the book.
5. The T-shirt is as bright as the trousers.

Übung 3
1. more expensive; 2. big; 3. healthier; 4. tall

Übung 4
1. b; 2. a; 3. c; 4. a

Übung 5
1. well; 2. fast; 3. beautifully; 4. hard

Übung 6
1. worst; 2. biggest; 3. best; 4. least

8

Übung 1
1. d; 2. b; 3. c; 4. a

Übung 2
1. d; 2. e; 3. b; 4. a; 5. c

Übung 4
1. vineyards; 2. wine; 3. suntan lotion; 4. the neighbours

Übung 7
1. have to; 2. don't have to; 3. have to; 4. didn't have to; 5. do we have to; 6. has to; 7. 'll have to

Übung 9
1. should; 2. shouldn't; 3. should

Übung 12
1. could / was able to; 2. couldn't / could not / wasn't able to / was not able to;
3. can / am able to / 'm able to; 4. can't / cannot / 'm not able to / am not able to;
5. could / was able to; 6. can't / cannot / 'm not able to / am not able to;
7. 'll be able to / will be able to; 8. 'll be able to / will be able to

Übung 14
1. I can't go. 2. He doesn't have to go. 3. She can't see us. 4. I mustn't work.
5. They might play. 6. They might play.

Übung 16
1. b; 2. e; 3. c; 4. a; 5. f; 6. d

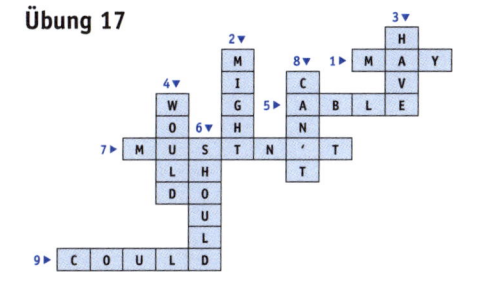

Übung 17

Across/Down crossword:
- 1▶ MAY
- 2▼ MIGHT
- 3▼ HAVE
- 4▼ WOULD
- 5▶ ABLE
- 6▼ SHOULD
- 7▶ MUSTN'T
- 8▼ CAN'T
- 9▶ COULD

Übung 18
1. They'll be able to relax on the beach.
2. They may buy some wine.
3. They could go sailing.
4. Sailing would be fantastic.
5. They should take suntan lotion.
6. They should take books.
7. Jane will have to speak French.
8. They mustn't forget the cat.
9. They don't have to buy many things in England.
10. They'll be able to buy a lot in France.

Test 8

Übung 1
1. mustn't / must not; 2. mustn't / must not; 3. have to; 4. mustn't / mustn't

Übung 2
1. had to; 2. must / have to; 3. have to; 4. have to / must

Module 8 bis 9

Übung 3
1. mustn't; 2. doesn't have to; 3. mustn't; 4. don't have to

Übung 4
1. I can swim. / I'm able to swim. 2. I can't dance. / I cannot dance. / I'm not able to dance. 3. I can't drive. / I cannot drive. / I'm not able to drive. 4. I can read. / I am able to read.

Übung 5
1. would; 2. might; 3. should; 4. could

Übung 6
1. Don't let me forget to feed the cat!
2. Don't stay out too late!
3. Tell him I called!
4. Go and buy some milk!
5. Let's have a party next Saturday!
6. Let's play tennis together tomorrow!

9

Übung 1
1. e; 2. h; 3. a; 4. g; 5. c; 6. b; 7. f; 8. d

Übung 2
1. b; 2. d; 3. a; 4. c

Übung 5
Gruppe 1: nicht zählbar
water, cheese, money, advice, information, wine

Gruppe 2: zählbar
apple, glass, dog, euro, child, towel

Übung 7
Gruppe 1: much
wine, advice, butter, time, money, information

Gruppe 2: many
bottle, computer, flower, house, car, apple

Übung 8
1. much; 2. many; 3. much; 4. many

Lösungen | Übungsgrammatik

Modul 9

Übung 10
1. a; 2. b; 3. b; 4. b

Übung 11
1. There are few apples.
2. There is little milk. / There's little milk.
3. I have little time.
4. He has few friends.

Übung 13
1. some; 2. some; 3. any; 4. some; 5. any; 6. any

Übung 15
1. everybody; 2. somewhere; 3. anybody; 4. something; 5. everywhere

Übung 16
1. few; 2. little; 3. much / a lot / any; 4. any / many; 5. some / a few / many;
6. many / a lot of / some / a few; 7. many / a lot of / any; 8. a lot of / much;
9. much / a lot of / any; 10. some / many / a lot of / few

Übung 17
1. nobody; 2. nowhere; 3. nothing; 4. many people / a lot of people; 5. every family;
6. a lot of time / much time; 7. every teacher; 8. not any dishes; 9. anywhere;
10. any time

Übung 18

K	M	U	C	H	Z	K	X	H	G	L	P
P	X	A	P	A	K	P	Z	X	P	I	X
F	P	P	N	N	N	N	K	H	P	T	K
E	V	E	R	Y	B	O	D	Y	E	T	W
W	P	U	P	W	S	B	T	A	X	L	T
P	U	X	C	H	P	O	P	H	Q	E	P
Q	K	X	M	E	X	D	M	B	I	W	K
Q	A	Z	E	R	K	Y	X	E	K	N	K
Z	A	K	L	E	S	S	O	P	P	T	G

Test 9

Übung 1
1. much / a lot of; 2. many / a lot of; 3. much / a lot of; 4. many / a lot of

Übung 2
1. few; 2. little; 3. few; 4. little

Module 9 bis 10

Übung 3
1. nowhere; 2. not anybody; 3. no one; 4. few things; 5. nowhere

Übung 4
1. b; 2. a; 3. c; 4. c

Übung 5
1. I do not have any time.
2. Nobody knows him very well.
3. They did not have much money.
4. They had few problems.
5. They did not have many problems.

10

Übung 1
1. d; 2. b; 3. f; 4. c; 5. a; 6. e

Übung 2
1. b; 2. e; 3. a; 4. d; 5. c

Übung 7
1. -; 2. at; 3. by / -; 4. in; 5. At; 6. -; 7. in; 8. At; 9. -; 10. on

Übung 9
1. in; 2. ago; 3. for; 4. ago; 5. in; 6. for; 7. ago; 8. in

Übung 11
1. on; 2. above; 3. under; 4. next to; 5. between

Übung 12
1. above / over; 2. opposite / in front of; 3. next to / by; 4. on

Übung 13
Through und **back to** beschreiben eine Bewegungsrichtung.

Übung 14
1. up; 2. past; 3. round; 4. across; 5. off

Übung 15
1. down; 2. along; 3. around / round; 4. towards / to; 5. through; 6. out of; 7. to; 8. past; 9. into; 10. off; 11. near

Lösungen Übungsgrammatik

Module 10 bis 11

Übung 16
1. for; 2. through; 3. at; 4. ago; 5. on; 6. in; 7. in front of; 8. to; 9. across; 10. along; 11. over; 12. among

Übung 17
1. along; 2. across; 3. through; 4. up

Test 10

Übung 1
1. on; 2. in; 3. in; 4. at; 5. at; 6. at; 7. in; 8. on

Übung 2
1. in / for; 2. for; 3. ago; 4. in; 5. for

Übung 3
1. between; 2. on; 3. under; 4. in front of

Übung 4
1. a; 2. c; 3. b; 4. b

Übung 5
1. next to; 2. in; 3. on; 4. under; 5. above; 6. between; 7. opposite; 8. behind

11

Übung 1
1. b; 2. e; 3. c; 4. d; 5. f; 6. a

Übung 2
1. a; 2. d; 3. e; 4. c; 5. b

Übung 4
1. These are Ben's trousers.
2. This is her air mattress.
3. Where is our air mattress?
4. Paul and Kate forget everything themselves.
5. I've got mine!
6. Kate packed it herself.

Übung 6
1. his; 2. their; 3. her; 4. our

Modul 11

Übung 7
1. my; 2. his; 3. your; 4. their; 5. its

Übung 9
1. our; 2. his; 3. theirs; 4. yours

Übung 10
1. This house is ours. / This is ours.
2. These shoes are mine. / These are mine.
3. This umbrella is yours. / This is yours. / This umbrella's yours.
4. These photos are theirs. / These are theirs.
5. This car is his. / This car's his. / This is his.
6. These trousers are hers. / These are hers.

Übung 12
1. This is Paul's car.
2. This is Kate's bike.
3. This is the children's tent.
4. This is the parents' bedroom.

Übung 13
1. my; 2. Mine; 3. yours; 4. 's; 5. yours; 6. 's; 7. our / my; 8. your; 9. our / my; 10. your; 11. their

Übung 15
1. myself; 2. yourself; 3. himself; 4. herself; 5. itself

Übung 16
1. yourself; 2. ourselves; 3. themselves

Übung 17
1. Yes, I made the dress myself. / Yes, I made it myself.
2. Yes, Jane did the homework herself. / Yes, she did it herself.
3. Yes, Paul and Kate did the garden themselves. / Yes, they did it themselves.
4. Yes, Louise and I made the cake ourselves. / Yes, we made it ourselves.

Übung 18
1. They bought their house five years ago.
2. I can do that myself!
3. He prepared everything himself.
4. The red car is theirs.
5. He likes his family very much.
6. He opened the door himself.
7. That bicycle is Ben's. / That is Ben's bicycle.
8. That is Paul and Kate's house. / That house is Paul and Kate's.

Übung 19

K	Z	D	P	M	W	H	M	W	K	I	O
G	P	B	H	I	S	E	Y	J	K	T	U
J	C	D	A	N	B	R	S	D	A	S	R
D	A	T	H	E	M	S	E	L	V	E	S
A	Z	H	I	M	S	E	L	F	Z	L	B
Y	O	U	R	S	E	L	F	C	A	F	G
P	B	Y	O	U	R	S	E	L	V	E	S

Test 11

Übung 1
1. our; 2. his; 3. your; 4. their; 5. my

Übung 2
1. mine; 2. yours; 3. his; 4. hers; 5. its; 6. ours; 7. theirs

Übung 3
1. your; 2. our; 3. yours; 4. ours

Übung 4
1. Ben's bike / Ben's bicycle; 2. Louise's bag; 3. Paul's car; 4. Kate's cat; 5. Jane's book

Übung 5
1. myself; 2. yourself; 3. yourselves; 4. themselves; 5. ourselves

12

Übung 1
1. c; 2. d; 3. a; 4. e; 5. b

Übung 2
1. g; 2. c; 3. j; 4. d; 5. f; 6. b; 7. i; 8. a; 9. e; 10. h

Übung 8
1. spoken; 2. been; 3. eaten; 4. driven; 5. told; 6. taken

Übung 10
1. seen; 2. put; 3. bought; 4. left; 5. packed; 6. read; 7. finished

Übung 12
1. for; 2. since; 3. since; 4. for; 5. for; 6. since

Modul 12

Übung 14
1. 've been / have been; 2. 've / have not gone / been; 3. went; 4. bought; 5. grilled; 6. was; 7. Have / have ... tried; 8. 's / has been; 9. 've spent / have spent

Übung 15
1. written; 2. drunk; 3. eaten; 4. read

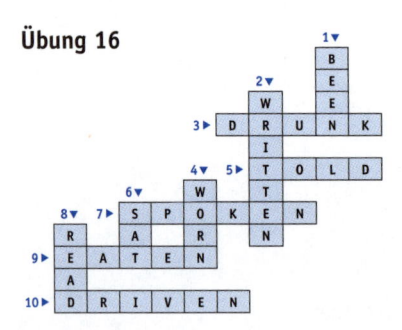

Übung 16

						1▼		
						B		
					2▼	E		
					W	E		
		3▶	D	R	U	N	K	
					I			
			4▼	5▶	T	O	L	D
		6▼		W	T			
8▼	7▶	S	P	O	K	E	N	
	R	A		R		N		
9▶	E	A	T	E	N			
	A							
10▶	D	R	I	V	E	N		

Test 12

Übung 1
1. written; 2. eaten; 3. read; 4. washed / cleaned; 5. slept

Übung 2
1. We've gone shopping. / We have gone shopping.
2. She 's spoken to her friend. / She has spoken to her friend.
3. He 's driven home. / He has driven home.
4. She 's bought apples. / She has bought apples.
5. They've taken pictures. / They have taken pictures.

Übung 3
1. for; 2. since; 3. for; 4. since; 5. for

Übung 4
1. c; 2. b; 3. c; 4. b

Übung 5
1. walked; 2. have worked; 3. has lived; 4. has known; 5. bought

Übungsgrammatik

Zielsprache/ Target language	Ausgangssprache/ Source language
A	
14th	14./vierzehnter
a	ein/eine
a few	ein paar
a little	ein bisschen
a lot	viel
a lot of	viel
about	über, ungefähr
above	über
across	über
active	aktiv
advice	Rat/Ratschlag
Africa	Afrika
after	nach/nachdem
afternoon	Nachmittag
again	wieder
age	Alter
ago	vor
air	Luft
air mattress	Luftmatratze
airport	Flughafen
all	alle
all day	den ganzen Tag
all evening	den ganzen Abend
all right	in Ordnung
along	entlang
already	schon
also	auch
always	immer
am	bin
American	amerikanisch Amerikaner/Amerikanerin
among	zwischen/inmitten/unter
an	ein/eine
and	und
angry	verärgert
another	noch ein/eine/einen
any	irgendein/irgendeine/ irgendeiner/irgendwelche
any more	nicht mehr
anybody	irgendjemand
anyone	irgendjemand
anything	irgendetwas
anyway	jedenfalls/sowieso
anywhere	irgendwo
apartment	Wohnung
apple	Apfel
apple pie	Apfelkuchen
apply	sich bewerben
April	April
are	bist/sind/seid
argue	streiten
armchair	Sessel
around	um/in der Gegend von um ... herum
arrive	ankommen
as	als
as ... as	so ... wie
as well	auch noch
ask	fragen
aspirin	Aspirin
at	auf, um, in/an
at all	überhaupt
at home	zu Hause
at most	höchstens
at night	nachts
at the moment	im Moment/momentan
ate	aß/aßt/aßen
August	August
aunt	Tante
Australia	Australien
author	Autor
Avignon	Avignon
B	
baby	Baby
back	zurück
back seat	Rücksitz
bad	schlecht

397

Übungsgrammatik

badminton	Badminton	bit	bisschen
banana	Banane	blue	blau
bank	Bank	book	Buch
barbecue	Grillfest, Grill	bored	gelangweilt
basket	Korb	boring	langweilig
bathroom	Badezimmer	boss	Chef
be	sein	both	beide
be able to	können	bottle	Flasche
be called	heißen	bought	kaufte/kauftest/kauften/ kauftet/gekauft
be lucky	Glück haben		
be used to	an etwas gewöhnt sein	boutique	Boutique
beach	Strand	bowl	Schale
Beatles	Beatles	boy	Junge
beautiful	schön	bread	Brot
because	weil	break	Pause, zerbrechen/ kaputtmachen
become	werden		
bed	Bett	breakfast	Frühstück
bedroom	Schlafzimmer	bright	grell/leuchtend
been	gewesen	bring	bringen/mitbringen
beer	Bier	brother	Bruder
before	vor, vorher	brought	brachte/brachtest/ brachen/brachtet/ gebracht
began	begann/begannst/ begannen/begannt		
begin	beginnen/anfangen	brown	braun
begun	begonnen	build	bauen
behind	hinter	built	baute/bautest/bauten/ bautet/gebaut
believe	glauben		
bell	Glocke	bus	Bus
belong to	gehören	bush	Busch
below	unter	but	aber
Ben Nevis	Ben Nevis	butter	Butter
best	besler/beste/bestes/ am besten	buy	kaufen
		by	an/bei, von, um
better	besser	by the way	übrigens
between	zwischen	bye	Tschüss
big	groß		
Big Ben	Big Ben	**C**	
bird	Vogel		
Birmingham	Birmingham	cake	Kuchen
birthday	Geburtstag	Calais	Calais
birthday card	Geburtstagskarte	call	nennen
birthday present	Geburtstags-geschenk	camera	Fotoapparat/Kamera
		camping site	Campingplatz

can	können	concert	Konzert
cancel	abbestellen	contact	kontaktieren/anrufen
cannot	nicht können	corner	Ecke
car	Auto	corner shop	Laden an der Ecke
card	Karte	cottage	Hütte/kleines Haus
careful	vorsichtig	could	könnte/könntest/könnten/könntet
carry	tragen		
cat	Katze		konnte
cellphone	Handy	country	Land
chair	Stuhl	course	Kurs
changing room	Umkleidekabine	cuisine	Küche
channel	Kanal	cup	Tasse
Channel Tunnel	Kanaltunnel	cycle	Fahrrad fahren
chat	chatten/sich unterhalten		
cheap	billig	**D**	
cheese	Käse	Dad	Papa/Vati
child	Kind	dance	tanzen
children	Kinder	daughter	Tochter
China	China	day	Tag
Chinese	chinesisch	dear	Lieber/Liebe
chips	Pommes frites	December	Dezember
Christmas	Weihnachten	decide	entscheiden/sich entscheiden
church	Kirche		
cigarette	Zigaretten	definitely	unbedingt
cinema	Kino	delicious	lecker
city	Stadt	dentist	Zahnarzt
clean	sauber machen/putzen sauber	desk	Schreibtisch
		dessert	Nachtisch/Dessert
clever	klug	did	tat/tatest/taten/tatet
cliff	Felsen	different	anders/unterschiedlich
close	schließen/zumachen	difficult	schwierig/schwer
cloud	Wolke	dining table	Esstisch
coat	Mantel	dinner	Abendessen
coffee	Kaffee	dishes	Geschirr
coffee bar	Café	do	tun
coffee table	Beistelltisch	doctor	Arzt/Ärztin
coke	Cola	doesn't	tut nicht
cold	kalt	dog	Hund
college	College	don't	nicht tun
come	kommen	done	getan
complain	sich beschweren	door	Tür
computer	Computer	Dover	Dover

down	herunter/hinunter	evening	Abend
drank	trank/trankst/tranken/trankt	every	jede/jeder/jedes
		everybody	jeder/alle
drawer	Schublade	everyone	jeder/alle
dress	Kleid	everything	alles
drink	trinken, Getränk	everywhere	überall
drive	Fahrt, fahren	exam	Prüfung
driven	gefahren	exciting	spannend/aufregend
driver	Fahrer/Fahrerin	expensive	teuer
driving test	Führerscheinprüfung	extra	extra/zusätzlich
drove	fuhr/fuhrst/fuhren/fuhrt		
drunk	getrunken betrunken		
during	während		
duty-free	zollfrei		

E

F

early	früh	fall	fallen
earn	verdienen	fall in love	sich verlieben
earth	Erde	fallen	gefallen
East Africa	Ostafrika	family	Familie
easy	einfach	famous	berühmt
eat	essen	fantastic	fantastisch
eaten	gegessen	far	weit
Edinburgh	Edinburgh	fast	schnell
egg	Ei	fat	dick/fett
egg salad	Eiersalat	father	Vater
eight	acht	fear	fürchten
either	auch nicht	February	Februar
eleven	elf	fed	fütterte/füttertest/fütterten/füttertet/gefüttert
else	sonst noch		
end	Ende	feed	füttern
England	England	feet	Füße
English	englisch Engländer/Engländerin	fell	fiel/fielst/fielen/fielt/gefallen
		fellow student	Kommilitone/Studienkollege
English course	Englischkurs		
enjoy	genießen	ferry	Fähre
enough	genug	few	wenige
escalator	Rolltreppe	field	Feld
essay	Aufsatz	fifteen	fünfzehn
euro	Euro	find	finden
		find out	herausfinden
		fine	gut/prima
		finish	beenden/fertig sein mit
		fireplace	offener Kamin

first	erster/erste/erstes	Germany	Deutschland
fish	Fisch	get	holen/bringen
five	fünf	Get better soon!	Gute Besserung!
flat	Wohnung	get in	hinein bekommen
flower	Blume	get into	einsteigen
follow	folgen	get married	heiraten
food	Essen	get out of	aussteigen
foot	Fuß	get stuck	stecken bleiben
football	Fußball	get up	aufstehen
football match	Fußballspiel	girl	Mädchen
for	für	glad	froh
forget	vergessen	glass	Glas
forgot	vergaß/vergaßt/vergaßen	glasses	Brille
forgotten	vergessen	go	gehen
found	fand/fandest/fanden/ fandet/gefunden	go ahead	tu das
		go for a walk	spazieren gehen
four	vier	go out	ausgehen
fourteen	vierzehn	go to bed	ins Bett gehen
France	Frankreich	go with	passen zu
French	französisch	golf	Golf
	Franzose/Französin	gone	gegangen
French fries	Pommes frites	good	gut
Friday	Freitag	goodness	Güte
fridge	Kühlschrank	got	bekam/bekamst/bekamen/ bekamt/bekommen
friend	Freund		
from	von	gotten	bekommen
fruit	Obst/Früchte	gravy	Bratensoße
fruit bowl	Obstschale	great	toll/großartig
frustrating	frustrierend	great aunt	Großtante
fun	Spaß	green	grün
furniture	Möbel	grill	grillen
further	weiter	guess	raten/denken
furthest	weitester/weiteste/ weitestes/am weitesten		

G

H

game	Spiel	had	hatte/hattest/hatten/ hattet/gehabt
garage	Garage		
garden	Garten	hairdresser's	Friseurgeschäft
garlic	Knoblauch	half	Hälfte, halb
German	deutsch	hang on	warte mal
	Deutscher/Deutsche	happen	geschehen/passieren
		happily	glücklich
		happy	glücklich

hard	hart	**I**	
has	hat	I	ich
have	haben	I'm	ich bin
have a look	nachsehen	ice cream	Eis
have breakfast	frühstücken	idea	Idee
have got	haben	if	wenn/falls, ob
have to	müssen	ill	krank
he	er	important	wichtig
healthy	gesund	in	in
heavily	stark	in front of	vor
heavy	schwer	in the afternoon	nachmittags
help	helfen	in the evening	abends
her	sie/ihr	in the middle of	in der Mitte von
here	hier	in the morning	morgens
hers	ihrer/ihre/ihres	inflate	aufpumpen/aufblasen
herself	selbst, sich	information	Information
high	hoch	intelligent	intelligent
hill	Hügel	interesting	interessant
him	ihm	internet	Internet
himself	selbst, sich	into	hinein/herein
his	sein/seine	Ireland	Irland
	seiner/seine/seins	is	ist
history	Geschichte	isn't	ist nicht
holiday	Ferien/Urlaub	it	es
home	nach Hause	Italian	italienisch
homework	Hausaufgaben		Italiener/Italienerin
hoover	staubsaugen	Italy	Italien
hope	hoffen	its	sein/seine
horrible	fürchterlich/schrecklich	itself	selbst
hot	warm/heiß		sich
hot chocolate	heiße Schokolade/Kakao		
hotel	Hotel	**J**	
hour	Stunde	January	Januar
house	Haus	Japan	Japan
how	wie	Japanese	japanisch
how about	wie ist es mit	job	Arbeit/Stelle
how many	wie viele	jog	joggen
however	wie auch immer	juice	Saft
hungry	hungrig	July	Juli
		jumper	Pullover
		June	Juni

just	*genau*	living room	*Wohnzimmer*
	gerade	local	*lokal/ortstypisch*
		London	*London*
K		long	*lang/lange*
key	*Schlüssel*	look	*schauen, aussehen*
kid	*Kind*	look after	*sich kümmern um*
kiss	*Kuss*	look forward to	*sich freuen auf*
kitchen	*Küche*	lotion	*Lotion/Creme*
knew	*wusste/wusstest/wussten/*	love	*lieben, Liebe*
	wusstet	lunch	*Mittagessen*
knife	*Messer*		
know	*wissen, kennen*	**M**	
known	*gekannt*	made	*machte/machtest/*
			machten/machtet/
L			*gemacht*
lake	*See*	magazine	*Zeitschrift*
large	*groß*	make	*machen*
last	*letzter/letzte/letztes*	man	*Mann*
late	*spät*	manage	*schaffen*
later	*später*	Manchester	*Manchester*
law	*Jura/Recht*	Manchester United	*Manchester United*
learn	*lernen*	many	*viele*
least	*am wenigsten*	map	*Karte*
leave	*verlassen*	March	*März*
left	*verließ/verließt/verließen/*	Margaret Thatcher	*Margaret Thatcher*
	verlassen	market	*Markt*
	übrig	married	*verheiratet*
lemon	*Zitrone*	Marseille	*Marseille*
less	*weniger*	match	*Spiel*
let	*lassen*	mate	*Kumpel/Freund*
let's	*lass uns*	maths	*Mathe*
letter	*Brief*	mattress	*Matratze*
library	*Bibliothek/Bücherei*	May	*Mai*
life	*Leben*	may	*könnten*
light	*hell*	maybe	*vielleicht*
like	*mögen*	me	*mir/mich*
list	*Liste*	mean	*meinen/heißen/bedeuten*
listen	*zuhören*	meant	*meinte/meintest/meinten/*
little	*klein, wenig*		*meintet/gemeint*
live	*wohnen/leben*	meat	*Fleisch*
Liverpool	*Liverpool*	medicine	*Medikamente*
		meet	*treffen*

men	Männer	**N**	
met	traf/trafst/trafen/traft/ getroffen	name	Name
mice	Mäuse	near	in der Nähe von
middle	Mitte	nearly	fast
might	könnten	need	brauchen, müssen
milk	Milch	neighbor	Nachbar
mine	meiner/meine/meins	neighbour	Nachbar
mineral water	Mineralwasser	never	nie
minister	Minister/Ministerin	new	neu
minute	Minute	news	Nachrichten
mistake	Fehler	newspaper	Zeitung
mobile phone	Handy	next	nächster/nächste/nächstes
modern	modern	next to	neben
Mom	Mama	nice	nett/schön
moment	Moment	nicely	gut/schön
Monday	Montag	night	Nacht/Abend
money	Geld	nine	neun
month	Monat	nineteen	neunzehn
more	mehr	no	nein, kein
morning	Morgen	no idea	keine Ahnung
most	am meisten	no one	niemand
mother	Mutter	nobody	niemand
motorway	Autobahn	normally	normalerweise
mountain	Berg	Norway	Norwegen
mouse	Maus	Norwegian	norwegisch
move	umziehen	not	nicht
movie theater	Kino	not ... yet	noch nicht
mph	Meilen in der Stunde	not any	kein/keine
much	viel	not at all	überhaupt nicht
Mum	Mama	nothing	nichts
music	Musik	November	November
must	müssen	now	jetzt
must not	nicht dürfen	nowhere	nirgendwo
mustn't	nicht dürfen	number	Nummer
my	mein/meine/meiner/ meines	**O**	
my goodness	meine Güte	o'clock	Uhr
myself	mich/mich selbst selbst mich/mir	October	Oktober
		of	von
		of course	natürlich
		off	herab/herunter

office	*Büro*	party	*Fest*
off-licence	*Wein- und Spirituosengeschäft*	past	*nach, an ... vorbei*
		pear	*Birne*
often	*oft*	pen	*Stift*
oh dear	*oh je*	people	*Leute*
OK	*in Ordnung*	per	*pro*
old	*alt*	perhaps	*vielleicht*
on	*auf, am, an/am*	person	*Person*
on earth	*auf Erden*	phone	*anrufen/telefonieren*
on Mondays	*montags*	phone book	*Telefonbuch*
on Sundays	*sonntags*	piano	*Klavier*
on the way	*unterwegs*	picnic	*Picknick*
once	*einmal*	picnic basket	*Picknickkorb*
only	*nur, erst*	picture	*Bild/Foto*
open	*offen*	pie	*Kuchen*
opposite	*gegenüber*	piece	*Stück*
orange	*Orange*	pink	*rosa/pink*
orange juice	*Orangensaft*	place	*Ort/Stelle/Platz*
organise	*organisieren*	plan	*Plan, planen*
other	*anderer/andere/anderes*	plastic bag	*Plastiktüte*
our	*unser/unsere*	play	*spielen*
ours	*unserer/unsere/unseres*	please	*bitte*
ourselves	*selbst, uns*	Portugal	*Portugal*
out	*aus/weg*	Portuguese	*portugiesisch*
out here	*hier draußen*	post office	*Postamt*
out of	*heraus/hinaus*	postcard	*Postkarte*
outside	*draußen/außerhalb von*	poster	*Poster*
over there	*da drüben*	potato	*Kartoffel*
overtime	*Überstunden*	pound	*Pfund*
own	*eigener/eigen/eigenes*	practice	*üben*
Oxford	*Oxford*	practise	*üben*
		prefer	*lieber mögen/bevorzugen*
P		prepare	*vorbereiten*
		present	*Geschenk*
pack	*packen*	primary school	*Grundschule*
packet	*Packung*	prime minister	*Premierminister/Premierministerin*
pants	*Hose*		
paper	*Papier*	probably	*wahrscheinlich*
parents	*Eltern*	problem	*Problem*
Paris	*Paris*	Provence	*Provence*
park	*Park, parken*	pub	*Kneipe*
parked	*geparkt*	pump	*Pumpe*

put	stellen
put away	wegtun/wegpacken
put in	hineintun
put up	aufstellen

Q

quarter	viertel
question	Frage
quiet	ruhig

R

radio	Radio
rain	regnen
raincoat	Regenjacke
read	lesen, las/last/lasen/last/ gelesen
ready	fertig
really	wirklich
recipe	Kochrezept
recognize	erkennen
red	rot
relax	entspannen
remember	sich erinnern
remind	jemanden erinnern
rent	mieten
retire	in Rente gehen
Rhine	Rhein
rice	Reis
ridden	geritten/gefahren
ride	reiten
right	richtig, also
road	Straße
roast	rösten
roast dinner	Bratengericht
roast potatoes	Röstkartoffeln
rode	ritt/rittest/ritten/rittet
roof	Dach
room	Zimmer
round	um ... herum
route	Route/Strecke
Russia	Russland

S

said	sagte/sagtest/sagten/ sagtet/gesagt
sailing	Segeln
salad	Salat
same	gleich
sandal	Sandale
sang	sang/sangst/sangen/sangt
sat	saß/saßt/saßen/saßt/ gesessen
Saturday	Samstag
saw	sah/sahst/sahen/saht
say	sagen
school	Schule
school bus	Schulbus
school holidays	Schulferien
Scotland	Schottland
sea	Meer
see	sehen
see you	bis bald
seen	gesehen
sell	verkaufen
send	schicken
sent	schickte/schicktest/ schickte/geschickt
September	September
Serengeti	Serengeti
set up	aufstellen
seven	sieben
Shakespeare	Shakespeare
she	sie
shoe	Schuh
shop	Geschäft/Laden einkaufen
shopping	Einkaufen
should	sollen
sign	Schild, unterschreiben
sing	singen
sir	Herr
sister	Schwester
sit	sitzen
six	sechs

sixteen	*sechzehn*
size	*Größe*
skirt	*Rock*
sky	*Himmel*
sleep	*schlafen*
sleeping bag	*Schlafsack*
slept	*schlief/schlieft/schliefen/schlieft/geschlafen*
slice	*Scheibe*
slow	*langsam*
slowly	*langsam*
small	*klein*
smoke	*rauchen*
so	*so*
so far	*bis jetzt*
soccer	*Fußball*
soccer match	*Fußballspiel*
sofa	*Sofa*
some	*einige/ein paar*
somebody	*jemand*
someone	*jemand*
something	*etwas*
sometimes	*manchmal*
somewhere	*irgendwo*
soon	*bald*
south	*Süden*
South of England	*Südengland*
Southern France	*Südfrankreich*
souvenir	*Souvenir/Andenken*
Spain	*Spanien*
Spanish	*spanisch*
speak	*sprechen*
spend	*verbringen, ausgeben*
spent	*gab aus/gabst aus/gaben aus/gabt aus/ausgegeben*
spoke	*sprach/sprachst/sprachen/spracht*
spoken	*gesprochen*
sports	*Sport*
stamp	*Briefmarke*
stand	*stehen*
station	*Bahnhof*
stay	*bleiben*
stay up	*aufbleiben*
steak	*Steak*
still	*noch/immer noch*
still	*still*
stood	*stand/standest/standen/standet/gestanden*
straight	*geradeaus/direkt*
street	*Straße*
strict	*streng*
study	*studieren/lernen*
stuff	*Zeug/Sachen*
stupid	*dumm/blöd*
sugar	*Zucker*
summer	*Sommer*
Sunday	*Sonntag*
sung	*gesungen*
sunny	*sonnig*
sunshine	*Sonnenschein*
suntan	*Sonnenbräune*
suntan lotion	*Sonnencreme*
supermarket	*Supermarkt*
suppose	*annehmen*
sure	*sicher*
swam	*schwamm/schwammst/schwammen/schwammt*
sweater	*Pullover*
Sweden	*Schweden*
Swedish	*schwedisch*
sweets	*Süßigkeiten*
swimmer	*Schwimmer/Schwimmerin*
swimming	*Schwimmen*
swimming costume	*Badeanzug*
swum	*geschwommen*

T

table	*Tisch*
take	*nehmen, dauern/brauchen, mitnehmen*
Take care!	*Pass auf dich auf!*
taken	*genommen*

talk	sich unterhalten/sprechen	ticket-office	Kartenbüro
tea	Tee	tidy	ordentlich
teacher	Lehrer/Lehrerin	tidy away	wegräumen
teaching	Lehramt	tie	Krawatte
teenage	im Teenageralter	time	Zeit
teeth	Zähne	tired	müde
television	Fernseher	to	zu, zur
tell	sagen/erzählen	toast	Toast
ten	zehn	today	heute
tennis	Tennis	together	zusammen
tent	Zelt	told	erzälte/erzähltest/ erzählten/erzähltet/ erzählt
Thames	Themse		
than	als		
thanks	danke	tomato	Tomate
that	das, dieser/diese/dieses	tomorrow	morgen
that long	so lange	tonight	heute Abend/Nacht
that's	das ist	too	zu, auch
the	der/die/das	took	nahm/nahmst/nahmen/ nahmt
theater	Theater		
theatre	Theater	tooth	Zahn
their	ihr/ihre/ihren	totally	total
theirs	ihrer/ihre/ihres	tourist	Tourist
them	sie/ihnen	towards	in Richtung
themselves	selbst sich	towel	Handtuch
		toy	Spielzeug
then	dann	traffic	Verkehr
there	dort, dorthin	traffic jam	Stau
there are	es gibt/da sind	traffic lights	Ampel
there's	es gibt/da ist	translate	übersetzen
these	das/diese	travel guide	Reiseführer
they	sie	tree	Baum
thin	dünn	trousers	Hose
thing	Ding/Sache	true	wahr/richtig
think	denken/glauben	try	probieren
thirteen	dreizehn	try on	anprobieren
this	das	try out	ausprobieren
those	jene	T-shirt	T-Shirt
thought	dachte/dachtest/dachten/ dachtet/gedacht	Tuesday	Dienstag
		tunnel	Tunnel
through	durch	TV	Fernseher
Thursday	Donnerstag	two	zwei
ticket	Karte	typical	typisch

U

UK	*Großbritannien*
under	*unter*
underground	*U-Bahn*
unhappy	*unglücklich*
uniform	*Uniform*
United Kingdom	*Vereinigtes Königreich*
United States of America	*Vereinigte Staaten von Amerika*
university	*Universität*
untidy	*unordentlich*
until	*bis*
up	*hinauf/nach oben*
us	*uns*
USA	*USA*
use	*benutzen*
usually	*normalerweise*

V

vacation	*Ferien/Urlaub*
vacuum clean	*staubsaugen*
vanilla ice cream	*Vanilleeis*
vegetables	*Gemüse*
very	*sehr*
vineyard	*Weingut/Weinberg*
visit	*Besuch*
	besuchen

W

wait	*warten*
waiter	*Kellner*
Wales	*Wales*
walk	*zu Fuß gehen*
	Spaziergang
want	*wollen*
wardrobe	*Kleiderschrank*
was	*war*
wasn't	*war nicht*
watch	*ansehen/schauen*
watch TV	*fernsehen*
water	*Wasser, gießen*
way	*Weg*
we	*wir*
wear	*tragen*
weather	*Wetter*
wedding	*Hochzeit*
Wednesday	*Mittwoch*
week	*Woche*
weekend	*Wochenende*
well	*nun/naja, gut*
went	*ging/gingst/gingen/gingt*
were	*warst/waren/wart*
what	*was*
what about	*was ist mit*
when	*wenn/als*
where	*wo*
white	*weiß*
white wine	*Weißwein*
who	*wer*
whose	*wessen*
why	*warum*
will	*werden*
window	*Fenster*
windsurfing	*Windsurfen*
wine	*Wein*
winter	*Winter*
winter coat	*Wintermantel*
wish	*Wunsch, wünschen*
with	*mit*
woman	*Frau*
women	*Frauen*
won't	*nicht werden*
wonderful	*wundervoll*
wore	*trug/trugst/trugen/trugt*
work	*Arbeit, arbeiten*
world	*Welt*
worn	*getragen*
worry	*sich sorgen*
worse	*schlimmer*
worst	*schlimmster/schlimmste/ schlimmstes/am schlimmsten*
would	*wäre*

write	*schreiben*	yes	*ja*
write down	*aufschreiben*	yesterday	*gestern*
written	*geschrieben*	Yorkshire puddings	*Yorkshire Puddings*
wrote	*schrieb/schriebst/ schrieben/schriebt*	you	*du/dich/Sie/ihr/dir/euch*
		you're right	*du hast Recht*
		young	*jung*
		your	*dein/ihr/euer*
Y		yours	*deiner/deine/deins*
yard	*Garten*	yourself	*dich/dir, selbst*
yeah	*ja*	yourselves	*euch, selbst*
year	*Jahr*		

Trackliste

1
Track 1 – Übung 1
Track 2 – Übung 2
Track 3 – Übung 5
Track 4 – Übung 5
Track 5 – Übung 8

2
Track 6 – Übung 1
Track 7 – Übung 6
Track 8 – Übung 9
Track 9 – Übung 11

Test 2
Track 10 – Übung 4

3
Track 11 – Übung 1
Track 12 – Übung 2
Track 13 – Übung 4
Track 14 – Übung 8
Track 15 – Übung 10
Track 16 – Übung 12

Test 3
Track 17 – Übung 2

4
Track 18 – Übung 1
Track 19 – Übung 2
Track 20 – Übung 3
Track 21 – Übung 13
Track 22 – Übung 16

5
Track 23 – Übung 1
Track 24 – Übung 2
Track 25 – Übung 4
Track 26 – Übung 9
Track 27 – Übung 14

Test 5
Track 28 – Übung 3

6
Track 29 – Übung 1
Track 30 – Übung 2
Track 31 – Übung 3
Track 32 – Übung 10
Track 33 – Übung 17

7
Track 34 – Übung 3
Track 35 – Übung 7
Track 36 – Übung 16

Test 7
Track 37 – Übung 4

8
Track 38 – Übung 1
Track 39 – Übung 3
Track 40 – Übung 8
Track 41 – Übung 9
Track 42 – Übung 13

9
Track 43 – Übung 1
Track 44 – Übung 2
Track 45 – Übung 3
Track 46 – Übung 10
Track 47 – Übung 12

Test 9
Track 48 – Übung 4

10
Track 49 – Übung 3
Track 50 – Übung 10
Track 51 – Übung 13
Track 52 – Übung 14
Track 53 – Übung 16

Test 10
Track 54 – Übung 4

11
Track 55 – Übung 2
Track 56 – Übung 3
Track 57 – Übung 12

12
Track 58 – Übung 1
Track 59 – Übung 3
Track 60 – Übung 6
Track 61 – Übung 8

Notizen

Notizen

RICHTIG SPRACHEN LERNEN VON ANFANG AN

PONS GROSSER SPRACHKURS ENGLISCH

Die erfolgreiche Lernmethode - da ist alles dabei, was Sie brauchen

Das gute Gefühl mit sicherem Englisch
Warum Sie mit diesem Kurs wirklich sichere Sprachkenntnisse erwerben?

- Ob Sie eine Reise planen, mit Bekannten kommunizieren wollen oder sich einfach für Land und Kultur interessieren: Sie erhalten hier Schritt für Schritt fundierte und umfassende Kenntnisse, die andauern
- sichere Lernmethode: in zwei Stufen leicht zum Ziel. Mit insgesamt 28 Lektionen, 10 Wiederholungseinheiten und dem Test erreichen Sie ein fortgeschrittenes Sprachniveau
- umfassendes Hörmaterial, gesprochen von Muttersprachlern (auch mit praktischen MP3- Dateien), macht Sie auch unterwegs schnell mit dem besonderen Klang der Sprache vertraut
- Grammatik und Wortschatz im Nu: in jeder der beiden Phasen steht Ihnen eine getrennte Grammatik und ein Mini-Wörterbuch zur Verfügung
- abwechslungsreiche Übungen helfen, alles zu lernen, was Sie benötigen: verstehen, sprechen, lesen, schreiben. Interkulturelle Tipps erleichtern es Ihnen, sprachliche Besonderheiten und Gepflogenheiten besser zu verstehen
- der extra Lernratgeber verrät, wie man am effektivsten lernt und unterstützt Ihren Fortschritt

Inhalt: 6 Audio-CDs (mit Audio- und MP3-Dateien)
+ 3 Lernbücher, + Ratgeber Sprachenlernen

ISBN: 978-3-12-561467-3

www.pons.de

RICHTIG NACHSCHLAGEN - AUCH UNTERWEGS

PONS STANDARDWÖRTERBUCH ENGLISCH MIT CD-ROM

Im Standardwörterbuch finden Sie zum Sprachenlernen:

- rund 75.000 Stichwörter und Wendungen
- den Prüfungswortschatz für das Europäische Sprachenzertifikat
- einen hochaktuellen Wortschatz aus allen Lebensbereichen
- wichtige Redewendungen für den täglichen Gebrauch
- ausführliche Infokästen zu Kultur, Land und Leuten
- viele Musterbriefe, die Ihnen beim Formulieren helfen

Mit extra CD-ROM zum mobilen Nachschlagen für PC, PDA und Smartphone

Format: 12,5 x 19,5 cm

ISBN: 978-3-12-517029-2

Pressestimme:
„This dictionary includes all the words required for the TELC certificate."
Spotlight 03/2008

PONS
www.pons.de

RICHTIG TRAINIEREN - ÜBERALL

PONS MOBIL SPRACHTRAINING-AUFBAU ENGLISCH

Sie besitzen bereits englische Grundkenntnisse und Sie möchten mehr dazulernen und mehr können? Mit diesem Audio-Training für unterwegs sind Sie richtig flexibel

PONS mobil Sprachtraining enthält 12 Dialoge und Interviews mit Menschen aus Großbritannien und den USA. Nach jedem Dialog bzw. Interview folgen Übungen, die Ihnen helfen

- gesprochenes Englisch leichter zu verstehen
- die Grammatik zu wiederholen
- Ihren Wortschatz auszubauen
- Ihre Aussprache zu verbessern

Inhalt: 2 Audio CDs + Begleitbuch 72 S.

Format: 13,5 x 18 cm

ISBN: 978-3-12-561366-9

www.pons.de